A KINDLY PROVIDENCE

A KINDLY PROVIDENCE

AN ALASKAN MISSIONARY'S STORY
1926–2006

by

Louis L. Renner, S.J.

IGNATIUS PRESS   SAN FRANCISCO

Cover photograph of Father Louis L. Renner

Cover design by Roxanne Mei Lum

Dedication
This autobiography,
A Kindly Providence,
is dedicated to Saint Ignatius Loyola,
founder of the Society of Jesus,
who, having been brought by his Jesuit companions
to the realization that his life as an instrument
of Divine Providence was not exclusively his own,
favored posterity with his autobiography.

CONTENTS

PREFACE

When I first began to write an autobiographical sketch, it was my firm resolve that it be seen only by such as would outlive me. However, around 1995, when I made known to several members of my immediate family and a few close friends that I was roughing out an autobiographical sketch, they asked to see it. Somewhat reluctantly, I yielded. Among my "close friends", I number Dr. Dorothy Jean Ray, my collaborator on the biography of Father Bellarmine Lafortune, S.J. (published in 1979). Upon receiving my autobiographical sketch, she intended at first, as she wrote me, merely to glance at it. However, as she further wrote me, "Once I started reading it, I couldn't put it down. Once into it, I had to finish. So I finished the whole thing late that evening. I'm so glad to have it. You have written in such a way as to bring yourself alive. We really get to know the inner man." She urged me to write a full-fledged autobiography. On April 11, 1986, she had already written to me: "I trust that you had a wonderful Easter with all your Ruby parishioners. I hope that you are keeping notes about all your experiences as a bush priest. With all your trips and your interesting sidelights of life in Ruby, it would make a wonderful story for your autobiography or biography."

Fortunately, in retrospect, I was, at the time, keeping notes and making diarylike jottings—just as I had all along in my priestly life—of most of my more important doings, goings, and comings. In my favor, too, as an autobiographer, was the fact that I had retained much of a voluminous correspondence, as well as articles written by and about me. I also had in my possession copies of all the tapes and transcripts of interviews of me. When my fifteen-year career as a member of the faculty of the University of Alaska–Fairbanks came to an end, the university, at my request, sent my complete personnel file to the Jesuit Oregon Province Archives. This was accessible to me, of course, as was an extensive photo collection to illustrate most aspects of my life.

Over the years, various readers of my writings encouraged me to write an account of my life. The editor of *Extension Magazine* editorialized in 1991: "Perhaps someday a young Jesuit following in Father Renner's footsteps will write a book about this dedicated Alaskan missionary." A former classmate, Father Armand M. Nigro, S.J., wrote to me before I left Alaska in the year 2002: "My last advice is—write a good biography of yourself, for the edification of young people for generations to come." Very Reverend John D. Whitney, S.J., father provincial of the Oregon Province of the Society of Jesus, during my annual colloquy with him on January 13, 2005, asked me, on his own initiative, to write my autobiography. A year later, he asked me how I was coming along with it and told me that he himself looked forward to reading it.

When, on April 17, 1991, Marjorie Van Cleve interviewed me as part of the University of Alaska–Fairbanks Oral History Project, I told her that, given my naturally shy nature, I would rather write a thousand words than speak a hundred. I can honestly say that the writing of these many thousands of autobiographical words, a quasi-reliving of my past life, has been for me a truly pleasant, satisfying experience. May the reading of this autobiography be for readers likewise a pleasant, satisfying experience.

By way of acknowledgements: For reading the manuscript and making many invaluable comments and suggestions, I thank very sincerely Sister Margaret Cantwell, S.S.A., who had been my collaborator on *Alaskana Catholica*. I thank very sincerely also Father David J. Leigh, S.J., a former student of mine at Seattle Preparatory School who is a specialist in matters pertaining to autobiographies and the writing thereof. Father Leigh, providentially, was on sabbatical leave from Seattle University just when my manuscript was at the stage to profit most from his insights and suggestions, and he, therefore, having a little slack time, favored me with these at length. Without his generous input, *A Kindly Providence* would simply not be the autobiography that it is.

Likewise very sincerely, I thank also Michael Rorholm for putting his computer-related expertise so graciously and unstintingly at my disposal. I would also like to thank the staff and freelancers of Ignatius Press for their help in bringing this book to publication.

Before concluding my preface, I want to mention that Jesuit Fathers Jules M. Convert and James E. Poole need to appear, if only in passing, in this autobiography, inasmuch as their lives touched my life, and so are part of it—this, in spite of later allegations that they engaged in sexual misconduct with minors, as is stated in the respective entries concerning them in my *Alaskana Catholica*.

Louis L. Renner, S.J.
July 31, 2007
Feast of Saint Ignatius Loyola

Chapter 1

Childhood on a North Dakota Farm:
1926–1937

In June 1975, I found myself standing on top of Little Diomede Island in Bering Strait looking across several miles of water to Big Diomede Island and beyond to the Siberian mainland. Had I been able to make a leap of about twenty-five miles, I would have been on that mainland and able to travel cross-country all the way to the region just north of the Black Sea. There I would have been able to visit the burial sites of several generations of my great ancestors. From there, I would have been able to go still farther west, to the south-western part of Germany, to visit more burial sites, of those many more generations of great ancestors. The sight of the Siberian mainland warmed my heart further, inasmuch as that landmass was the home also of former White Russia, to which I, as a Jesuit, owed a great debt of gratitude for allowing the Society of Jesus to exist in its domains when elsewhere it had been suppressed by papal decree in 1773.

I trace my more immediate ancestry on my father's side as follows, beginning with Johann-Martin Renner. He was born of Catholic parents—as had been his ancestors of many generations—in Steinweiler, Palatinate, Germany, on May 30, 1766. In 1809, he emigrated to Karlsruhe, near Odessa in southern Russia. A few decades earlier, Catherine II, Catherine the Great, czarina of Russia (1762–1796), had invited

1

German farmers to come to Russia to set an example of good farming for Russian farmers. In Karlsruhe, in 1818, Andreas, the son of Johann-Martin, was born. Andreas was the father of Joseph Renner, born on January 6, 1875, also in Karlsruhe. On May 3, 1893, Joseph, having sailed from Bremerhaven, Germany, arrived in New York. A year later, he settled on a farm eight miles due west of Saint Anthony, North Dakota. Joseph—married, in 1898, to Margaretha Forster—was the father of John Joseph Renner, my father, born in Saint Anthony on September 19, 1899.

The ancestors on my mother's side, the Gustins—likewise Catholic for many generations—came originally from the same area of Germany as did the Renners and similarly immigrated to the same general area in Russia as did the Renners. Lorenz (Lawrence) Gustin, my mother's father, was born on July 7, 1860, most likely in Karlsruhe, Russia. Margaretha Röther-Gustin, my mother's mother, was born in Karlsruhe on March 1, 1862. They were married on January 25, 1882, in Halbstadt, Russia. For nineteen years, they lived in Russia, presumably in Halbstadt. Meanwhile, their friends and relatives were selling their properties and immigrating to the United States. Reasons given for the emigration were that farmland for the growing families was getting harder and harder to come by and young men were beginning to be conscripted to serve in the Russian military. By early December 1901, the Lawrence Gustin family—consisting now of the two parents plus seven boys and two girls—were in Fallon, North Dakota. The following year, they settled on a homestead four miles northeast of Flasher. (Fallon and Flasher, about four miles apart, are some thirty miles southwest of Mandan-Bismarck. Saint Anthony is halfway between them.) It was on that homestead that, on January 6, 1904, my mother, Rosa (Rose), the last child to be born to that family, came into this world.

My parents, John Renner and Rose Gustin, the offspring of ancestors twice pioneers, were married on October 23, 1923, in Saint Anthony. (At that same Mass, Frank Gustin, my mother's next-older brother, and Anna Yantzer were married.) For the next five years or so, the John Renner family made its home on a farm near Saint Anthony, living in "the stone house". My older brother, William (Bill), was born in Mandan on February 11, 1925. I was born in Saint Alexius Hospital in Bismarck on April 25, 1926. Presumably because I seemed to be in less-than-perfect health, I was baptized in the hospital shortly after being born. (During my earliest years, I was not particularly healthy. I did survive a severe case of pneumonia. I suffered from nosebleeds and had to undergo cauterization. For a time, I was given daily a spoonful of cod liver oil—the taste for which I never acquired, and the taste of which I did not soon forget.) My parents wanted my baptismal name to be Louis. The Benedictine sister on the hospital staff, however, persuaded them to have me baptized Aloysius, after the young Italian Jesuit martyr of charity, Saint Aloysius Gonzaga, arguing that the two names were really one and the same and that they could, therefore, still call me Louis. The name Aloysius was entered on my baptismal certificate, and Saint Aloysius has been my patron saint ever since. (My secondary patron is Saint Lawrence. For my confirmation name I took that of my maternal grandfather, Lawrence Gustin.) Though neither was present at my baptism, my uncle George Renner was designated my godfather, and my aunt Anna Yantzer Gustin my godmother. (Born on October 5, 1903, she died on July 10, 2005!)

My next-younger brother, Richard (Dick), was likewise born in Bismarck, on August 23, 1927. By the time Leonard (Len), the fourth of the Renner boys, was born, on April 29, 1929, the family had moved to a farm three miles north of Flasher.

My sister Julia Rose (Julie) was born on November 5, 1930; my sister Adella (Della) on March 9, 1932; and my brother Albert (Al) on October 8, 1933. So large a family needed its own little intercessor in heaven. This was granted the family in the person of Delores Marie, the eighth and last child born to the family. She was born, baptized, and died all on the same day, February 16, 1935. We seven Renner children were all born in a relatively short time frame, and we have throughout the decades remained an unusually close-knit family but, at the same time, also a family not without the tensions, conflicts, and squabbles typical of any large family.

Many decades after the family had made the move to the farm north of Flasher in early 1929, I astounded Mom by telling her my recollection of our drive from the Saint Anthony farm to the Flasher one. I recalled how we were driven to the farm site in the loaded-down gray Chevy sedan. Grandma Renner was at the wheel, Mom in the passenger's seat, Dick and I in the back seat. I was a three-year-old at the time. She marveled at the accuracy of my memory. I have, it is true, been blessed with a good memory, an asset for historians and autobiographers. In my writing, this gift of memory—supported by an extensive photo collection and many saved documents and letters, as well as by a variety of diarylike notebooks I kept over the years—has served me well.

I came within seconds of not being around to make that drive to the Flasher farm. One day, while the family was visiting the Grandpa Renner farm, I reached for something in the horse trough and fell in. I was alone at the moment. In the nick of time, Uncle Albert, Dad's youngest brother, happened along. He fished me out. By then, I had turned blue. Fortunately, they were able to revive me. What water in a horse trough at Grandpa's farm did not do to me—end my life—a horse's hoof almost did a few years later, on the Flasher farm. Dick and I were riding along one day, he in the saddle, I behind it. We came to a gate. He got off to open it. Fuchs, our spirited young saddle horse, did not like the feel of someone sitting on him behind an empty saddle. In a second, he made an explosive buck, throwing me headlong out in front of him as he bolted off straight ahead. I landed on my back. Just inches from my head, he left a two-inch-deep hoofprint. Spared again, this time by inches—and God's kindly Providence!

I have never considered myself as being accident-prone, though I have had some close calls and I have done some very foolish things in my life. Once, as a toddler, I climbed up on the washing machine and stuck my left arm into the rolling wringer. As it began gouging a hole into the inside of my elbow, I let out a loud scream. Mom ran up, and, instead of immediately hitting the release knob, she, in her frenzy, first hit me on the head with the stick she had been using to fish wet clothes out of the machine. The pronounced scar never left me. Of lesser vintage is the little scar on my chin. One fall day, early in the morning, I went on a duck hunt with Dick. Sitting next to him as he did the driving, I had the loaded shotgun resting at an angle between my legs. We came to a frost-covered wooden bridge, skidded, and hit the guardrail with full force. My head went up, the shotgun swung over, and, with my chin, I came down on the end of the barrel. Luckily, the gun did not go off.

To end this far-from-complete list of my foolhardiness, I can add the following. Once, while on a swimming outing during summer vacation at the Jesuit villa at the mouth of Oregon's Nestucca River, I dove off a sandbar into murky water, assuming I was diving off a steep bank. I was not. For many days, I had a very stiff neck. More than once, God, in

His divine Providence, saw fit to spare my life so foolishly put at risk by me.

Our family was the first one to live on that Flasher farm; in fact, we created it. The family home was a onetime schoolhouse moved to the site from nearby. It was a one-story building but was placed on a full basement. The coal bin was at one end of the basement. Shelves holding jars of canned vegetables, meats, and jellies—the yield of our gardens, our farm, and the wild plum and chokecherry trees growing in two of the three gullies on the farm—put up for the off-seasons and winters occupied a good part of the other end. A chamber pot, too, for night and winter use, had its place in the basement. An outhouse was a standard farm fixture. There was no indoor plumbing. Water for every use had to be carried to the house from a well. Well water could be pumped by hand when there was not wind enough to get the windmill pumping. Carrying water from the well to the house was one of the basic chores of us boys as soon as we were able to carry a half-gallon pail (a onetime syrup pail) full of water. From that, we graduated to a gallon pail, or two of us to a three-gallon bucket.

In addition to the white family house, the well, and the outhouse, the farm had also a one-story barn, a white building with a steep enough pitch to the roof to provide a hayloft. A chicken coop was built onto one end of the barn. The barn building proper, too, was a former schoolhouse. A granary, built by Dad and painted red, was the third major building. For a time, we had also a "straw barn", an oblong animal shelter made out of double rows of poles all around—except for an entrance gate—faced with big-mesh wire. Straw was stuffed between the double rows of wire-faced poles. The roof, too, was made out of poles, wire, and straw. Even in extremely cold weather, the structure provided a warm shelter. Its one drawback was that the cows were able to get their noses through the bigger meshes and eat a good amount of the straw. This could, of course, be easily replenished.

With the family home, barns, and outhouse all relatively close to one another, it was inevitable that, especially during summers, a plague of flies would be an inescapable part of farm life. For me, personally, the flies were a mixed blessing. Bargaining with Mom, I was promised a cookie for every twenty flies I swatted in the kitchen. There were times when I ran out of flies before I had my cookie's-worth quota. Sensing that Mom was counting the thwacks, I had to hit the wall enough extra times, plus a few for good measure, to make up the deficit. She was on to my trickery, and I knew it. But with both of us knowing that the other knew the facts of the case, there was no real deception, and the battle against the flies went on with neither reproach on her part nor confession on mine. Having just the right touch—that is, swatting the flies just hard enough to kill them but not so hard as to paste them to the wall—I was the fly-swatter of her choice.

Though only a one-story building, our house did have a full attic. One end of this was made into a bedroom with a register in the floor to let heat up from below. The other end, where we boys slept, remained in the rough. One had to be careful not to scratch his head on the shingle nails coming through the roof. Winter blizzards blew snow through the tiny holes in the roof. However, under a feather quilt, and with always at least two of us to the bed, we were seldom cold. During extremely cold nights, we were bedded down on the floor in the living room near the coal stove glowing red-hot. On the roof, Dad had rigged up a propeller to drive an electric generator, which charged the batteries used to light up a single car-headlight bulb, providing the only electric light we had. On an especially windy night, the rattle of the propeller could disturb sleep. Throughout our years on that farm, except for that little light bulb, which glowed only when the wind blew and the batteries were charged up, illumination was provided solely by kerosene lamps, Coleman lamps, or lanterns. The lamps called for careful attention. It was all too easy to break a smoked-up lamp chimney while trying to clean it or to break the delicate mantles of the Coleman lamp.

Our farm was one of the better ones in that general area. We owned 320 acres of land and leased some on the nearby school section. Our well yielded limitless, clear, drinkable water. The fields were relatively fertile. Rolling hills provided good pasturage. Special features of the hills were the three gullies that provided shade and drinking water for the cattle. Two of the gullies had water holes fed by natural springs. Chokecherry and wild plum trees grew in the gullies. The juice of boiled chokecherries strained through a white flour sack made excellent jelly. Some years, when there was enough rain, a profusion of wildflowers, especially of wild roses, brightened the landscape with welcome color. Flowers were also grown around the house.

Ours was "mixed farming". We grew various grain crops such as corn, wheat, barley, and oats, and also forage crops such as alfalfa. We raised cattle and hogs. Most of what we grew or raised was for home consumption. It was eaten either fresh or after having been preserved in one form or other. Slabs of bacon, hams, sausages, and head cheese were cured in the smokehouse. Some meats, chicken and beef, were preserved in jars, as were different kinds of vegetables. Sauerkraut was a staple in a German's diet. Surplus grains and some beef and hogs, as well as cream and eggs, were sold or traded for credit at the grocery store in Flasher. More than once, the Flasher grocer was out to our farm to take part in the butchering of a hog or some beef cow or calf.

Gardens, too, were a major part of our farming operation. As with the meat, most of the garden yield was consumed by the family, either directly out of the garden or after having been preserved in jars for later consumption. An annual hot summer's day treat was a big slice of watermelon. There was no refrigeration on the farm, but we cooled things such as watermelons, butter, and other foods in waterproof containers in a barrel through which fresh water flowed from the well and into the cow tank.

All in all, our "mixed farming" was what one might call "a rather mixed bag", both as to what we grew and raised and as to the degree of success, or lack of same, with which we did so. There were years when a rainstorm or hailstorm would flatten a stand of wheat ready for the harvest. There were years of drought and years when grasshoppers devoured anything green. Chicken hawks took their toll, as did other predatory animals. Fowl and animal diseases were a problem. One year the government, in hopes of raising cattle prices, demanded that farmers thin their herds to a bare minimum. Calves had to be slaughtered. That year we "jarred" some veal and fed some slaughtered calves to the hogs. And yet, for the most part, ours was a viable farming venture. We never went hungry. Life was, perforce, kept simple. Our clothes were of the barest essentials. In summer, we boys wore only suspender overalls, nothing else, not even shoes. Before going to bed at night, we took a dip in a barrel full of water. In general, the lot of the North Dakota farmer of the 1930s was not an easy one. The Great Depression continued to have its negative impact on him. Many farmers were ruined, or came close to being ruined, by the prolonged and severe spells of drought that occurred all too frequently.

I have talked about us as farmers and about "our" farming, and with justification. For we children, from our earliest years, to the extent that strength and skills allowed, all contributed something to the farming effort. We weeded in the garden; gathered eggs; carried water; gathered "buffalo chips" (dried cow manure) for the kitchen stove; carried coal up from the basement; carried out ashes; emptied the chamber pot; fed the calves, hogs, and chickens; rounded up the cows for milking; and helped with the general housekeeping. I was milking cows before I began grade school. While still less than ten years old, on a dump rake pulled by Jess, an old white mare, I was raking hay behind Bill, on a hay mower pulled by two black horses, Big Prince and Little Prince. At that age and under those conditions, however, we hardly knew how to distinguish between what was work and what was play. My early years of life and work on a family farm instilled in me, among other personality traits, a sense of orderliness, of harmonious collaboration, of "getting the job done"—traits that were to stand me in good stead throughout my subsequent life.

But life on the farm brought with it also real play and amusement. With a softball and a pitchfork handle for a bat, we played "long ball". We played with marbles. In winter, we sledded on the hill in the cow pasture. We romped in the straw stacks. On some summer days, the family piled into the car and drove to the Little Heart River for a swim and picnic. One Fourth of July, Dad took us older boys to Flasher to see the celebrations there. I remember watching the fatmen races and the gunny-sack races. There was the popping of firecrackers. In all respects, life on the Flasher farm was a life simple and basic but aglow with family warmth.

We were, indeed, a close-knit family. When we were not in school, our parents had complete control of what entered into our lives. We did have a radio. And we did have a telephone, a one-liner, a crank model predating the dial and touch models. The telephone line, strung out along the top of the cow fence, ran up to Uncle Frank Gustin's farm, two miles to the east of ours. If we wanted to contact someone beyond his farm, we had to phone his place and have someone there relay the message through their "party line" to the party we hoped to contact. Often our phone was out of commission; generally, this was because the line was down, thanks to some fence-breaking cow, or because a bolt of lightning had knocked it out. For many years after we left the farm, I could still hear the rise and fall in volume of the hum droning over the phone into our house then receding again. This was especially pronounced on cold nights.

Religion was a major, an essential, part of our family life. A picture of the Sacred Heart hung on the wall in the kitchen above the dining table. Before it, with hands piously folded, we said grace before and after meals. There were morning prayers, and there were night prayers. On one of the living room walls hung a picture of Pope Pius XI. That, and going faithfully to Sunday Mass at Saint Lawrence Church in Flasher—sometimes by car, sometimes by wagon or sledge, depending on weather and road conditions—gave us kids a broader sense of religion. During our latter years in North Dakota, the evening Rosary became part of family devotions. One evening, on the radio, we boys were listening to a boxing match between Joe Louis and James Braddock. After a few rounds, Mom told us it was time for the Rosary. Reluctantly, we turned the radio off—and said Hail Marys with a speed never matched thereafter. (Joe Louis won the fight and, with that victory, the world championship.)

Religion was practiced in the home rather than preached or formally taught. For systematic training in the Catholic Faith, we were sometimes sent to summer catechism classes in Flasher. One summer, while preparing for my First Holy Communion, I was staying with my cousin, Nicholas J.

(Nick) Gustin, and his wife, Aunt Emelia, in Flasher. By this time, I had, for a year, attended the Catholic school in Fallon, a small settlement some four miles east of our farm. This school was staffed by Benedictine sisters, who taught us catechism formally and systematically. One morning, convinced that I had little new catechism to learn in Flasher, I got up early and, without saying a word to anyone, walked the three miles home. The family was quite surprised to see me there for breakfast. There was no scolding. They may have assumed that it was homesickness for them that prompted me to cut short my stay in Flasher. I am sure it was not homesickness that motivated my self-authorized departure from Flasher. Homesickness, in spite of my life-long and deep attachment to all my family, has, throughout my life, been but a rare personal affliction. The one time in my life that I experienced a genuine kind of prolonged, painful "homesickness" was during the first several years after I made the permanent move out of Alaska in the year 2002.

From the outset, one of our parents' major concerns was that we children receive a Catholic education. Flasher had no Catholic school, which is why I went to Fallon, where the Benedictine sisters of Richardton, North Dakota, operated a school for day scholars and boarders. For all practical purposes, this school was the parish school of Saints Peter and Paul Church in Fallon. I first began attending it in the fall of 1933. That year, my brother Bill also attended it. The next year, Dick joined us, and the year after that, Len. We boarded at the school during the five school days and were home from Friday evenings till Monday mornings. We did spend a few weekends there when blizzards made travel virtually impossible. Dad drove us to and from Fallon, sometimes by car, sometimes by horse-drawn wagon or sledge. There were Monday mornings when I arrived at the school so chilled to the bone that I had to stand next to the hot-water radiator for quite some time before I was warm again.

The Fallon of the 1930s, before it disappeared entirely off the map, was not much of a settlement. In addition to the school building, there was Saints Peter and Paul Church, the parish house, the cemetery, a one-pump gas station, a little store, a meeting hall, a blacksmith shop, and several private homes. The school building—a wooden-frame former public school building—had four levels, which included a full basement with laundry, a kitchen, separate dining rooms for the sisters and the children, and the furnace and the well rooms. There was no indoor plumbing. Water was hand-pumped. Chamber pots and outhouses completed the "plumbing" facilities. Classrooms and a chapel were on the first floor; a dormitory for the girls and sisters was on the second floor. The boys slept in the attic. Hot-water radiators heated all but the attic. The furnace was coal-fired. The building had no fire escape.

One night, the whole school building could easily have burned to the ground with the loss of lives. Whoever stoked the furnace for that night left a layer of coal so fine on top of the glowing coal that, at a given point, the coal exploded into flame, blew open the furnace door, and spewed hot embers over the wooden floor, which soon began to smolder and send smoke up to the floors above. The smoke awakened my cousin, Elizabeth (Betty) Gustin (Uncle Frank's oldest), who alerted one of the sisters. The fire was soon put out. For her valor, Elizabeth received a medal, a simple medal of devotion, from one of the sisters.

As may readily be guessed, both room and board at Fallon were simple, almost primitive. Sharing a bed with a sibling was common. Food for the boarders was provided by their families. On Friday, before the boarders went home for the weekend, whoever came to pick them up was given a list of foods that that family was to bring with it when it returned on Monday. Bread and cereals were staples. The weekly fare was so plain and bland that, generally, a sister was in the dining room to make sure we all ate enough.

Sister Helen Schwindt—one of my teachers at Fallon, and with whom I, as a priest, corresponded till she died in her nineties—later wrote me that Fallon was the last place to which any of the sisters ever wanted to be assigned. For all that, the sisters were competent and committed teachers, dedicated to the academic and religious formation of the children entrusted to their care. In their efforts, they had the full support of the rather strict German pastor, Father F. X. Mueller, and of the parents.

All the children attending the Fallon school were from German families. Many of us, myself included, first began to learn English at the school. In the classroom, English was the language; outside the classroom, we spoke German. On the school roster, in addition to the names Renner and Gustin, there were names like Gerhardt, Barth, Scholl, Kuntz, Hopfauf, Messer, Friez, Eckroth, Schmidt, Kautzmann, Bullinger, and Bohl. Day scholars came from the nearby farms. Some walked to the school; some came in horse-drawn wagons or buggies; some came in old Model-T cars. Some of the boys were considerably older than typical grade-school children. Work on the farm slowed down their education process, keeping them from advancing through the grades at the usual rate of one grade per year. There was one older boy, who tended his trap line on the way to and from school. One day, he came to school so reeking of skunk odor that Sister had to send him back home again.

Discipline at the school was in keeping with the discipline generally in vogue at the time in the homes. It had a distinctive "German" touch to it: firm, no-nonsense, but not cruel. The yardstick was put to use, at times, to serve purposes other than to measure the yard; the pointer, to do more than point out the verb in the sentence on the blackboard. For fooling around in class or during the evening study hall, I felt the tap of both more than once, as well as spent time standing in the corner. We took the discipline in stride and did not chafe under it.

I enjoyed the games we played at Fallon: Red Rover, fox and geese, tag, hide-and-seek, marbles, and other kid games. We competed aggressively for the swings on the playground. When snow conditions were right, we formed sides, built forts, and had snowball fights. During free time in the classroom, I could easily lose myself in the geography book, reading about far-away places and travels on the oceans.

In spite of the rather primitive conditions of the Fallon school, the basic schooling we received was unquestionably solid. When my brothers and I moved on to attend parochial schools in Tacoma, Washington, we had no trouble whatever making the grade. Our command of English was adequate— though I was, for years, teased by classmates because of my "dat's" and "dem's" and the like. In retrospect, I can honestly say that, all in all, my recollections of the four school years I spent at Fallon are wholly positive.

However, our parents did not send us to the Fallon school to be disciplined, to play games, or even to get a solid basic education. Their principal concern was that we get a thorough grounding in our Catholic Faith. This we got. Catechism class and Bible readings were part of the daily curriculum. There was daily morning Mass. There were weekly confessions, prayers before and after meals, morning and night prayers, the Angelus, the Stations of the Cross during Lent, Rogation Day processions, and various other devotions. I took part in these with a religious fervor matched only by the patriotic fervor with which I pledged allegiance to the flag. In both cases, I went through the motions as prescribed: routinely, perfunctorily, with neither devotion nor protest. A certain personal spiritual awakening was yet to come into my life. The bases for that, however, were laid in the home and in the Fallon school.

One day, at Fallon, life took on a new meaning for me. That was the day I saw, for the first time, life's opposite—death. I can still see the elderly woman, dressed in black, lying in a plain, homemade casket flanked by six flickering dark brown candles. Hushed silence filled the room that evening. Then, the next morning, there was the Requiem Mass, with its black vestments, incense, and singing. This was followed by a solemn procession to the cemetery, led by a cross-bearer and two acolytes, as the *Dies Irae* was sung. Graveside memories stayed with me: the priest in a black cope, the chanting of the *Benedictus*, a final sprinkling of holy water. The hollow thuds of the first shovelfuls of damp earth landing on the wooden casket set a somber tone and made a deep, sobering, lasting impression on my preteen imagination.

There was the day, too, when we kids at Fallon saw our first airplane—and close up at that. In his little yellow biplane, Jack Stegmueller, a crop duster, landed right in the middle of the fenced-in school ground. We swarmed around the plane to hear Jack, beaming with pride, tell us all about planes and how they fly. Then we helped him push the plane as close to one end of the playground as it would go, so that, upon takeoff, he could safely clear the fence at the opposite end. With a great roar, he was off, cleared the fence, and, with a tip of the wing in salute, was soon a mere speck in the western sky.

Chapter 2

Adolescent Years in Tacoma, Washington: 1937–1944

The Great Depression of the 1930s, in and of itself, already made the life of the North Dakota farmer a difficult one. In addition, those same years were also North Dakota's Dust Bowl Era, when, owing to frequent prolonged and severe droughts, nothing but Russian thistles seemed to grow. Crop failure in a given year meant no seed for next year's planting. With die-hard hopes, farmers kept taking out "seed loans" to buy seed for another spring planting. This happened year after year during the 1930s. Our family was part of the pattern. For years after we moved to Tacoma, Washington, Dad was paying off seed loans.

Given the depressed economy, the seemingly endless series of droughts, and the fact that, though his ancestors had for countless generations been successful farmers, Dad himself—by his own admission to me in later years—hated farming, it was not surprising, then, that, in the spring of 1937, he entertained the thought of getting away from it all. As coincidence—rather, a kindly Providence—would have it, that spring, his next-younger brother, Uncle Ralph, now living in Salem, Oregon, happened to visit North Dakota. Dad began to think West and decided to accompany Ralph on his return trip to Oregon. This he did, in June. Salem, unfortunately, offered little by way of suitable job opportunities.

However, at this time, Uncle Adam Gustin and family were living in Tacoma. This prompted Dad to go there in hopes of finding a suitable job. Men from North Dakota working at the Tacoma Smelter had the reputation of being able, reliable workers. Dad applied for a job there, was hired on, and worked at the Tacoma Smelter till he reached retirement age. He and all our family were blessed in that this proved to be a permanent, satisfying job for him. With a steady job secured, he had Mom sell what the family had, pack up us kids, and come to Tacoma.

We left North Dakota from Mandan on the Northern Pacific Railway on July 28, 1937. I was then eleven years old. My last night in North Dakota I spent at Grandpa Renner's place. The next morning, the family all met at the train station. There, a group of Indians, all outfitted in war regalia and brandishing tomahawks, put on a whoopin' and hollerin' war dance as the train from the east, our train, with whistle blowing, bell ringing, and steam belching, pulled in. Nervous excitement on the part of us kids—certainly on my part—reached fever pitch. Not having slept well the night before, I was ready to burst. Great, then, was the peace that settled over me shortly after we were under way, and the rocking of the train to the clickety-clack, clickety-clack rhythm of the rails worked its soothing magic. By the time I woke up, the conductor was coming through our car announcing the next stop: "Glendive, Montana! Glendive, Montana!" As dusk began to settle over central Montana, the porter, a black gentleman, came through the car offering: "Pillows! Pillows!" We had our own food along and ate when hungry; slept on the seats when sleepy; and were entertained by the ever-changing scenery, especially that of the majestic Rocky Mountains, as we chuffed our way slowly up and through them. We arrived in Tacoma, at Union

Station, on the morning of the thirty-first, the feast of Saint Ignatius Loyola, founder of the Society of Jesus, the Jesuits.

While hopes of general economic betterment and employment personally more satisfying than farming strongly motivated Dad to move the family west, it was the assurance of a Catholic education for the children in Tacoma, more than anything else, that influenced the parental decision to begin life anew in Tacoma. As mentioned above, we kids attended the Fallon school as nonparishioners. By 1937, the school no longer accepted nonparishioners. By this time, we were seven children. For the four of us already in school, there were no prospects of our being able to continue on in our Catholic education in North Dakota; nor was there hope that the three not yet in school would be able to receive a Catholic education in North Dakota.

Our first home in Tacoma placed us in Holy Cross parish on the north end of town. However, we spent only the months of August and September there before we moved to within three city blocks of Holy Rosary parish, fairly close to downtown Tacoma. Holy Rosary School was staffed, as was the Fallon school, by Benedictine sisters. We lived in Holy Rosary parish for only two years, long enough for me to complete my fifth and sixth grades. When we first began to attend Holy Rosary, we Renner boys were still wearing, to our embarrassment, "prairie pants", blue overalls with suspenders. At the time, the family was entitled to the benefits of the Federal Relief Act. We were relieved to receive fairly early on, at no cost, the type of corduroy pants worn by our peers. We benefited from the Act, too, in terms of food. I can still see the round, gold-colored tins of canned meat with NOT FOR SALE stamped on them in black letters.

It was while we were members of Holy Rosary parish that I first heard of Saint Thérèse, "the Little Flower". Routinely, on Tuesday evenings, along with other family members, I attended the "Little Flower devotions".

From Holy Rosary parish, the family moved to a home that put us in Sacred Heart parish on McKinley Hill. At this time, although Dad was employed full time at the Tacoma Smelter, given the large, young family, it was impossible to make ends meet. The move to this particular home, despite its being still farther away from the smelter, was made because, in addition to the house, the place, being a two-acre plot, had on it also a garage, a small barn, and fruit trees, plus adequate ground for a garden and enough land to support a milk cow. Spotty was the family cow, and she was entrusted to my care. Years later, Dad remarked to me how well she and I took to one another and how good a provider of milk for the family she was.

The cow, the fruit trees, and the gardens helped considerably toward feeding the family. At this time, too, Dad also worked part time for the WPA (Works Progress Administration). Nevertheless, family debits continued to outweigh credits, so much so that Bill, after finishing his junior year of high school, had to go to work full time, likewise at the smelter. To earn money to buy our school clothes and to contribute nickels and dimes to the family purse, my next-younger brothers and I picked blackberries and raspberries in our next-door neighbor's berry patches. I delivered newspapers from door to door, covering my spread-out paper route on my bicycle. While still living in Holy Rosary parish, I had sold the *Tacoma Ledger* on Sunday mornings on a downtown street corner. I had also sold magazines and magazine subscriptions from door to door. There was nothing all that unusual about this. Other boys of my age did likewise. These were not my first ventures into wage earning. As a kid on the North Dakota farm, when I saw Uncle Frank in his

Model-A coming down the hill through our cow pasture toward our farm, I would run up to open the gate next to the cow tank for him. He was always prepared to pay me a just wage for that service: one penny!

I rounded out my elementary education by attending Sacred Heart Grade School for the seventh and the eighth grades. The school was staffed by Sisters of Providence, well-qualified, dedicated, no-nonsense teachers. When Sister Michaeleen Begley, S.P., my teacher during those two years, addressed me by my full name, I knew the matter at hand was serious. When she walked out to the mound during one of our parochial league softball games and shook her forefinger vigorously before the umpire's face, he knew the point at issue was a serious matter. We did well as a softball team, but it was in basketball that we really made our mark—by winning the Tacoma Parochial League championship that year, 1941, for the first time in the history of the school. As a starter on the team, I was genuinely proud of the little *SH* letters awarded us for our achievement. Those little letters, and a letter for frosh basketball at Bellarmine, were the extent of my lettering in that sport. I did, however, play much basketball throughout the years of my Jesuit training; and, even during the early 1990s, I enjoyed shooting baskets on the outdoor court by the high school next to Saint Aloysius Church in Tanana, Alaska.

As at Fallon and Holy Rosary, so, too, at Sacred Heart— the extracurricular, the academic, and the devotional training was solid. Again, I experienced no discernible attraction to either the clerical or to the religious life as such. I attended Mass routinely with the student body but rarely served it, mainly because the shoes the altar boys were expected to wear—along with cassock and surplice—were too small for my feet. The study of geography and John J. Considine's book

When the Sorghum Was High, a biography of Gerard A. Donovan, a Maryknoll Father and China missionary, read aloud to the class, continued to make faraway places look attractive to me.

In late May 1941, I found myself standing on the stage in the Sacred Heart School auditorium. Behind me sat my fellow graduating classmates. Before me, in the front rows, sat the pastor, Father Albert H. Allard, the sisters, our parents, and family members. In my shaking right hand, I held a one-page farewell address written by Sister Michaeleen. I was told, by one who had witnessed my nervous ordeal, that, by the time I had finished reading that address, I had clawed my left pant leg up to above my knee.

"Reverend Father, dear Sisters, Parents, and Friends", it began. "Once more the passing of the school year has brought us to the month of the Sacred Heart, and to twenty of us it means the completion of the elementary school course, which marks the first milestone in our lives." It went on to express gratitude to the pastor, teachers, and parents for "the invaluable gift of a Catholic education". It spoke of fidelity to God and country, of "high ideals". It ended: "That the blessing of the Sacred Heart with all its peace and love may rest upon you is the prayerful wish of this year's graduating class. Thank you, and God bless you all!" Later, as a priest, I corresponded fairly often with Sister Michaeleen and once visited her after her retirement.

My natural North Dakota farm-boy shyness and proneness to stage fright haunted me throughout my life. As a classroom teacher, after meeting a class once or twice, I had no trouble facing it thereafter. But those firsts, whether in the classroom, or in the pulpit, or before a new audience, were always stressful times for me. Along with that Sacred Heart graduation ordeal, I might here mention two other occasions when my nerves came close to getting the better of me. In 1959, I was assigned to give the sermon (a "homily" was still an unknown at that time) during the Holy Thursday Mass in the small Church of the Immaculate Conception in Fairbanks, Alaska. There I was, standing in front of the high altar, not even a reading stand to hang onto, before a packed church. To my left sat Bishop Francis D. Gleeson, S.J., Vicar Apostolic of Alaska—all done up in purple and lace—and Father George T. Boileau, S.J., pastor of the parish and preacher esteemed well above the ordinary. There were times in the course of that sermon when I had to pause to chew my tongue to get some juice into my mouth. On July 24, 1988, in the big front living room of my sister Julie's and brother-in-law Duncan McMillan's home, I offered a Mass of thanksgiving for Dad and Mom as they celebrated their sixty-fifth wedding anniversary. The room was quite filled with immediate family, close relatives, and longtime family friends. It was really just one grand family affair. And yet I was so nervous that, at homily time, I literally felt my knees shaking, so much so that I glanced down to see if it showed. In my heart, I had occasion to thank God for the long, full, white alb I was wearing. Insurmountable natural shyness can be a great cross.

After finishing grade school, I moved up from being a paperboy to being a messenger boy. During the summer of 1941, I went to work for the Western Union Telegraph Company. This meant riding my bicycle all over hilly Tacoma or running around to downtown offices to deliver telegrams, all for thirty cents an hour. However, it also meant that I was no longer tied down every day after school by a paper route and could, therefore, turn out for football, when I entered Bellarmine Preparatory School in the fall. Throughout my freshman year at Bellarmine, I continued on at Western Union but worked only on weekends and holidays.

Sunday, December 7, 1941, was a day I—along with count-less others, for that matter—did not soon forget. On that day, upon my return after delivering a batch of telegrams, as I walked into the Western Union office, Joe Hoffman, the super-visor on duty, said to me, "The Japs just bombed Pearl Har-bor!" The full import of those words took on meaning for me only gradually, as night blackouts and notices on movie screens ordering all military personnel to report immediately to their bases became routine—and as upper classmates left school early to enter military service, some even to lose their lives on battlefronts.

In the early evening of Christmas Eve 1941, the Western Union office was swamped with Christmas telegrams urgently needing to be delivered. Again, Joe Hoffman was on duty. In a low voice, I asked him if I could get off early. Rather brusquely, he wanted to know why. "I want to go to confes-sion", I told him. *"Fishin'*, to*night*, of all nights?" he exploded. I clarified my need. Being himself a Catholic, of sorts, he understood, and he let me sign out.

At this time of my life, I already sensed some kind of a vague, almost subconscious, call to the priestly, the reli-gious, life. On some days, after having delivered the last tele-gram on a particular outing, as I was riding my bike along the Tacoma waterfront breathing in the salty, tangy, moist sea air at low tide, listening to the shrieking seagulls and watch-ing ships come and go, I felt so strongly drawn to a future on the high seas that I found myself actually praying that I did not really have a call to the priestly, the religious, life.

As a freshman at Bellarmine, I took the basic first-year high school courses: religion, English, Latin, algebra, and history. These were taught by Jesuit priests and Jesuit seminarians, "scholastics", still on their way to the priesthood. This was the first time I came in close contact with the Jesuits. I was pretty much an average student, motivated less by scholarly ambitions than by the need to keep my grades up so as to be eligible for sports. That first year, I earned letters playing right guard on the "Reserves" football team and on the frosh basketball team.

With World War II in full swing by early 1942, there was a general labor shortage giving rise to multiple-choice job opportunities, even for high school kids. Carstens Meat Packing Company on the Tacoma tide flats was recruiting workers. One could work any hours, day or night, weekdays or weekends. The beginning wage was eighty-seven cents an hour. Compared to Western Union's wage of thirty cents an hour, that was big money in my eyes. My buddy and I applied. According to a child labor law, one had to be at least sixteen years old to work at a place like Carstens. During the interview, the hiring boss asked me my age. Being honest—and a little naïve—I answered, "Fifteen." "Good, sixteen", he muttered to himself, and started to write down "16". "No," I came back, "*fif*teen!" At that, my buddy, being wise to the game, kicked me in the shin. Amazingly, then and there, I suddenly "aged" another year. "Correcting" myself, I agreed, with emphasis, "Uh ... yeah, *six*teen." On the spot, we were hired to work in the fertilizer department. This meant hauling in wheelbarrows or shoveling into bags "sheep guano", or dried, ground-up fish remains, or pulverized rock. The wages were good; the hours: "Whenever, and as long as you want!" Occasionally, we treated ourselves to a steam-boiled wiener or two—courtesy of the company, presumed. The work was smelly, and so dusty that "No Smoking!" signs were posted all over, lest there be explosions. It was also hard work. At times, I stacked or loaded for shipment 40-pound bags; at other times, 120-pound bags. Handling many of those bags kept me in good condition for football, and that was important to me. During that second semester of my freshman year of high school, I put in many hours at Carstens. The results: good take-home pay, good muscles, little-better-than-average grades on the report card.

During the summer between my freshman and sophomore years, I worked for the Northern Pacific Railway in its South Tacoma yard. At first, I was assigned to loading out of boxcars twenty- to twenty-six-foot-long one-by-fours and one-by-sixes. This was easy work but so insufferably boring that the midmorning coffee break seemed like a major vacation. Fortunately, before the summer was very far along, I had a more interesting job, as a member of the "crane crew". This meant heavier, more dangerous—but less tedious—work. The crane, an old coal-fired steam model, was kept operable thanks only to much welding and soldering. Whenever it exerted itself, it belched forth a thick cloud of billowing black smoke. It should have been condemned as unsafe long before I, along with three others—not counting the crane's operator, a little man with a limp known to us as "Shorty"—began to crew it. But that was wartime. The crane was used principally to offload big timbers and telephone poles from flatcars. Standing on a pile of telephone poles, with another pole swinging precariously over our heads as it was about to be lowered, so that my partner and I could guide it into its place on the pile, was for both of us always a tense moment. After the 1942 football season, I went to work for Safeway as a shelf stocker and a "Box out!" boy.

The fall semester of my sophomore year was for me a semester of major achievement, not simply because I earned passing grades on my report card, but because I ended the football season having played enough minutes on the varsity football team to earn that big Bellarmine "B". I proudly sported it on my new, tailor-made, navy blue pullover sweater with the white stripe on the upper left sleeve. Ever since that fall semester, I have had warm feelings toward Issaquah, Washington, for it was there that—on a drizzle-dreary afternoon, on a field chalked out on a cow pasture—we Bellarmine Lions defeated the Issaquah Indians. So weak were those Indians, that I got to play much of the game, logging there most of the minutes I needed to qualify for a letter. I was one of only two sophomores to earn a varsity letter in football that year, 1942. Joe Ferry—a short, fast, sticky-fingered guy playing end—was the other. To my sorrow, he died of malaria two years later in the Philippine Islands.

During the 1943 season, I was a starter on the team, played a number of entire games, was co-captain toward the end of the season, and missed winning the Most Inspirational Player Award by one vote. Had I voted for myself instead of for Frank Taylor, the winner, I would have been the winner. That year, too, I was elected to the Tacoma All-City Team, second string. (If the truth be told, this was not really much of an honor, since there were only three teams in the Tacoma City League at that time.) Those may not seem like great achievements, but, when one is a junior in an all-boys high school, one does, quite naturally, attach a certain importance to the likes of them.

One of the entire games I played during that 1943 season was the one against Seattle's O'Dea High, a school staffed by the Christian Brothers. It had a powerhouse team that year. In connection with that mid-October game, I was referred to in a newspaper article as "Woodpecker Louie". The story behind that nickname was written up by me in February 1944. For over thirty years, it was in Mom's possession. In 1978, I received a photocopy of it.

The story in summary: My brother, Dick, and two of his classmates decided to spend the Sunday before that O'Dea game in the Weyerhauser Timber Lands in the foothills of Mount Rainier, near Eatonville, a logging town thirty-five miles southeast of Tacoma. I invited myself along. Dick and his buddies had each a .22-caliber rifle; I sported a .16-gauge double-barreled shotgun. Deer season being open, we had deer tags along, just in case. Mainly, however, we intended simply to do some small-game hunting.

We arrived at our destination around seven in the morning, parked the car at the end of a logging road spur, and took off into the virgin timber. Well before noon, we decided to head back to the car for lunch. To our surprise, each of us wanted to go in a different direction. Staying together as a group, we searched for the car, but in vain. We spent Sunday night sleeping under the trees. On Monday morning, giving up all hopes of finding the car and knowing that water would eventually lead us out, we began our hike downstream. That morning, Dick shot a woodpecker out of a tree. With food ever more on my mind, I picked it up and put it in my pocket. In the late afternoon, we made a makeshift camp for another night in the woods. By then, as I wrote in my story, the bird "was pretty stiff. But roasted, it tasted just like chicken."

By Tuesday afternoon, we had hiked out of the heavy timber to the road leading to Eatonville. Shortly after we reached the road, the Eatonville marshal came along, had us hop in, and drove us into Eatonville. From there, the county sheriff drove us to Tacoma. He told us that over a dozen men—among them all our dads and fellow workers—were out looking for us, and more were ready to go. Our neighbor brought Dick's car home.

I spent the Wednesday after that two-day ordeal in the wilderness at home, resting up. On Thursday, I was back in school. On Friday, I played the entire game against O'Dea High. Let woodpecker power not be underrated!

During the summer of 1943, I had had the one pre-Jesuit job that I can honestly say I genuinely loved: working as a deckhand for the Foss Tug & Barge Company. When I told a young man, also working for Foss, that I planned to work for the company only till the end of summer, then return to school, he assured me that I would change my mind and make tugboating my life's career. The temptation was there. To begin with, I was stationed at the Foss home port, in the Port of Tacoma harbor on Commencement Bay in Puget Sound. Along with other Foss employees, I was given room and board by the company in a floating bunkhouse. This could be at different sea levels, varying by as much as thirty feet, depending on the tides. One day, a couple of us took to diving off the roof of the bunkhouse. "Don't you guys know that that water is sixty feet deep?" the office manager warned us. Well . . . at least there was no danger of us hitting our heads on the bottom.

While stationed in the harbor, I worked on smaller tugs generally crewed by only the skipper and me. Small aircraft carriers were being built in Commencement Bay at the time. Heavy oblong contraptions on wheels were used to test the carriers' catapults, which were eventually to launch real fighter planes. When these makeshift "planes" were catapulted, they first zipped along the deck, then flew off into the water. It was our job to tow them back to alongside the ship, where a crane could haul them back up on deck for further tests. During lulls between tests, I was free to nap. Remarkably, despite the din created by the riveters and the roar of the torches of the welders as they worked on the ship's steel hull, I was able to nod off a few times.

Often, we also towed scows loaded with sawdust from lumber mills from place to place. Logging was big in western

Washington. With a heavy toggle chain over my shoulder and a pikestaff in hand, I spent much time walking around on logs while rafting them up to be towed to places near and far. This was anything but terra firma. Logs are round, roll easily, and bob in even a slight swell. One night, I had an immersion bath when I went down between two rafted-up logs. Fortunately, the raft was loose enough to enable me to come up through the logs again rather quickly. The ordeal soaked my body and dampened my spirits, but I continued on with Foss. Not too long after that misadventure, I was advanced to boats serving beyond the confines of Commencement Bay.

Still a deckhand, I now found myself on bigger boats, boats likely to go to any place on Puget Sound. To pick up a raft of logs, we once made a memorable trip to the western extremity of Puget Sound, to Shelton. On such longer trips, after swabbing the stern deck, I would do calisthenics to get into better shape for the upcoming football season. One day, we took a raft up to Quilcene at the end of Hood Canal. That night, at high tide, we anchored. The water was pleasantly warm. We younger crew members had ourselves a refreshing impromptu skinny-dip by the light of a full moon. When the Tacoma Narrows Bridge, having buckled and come down in a windstorm, was in the final stages of being dismantled, we worked on that project.

On one of our more memorable trips, we towed a scow loaded with sulfur from Tacoma to the Port Angeles pulp mill. On the way up, we stopped at Port Townsend to wait out the weather and to take showers. By the time we left Port Townsend, the windstorm had pretty well blown itself out, but there was still a very heavy head-on swell running, so much so that boats ahead of us appeared and disappeared as the swells rose and fell. With windows open and a distant horizon to focus on, I, in the wheelhouse taking my turn at the wheel, was able to hold my own during the first part of that trip. But when I had to go down into the closed-in engine room to do a routine oiling job, the up-and-down motion of the boat and the smell of diesel fumes made matters go from bad to worse. One need not be on the high seas to experience seasickness. I was to experience it again some twenty years later while crossing the English Channel from Ostend, Belgium, to Dover, England.

Once that summer, we took a tow all the way up into Canadian waters. This was during the war years. On top of the wheelhouse, we had a specially coded sign painted to identify us as a friendly American boat. Several times, we took boom logs through Seattle's Lake Union and the Lake Washington locks on into Lake Washington for the fresh water to kill the barnacles encrusting the logs. Little did I realize then that, fewer than ten years later, while teaching at Seattle Preparatory School, I would be looking out of my faculty house room window over to those same lakes and locks.

As the days on Foss tugs followed one after another, I came to see how one could readily get addicted to a life of tugboating. The boats themselves were cozy, secure little homes. One was, generally, under way, yet always at home. I got along well with fellow crew members. Thanks to the variety of duties and the endless goings and comings, the work was never boring. Moreover, it was life close to nature. Even a night watch at the wheel—as, with eyes fixed on the softly lit compass, one fought off sleep induced by the steady drone of the engine struggling to move forward a heavy tow of logs—had its little compensations: the moonlight playing on the water, the star-studded sky above, the silvery wake aglow with phosphorus. The mournful sound of the foghorn in the distance and the predictable flash of the lighthouse beacon were reassuring. It was an atmosphere well suited to spiritual meditation, though I do not recall doing much of that. And yet I am sure I felt the presence of God and actually did pray. As implied earlier, life in and on the water was all but connatural to me. Nevertheless, I knew I was not called to make a career of tugboating. In late August, as preseason football practice was about to begin, I stepped off a Foss tug for the last time.

At the beginning of my junior year at Bellarmine, in the fall of 1943, I was elected class president of my half of the junior class. That was the highest office to which I was ever to be elected or appointed in my life. During this time, I was also a member of the school's Quill and Scroll Club, a club for aspiring journalists. As such, I wrote a number of articles for the school paper, the *Bellarmine Lion*. In addition, I was also a halfhearted member of Our Lady's Sodality. I made the annual on-campus retreats with the rest of my classmates. My grades continued to be solid average. It was wartime. Many students had after-school or weekend jobs. Academic standards were below what one might have expected at a college preparatory school.

Sometime during my sophomore year, I already found myself, on rare occasions, attending a Mass in the faculty house chapel before the day's first class. Generally, I was alone or in attendance with only one or two others. One morning, while Father Joseph A. Lynch, the spiritual father to the Bellarmine students, was unvesting after Mass, he pointed to the *Mementote*, the list of the dead of the Oregon Province hanging on the sacristy wall, looked at me, and, in a matter-of-fact tone of voice, said simply, "Someday your name will be on that list."

At the time, I was far from seeing myself a Jesuit. Service in the U.S. Navy seemed the more immediate, obvious choice for me. In all honesty, I admit that it was not a matter of patriotism on my part. Rather, it was the thought of adventure on the high seas that Navy life was expected to bring with it that motivated me. Likewise, it was the prospect of adventure in Alaska that set my heart aglow one day, when, in the school library, I read an article by an Alaskan missionary in the *Jesuit Seminary News*.

At that time in my life, the thought of marriage had never entered my mind. Nor did it ever, subsequently. Except for taking a classmate, an eighth-grade girl, to a movie once, I never dated. During my junior year, I attended most of the Bellarmine high school dances. In fact, several months before I left for the Jesuit novitiate at Sheridan, Oregon, I was still taking dancing lessons at the Merrick Studio of Dance on Sixth Avenue, having let myself be talked into joining my brother Dick and two classmates, who had decided to take them.

After the 1943 football season was over, while continuing on as a junior at Bellarmine, having been duly bonded as required for the job, I went to work for the U.S. Postal Service at the Tacoma downtown station. I was assigned to the parcel post section. Mostly, this meant pitching packages into mailbags hung on racks on casters. As Christmas drew ever nearer, more and more packages addressed to people in the military on far-off warfronts came through our department. There were the pinup-girl calendars, of course; but mostly it was cookies or framed, glassed-in photos of loved ones. It was rather heartrending for me to have to handle so many packages—packages already coming apart and leaving a trail of crumbled cookies and broken glass—addressed by mothers, wives, and girlfriends to dear ones in places unknown. Some of the packages were beyond salvage. It was wartime.

One evening, after I had helped load many mail pouches into the back of an old van, I was given a .45-caliber side arm and told to hop into the back of the van and guard the mail.

I was then told by the driver that the "mail" I was sitting on was literally millions of dollars. It was the payroll, in small bills, for military personnel stationed at Fort Lewis, Washington. Our job was to get it safely to Tacoma's Union Station, where a train would take it on to Fort Lewis. Before he went up front to hop into the cab, the driver said to me, "If anyone tries to hold us up, let 'im have it!" When I asked what he meant by "it", he did not answer, leaving the decision up to me. Fortunately, it was a decision I never had to make. That van was so old and beat up that no one would ever have suspected what it might be hauling.

The time between the end of the 1943 football season and the day I was approved for entrance into the Society of Jesus turned out to be the most difficult time of my entire life, and Christmas 1943 was the most difficult Christmas of my entire life. Exactly four months from that Christmas, I would celebrate my eighteenth birthday and would have to register for the draft. Once registered, I would be subject to being called up for active military service at any time. Great was the pressure upon me to come to some kind of a decision regarding my future, and soon. That same Christmas, my brother Bill and my close friend and classmate since the seventh grade, Tommy Creedican, were home on leave, both wearing the navy uniform and talking navy. At the same time, I felt mysteriously, forcefully drawn to life as a priest in the Society of Jesus. My mind was in such a state of turmoil at the time that any rational decision concerning just about anything was beyond me. I could neither think straight, nor pray in any meaningful way. It was, in truth, a case of a teenager going through "the dark night of the soul"—without his ever having heard of such a spiritual trial.

Christmas vacation over, I went back to Bellarmine to begin the second semester of my junior year. My mental confusion continued unabated. I could not concentrate on my studies. Sometime in January, rather spontaneously, I went to see Father Lynch, a wise and shrewd judge of youth, who by then had known me personally for several years. When I first decided to see him, my hopes were not at all that he would pave the way for me to enter the Jesuits but that he would put my mind at ease by assuring me that, yes, in his judgment, I would be doing the right thing by joining the navy. After I had unburdened myself to him, he, reading my heart and discerning God's will for me, strongly counseled that, instead of joining the navy, I apply for acceptance into the Society of Jesus. I then told him, "But I get this strong urge to join the navy." He nevertheless continued to counsel me to enter the novitiate, pointing out to me that it was more logical for me to go there first rather than to think of going there after having served in the navy. If, after some time in the novitiate, he reasoned, it was determined that I definitely did not have a true vocation, I could still go and serve my country in the navy. Using the very same words, I again told him, "But I get this strong urge to join the navy." To that, he more or less simply repeated his reasons as to why I should apply to be accepted as a candidate for the Society of Jesus. Finding his logic persuasive, and being unerringly guided by a kindly Providence, I, then and there, applied. The process leading to my eventual acceptance was begun. With that, the storm in my soul was hushed to a gentle breeze.

There is no other man to whom I have ever owed a greater debt of gratitude than the one I owe to Father Lynch. I had come to a major fork in the road of my life, was faced with a choice that would affect radically the whole of my life— and the whole of my eternity—and he, as God's instrument, persuaded me to take what proved ever after to be the right road for me. I should mention here, too, that I have ever after been singularly grateful to God for giving me that "urge to join the navy" and for my explicitly mentioning it not once, but twice. Doing so forestalled any possible future anxious thoughts on my part that I might have entered the novitiate to avoid military service or that I was a "draft dodger" seeking monastic security during very troubled times. This is not to deny that, while I have throughout most of my life been drawn to faraway places of adventure, I have, at the same time, found images of security, such as a snowed-in cabin, or a tent in the wilderness, or an oasis in the desert, or a ship in a sheltered cove off a stormy sea, or a covered wagon on the Great Plains, naturally attractive. As do most people, I, too, relate warmly to words like "home" and "haven"—and, yes, "heaven"!

On January 20, 1944, Father Albert H. Allard, pastor of Sacred Heart parish in Tacoma, wrote to Father Lynch: "I am very glad to be able to recommend Louis Renner of this parish for entrance into the Jesuit Order. This young man, Louis Renner, has always been a studious and obedient pupil here at Sacred Heart School. I found him rather pious, somewhat above the average. He is of good moral character. I believe he is the type of boy who would be a good religious." On February 25, 1944, Father Henry J. Schultheis, rector and president of Bellarmine, wrote to Father Mark A. Gaffney, master of novices at Sheridan, "I believe you will find Louis Renner a very fine lad. Liked by everyone, he is a very quiet boy." (In his 2004 Christmas card to me, Brother Robert J. Ruzicka, O.F.M., veteran Alaskan missionary, was to refer to me as "the quiet giant" in his spiritual life.)

It was from Father Allard that my parents first learned that I was going to the novitiate. "I hear your boy is joining the Jesuits", he told them in a casual conversation. Why I never told them myself, I really could never say. The news came as a considerable surprise to them and the rest of the family. I remember distinctly the evening we were sitting around the dinner table, with me facing Dad at the opposite end, when he said, "I thought you were gonna join the navy." My parents were, of course, pleased at my decision to join the Jesuits. They had never talked to me about becoming a priest, but Mom told me some time later that she had often prayed that one of her boys might decide to become a priest.

To give an account of one's calling to religious life, or to the priesthood, is, for most religious and priests, not all that easy. (Few of us are a Saint Matthew, who, in the brief autobiographical sketch of his vocation, could write simply: "I was sitting there collecting taxes, when along came Jesus and told me to follow Him. I, then and there, got up and followed Him.") In my case, I have never been able to give logical, concrete, humanly understandable reasons for my having entered upon the path that led to my taking religious vows and going on to the priesthood. I was clearly not running away from anything. I did not enter with the conscious intention "to save my soul"—as I had no reason to believe that it was in jeopardy. I had only a general, vague idea of what vowed life really entailed. I cannot, with any truth whatever, say that I had great aspirations of "saving souls". In general, I admired the sisters, priests, and Jesuits who had, up to then, been a part of my life at one time or another, but I cannot say I felt myself drawn to emulate them. Yes, the thought of a future in Alaska was attractive, but it was Alaska as a place of far-off adventure rather than as a field where I might exercise my missionary zeal— for, if the truth be told, I had no such zeal. Even when I celebrated a Mass of thanksgiving on the occasion of the fiftieth anniversary of my entrance into the Society, I could not give any clear reasons as to why I had entered the Society. I spoke of being "strangely, mysteriously drawn", of

being, so to speak, "vacuumed" into religious life. Whatever the reasons I gave the four who examined me before
I was accepted as a candidate for the Society, they must have
been adequate, for all four approved of my being accepted.

It has always been a consolation to me that, never having
been able to give a plausible, natural explanation for my calling to be a Jesuit priest, I have, happily and gratefully, been
forced to conclude that my vocation can only be accounted
for as a call, ever so mysterious, from the Lord Himself to
follow Him. His consoling words, "You have not chosen me;
I have chosen you", keep reechoing in my mind and heart.
Flawed instrument of Divine Providence that I am, I see my
vocation as all grace, all gift, all favor. What have I that I
have not received? What return can I make to the Lord, Who
"called me by His grace"? How to express my gratitude?

Chapter 3

The Novitiate, Sheridan, Oregon: 1944–1946

Well before I actually entered the novitiate, Father Leo J. Robinson, the father provincial of the Oregon Province, and Father Mark A. Gaffney, master of novices, agreed that I should enter on March 24, a month before my eighteenth birthday, April 25, the day on which I would have to register for the draft and become subject to being drafted into the military. The twenty-fourth of March was decided upon, so that the following day, the feast of the Annunciation, would be my "vow day" two years later. (In the early 1940s, it was customary to have candidates for the Society of Jesus enter the novitiate as members of a group and on the eve of some Marian feast. August 14, the eve of the Assumption of the Blessed Virgin Mary, and September 7, the eve of the Nativity of the Blessed Virgin Mary, were the usual entrance dates.)

About the twenty-second of March 1944, I packed a small bag mostly with some clothes, including the two letterman sweaters—minus the letters. (The sweaters were sent to Germany immediately after the war, when the great need for clothes of all kinds there became known.) There were no farewell parties. On the morning of the twenty-fourth, Dad, having said good-bye with a handshake the evening before and having assured me that I would be welcome back home anytime, went to work, as usual, before I was up. Bill was off in the South Pacific. The rest of the family went through their usual routine before heading off to school. About the same time, I grabbed my bag, hugged my tearful mother farewell, and walked up to the McKinley Hill busline to take the bus downtown to catch a bus for Portland, Oregon.

The trip to Portland was uneventful. Lost in my thoughts, as I was crossing a new, and major, threshold in my life, I hardly noticed the scenery whizzing past my bus window. Sometime before we crossed the Columbia River into Oregon, we stopped for lunch. In the late afternoon, in Portland, I boarded the bus for Sheridan. It was getting dark by the time we arrived at Sheridan. There I was met by Brother Benjamin A. (Benny) Trautman, who asked me if I was the new "postulant" coming to the novitiate. "Postulant?" That was a new word for me. Still, I told him, yes, I was the new postulant—whatever that might be. In a small gray pickup truck, he drove me past fields still fallow, across Rock Creek, through prune and apple orchards, and on up the high hill to Saint Francis Xavier Novitiate crowning the hill and overlooking the broad Yamhill River Valley below.

On the front steps of the big cement novitiate building, I was cordially welcomed by Father Mark A. Gaffney, master of novices—a saintly man to whom I related well—and David B. Collins, a second-year novice, who, as my "guardian angel" during my twelve days of postulancy, would introduce me to novitiate life. The moment I stepped through those novitiate doors, a sense of profound peace came over me, a peace born of the firm conviction that Jesuit life was the only life for me. That sense of deep interior peace was never to leave me. Nor was an equally profound sense of gratitude for that peace ever to leave me.

My first night at Sheridan was the first night in my life that I slept between white sheets. From the outset, I liked my little cubicle, one of seven in a long room. Cubicle partitions, being only six feet high, did not go up to the ceiling of the room. Each cubicle had its own draw curtain. Between the outside wall of the room and the cubicles there was a narrow passageway. The cubicles were furnished with utmost simplicity: a cot with army blankets, a desk, a chair, a little stand for clothes and personal items, a few hooks on one wall for hang-up clothes, a simple kneeler (not a prie-dieu), and a gooseneck lamp. The floors throughout the novitiate building at that time were all still bare concrete. Rooms at the ends of the second and third floors housed two urinals, several toilet stalls, tin-bottomed shower stalls, and a long metal trough with washbasins hanging along it. The basins served as sinks. Our meals were taken in the dining room in the one-story wooden bungalow that had housed the novitiate before the permanent novitiate building, the concrete building next to it, went up. The meals were hardly gourmet but wholesome enough, plentiful, and adequately prepared. The heart of the novitiate as a physical plant was the chapel. This, with its lofty ceiling, Gothic arches, and stained-glass windows, was a gem in the best sense of the word. Except for the chapel, all else about novitiate life was rather plain and simple. I, personally, however, had no trouble whatever adjusting to it. My background on the farm and at the Fallon boarding school, as well as my family life, in general, had prepared me well for the externals of novitiate life.

At the end of my twelve-day postulancy, having been initiated, to a degree, into the novitiate routine and taught the rudimentary mechanics of making a meditation by my "guardian angel", I was ready to receive my cassock. Since I was a class of only one, the "Cassock Day" ceremony was of the utmost simplicity. In his office, in my presence and that of Brother Collins, Father Master made the Sign of the Cross over the cassock lying on his desk, gave it a few sprinkles of holy water, then told me: "It's yours." He went on, however, to explain that it was not really mine but one of Father Rector's, a make-do cassock for me until one tailored to me would be ready some weeks later. The trouble was that Father Rector, Father John S. Forster, was a good six feet tall, and the cassock had been made to fit him. However, with some noticeable tucking up and cinching in, and some practice, I was soon able to move about in it without walking up the front inside of it. In all honesty, I must admit that I did not wear that cassock with all that much pride. However, it was cassock enough to put me into "the long black line", and that made me feel good. It was wartime.

On April 25, 1944, my eighteenth birthday, accompanied by fellow novice Paul B. Mueller, I took the bus to nearby McMinnville to register for the draft. As a seminarian, I was granted A-4 status, which exempted me from active service.

During my novitiate days already, as well as throughout my subsequent years in the Society, I considered myself blessed in always having companionable, congenial fellow community members. As of August 31, 1944, we numbered twenty-four novices: fourteen in the first year, ten in the second. Two of the first-year novices were lay brother candidates. Virtually all of my fellow novices had entered the novitiate as graduates just out of high school. Several of us had entered out of our junior year. We all had much in common. On the surface, we seemed to be a contented group of young men. But underneath, we all had our individual inner battles to fight. The basic battle, of course, was the matter of one's vocation. The novitiate was the time for us, as individuals, to determine, as far as was humanly possible, whether or not we had a genuine calling to life in the Society of Jesus. In my case, I can truthfully say that, from the day I first entered the novitiate, I was certain beyond a doubt that Jesuit life was the only life for me. I had fought my battle two months previously. Being blessed with inner peace myself, it pained me when I sensed fellow novices anguishing over the matter of their vocation, only eventually to leave the novitiate.

At the time of my entry, the whole novitiate community numbered sixty-eight. Given such numbers, there was considerable diversity among us. In addition to the novices, there were also priests, lay brothers, and the "juniors", men who had completed their noviceship and taken vows. Still, we were one big family in the Lord—though a family of humans, with the customary shortcomings of humans and the consequent tensions and conflicts.

I entered the Jesuits with the express hope that I would one day be assigned to serve in Alaska. One of the two lay brother candidates referred to above was Ignatius J. Jakes, an Iñupiat Eskimo from the Seward Peninsula in northwestern Alaska. Inasmuch as he was for me a flesh-and-blood link to Alaska, the land where I aspired to spend most of my Jesuit life, he was of great significance to me. Brother Jakes and I were to celebrate our golden jubilees as Jesuits together at the Saint Mary's mission on the Andreafsky River, Alaska, on April 22, 1994. At Sheridan, I played my first games of chess with him; in Fairbanks, Alaska, during the last years of his life, I was to play my final games with him.

While Brother Jakes made Alaska physically present to me, I, as a novice, was, at the same time, in contact also with Jesuit priests in far-off Alaska, exchanging letters with them and sending them religious articles, such as scapulars, holy cards, and Sacred Heart badges. Among the highlights of my years at Sheridan were the visits paid us by Jesuit Alaskan missionaries Fathers John B. Baud, Paul C. Deschout, and Paul

C. O'Connor, as well as the movies on Alaska shown us on several occasions by the "Glacier Priest", Father Bernard R. Hubbard.

Being basically an uncomplicated person, relatively easily satisfied, and able to make do with whatever resources are at hand, I took to most aspects of novitiate life quite naturally and with enthusiasm. The more temporal aspects of that life, such as helping out in the laundry, carrying slabwood for the furnace, splitting oak for the kitchen stove, helping the cook, setting tables, waiting on tables, washing dishes, sweeping corridors, picking prunes and apples in season, and working in the hayfields, were not all that new to me. In general, I enjoyed attending to such tasks. I liked to see my efforts produce tangible, measurable results.

Some of the novices had more specific, long-range assignments. One novice, having a background in music, was assigned the role of organist. Several others, somewhat arbitrarily, were appointed barbers. In passing, I might mention that I was a priest before I ever went to a professional barber. Before I entered the novitiate, Dad always cut my hair. Thereafter, fellow Jesuits barbered me. Since around 1970, all my haircuts have been self-inflicted. Only a few of the few to whom I ever made this known had the courtesy to act surprised upon learning it.

While we were taught a little Latin, Greek, and English composition in the novitiate, the primary purpose of the novitiate—a kind of spiritual boot camp—was to introduce us to matters of the spirit. The emphasis was on spiritual formation. Through regular conferences on the spirituality of Saint Ignatius, the reading of the lives of Jesuit saints, and reflecting and meditating on these, we were introduced to the Jesuit way of life. The daily order, signaled by the ringing of bells, was rather rigid: rise at 5:00, wash up, visit the chapel, do an hour of meditation, attend Mass, stay for a period of thanksgiving after Mass, eat breakfast, do chores, read in Alphonsus Rodriguez' *The Practice of Perfection* for thirty minutes, hear a forty-five-minute conference by the master of novices, take a break; read for fifteen minutes in *The Imitation of Christ* by Thomas à Kempis, take a break; make a fifteen-minute examination of conscience, eat dinner, do chores, have recreation, take a siesta, engage in walking (with assigned partners) or outdoor games (handball or softball), do a thirty-minute afternoon meditation, eat supper, do chores, have recreation, do thirty minutes of spiritual reading (lives of Jesuit saints), make an examination of conscience, have private prayer in the chapel, go to bed at 9:30. During so-called regular order, that was the daily schedule. It took a degree of self-discipline on one's part to put mind, heart, and soul into it.

Novitiate life, however, was not all work and prayer. Time was allotted, too, for recreation and play. I learned to play chess as a novice, also handball, two games of which I became quite fond. I looked forward to our softball games. Novitiate recreational highlights for me were the long hikes—with assigned companions—I took in the hilly, wooded surroundings. On Thursdays, we had "villa day". Generally, on villa day, we went to a cabin in the woods for a picnic-style noonday meal. Often, on villa days, before we went on to wash up and make our afternoon meditation, we would gather around the piano, played with expertise by Father Gaffney, and sing a considerable variety of songs, sacred and profane, opera and popular. The more common, simple walks along the roads on novitiate property, too, were pleasant changes from the indoor, interior life. As did my fellow novices, so I, too, found devotion in stopping to pray at the little shrines on the novitiate property. Among these was a very unostentatious one honoring Saint Thérèse, "the Little Flower".

Most of the formal devotions of novitiate life—the Mass, the Way of the Cross, the Rosary, the Angelus, standard prayers—had long since been part of my prenovitiate days. Formal mental prayer, meditation, a systematic examination of conscience, and spiritual reading were new to me. One of the main functions of the novitiate was precisely to form the novices in these spiritual exercises. Written large, the spiritual exercises in question here are the *Spiritual Exercises* of Saint Ignatius of Loyola. These were at the very heart of what novitiate life was all about. Throughout October, as first-year novices, we were engaged in making these spiritual exercises, called also "the thirty-day retreat" or "the long retreat". Most of us, not being even fledgling mystics, found thirty days—punctuated by only three "break days"—of five conferences a day, plus the meditations, prayers, and reflections, a demanding, tiring undertaking. I do not remember receiving any special graces or illuminations during that retreat. I might, however, mention here one grace received (whether during the retreat or after it, I can no longer remember). It was that of having a bout with scruples. While having scruples can be painful, I, as a priest, consider having had them a grace, a favor; for, once having experienced them myself, I was better able to understand people who came to me for help with that spiritual affliction.

During that thirty-day retreat, along with fellow retreatants, I picked many an apple in the novitiate orchards. Apples, applesauce, and apple pie were novitiate staples. It was a beautiful October, with a variety of trees richly adorned in full autumn colors. That October also marked a big step forward for the novitiate building as such. Its raw concrete exterior received its first coat of tar. Through open windows, we could hear the man up on the scaffold yelling down to the man on the ground: "Hey, Eddie, another bucket of hot!" The smell of hot tar, a pleasant smell to me, was, throughout my subsequent life, always to evoke memories of that first retreat.

"Dear Mom, Dad, and All," I began a letter dated December 19, 1944.

> Just a line to extend my greetings to you all. A Merry Christmas to you all and a joyous and blessed New Year. You too must be pretty busy, as I am. Two other brothers and I are decorating a room about as big as the Bellarmine gym, and we are carrying half of the countryside in. We'll have about twenty trees, and lots of moss and ferns. Around here they really do things up for Christmas. Everybody is busy practicing singing, etc. I myself will be a torchbearer during the solemn High Midnight Mass.
>
> Drop me a line sometime so I'll know I'm not addressing mail to a haunted house.
>
> Your loving son and brother, Lou

Mom kept that letter for many years before it got back to me. Even without it as a memory refresher, I would never have forgotten how three of us transformed that common room with slabwood and greenery. What the decorations lacked in artistic finesse they made up for in sheer bulk. In retrospect, I believe the decorating frenzy, the singing practice, and other occupations were meant, in part, to keep us from dwelling on Christmases past and getting homesick.

In the above letter, I remarked that I was to be a torchbearer that first Christmas at Sheridan. Though having always had a good ear for music and, from the late 1940s onward, an abiding fondness for classical music and opera, I never had the hint of a singing voice. Throughout my years of Jesuit training, I was never in the choirs. Happily, I left the singing to those who could sing, while I bore the torches and served the solemn High Masses. As a performing artist, apart from being able to play a few recognizable tunes on the harmonica, I could also tap out with one finger a passable rendition of "Twinkle, Twinkle, Little Star". With that, I also pretty well reached the outer limits of my ventures into astronomy. And yet, with the German philosopher Immanuel Kant, I, too, can, in truth, say that there are two realities that never cease to fill me with awe and wonderment: the starry heavens above me and the moral law within me.

After that Christmas season of 1944, there followed another lengthy period of "regular order". The daily routine varied little from day to day. Somehow, time, during those periods of regular order, seemed to go by surprisingly fast for me. I took them in stride, as I did most all of novitiate life. My second year of novitiate, shortened by three months, more or less, paralleled the first year, the major difference being that, unlike during the first year, when I made the thirty-day retreat, during the second year, I made only an eight-day retreat.

What kind of a novice was I in the eyes of my novice master, Father Gaffney? In his monthly report for May 1945 to Father Provincial, he wrote concerning me: "He likes it cold, part of his vocation to Alaska. On the swim picnic he was challenged to prove he loved the cold water. He played around in it like an old hippo." In his September 1945 report, he wrote concerning me: "Solid as can be. Dreams Alaska. Making a fine retreat. Is a good hard worker, quite efficient. Has a lot to learn about reading; his English is poor owing to the fact that he talked German in childhood."

Chapter 4

The Juniorate, Sheridan, Oregon: 1946–1948

In early January 1946, I moved over to the east wing of the novitiate building for what in Jesuit parlance at that time were called "juniorate studies", or simply the "juniorate". Not having yet taken my vows by then, I was still a novice but designated now as a "skullcap junior". On March 25, 1946, in a low-key ceremony during the morning community Mass in the domestic chapel, I took the simple, but perpetual, vows of poverty, chastity, and obedience that constituted me a full-fledged member of the Society of Jesus. After the Mass, I was given my "vow crucifix" and began wearing a biretta. What made my "vow day"—a day of much spiritual joy and consolation—further memorable was the visit paid me that day by Dad and Mom and my sisters, Julie and Della.

Given my early years on the farm and my German heritage, the vows of poverty and obedience presented no particular difficulties for me. Regarding the vow of chastity, I wrote in a short article published in the 1990 issue of *Laborers in His Harvest*:

For close to half a century, I have experienced chastity as a personal gift, as a treasured gift from the Lord Jesus. I have experienced this gift also as a profound mystery. The call to vowed and lived chastity and the love of the Lord Who has called me to a life of chastity are both equally mysterious to me—accepted, however, unhesitatingly, embracingly, without shadow of doubt, as inestimable, mysterious graces. While I esteem my gift of chastity as a personal gift, I esteem it no less as a gift given for the sake of the Kingdom, as an apostolic gift, conferred also for the spiritual benefit of the people of God.

When I entered the novitiate, it was still wartime. Metal vow crucifixes were hard to come by. However, in Hooper Bay, Alaska, on October 20, 1940, veteran Jesuit Alaskan missionary Father John B. Sifton had died suddenly of a heart attack. Knowing of the need for vow crucifixes at Sheridan, Father John P. Fox, missionary at Hooper Bay, sent Father Sifton's vow crucifix to Sheridan. In need of repair, the crucifix was sent to my Dad in Tacoma, where he saw to it that it was restored to good condition. Since March 25, 1946, the onetime Father Sifton vow crucifix has been my vow crucifix.

The courses in Latin, Greek, and English that were taught us in the novitiate were of a very limited scope. Spiritual, rather than intellectual, formation was what the novitiate was all about. In the juniorate, the emphasis was heavily on the classics and humanities: Latin and Greek, English literature and composition, and history. The juniorate studies marked the beginning of my awakening to the intellectual life for its own sake. Prior to that, high school and novitiate studies— except for some of the English literature we read in high school, which I enjoyed—were simply hurdles taken as par for the course. I can honestly say that I developed a natural liking for, and genuinely enjoyed, the classics and English literature. On my own, I read many English and American novels, Virgil's *Aeneid* in Latin, and the sixth book of Homer's *Iliad* in Greek. Dante's *Divine Comedy* was of special interest to me. I read the whole of it in an English translation and many parts of it in Italian. An old 1837 Italian edition of Dante's *La divina commedia* is one of the few non-Alaskan books I took with me when I left Alaska. By the time I was nearing the end of my juniorate studies, I had become so enamored of the great works of literature and so wanting to read more of them, and in depth, that I, quite seriously, discussed with Father Provincial Harold O. Small the possibility of my staying on at Sheridan an extra year just to read at leisure and at length more of the world's great literature. Wisely, he had me move on with my class to philosophical studies.

During my first summer in the juniorate, we were taught a course in elementary German. I did well in this, though I was faulted on the basis of my plattdeutsch accent. During the other two summers, we were taught courses in French and Washington state history. This latter course we took as a prerequisite for our anticipated certification as teachers in the state of Washington. Along with teaching us this course, John H. Wright, still a Jesuit seminarian, introduced us to classical music, using as an example thereof Mozart's Symphony no. 40 in G Minor. This was my first introduction to classical music, music that has ever since been an integral, indispensable part of my life. As for the course in French, while elementary, it did enable me to make my first attempt at reading Saint Thérèse's autobiography, *Histoire d'une âme.*

However, juniorate life was not all prayer and academics. There was also some manual work but less than in the novitiate. We helped with the annual hay harvest, something to which I always looked forward. I continued to enjoy splitting stove wood and working in the orchards. There was more play. In addition to handball courts, we had, by now, also a basketball court set up. I much preferred basketball to handball. We played softball, took long hikes, and occasionally went swimming in the nearby river. Thursdays, as in the novitiate, were villa days. During our evening recreation periods, we generally strolled, speaking Latin the while. During some recreation periods, we played chess or bridge, the latter something newly introduced into juniorate life. I took to bridge with enthusiasm and stayed with it for years, winning some second prizes in it while in philosophical and theological studies. In the family circle, I had played kid card games with my brothers, but bridge was something new.

The Oregon Province has been blessed from its inception with wonderful villas. At the mouth of the Nestucca River on the Pacific Ocean, near Tillamook, the juniorate had its villa. The accommodations bordered on the primitive, but wild nature—the river, the ocean, the immense evergreens, the wild birds and game—more than compensated for what we lacked in amenities. Those three-week annual major vacations of boating, swimming in the river, jumping in the surf, and catching and boiling and eating crabs on the spot were among the true high points of my juniorate years, years of intensive study. Some of us gave a new twist to the words of Saint Stanislaus, the Jesuit saint who died at an early age, who said, *"Ad majora natus sum"* (I was born for greater things), translating them, "I was born for majors."

At the end of my first year in the juniorate, on December 30, 1946, I wrote to Father Paul O'Connor:

A few weeks ago, Father [Leo J.] Robinson [provincial of the Oregon Province at the time] made his annual visitation. In a long colloquy with him, he assured me that, if he was in office when my time for regency [the Jesuit term for the normally three-year teaching practicum] came, he would send me to Alaska. If out of office, he promised me a good recommendation. Since I entered with the intention of going to the missions, he told me that it is quite certain that I would be sent there as a priest, even if I wouldn't go as a regent.

Near the end of that letter, I added, "I myself am as healthy and happy as ever, and all fired up over Alaska." Here it might be wondered, "How long will that youthful fire burn before it burns itself out?"

On April 22, 1948, I wrote to Father Provincial Small:

Long before I ever thought of entering upon the religious life, I found anything about Alaska of particular interest. True, it was little more than a boyish attraction for adventure, but from that desire of adventure grew the attraction for the foreign missions. During my three years of high school, the desire for the Alaskan missions was frequently before me, and it was finally that same strong desire that moved me to apply for admittance to the Society. Before entering, I already told one of my examiners that I wanted to go to Alaska. Since my entrance into the Society, the desire of serving God there has never left me.

By this time, I had exchanged letters on the subject of my one day serving in Alaska also with Father General John B. Janssens in Rome. Here it might be wondered, too, "How long will that 'strong desire' last?"

A year later, on April 27, 1949, as I was nearing the end of my first year of philosophical studies at Mount Saint Michael's on the outskirts of Spokane, Washington, I again wrote to Father Small: "Since you already told me to prepare for Alaska last December and promised to send me as a scholastic [Jesuit seminarian] if no serious obstacle arose, this letter is hardly necessary. However, I see no harm in writing to you on this day of renovation of vows and again making known to you my ardent desire of going to Alaska, even as a scholastic."

During the latter part of August 1948, after having taken my third major vacation at Nestucca and having made my annual eight-day retreat, I was ready to leave Sheridan for three years of philosophical studies at Mount Saint Michael's. Sometime during the third week of August, my brothers Bill (the driver) and Len drove me from Sheridan—via Mount Rainier, where we lunched and stretched our legs—to Tacoma. With us we had my classmate J. Patrick Hurley. This was my first visit home since I had left over four years earlier. After I had spent three days visiting my family, Bill drove me to Seattle. There, in the Kindall home, I spent a short time with classmates John J. Kindall and Hurley before we boarded the night train for the trip to Spokane, where, early the next morning, we were met by classmates Joseph L. Showalter and Patrick F. King, who drove us to the home of Showalter's aunt Agnes for breakfast. After giving us a tour of Spokane, in the later afternoon, they drove us up to "the Mount".

Chapter 5

Mount Saint Michael's, Spokane, Washington: 1948–1951

Upon my arrival at Mount Saint Michael's, it was immediately evident to me that "the Mount" and I seemed to have been made for one another. There was the place itself. In the big main building, I had my own room instead of a little cubicle, as at Sheridan. There were the swimming pool, the ball fields, the basketball courts, and the ice skating and hockey rinks. And there was the surrounding farm country, ideally suited for long rural walks and hikes. And there were the small villa cabins in the vicinity, as well as the major villas in Idaho. All this created a kind of natural physical habitat for me. Indoors, we had the music room, with its many classical music records; and the radio, on which we listened to the Saturday Metropolitan Opera broadcasts. There were the bridge tables and chessboards. And there were new-release movies at fairly regular intervals.

My social life and my view of and understanding of the Society of Jesus were significantly broadened by the presence at the Mount of classmates, in addition to my fellow Oregonians, from other U.S. provinces, mainly from California, but also from several South American provinces. We now addressed one another as "Mister" instead of as "Brother", as had been the custom at Sheridan. In retrospect, I see the three years we young Jesuits spent at Mount Saint Michael's as a quasi-adolescent period, a period of maturation, in our spiritual and intellectual training as Jesuits. The study of philosophy itself, the larger community (139 Jesuits), and a greater exposure to the outside world contributed to this. Some of us taught catechism to children in the parishes below the Mount or helped decorate parishes for Christmas. In contrast to the Mount, Sheridan had been somewhat of a hothouse. Life had been sheltered, isolated. Except for visits to a dentist or doctor, or a stay at the ocean villa during major vacations, we had never gotten away from the place. The rare visits paid us by members of our immediate families had been our only contact with outsiders. We had never seen a newspaper. From time to time, Father Gaffney had informed us on major World War II developments. At the Mount, newspaper clippings on the bulletin board kept us posted on important events, such as the Korean War (1950–1953). This interested me without preoccupying me. In general, life at the Mount was freer, less regimented, and left more decisions up to us as individuals.

As at Sheridan, I had, from the outset, good rapport with the faculty and the whole community, in general. We were ninety-seven "scholastics". Each of the three years had roughly the same number. In keeping with our personal temperaments and interests, we tended to form subgroups. The swimming pool, the ball field, the handball and basketball courts, the music room, the bridge tables and chessboards all had their devotees. During my first year, my interest in chess brought me into close contact with Arthur E. Swain, a third-year Californian, an excellent chess player, and an outstanding student, majoring in philosophy. We enjoyed many a session at the chessboard; but of far greater importance to me was his ever readiness to be a personal tutor to me in the matter of philosophy. From him, I learned not only about philosophy but how to philosophize, how to think about and reflect on reality on a new level, on the level of metaphysics. It is no exaggeration to say that, in my formation as a philosopher, I owed as much to him as I did to my professors. All in all, they were good, and I related well to them. All too often, however, they did little more than relay to students what was already in textbooks. Textbooks and lectures were in Latin. Juniorate studies and the speaking of Latin during the evening recreation periods at Sheridan had given me an adequate command of Latin.

At Mount Saint Michael's, as at Sheridan, domestic chores—setting and waiting on tables, washing dishes, doing general housekeeping, helping harvest potatoes, working on the grounds—were also part of the daily routine. Some of us had more-demanding job assignments. Shortly after my arrival at the Mount, I was assigned the role of "tombstone engraver". This meant engraving key dates on headstones, upright slabs of marble, of recently deceased Jesuits buried in the Oregon Province cemetery at Mount Saint Michael's.

During my years at the Mount, I served also first as sub–villa minister at the major villa at Twin Lakes, Idaho, then as head villa minister at the major villa on Lake Pend Oreille, Idaho. It just so happened that, during my two years as villa minister, the move was made from the one villa to the other. I played a major role in the closing of the former and the opening of the latter. As villa minister, I was kind of a quartermaster. During the Lake Pend Oreille villa season, I made sure I had time to allow myself to do some leisurely trolling for trout, mostly silvers. I caught my share. Sport fishing was not new to me. By the time I entered the Jesuits, I had done a fair amount of it in Commencement Bay and in lakes near Tacoma. Among the off-season perks of being villa minister was getting to spend time, along with a handpicked crew, at Twin Lakes during some winter months sawing blocks of ice out of the frozen-over lake and storing them in the icehouse, where, imbedded in sawdust, they kept till needed in the summer. Felling old, tall timber, sawing it up, and splitting it for stove wood was another perk. Daniel J. Tainter (Missouri Province) and Daniel Fontana (Turin Province) were members of my crews. For seven years, Tainter and I were to be co-missionaries in Alaska. Fontana and I were to be fellow teachers at Seattle Preparatory School for the 1951–1952 school year. A decade later, in his native Italy, he was to be my traveling companion and tutor in Italian.

Philosophy, along with ongoing spiritual formation, was what life at Mount Saint Michael's was all about. Some took it in stride; others merely endured it as an essential part of Jesuit training. In my case, vis-à-vis philosophy, it was love at first sight. Before I left Sheridan, I had declared German as my major. At the Mount, in short order, and with the permission of superiors, I switched to philosophy. Metaphysics, ethics, and natural theology were the three branches of philosophy that interested me in particular. They especially, I found subsequently, prepared me well for theological studies. Aristotle and Saint Thomas Aquinas were the big names in Jesuit philosophical studies at the time. It was not only what I learned at the Mount that prepared me well for theology. The very studying of philosophy, as a mental discipline, was a good preparation.

During my second year at the Mount, I was proficient enough in metaphysics to be chosen by my professors to participate in the annual, hour-long, formal "disputation" as one of the two objectors, or "adversaries", to the thesis being defended. There I was, up on the stage, sitting at a little table—along with a classmate, likewise an objector, at his little table—before the whole community, trying to shoot down a thesis being defended by a third classmate at his little table.

This entire academic display, in Latin, was staged, of course, and totally lacking in spontaneity, with rather strict rules governing it. Still, to be part of it was a bit of an honor, a feather, albeit a little one, in my academic hat.

During one summer, we philosophy majors were taught a course in aesthetics, a course based on French philosopher Jacques Maritain's *Art and Scholasticism, The Frontiers of Poetry,* and *Creative Intuition in Art and Poetry.* These three works became part of my personal library ever after. They, and the course, were to stand me in good stead later, when, at the University of Alaska–Fairbanks, I was to teach a course for the philosophy department entitled "Unity in the Arts".

While at the Mount, during one semester, along with courses in philosophy, I took an obligatory course in basic physics; during another semester, I took a basic course in chemistry, likewise obligatory. The physics teacher asked me to consider majoring in physics. The chemistry teacher eased me by with a C.

By the end of my third year at the Mount, I had my M.A. degree in philosophy, conferred upon me by Gonzaga University in Spokane, Washington. "Order in the Life of Man through Finality" was the title of my qualifying dissertation. Shortly before leaving the Mount, I received the tonsure, constituting me a cleric, and the minor orders of acolyte, exorcist, lector, and porter. I was now ready to go into "regency", generally, at the time, a three-year period of teaching in one of the Oregon Province high schools or a two-year period of prefecting boys at the Holy Cross mission in Alaska.

Where to go for regency? How stood matters now with my being "all fired up over Alaska" and with that "ardent desire" to serve there that had "since my entrance to the Society never left me" and was still alive as late as April 27, 1949? By

December 8, 1950, philosophy and the academic life had, for some time already, clearly won out. Alaska was now no longer on the horizon of my active apostolic interests. On that day, I wrote to Father Provincial Small:

> This is one letter that I'm sure you never expected to receive from me. After all my talk about Alaska, I write telling you that (what I long suspected, but was never so convinced of as now) I do not think that God wants my services in Alaska as much as in the Province. This is not a hasty judgment. I have given it considerable thought and prayer. The reasons for staying in the Province far outweigh those for going to Alaska. I would prefer to discuss these reasons during your next visitation rather than mention them here. However, in all things, my only hope for peace and joy will consist in perfect submission to the holy will of God as manifested to me through you.

Chapter 6

Seattle Preparatory School, Seattle, Washington: 1951–1954

For my regency, I was assigned to teach at Seattle Preparatory School—still an all-boys school in the 1950s—in Seattle, Washington. After attending a summer school in philosophy at Gonzaga University, followed by close to three weeks of vacationing at Gonzaga's villa on Hayden Lake, Idaho, and an eight-day retreat at Omak, Washington, I found myself, in late August 1951, on the Seattle Prep Panthers bus, along with fellow regents, headed for Seattle. I knew Seattle only somewhat, having played football there against Seattle Prep and O'Dea. I had been there, too, while in high school, trying, without success, to find a job on some fishing boat due to sail north soon to some Alaskan fishery.

Throughout my three years at Seattle Prep, I taught English, Latin, and religion to sophomores. I also taught geometry one year, and German another, to juniors. German was a "natural" for me. Geometry, however, for one who never rose above C-level in mathematics, was another matter. Nevertheless, both students and teacher survived it, and both with a passing grade. All in all, I was a happy teacher and was rated a good one by both students and faculty—in spite of my soft, rather weak voice. When Father Christopher J. McDonnell, S.J., Prep's principal, learned that my 2-B Latin class had placed among the top such classes in the Oregon

Province high school exams, he muttered something about my voice and just shook his head.

I liked the subjects I taught; and I liked the students I taught. In keeping with the Jesuit principle of pedagogy, *cura personalis alumnorum* (a personal concern for the students), I tried to know and treat each student as an individual.

As a member of the teaching faculty, each one of us was, by that very fact, also officially an "assistant prefect of discipline". As such, we were expected to help keep order in the hallways, classrooms, and study halls. At times, keeping order in a sixth-period study hall full of restless sophomores presented me with a bit of a challenge. However, for the most part, I rose to it, once even letting one of my fellow regents know that I thought myself a good disciplinarian. With a big guffaw and laugh, he said, "Do you know what your students call you behind your back? The 'blond *dove*'!"

Throughout my three years at Prep, I was property room manager. That meant that, with one or two student assistants, I spent the seventh period of each school day in a small room in the basement of the school handing out practice uniforms to the athletes: football in the fall, basketball in the winter, baseball and track in the spring. For the next several hours, then, while the athletes did calisthenics, practiced, and scrimmaged, I might be down at the practice field with them. Sometimes, during a nonbasketball season, I might be in the gym getting some exercise shooting baskets or playing in some pickup game. After the day's practice session, when the athletes returned to the dressing room to take off their practice gear, to shower, and to dress for home, my assistants and I would take the uniforms back in, hang them up to dry, and hand out and take back towels. At regular intervals, the dirty uniforms and towels had to be taken down to the basement of the faculty house to be laundered, then carried back up to the property room. The elevation difference between the two was equal to about seven stories.

One of my property room assistants, Michael Wyne—as a sophomore, also a student in my Latin class—proved to be an exceptionally good assistant. We became close mutual friends and corresponded with one another for decades. (We will meet him again in chapter 8.) David J. Leigh, to whom I taught Latin and handed out basketball uniforms, went on to become a Jesuit and a specialist on the subject of auto-biographies and the writing of the same. (Thanks to his suggestions and comments, this autobiography is considerably improved.) Little did I think, in the fall of 1953, when I handed out a varsity football uniform to sophomore Francis E. (Frank) Case, another of my students, that he would go on to become a Jesuit priest, the father provincial of the Oregon Province, and, by the year 2005, the number-two man, as executive secretary, in the governance of the Society of Jesus. While on the subject of students, I might mention here the most brilliant one I ever had in class, namely, John M. Hutchinson—not an athlete. He was a straight-A student at Seattle Prep, at the College of the Holy Cross, and at Stanford University before he graduated with top honors from the Harvard School of Law. He was a charter member of the Orphean Club (see below). As close mutual friends, we carried on a lifelong correspondence. When, in early 2005, I was soliciting contributions to help the Oregon Province finance the publication of my history of the Catholic Church in Alaska, *Alaskana Catholica*, John gave us an exceptionally generous assist.

Generally, games were played on Friday nights. With special care, my assistants and I saw to it that game uniforms and all else needed, or possibly needed, for the upcoming game were checked over, bagged, and loaded into the bus. I always accompanied the teams to the games or track meets. During the games, I sat on the bench with team members, the coach, the athletic director, and my assistants. With rare exceptions, we were driven to the games in the old Seattle Prep Panthers bus. During my first year at Prep, this was driven by fellow regent Gordon L. Keys. (I was to replace him at Monroe Catholic High School in Fairbanks, Alaska, in 1958.) During my second and third years, it was driven by fellow regent Vincent J. (Vince) Beuzer. (At Sacred Heart Grade School, he and I had been in the same classroom together, he in the eighth grade, I in the seventh.) On trips to and from games, I commonly sat with the head coach. Throughout my three years at Prep, I had good rapport with the coaches, as well as with the players. Knowing them so well, I enjoyed watching the games—even when we lost. My being manager of the property room had as a plus the fact that it gave me contact also with upper classmen, which would not have been the case otherwise, since I taught mostly sophomores.

My years at Prep, however, were not spent only, or always, in either the classroom or in the property room. While a full teaching load and the property room did keep me occupied, more or less, full time, I was able, nevertheless, to find enough time, mostly on weekends and holidays, to organize what we named the "Orphean Club". My article about the club appeared in *America* on December 17, 1955. "It all began", the article begins,

one day after Latin class, when a sophomore [Patrick J. (Pat) Geraghty Jr.] came to my desk and told me he had heard I liked classical music. Then I told him of my idea of a club. From then on he gave me no peace unless there was ferment and progress. The idea had to become a concrete reality. We ferreted out others interested in the arts and, with their help, gradually transformed the old third-floor bookstore into a clubroom, complete with indirect lighting and acoustical tile.

Now that there was a clubroom and club members, members of the student body began to talk about a "Fine Arts Club", a "Culture Club", and worse. At that time, the line between aestheticism and athleticism was still sharply drawn. To many, the two seemed mutually exclusive. From the outset, it was important to make clear that there was nothing special about someone's being familiar with names such as Bach, Verdi, Mona Lisa, Chartres, Faust, and Unfinished Symphony as well as with names like Knute Rockne, Babe Ruth, Joe Louis, James Naismith, and Madison Square Garden. We were not favoring a given art form, or period, or movement— just the fine arts in general. Seeking a somewhat generic name for the club, we named it after Orpheus, poet and musician of ancient Greece.

Next we drew up a charter. It covered such items as dues, membership, meetings, and penalties. But, most important, it stated our objective. This was roughly twofold: to help the student body, in general, and club members, in particular, toward a better understanding and appreciation of good art. In the clubroom, during the noon hour and after school, any and all students were welcome to listen to recorded music and to read or merely flip through books on music, architecture, painting, the philosophy of art and beauty, and the like; or simply to sit around, eat lunch, play chess, and do homework. On a bulletin board, we kept rotating articles and pictures from *Time* and *Life* to keep us up on contemporary developments in the arts. This informality surprised some. In reality, however, it was well suited to the principal objective of the club: "to increase our knowledge of the arts, to deepen our appreciation of them, and to develop good taste by living with and enjoying good art."

Thanks to dues and generous parents, we eventually had a sizable collection of records and books. The high school library gave us the better part of its art section. The local art museum offered us exhibits. Occasionally, we had guest lecturers. Discussions followed the lectures. We also served the student body by sponsoring several art contests. These were well received. In one, three of the first four prizes went to nonclub members. This was good. It was especially good to see our all-state fullback get a prize.

The article in *America* ends: "Life with the 'fit and the fair' was an education and a joy. It was its own reward. But, what is more important, it taught us in a most pleasing manner about the Author of all beauty, and from afar off prepared us for that everlasting vision and happiness with Beauty ever ancient, ever new."

During my years at Prep, I had occasion to attend concerts at the University of Washington and at the Seattle Art Museum in Volunteer Park on Capitol Hill just above Seattle Prep. In a downtown Seattle theater, along with Father Robert V. Renner, S.J. (no relation), I saw the screen version of *Il trovatore*, an opera that was to become one of my favorites. With one of my students, Nicholas J. Bez Jr., also an Orphean Club member, I attended my first real live opera, Mozart's *Le nozze di Figaro*, likewise in a downtown Seattle theater. After the opera, the two of us had dinner at the Washington Athletic Club—all courtesy of Nicholas' mother. These were big first steps into the world of grand opera for this onetime North Dakota farm boy. Nicholas, too, contributed with exceptional generosity toward the publication of *Alaskana Catholica*. His parents had donated the life-size bronze statue of Saint Thérèse that stands near the chapel at the Shrine of Saint Thérèse, north of Juneau, Alaska.

My three years of regency at Seattle Prep ended in May 1954—with loss and gain. During the earlier part of that month, I lost my appendix, courtesy of Stephen J. Wood, M.D., team doctor of the Seattle Prep football teams and brother of fellow Jesuits, Fathers Francis P. and John J. Wood and Brother James B. Wood, a classmate of mine. That same May, while convalescing and studying on my own, under the direction of Father Edward S. Flajole, S.J., I earned ten credits "by examination" in intermediate German from Seattle University.

As my teaching years at Seattle Prep were coming to an end, I saw myself going on to eventually getting some kind of advanced degree and spending my active years in the classroom. During my third year of regency, I had considered seriously the possibility of making my theological studies in Innsbruck, Austria, and had even written to Father Provincial Small about it. In his mind, however, it was clear that Alma College, near Los Gatos, California, was the best place for me to make my theological studies. I herewith acknowledge a lasting debt of gratitude to him—and to a kindly Providence—for that thinking of his; for, at Alma, we had as our spiritual director Father Edward H. Hagemann, a man ideally suited for that sensitive post. I profited greatly from his guidance. Being given to a rather excessive amount of introspection and of caring about what might lie ahead, I was very much helped by his terse, down-to-earth advice: "Wear your cares like an old shirt."

So Alma it would be! After spending a leisurely summer at Gonzaga, followed by my fourth major vacation at Hayden Lake, I made my annual retreat at Gonzaga, from the seventeenth to the twenty-fourth of August. After spending some time, then, with my family in Tacoma, I was ready for the trip south. It proved to be a wonderful trip. All it cost me—

or, rather, the Society—was the price of gas and lodging in simple motels. I happily sat in the backseat, with Dad and Mom up front. For our first night, we were in Eugene, Oregon. The second day, after stopping off at Crater Lake, we visited my cousin Elizabeth Gustin—by then married and known as "Betty Creedican"—in Klamath Falls before crossing the border into California to overnight in Dunsmuir. The next day's drive took us to a small town just north of San Francisco, where we spent the night. The following day, we crossed the Golden Gate Bridge into San Francisco and took in the sights of that world-class city, among them Golden Gate Park and Fisherman's Wharf. After a night in San Mateo, we drove on to Alma College. I was the first of the new men to arrive there. For this, I had to take some ribbing. According to tradition, it was fashionable to arrive at the last minute on the appointed date, just before the evening dinner.

Chapter 7

Alma College, Los Gatos, California: 1954–1958

Alma College, in part once the beautiful estate of a wealthy man, was tucked away among giant redwoods and other evergreens in the Santa Cruz Hills only a few miles south of Los Gatos. The main original building, built out of redwood lumber, housed some faculty members, some chapels, and the recreation rooms—complete with magazine racks, pool and bridge tables, chessboards, and the like—as well as the kitchen and dining room. We ate well at Alma. Frame buildings added to the campus also housed some of the faculty, as well as all the theologians. Those buildings were of the simplest kind, described by one Alma College alumnus as "shacks". They were firetraps. Ropes tied to radiators in the third-floor rooms of the tallest building were intended to serve as emergency out-the-window fire escapes. The classroom building was a large, rather barnlike building. When, on rare occasions, such as World Series time, TV was allowed, or when movies were shown, the venue for them was in one of the classrooms. The main chapel building was adequate in size and décor. The gem of the whole complex was the new library building, a place made especially attractive on a cool, damp day by the radiant heat in the tiled slab of the lower floor.

For those seeking relaxation or exercise, Alma College and its surroundings left little to be desired. There were two small lakes and a "Roman Plunge", an ornate swimming pool, on the property, plus a softball field, a small gymnasium, and handball and pelota courts. There were a variety of paths and trails through the surrounding redwood forest and the nearby grape fields. Within easy walking distance, there were small cabins. During the rainy season especially, they served as cozy Thursday villa-day refuges. The Santa Cruz Hills offered many opportunities for the hikers. On some villa days, we took hikes of up to twenty miles. And there were the major villas. During my first two years at Alma, we had a villa, named "Phelan Park", at Santa Cruz, right on the Pacific Ocean. There we spent our major vacations, as well as many Thursday villa days. During my last two years at Alma, we had a villa at Applegate, north of Sacramento. Several times during my four years at Alma, we had the opportunity to visit one or other of California's famous old missions. The only other occasions for leaving the campus or its immediate surroundings were trips to San Jose to donate blood; to prepare "Mexican kids" for First Holy Communion, as I did in 1956; or to see a doctor or dentist.

However, theology and preparations for the priesthood were the focal points at Alma College. Before I had come to Alma, my personal priesthood had always seemed somewhat remote to me, something that had reality only in my subconscious mind. Now, however, with the study of theology and the more immediate preparations for the priesthood and with the "fourth-year fathers" (men ordained only a few months previously, men whom I had known since novitiate days, members of our "long black line") the priesthood began to be in the forefront of my consciousness.

After the hectic pace of the three years of regency in the metropolis of Seattle, I found the quiet, somewhat rural, semi-monastic life at Alma rather pleasant. I was happy to renew old friendships. The men I was now with, mostly men with whom I had been at Mount Saint Michael's, were, after three years of regency, noticeably more mature. Some of them saw theology, in general, as a sacred science worthy of study for its own sake; others saw it as just another hurdle to be cleared along the road leading to the priesthood. I myself saw it as both. Moral theology and canon law, for example, were for me little more than hurdles; likewise, the smattering of Hebrew. Most of the other courses, all taught in Latin, did engage my academic mind, however. Courses in Sacred Scripture opened whole new vistas for me, providing me with a solid base for future sermons and homilies. The three years of philosophical studies at Mount Saint Michael's had prepared me well for theological studies. Having learned to think analogically during the former was of special help to me with the latter.

The Alma College faculty was competent enough to teach those traditional, mandated pre–Vatican II courses. Much of the material was little more than simply relayed to us out of textbooks and off mimeographed pages. We referred to our canon law teacher as "Arizona": predictably clear—and dry. By around the mid-1950s, however, certain Europeans had achieved prominence as theologians. We found it stimulating to hear them quoted in our classes and to read some of their works. Among them, a number were to play major roles as participants in the Second Vatican Council. To mention but a few: Yves Congar, Jean Daniélou, Henri De Lubac, and Karl Rahner.

My first year at Alma, with much of life new and different, passed rather quickly. The second year, with most of the novelty worn off, was somewhat of a drag. The third year was quite another story. There were the routine classes, of course; but, suddenly, during the second half of that year especially,

the priesthood seemed almost at hand, as we began practicing hearing confessions, baptizing, offering Mass, and singing a solemn High Mass. Having our pictures taken for our
ordination cards, working on invitations, and much else that
preoccupies those soon to be ordained helped further to accel-
erate the pace. During the spring of that year, Dad and Mom
visited me for a few days to discuss invitations and some of
the doings that were to follow the week after my ordination, when I would be in the Northwest.

During the earlier part of the second week of June 1957,
my fellow ordinandi and I were ordained subdeacons and deacons in Menlo Park, California, by Merlin J. Guilfoyle, aux-
iliary bishop of San Francisco. On the thirteenth, out of
Oakland and via San Francisco and Seattle, we flew to Spokane. This was my first time in the air. It only added to the
general excitement of that momentous week. We spent the
nights at Mount Saint Michael's. There was a lengthy rehearsal
on the fourteenth. On Saturday the fifteenth, in Saint Aloysius Church, my six fellow ordinandi and I were ordained to
the holy priesthood by Bernard J. Topel, bishop of Spokane.
What was printed on the invitation card announcing my ordination, "Thou art a priest forever", was now realized in me.
In passing, I note, with humble gratitude, that the seven of
us ordained in Spokane, along with the five other classmates ordained elsewhere that same year, all, by the grace of
God, persevered as faithful priests.

All my immediate family and my niece Cheryl (Bill and
Bernice's eldest) were present at the ordination Mass. Immediately after the Mass, at the altar rail, beginning, naturally,
with my Mom and Dad, I gave them all my first priestly
blessing. Not all eyes remained dry. A breakfast at Gonzaga
with the family followed the Mass. That afternoon, some of
us newly ordained priests went to Sacred Heart Hospital in

Spokane to bestow first blessings on some of the sick. Among them was Father John P. Martin, a fellow Jesuit. He died four days later, at the age of forty-four. On the evening of ordination day, there was a Jesuits-only festive dinner at Mount Saint Michael's in honor of us newly ordained priests. After the dinner, wearing white stoles over our cassocks, we bestowed first priestly blessings on each and every one of the assembled. I went to bed early that night but slept very poorly.

The following day, Sunday morning, in the presence of all the immediate family, in a classroom at Mount Saint Michael's transformed into a chapel, I offered my first Low Mass. At this, Cheryl made her First Holy Communion. Father Neill R. Meany, S.J., a Bellarmine graduate ordained three years before me, was my assistant priest. After Mass, we all had breakfast together in the Mount's dining room. Soon after breakfast, with Dad and Mom in the front seat, I in the back, we were on our way to Tacoma. Slowly, I began to unwind, to relax—somewhat. All the doings and the nervous excitement of the previous days, along with general fatigue and the consequent insomnia, had taken their toll.

In Tacoma, I saw, for the first time, Dad and Mom's new home, an apartment in a tenement house that they were buying and operating a block downhill from Saint Patrick's Church. After showing me their apartment, they presented ordination gifts that they and others had waiting for me. Among them were a priest's pocket stole, a pocket ritual, and a big suitcase. I admired the gifts and thanked the givers, but I was so exhausted that my performance was rather perfunctory. Everyone understood. Soon Dad drove me up to Bellarmine, where I was to spend my nights while in Tacoma. Fellow Jesuits at Bellarmine received me warmly and extended sincere congratulations. One of the Fathers, recognizing my fatigue, assured me that, because of it, I was dispensed from saying the breviary for the time being. Wisely, and without scruple, I laid it aside for a few days. I tried to relax and get rested up for my first solemn High Mass and the reception to follow, now just a few days off, but was unable to do so. My brother Bill to the rescue!

At that time, Bill and family were living at Lake Cushman on the Olympic Peninsula. Bill, an employee of the City of Tacoma Power and Light, was stationed at the Cushman Dam. He invited me to spend a few days with him and his family. This I did. Their warm hospitality, the lake, and the hikes in the surrounding mountainous country worked their magic. I began really to relax and sleep well, and by the middle of the week, I was a new man, ready to return to Tacoma and make final preparations for my first solemn High Mass, due to be celebrated in Saint Patrick's Church on June 23, Trinity Sunday.

Everything regarding that first solemn High Mass came off beautifully. Father Allard assisted as deacon, and my cousin Father Arno Gustin, O.S.B., as subdeacon. Father Edward J. McFadden, pastor of Saint Patrick's parish, was assistant priest. My classmate since novitiate days, Father Armand M. Nigro— ordained a year ahead of me, having had only two years of regency, because he had made it at Holy Cross, Alaska— gave the sermon. Pat Geraghty (met already in chapter 6, in conjunction with the Orphean Club) was master of ceremonies. Family, friends, former students, and parishioners filled the church. Solemn Benediction took place immediately after the Mass. This was followed by my blessing those who had not yet received my first blessing. Brunch for family and friends, graciously hosted by Father McFadden in the church basement, capped the doings at Saint Patrick's.

During the afternoon of that memorable day, in the cafeteria at Bellarmine, a formal reception took place. Many family members and relatives—among them my godmother, Aunt Anna Gustin—from near and far, as well as fellow Jesuits, former students, and friends, attended the reception. Many hugs and handshakes added further warmth to that already warm June day. More first blessings were given; professional photos were taken. Much of the self-inflicted pressure was now off. It was truly a happy, enjoyable afternoon.

My sister Della's expected baby—who had had the courtesy to put off his entry into this world just long enough to enable her to attend the major events of the previous octave—was born on Monday, June 24. The following day, in Saint Joseph's Hospital, I baptized a baby boy, my nephew, David Carlin—my first baptism.

One morning during my days in Tacoma, I offered Mass for a few Benedictine sisters at Holy Rosary parish, where I had attended the fifth and sixth grades. Dad and Mom were with me. After Mass and thanksgiving, we had breakfast with the sisters. I was often to say Mass for various groups of sisters and, then, after making my thanksgiving, enjoy the breakfast their hospitality served me. The trick on those occasions was to make my thanksgiving long enough so as not to disedify the sisters but not so long as to let the breakfast get cold.

On the twenty-sixth, I went to Sheridan to offer Mass and to bless individually all the members of that community. Among its members were eight former Seattle Prepsters, most of whom I had had in class during my years at Prep. On the twenty-eighth, early in the morning, Uncle Ralph and Aunt Helen Renner, who had attended my solemn High Mass and the reception in Tacoma, came by to drive me back to California, to the villa at Applegate. It was one marathon of a drive, ending in the wee hours of the following day.

After some days at the villa, I was back at Alma for a final year of theological studies. However, I was a different man

now. I was now one of the "fourth-year fathers". We offered
Mass every morning, prayed the Divine Office, and had our
own special table in the dining room. During the remainder of that summer, we "rookie priests" had "weekend supply calls". That meant that we left Alma, generally on Friday
or Saturday, to help out with confessions and Masses in some
parish in the general area. Upon our arrival at the given parish, we were almost invariably introduced as "the young Jesuit
father from Alma College". Those weekend supply calls gave
us valuable hands-on experience in priestly ministry.

Weekend supply began for me with a short notice on the
bulletin board: "Emigrant Gap, July 7, Father Renner." On
Friday the fifth, I checked the old army Mass kit loaned to
me, to make sure it had everything needed for Mass, and packed
my small weekend suitcase for the first time. On Saturday, I
was driven to a Boy Scout and Girl Scout camp at Emigrant
Gap, fifty-five hundred feet up in the High Sierras, near Lake
Tahoe. I ate with the boys, then heard confessions before retir-
ing to a tent of my own for the night. On Sunday morning,
I offered the first Mass of the day at the boys' part of the camp.
My "church" was the tent, with flaps tied back, that had served
as my confessional and bedroom the night before. After Mass
and breakfast, I was driven over the bumpiest road in the High
Sierras to the girls' part of the camp. After setting up my
"altar" on a table under the trees, I put on a stole and, perched
on a rock, heard Girl Scout confessions. Confessions heard, I
vested and began Mass: *"In nomine Patris. . . . Introibo ad altare
Dei."* No response. "Oh, of course!" I thought to myself. "This
is a *Girl* Scout camp!" Those were pre–Vatican II days. No
"altar girls" yet. In Latin, I continued to dialogue with myself.

Two weeks later, my supply call took me to the cathedral
in Fresno. Living quarters, one-hundred-degree-plus temperatures, and cathedral splendor were in sharp contrast to

Emigrant Gap; but the essentials were the same. In the cathedral confessional, I received a veritable baptism of fire. It was fiercely hot in that virtually airtight box. The following week's call took me down to sea level, to Carmel-by-the-Sea and the famous old mission of San Carlos Borromeo, founded in 1770. Pacific Grove, too, saw my priestly services that weekend.

In the fall, school bells began ringing once again, calling us daily to study and to class. Supply calls were now on hold until Christmas and Easter. In class, we took up where the penny catechism left off: "How many gods are there? How many persons in God? What are the four last things? What does the Bible tell us?" Our professors offered answers to these questions—at some length, you can be sure, and in Latin—in the treatises "God Is One and Triune" and "The Last Things". In Scripture classes, we took a deep look into the historical and prophetical books of the Old Testament.

My first Christmas as a priest I spent close to home, at the Los Gatos parish, where I helped the pastor with confessions and then offered the Midnight Mass. For my first Holy Week and Easter as a priest, I was a little farther away, at the Jesuit parish of Saint Joseph in San Jose. There, too, I helped with confessions and the pre–Vatican II Easter liturgies.

During my final semester at Alma, those of us still in the "long course"—meaning, among other things, that our classes were conducted in Latin and that we had maintained a certain grade level—had fewer classes to attend and were given more out-of-class time to spend preparing for the *ad gradum* examination, a two-hour oral exam in Latin, before a board of four examiners, covering the three years of philosophical and the four years of theological studies we had gone through. My exam was moved up several weeks, because I was wanted at Mount Saint Michael's to help out with the oral examinations of the philosophers there. I did not pass what we generally referred to as the "ad grad" exam. That I "went down" was something I found out only four years later, when the time came for me to take my final vows. However, by the end of my four years at Alma, I had fulfilled all the requirements leading to the licentiate and master of sacred theology degrees. These were conferred upon me by Santa Clara University in June 1958. To qualify for the M.S.T. degree, we had to write a modest dissertation. Mine was entitled "Saint Irenaeus' Development of Saint Paul's Doctrine (Eph 1:10) of the ἀνακεφαλαίωσις (Anakephalaiosis), or of the Recapitulation of All Things in Christ; That Is, How Christ, as the New Adam, Renews All Creation and, under His Headship, Leads It Back to Its Author through the Incarnation and the Redemption". During the latter part of May, I left Alma College for Mount Saint Michael's.

At this point, readers might again wonder about how things now stood with me and my interest in Alaska, about my at one time having been "all fired up over Alaska", and about my expressed "ardent desire" to serve there one day. They might recall, too, that I once wrote that, by December 8, 1950, "Alaska was no longer on the horizon of my active apostolic interests."

By the mid-1950s, changes had taken place in Alaska. In 1955, Jesuit-run Monroe Catholic High School had opened in Fairbanks. Father Bernard F. McMeel, a fourth-year father at Alma when I first arrived there, was its first principal. He was also a ham radio operator. As principal of Monroe, he, along with other men in Alaska at the time, had regular radio contact with the Alma "Alaskani", men who had been at Holy Cross as regents. I began to take part in their regular ham radio sessions. The enthusiasm they radiated for all things Alaskan was infectious. This rekindled my interest in Alaska, in general. The natural allure of Alaska had never left me.

However, what, in particular, got me "all fired up over Alaska" again was the reality of Monroe High and the real possibility of my one day teaching there. That, plus ministry at the University of Alaska–Fairbanks as Newman chaplain, I now saw as a golden opportunity to be both in Alaska and, at the same time, to pursue my undeniable academic inclinations and interests.

On December 7, 1956, I had already written to Father Henry J. Schultheis—one of the four examiners who had approved me as a candidate for the Society back in 1944, and now provincial of the Oregon Province—as follows:

Very Reverend and dear Father Provincial,
By way of a short memorandum:

In the peace and quiet of this renovation triduum [three days of recollection made by Jesuits still in formation before renewing their vows], my thoughts again turn to our Alaskan missions. After praying over it and trying to apply the Rules for the Discernment of Spirits, I feel that I ought again to tell you of my intense desire to serve God on our Alaskan missions. Again I offer myself for this work.

Praying and trusting that God in His Divine Providence will guide and direct us both to that end which is most to His honor and glory, I remain

Your Reverence's obedient servant in Christ,
Louis L. Renner, S.J.

Chapter 8

Saint James Cathedral, Seattle, Washington: The Summer of 1958

After helping out with the oral examinations at Mount Saint Michael's during the latter part of May 1958, I spent some time with my family in Tacoma. On June 7, in Saint Patrick's Church, I offered the nuptial Mass at which my cousin Noreen Schmidt was united in holy matrimony to Raymond Marostica. This was the first wedding I witnessed as a priest. On July 11, likewise in Saint Patrick's Church, I was to offer the Mass at which my brother Albert married Joanne Charleson.

The second week of June, I began my eight-week summer assignment as an assistant priest at Saint James Cathedral in Seattle. On Sunday the fifteenth, I preached at the two Masses I offered, as well as at the other four Masses offered that day. After the noon Mass, I baptized seven infants, most of them accompanied by sponsors, parents, and family members. It was a crowded baptistery that day.

During the first three weeks of my cathedral assignment, my principal duties were to render chaplain services to the seven hospitals in the immediate vicinity. Living in the cathedral rectory, I was on call around the clock. At all hours of the day and night, with stole and holy oils in my pocket, I found myself running to one or another hospital, in response to an emergency call. In one of those hospitals, I administered for the first time what then was still commonly called the "sacrament of extreme unction". On the top floor of King County Hospital, I baptized and confirmed a dying infant girl. Being new to this kind of ministry and never knowing what might come next, I found it a somewhat stressful one. But I was a real young priest then, fit and zealous.

The summer of 1958 was an unusually hot one for the Pacific Northwest. Wearing a black woolen clerical suit and a Roman collar while hastening to some bedside in a hospital, I often arrived gasping and mopping my brow. The plus side of the uncommon heat was that the waters of Puget Sound were warm enough to allow for comfortable swims of up to an hour or so. Several evenings, Father James B. Reichmann, S.J., a Seattle University faculty member, and I treated ourselves to such refreshing swims.

Requests for my priestly ministrations came not only via telephone calls from some hospital or at the ring of the rectory doorbell. One hot day, wearing my black cassock, as usual, when at the rectory, I was pacing back and forth on the shady north side of the cathedral rectory, praying the Divine Office, when I noticed a big, black limousine pull up to the curb. Out stepped a man in a black suit. He unloaded a wheelchair, then helped a lady, likewise formally dressed, out of the backseat of the limo into the wheelchair. Several other people, including the chauffeur, also stepped out. I, minding my own business—for the most part—kept on pacing and praying. Then the man in the black suit approached me and asked if I was a priest. I nodded yes and asked what I might do for him. "We want to get married", he answered. "Fine", I said. "When and where?" "Here and now", he answered. With sympathetic apologies, I had to inform him that getting married in the Church was a little more complicated than a simple, impromptu curbside ceremony in the presence of a priest.

On June 20, I found a note on my door asking me to phone a certain Winifred Burns at a given number. I had no idea who Winifred Burns was. I phoned her and introduced myself. She, in turn, introduced herself and, giving me an address, asked if I could come up to the rooming house she was running several blocks from the cathedral. She told me that there was a man there suffering from cancer who wanted to see a priest. I found the rooming house easily enough. It was an old three-story building faced with beige-colored imitation brick, a fair amount of which had already peeled off, exposing tarpaper and even bare, dried-out, warped boards. I rang the doorbell and was met by Winifred, who took me up two flights of stairs to a third-floor room. She knocked. We were invited in. There, on a sagging bed, sat a man, who looked to be beyond his middle years but was clearly not yet an old man. Winifred introduced me to him. His name was Byron Gratton.

Byron had spent most of his adult life on ships sailing the seven seas of the earth. He was now afflicted with terminal cancer. He told me he wanted to "make things right with God". He had never been baptized. Winifred, a Catholic, had told him that he needed to get baptized. Could I help him? I told him I surely could, and that, yes, he needed to get baptized and that I would help him prepare for baptism and then baptize him. He was most willing to go along with whatever I proposed. By the following day, I had hunted down a rudimentary catechism that very much resembled a child's coloring book, but it contained all the basic tenets of our Faith. I brought this to him, apologizing and explaining to him that that was the best I could offer him under the circumstances. He assured me that he was only too happy to get it, that he would study it very carefully. This he did. A few days later, when I visited him again, I was able to assure myself that he had acquired enough understanding of the basic Catholic beliefs so that I could, in good conscience, baptize him. In his room, on June 25, with Winifred as his godmother, I baptized him, my first "convert".

For some weeks more, Byron lingered on in his tenement house room. Routinely, I brought him Holy Communion and visited with him. His childlike simplicity and faith impressed me deeply. He always called me "my Father". Toward the end of his days in the tenement house, he was no longer able to go to the common facilities at the end of the corridor. He was provided with a five-gallon bucket to serve him as a toilet. Occasionally, I emptied and rinsed this out for him. Our secret!

By sometime in July, he needed hospital care and became bedridden in King County Hospital, where I kept visiting him, from time to time, and bringing him Holy Communion. He was always most humbly grateful for my visits. Toward the end of July, when my assignment as an assistant priest at Saint James Cathedral neared its end, I introduced another of the assistants to Byron. He took over where I left off. Byron died a peaceful, happy death soon thereafter.

(Sometime in the early 1990s, as I was rummaging through an old steamer trunk that, over a decade earlier, I had jammed under the steps in the basement of the Diocese of Fairbanks chancery building, I found in one of the corners a long-forgotten item, an old two-bladed pocket knife. The larger blade was dull and somewhat rusty, the smaller one still fairly shiny and with an edge. From one side of the knife, the black, dimpled bone covering was gone, revealing the smooth brass inner case. As I contemplated that knife, it all came back to me.

One day, while he was still in the tenement house, Byron had shown me that knife. He told me he was keeping it on hand, so that, if the pain caused by his cancerous condition became unbearable, he could end his life by slitting his wrists. I impressed upon him that that would be wholly contrary to God's will for him and assured him that God's sustaining grace would take care of him in his hour of special need. Then and there, he held the knife out to me. I told him I would leave it with him, that I trusted him completely not to use it for any bad purpose. In late September 1958, in Fairbanks, Alaska, I found a tiny package at my door. It was addressed to me. Inside it was the note: "While Byron was still in his room here, he gave me this knife. He told me, 'Send it to my Father when I die.' " The note was from Winifred Burns.)

On July 21, in Saint James Cathedral, after having instructed Ann Godefroy, the wife of Michael Wyne, in the Faith, I had the joy of baptizing and receiving her into the Church. (You may remember Michael Wyne from chapter 6.)

Ten days later, my Saint James Cathedral assignment came to an end. It was the feast of Saint Ignatius Loyola. On that day, one of the major surprises of my life awaited me. In the forenoon of that red-letter day, I received a phone call from my classmate Father Carmine J. Sacco, who was just terminating his summer assignment at Our Lady of Mount Virgin Church in Seattle. At the beginning of our conversation, there was the customary small talk. He then told me that the "annual status", the listing of new assignments for the men of the Oregon Province, was out. That was news to me. He went on to tell me who was going where. I showed only casual interest, since I had taken it for granted that I would, within a few weeks, be going to Port Townsend, Washington, for the final year of my formal training as a Jesuit, for the year known as "tertianship". My last contact with Father Provincial Schultheis had given me reason to assume as much.

My trunk was already addressed to Port Townsend. Father Sacco, suspecting by now that I was unaware of *my* status change, blurted out, "And *you*, you are going to *Alaska*!" That was the first I heard of it. Naturally, I was greatly excited and pleased at hearing that good news. It will be recalled from the previous chapter that, in my December 7, 1956, letter to Father Provincial, I had again made known to him my "intense desire to serve God on our Alaskan missions".

Some time later, I found out the reason for my rather abrupt change of status. Father Gordon L. Keys, S.J., who, in the spring of 1958, had finished a year of teaching at Monroe High School in Fairbanks, for reasons of his own, had requested a new assignment. Someone, therefore, was needed to replace him. Thanks to a kindly Providence, I was the fortunate one.

During the early part of August, with considerable excitement, I visited my family in Tacoma, readdressed my trunk, went to Spokane to make my annual eight-day retreat, and then, by the third week of August, was on my way to Fairbanks. My one and only nonjet flight to Alaska was that first one, made in a four-motor, DC-6 piston-engine Alaska Airlines plane. The fact that that flight, a nonstop flight, took seven and a half hours made Alaska seem all the more remote, all the more exotic, to me.

Some days after my arrival in Fairbanks, I received a five-dollar bill from my brother Dick with the note, "You win!" It took me a moment to recall that, while we were still in high school, we had made a wager: "I bet you five dollars I'll get to Alaska before you do!"

Alaska became the forty-ninth state of the union in January 1959. During my Alaskan years, it often gave me a degree of smug satisfaction to remind people, "latecomers", that I first came to Alaska "back in Territorial days, before statehood".

Chapter 9

Monroe High School, Fairbanks, Alaska: 1958–1960

Upon my arrival in Fairbanks in the late afternoon of a day near the end of August 1958, I was met at the airport by Father Lewis N. Doyle, S.J., principal of Monroe High School, who drove me to Loyola Hall on Betty Street, just across the street behind Monroe. (Monroe was named for Father Francis M. Monroe, S.J., founder of Immaculate Conception parish, Fairbanks, in 1904. In later years, the school became known as Monroe Catholic High School.) At that time, Loyola Hall was the residence of the Jesuits on the Monroe staff. In addition to Father Doyle and me, there lived in Loyola Hall also Father Charles A. Saalfeld, fellow teacher, and Brother Aloysius B. Laird, furnace man and general custodian—and often my formidable competitor at the chessboard, as well as my driver. During my first year at Monroe, Bishop Francis D. Gleeson, vicar apostolic of Alaska, also lived in Loyola Hall. Mrs. Erna Meier, from Switzerland, was our cook for the evening meals.

I was to find my two years of living in Loyola Hall and teaching at Monroe most happy, all-around-satisfying ones. At Monroe, as at Seattle Prep, I was blessed with working with congenial fellow faculty members and responsive students, this time boys and girls. Monroe was a co-ed school. While it was basically a parochial, a parish, school, it nevertheless welcomed students also from military families stationed at the

86

two nearby bases: Ladd Field—an army base, subsequently known as Fort Wainwright—and Eielson Air Force Base. The military chaplains at the bases were highly supportive of Monroe and of Immaculate Conception grade school, connected to Monroe by a hallway. Students from the military gave the school more of a cosmopolitan, less of a parochial, atmosphere.

Monroe's core teaching faculty was composed of three Jesuit priests, two Sisters of Providence, and several laywomen and laymen. We faculty members had good rapport with one another, as well as with the students' parents, whom we got involved in school affairs and whom we kept informed as to how their sons and daughters were doing. We Jesuits were often invited out to dinner by the parents of our students. During my first year at Monroe, the school had a total enrollment of only seventy-one; the following year, of ninety-five. Given the small numbers, everybody knew everybody. The spirit of the school was that of one big, happy family.

The small class sizes allowed even the slower students to receive enough personal attention to enable them to make the grade. I do not recall ever having had to flunk anyone during my stint at Monroe. As at Seattle Prep, so at Monroe: When I sensed a given student might fail a given course, I would call the parents in good time and tell them that I thought they would prefer I call them, then and there, and let them know why their son or daughter might fail a given course rather than that they should have to call me at the end of the semester to find out why he or she failed. Invariably, parents and student alike were most grateful for the forewarning and the forestalling of impending failure.

Whereas at Seattle Prep I taught mostly sophomores, at Monroe I taught mostly seniors. I taught them English, religion, history, and civics. During my second year, I taught religion also to sophomores. Those sophomores and I took well to one another, so much so that, in all seriousness, they voted to make me an honorary member of their class, an honor I appreciated.

During my first year, in addition to classroom teaching, I served also as "spiritual father" to the whole student body and as "senior advisor" to the six seniors. During my second year, I again served in those two capacities, as well as moderator of the Sodality and of the German, chess, and music appreciation clubs. As spiritual father, I routinely heard the confessions of the students and offered Mass for them. I was close to most all of the Monroe students and took part in their various extracurricular activities. I played basketball and chess with and against them. I attended their basketball games, bowled with them, and chaperoned—along with other faculty members and parents—their dances. I went sledding, hiking, and swimming with them. In the spring of 1959, I accompanied a busload of students to Copper Valley School for a festival of competitions: basketball, drama, choir, oratory, and maypole dancing. Given the all-around relatively small numbers, my assigned workload at Monroe was not nearly as demanding as the one I had had at Seattle Prep.

In addition to the work we did at the school, we priests also regularly helped out at Immaculate Conception parish, principally by offering Masses and hearing confessions. Sometimes we offered Masses for the Sisters of Providence in their chapel in Saint Joseph's Hospital. I did somewhat less helping out in the parish, since the Newman Club chaplaincy at the University of Alaska–Fairbanks was my chief non-Monroe-related assignment. Routinely, every Sunday forenoon, after first hearing confessions in the big classroom on the second floor of the Eielson Building, I offered Mass there for University faculty and staff members, students, and a few people living near the university. Generally, on Monday evenings, on campus, I met with Newman Club members for informal discussions and some socializing. A few times, we had a guest lecture followed by discussion. That I took my Newman Club chaplaincy seriously enough, maybe too seriously, is clear from what my local superior and pastor of Immaculate Conception parish, Father George T. Boileau, a most ardent supporter of Fairbanks' Catholic schools, wrote to Father Henry G. Hargreaves, general superior of Jesuits in Alaska, on November 6, 1958: "Father Renner seems to be working out well. He has to be held down, since he would eagerly spend all his time at the University Newman work. Right now he spends part of three days there. We shall have to cut that down to two, since the high school comes first."

While still in high school in Tacoma, I had already begun taking driving lessons from my brother Dick. But those were the World War II years, and gasoline was rationed tightly. There was none to spare for driving practice. I entered the novitiate without having a driver's license. Near the end of my third year at Mount Saint Michael's, I again thought it advisable that I learn to drive and get a license, in case I needed to drive during regency at Seattle Prep. A classmate since Sacred Heart Grade School days, Vince Beuzer, was now my coach. One day, with him at my side, I drove from the Mount down to Gonzaga. I did not then go on to get a license. Luckily, it turned out that I did not, after all, have to do any driving during my three years at Seattle Prep. I dropped the pursuit of a driver's license. I had no need, nor desire, to drive while at Alma. So, in the fall of 1958, I found myself in Fairbanks with limited, outdated driving skills and no license. I was urged to learn, once and for all, how to drive and to get a license. Jerry Johnson—a junior at Monroe, a student of mine, and the son of Rita Johnson, a fellow Monroe faculty member—agreed to be my driving coach. Accordingly, during after-school hours, the two of us spent time in the big green station wagon that served the Loyola Hall Jesuits as their basic means of transportation. The day came when Jerry thought I was ready to drive the length of Cushman Street, the main thoroughfare through the heart of downtown Fairbanks. Taking the wheel, I made that drive. That was the last time I drove that wagon—for a while. By then, another Alaskan winter, with its short, dark days and icy road conditions, was fast approaching. Never, in any case, having had a great natural desire to drive, I lacked the heart to go on, under those conditions, with my practice driving until I felt qualified to try for a license.

Fortunately, there was, in the final analysis, really no compelling reason for my being a licensed driver. Brother Laird was a good driver and liked to drive. From time to time, he drove me to visit an elderly Alaska Native shut-in to hear her confession, to bring her Holy Communion, and to visit with her. During my second year in Fairbanks, when I played on the Immaculate Conception Church basketball team, one of the teams in the Fairbanks Churches League, he drove me to the games. Routinely, he drove me to the university, a one-way drive of some four miles, for the Sunday morning Mass. One Sunday morning, he knocked on my door and, in a voice so hoarse I could hardly understand him, told me that he would not be able to drive me to the university for the scheduled Mass. What to do? The obvious—license or no license! I knew where to find the keys for the old station wagon. With them in hand, I went to the heated garage built onto one end of Loyola Hall, opened the big back door, started the wagon, backed it out, closed the door, and drove off to the university—very cautiously. There I offered Mass, as usual, then drove back to Loyola—again, very cautiously. Everything came off without incident. That solo drive, while it was not licit, *was* valid! That was the last time I ever sat in the driver's seat of a vehicle in motion. Throughout that drive to and from the University, I had the strange feeling that it was not actually I who was driving that old station wagon, but that, rather, I was being hauled around in it. That venture has served me as a kind of analogue of most of my life, for, throughout most of my life, I have generally had the feeling—if only a subconscious feeling—that my life has been other-directed, that a kindly Providence has hauled me along all the roads of life I have traveled and guided all my affairs.

An article about me in the April 29, 2002, issue of the *Fairbanks Daily News-Miner* reads in part: "Renner has always preferred walking, no matter what the weather, to piloting a car through snow, dark, and ice fog. He has never had a driver's license. His only regret on that score, he said, is that he has missed picking up guests from the airport or rendering the courtesy of driving people here and there."

On December 21, 1958, I wrote Dad and Mom: "Just a short note to wish you a blessed and joyous Christmas! I will be remembering you especially on Christmas—in Seward." On the twenty-second, I flew to Anchorage. The following day, I was to fly on to Seward. However, the weather was not safe for flying, so the airline had me go with the man driving the mail in a big station wagon to Seward. There, Father Arnold L. Custer, S.J., pastor of Seward, introduced me to the small church-rectory building before he left to offer Christmas Masses at his outlying stations on the Kenai Peninsula. On Christmas Eve, I heard confessions and celebrated the Midnight Mass. On Christmas Day, I celebrated another Mass at 11:00 in the morning. Toward evening, I heated up a can of stew for my Christmas dinner. Due to some misunderstanding, several parties had assumed that the other was inviting me to dinner. I had, by this time, come down with a rather bad cold, so I was perfectly content to have a quiet, simple snack by myself. After it, I took a brief stroll around the town, then went to bed early. The next morning, when I stepped out of the bedroom, I found Father Custer on the living room sofa sound asleep. When he awoke, we visited for a short while, comparing our Christmas experiences. He apologized for my not having been invited out to a Christmas dinner. By the evening of that day, the twenty-sixth, I was back in Fairbanks. In anticipation of being in Europe for Christmas 1960, I spent Christmas 1959 with my family in Tacoma.

On February 9, 1959, Father Boileau wrote to Father Provincial Schultheis: "Looking ahead to the summer and planning for the men who will be needed to handle the work here during those months, I felt it best to write you about it. Father Renner has been approached by Father Leary to teach at the summer session at Gonzaga." Nothing was to come of that. In the same letter, Father Boileau wrote also, "I presume that Father Renner will be with us for another year. He has done remarkably well both in teaching here at Monroe and with the Newman Club at the university."

On May 29, 1959, from Copper Valley School, I wrote to my classmate Father Nigro, studying theology in Rome at the time:

> Here goes I know not what. I'm at Copper right now about to make my triduum; came from Anchorage yesterday, where I spent one day with Father Doyle. We drove to Seward to visit Father Custer. The scenery down that way is magnificent, also that between here and Anchorage. People find it hard to leave Alaska. I understand. Love this place, the work, the spirit, the people, the moose, the porkies [porcupine], the ducks and geese, the sheep on Sheep Mountain, the waterfalls and

glaciers, the fellow missionaries, the northern lights, the snow, the bush planes, even the mosquitoes that serve their slap-happy purgatorial purpose. A visiting priest will be in my room in Fairbanks, so I have to stay here till about June 8. Fine by me. I have enough German books here to prepare my classes for the summer school language program Father Boileau has under way for this summer.

Later on in that letter, I wrote, "This next year I will again be at Monroe, and happy to be there, though I wouldn't mind being finished with the training years. My present plan and Father Boileau's is that I get a degree when I go somewhere for tertianship."

On July 17, 1959, via air mail, Father Nigro responded to my letter. Assuring me that I belonged in university work, he urged me in the strongest terms to make my tertianship in Europe and to do doctoral studies there. In a letter written two days later, I made his views known to Alexander F. McDonald, the new father provincial. He, in turn, on July 22, 1959, wrote to me: "Your proposal for tertianship in Europe and for studies for the doctorate is quite acceptable to me. I shall put you on the list to go to tertianship next year. It is a little early for me to know now where there is an opening. We can apply in France and Germany to find out. In the meantime, you can work on the specific details of your program and let me know the results in good time."

During the summer of 1959, a summer foreign language institute was offered at Monroe for students interested in learning elementary Latin, French, German, or Spanish. Sixty-minute classes in all four of those languages were offered on the grade-school level. Enrollment was limited to twenty-five students per class. There was offered also a ninety-minute class in German on the high-school level. This was open to all comers, adults included. Predictably, I taught the two German classes.

One of the adults attending that high-school-level German class was Mrs. Donald Toussaint, Wilda. The Toussaint family lived a few doors from Loyola Hall. They frequently had us Jesuits over for dinner, did some laundry for us occasionally, and put up Jesuits from the bush when Loyola Hall ran out of room. During my years in Europe, I was to write rather frequently to the Toussaint family. (Fortunately, Wilda kept those letters, until the year 2002, when she gave them to me. Lengthy quotes from them have found their way into some of the following chapters.)

Some of the students taking the high-school-level German class liked it so much that they requested it be continued on Saturdays during the following fall semester. Happily, I was able to oblige them. Recorded German songs and sing-alongs were favorite features of the classes.

About 40 percent of the students taking one or other of the four languages were not Catholic. Most of them came from prominent Fairbanks families. The institute thus had a favorable impact on the broader Fairbanks community. Local press coverage was positive and generous.

The article in the *Fairbanks Daily News-Miner* about the foreign language program, accompanied by pictures of me with my class, caught the eye of longtime Fairbanksan Ernest (Ernie) Hanauer, a German-born, Jewish, widely traveled furniture upholsterer and bachelor. One day, wanting to meet me, to talk with me, and to give me a German book, he invited me to his place for conversation over a one-pot bachelor's dinner. We hit it off well right from the outset and talked about many things. At one point, when we were well along in our conversation, he somewhat abruptly stopped talking, looked at me intently, and then said, "You seem to be so self-assured, so happy with your life and with what you are doing. How do you account for that?" I told him that I felt I was what God wanted me to be, a Jesuit priest, and doing what He wanted me to do at that stage in my life. "You know," he then said, "on a trip I once took to the South Seas, I visited a leper colony. There was a sister working there. She, too, seemed so happy and content in her work. I asked her the same question I just now asked you. And you know, she gave me almost the exact same answer you just gave me."

During the first week of August 1959, after a drive from Fairbanks to Anchorage via Copper Valley School, I flew to Bethel, where I spent part of a day and a night with Father William T. McIntyre, S.J. From Bethel, on an old red Alaska Airlines Norseman, I flew to the Saint Mary's mission on the Andreafsky River to make my annual eight-day retreat. I finished this on the fifteenth. That proved to be a long, but memorable, day. With most of the mission personnel on board the mission boat, the *Sifton*, we went out the mouth of the Andreafsky into the Yukon and on down to Mountain Village for the dedication of its new church and the celebrations for the feast of the Assumption. That evening, in an overcrowded, overheated old hall, dimly lit, I saw Eskimo dancing for the first time. It left a lasting impression.

Two days later, on the seventeenth, from Saint Mary's, I wrote to classmates interested in Alaska:

The retreat was my first one by myself. I came out of it so well rested that I wonder if I made a good one. The weather was excellent. I had four fine swims. I tramped over the hills quite a bit and ate many a blueberry. Counted seven different kinds of berries. The tundra is a difficult terrain to walk on, worse than sand; but I was enchanted by the rich growths of vegetation, berries, and birds and was purged by berry and mosquito in body and in soul. Felt sorry for the poor Protestants who don't believe in purgatory.

After a delay of two days at Saint Mary's, while the outboard motor of Father Astruc's boat was being worked on, French Jesuit father René Astruc and I headed downriver. A long day's "kickerboating" brought us to Chaneliak, where we spent the first night. Our second night we spent at the historic old village of Saint Michael. For dinner there, we had a cast-iron pan full of fried potatoes. It was at Saint Michael that I first became acquainted with the French painter George Rouault, whose painting *Christ and the High Priest* was to become one of my favorite paintings. Father Astruc had at Saint Michael a book of Rouault's paintings, which we perused leisurely that evening. After passing the night at Saint Michael, we spent most of the next day traveling up the coast to Unalakleet. There, we visited around the village for a while; then, after enjoying an evening meal as guests of a Catholic family, we spent the night in the tiny mission chapel. The following morning, I flew from Unalakleet to Nome, where I was hosted by the pastor, Father Lawrence A. Nevue, S.J. After visiting around the town, he and I visited the Little Sisters of Jesus in their home in King Island Village about a mile east of Nome. By the twenty-second, I was back in Fairbanks for my second year of teaching at Monroe.

My second year at Monroe resembled, in most respects, pretty much the first. One significant difference was that, instead of having only six seniors to teach, as I did during my first year, I now had seventeen. Additionally, I now also taught the sophomore religion class. I was still Newman Club chaplain.

By this time, too, I was also a member of the Fairbanks Junior Chamber of Commerce. In part, I had allowed myself to be talked into joining it in hopes that it would help me to overcome somewhat my natural shyness, to make it easier for me to get up and speak before a crowd. I would have done better to save my time and dues.

My first Easter in Alaska, that of 1959, I spent in Fairbanks. For my second Alaskan Easter, that of 1960, I was flown, on Holy Thursday, in a small two-seater bush plane, to Suntrana, a coal-mining camp across the Nenana River from present-day Healy. Before eating and spending the night in the company bunkhouse, I was given a tour of one of the mineshafts by one of the foremen. Once down in the shaft, we were surrounded on all sides, as well as top and bottom, by absolutely nothing other than black coal. Occasionally, we heard a distant thunderlike rumble as blasting took place. We did little talking. He did tell me, however, that there were several miners buried somewhere in the mine, victims of a cave-in of one of the shafts. Given only the beams of our headlamps for illumination, and being naturally somewhat prone to claustrophobia, I found that tour an eerie, somber, sobering experience, a sharp contrast to the brilliant light and liberating glories of what Easter is all about.

In reference to my second year at Monroe, Sister Pauline Higgins, S.P., in her book *Providence in Alaska* wrote, "The 1959–1960 Monroe yearbook, *Aurigena*, carried students' appreciative comments on the 'lively discussions and friendly arguments' that characterized Father Renner's classroom style." On January 11, 2006, Robert Nelson, a member of Monroe's first graduating class and one of the brightest students I ever taught, wrote to me: "You are the one of all my teachers for whom I felt more than the ordinary benignly adversarial relationship. You seemed to me, and I think to the entire class, to be a sort of magisterial colleague. Perhaps it had something to do with your youth at the time." (For Father Doyle's evaluation of my performance during my two years at Monroe, see chapter 14!)

In that February 9, 1959, letter to Father Provincial Schultheis cited earlier in this chapter, Father Boileau wrote also, "Should Father Renner come back to Alaska, it might be wise for him to have a doctorate in philosophy. This would give him knowledge and prestige, which he could use to great advantage with those public educators."

As my second year at Monroe began, I already had good reason to believe that it would be my last one there and that the following year would find me in Europe making my tertianship in Paray-le-Monial, France. Accordingly, as time and occasion allowed, I worked on my French.

Busy as I was with the work at hand and with preparations for the year ahead, my second year at Monroe passed very quickly. Monroe's second commencement exercises took place on May 20, 1960. Three days later, on a Pan Am flight, in a Boeing 707—a "wonderful flight", according to my diary entry—I flew to Tacoma to spend time with my family before leaving them for what I anticipated would be a period of some years.

Chapter 10

The Summer of 1960

The 1960 visit—May 23 to June 10—with my family in Tacoma turned out to be one of my longer ones with them. We were not to be together again until over five years later. While in Tacoma, I spent the nights in Saint Patrick's rectory and helped out with some of the parish Masses. On the twenty-seventh, I made a trip to Port Townsend to discuss travel plans with Fathers Richard A. (Dick) Hill and Joseph M. (Joe) Powers—California Province Jesuits and close friends of mine ever since our days together at Mount Saint Michael's— who were just finishing their tertianship. We were scheduled to sail on the same ship for Europe a month later. I spent four relaxing days with Bill and family at Lake Cushman. We had a family picnic there the fourth day. I did some fishing in Commencement Bay with Dad and Dick, bowled with Dad, and saw a stage performance of *Oklahoma!* I also had some dental work done. On June 9, there was a farewell party with most of the Renner clan present. The following day, Dad and Mom drove me to Spokane, where I wanted to consult with fellow Jesuits who had been in Europe for tertianship and doctoral studies.

On Saturday, June 11, I attended the ordinations of fellow Jesuits to the priesthood in Saint Aloysius Church, had lunch with Dad and Mom, and attended the ordination dinner at Mount Saint Michael's. On the thirteenth, I boarded the train for Saint Louis, where I arrived on the fifteenth. There I visited two of my former Seattle Prep students, Larry Grant and Tommy Wood, now in their philosophical studies. Together we saw the musical *Meet Me in Saint Louis*. I remember the Saint Louis weather as having been extremely hot and humid.

June 17 found me back on the train again, this time bound for Washington, D.C., where I arrived the following day. Mary, the wife of George W. Sundborg Sr.—executive secretary to Ernest Gruening, senator from Alaska—and her son Stephen (Steve) met me at the train station and drove me to their parish church. After I offered Mass, they brought me to their home to be their houseguest during my week in Washington. Steve had been a member of my sophomore religion class at Monroe during the 1958–1959 school year. After graduating from Georgetown Prep in 1961, he joined the Oregon Province. From 1990 to 1996, he was its father provincial. His younger sister, Sarah, too, I got to know at Monroe. In the Sundborg family, I had perfect hosts; in Steve, a perfect companion and tour guide.

On the day of my arrival in Washington, June 18, Steve and I had lunch at the Washington Press Club and visited the National Shrine of the Immaculate Conception and the houses of John D. Rockefeller and then Vice-President Richard M. Nixon. The following day, I offered Mass in Our Lady of Victory Church before we did some more "touristing" and attended a performance by the United States Marine Corps Band in the evening. On the twentieth, we took in, along with things of lesser importance, the National Gallery of Art, the National Archives, and the Ford Theater. We attended the Washington Ballet. A mere hint, and George had tickets in our hands for the given day's or evening's performance. We were back in the National Gallery again the next day. It was a thrill to see the originals of paintings I had previously seen only in art books. That day, we visited also the Smithsonian Institution and Georgetown University as well as attended a concert by the United States Army Band and Chorus. Music again capped the day—as well as my stay in Washington—when, on the twenty-third, we attended a performance by the United States Air Force Symphony Orchestra.

By the time I left Washington, Steve and I had visited also the Supreme Court; the Library of Congress; the Iwo Jima, Jefferson, and Lincoln memorials; and Arlington Cemetery. We had toured the Capitol and the two Houses and had seen Nixon preside over the Senate. We had visited Alaska senator Ernest Gruening in his office. (Some years later, when I was teaching German at the University of Alaska–Fairbanks, Senator Gruening was to drop in, unexpectedly, on me and my class in our classroom in the Gruening Building.) We had also visited E. L. "Bob" Bartlett, our Alaska senator. And we had taken a boat ride on the Potomac River.

Forty-five years after our days together in Washington, Steve, now president of Seattle University, wrote to me: "Those were the days! What I most remember was how YOU introduced me to great European art at the National Museum (Mellon) and how that became a lifelong interest of mine and was greatly advanced by my European years." (In passing, but in a spirit of sincere gratitude, I should mention that, during his European years, Steve, very competently, did some major Alaska-Jesuit-related research for me in the Jesuit archives in Rome.)

On June 24, on a Greyhound bus, I left steamy-hot Washington, D.C., for what turned out to be an equally steamy-hot New York City. In New York City, I stayed in the Leo House, a kind of hospitality house for traveling clergy and religious. It had a chapel, so I was able to offer daily Mass there.

About the first thing I did upon my arrival in New York was to see the city from the top of the Empire State Building. At Campion House, the home of *America* magazine and staff on 108th Street, I visited with Father Neil G. McCluskey, an Oregonian, who had taught at Bellarmine Prep and was then a writer on the staff of *America*. During my six-day stay in New York, I also visited the Metropolitan Museum of Art, the Museum of Modern Art, and the Frick and Guggenheim museums, as well as the Metropolitan Opera. I strolled in Central Park. I visited both Saint Patrick's and Saint John the Divine cathedrals. I toured the United Nations Headquarters Building. I saw the movie *Ice Palace* and a movie version of *Swan Lake* by the Bolshoi Ballet. With Fathers Hill and Powers—with whom I met up soon after my arrival in New York—I took in the Broadway play *Take Me Along*, starring Jackie Gleason. One day, Father Richard Maher, a Californian studying at Fordham University, gave us a tour of the university, then took us on a drive around the city. That evening, in Leone's, one of New York's top restaurants, the four of us splurged to enjoy a gargantuan dinner together—including something French on the half shell.

On June 30, after an almost-frenzied pace of sight-seeing in hot, muggy New York, with a sigh of great relief, I made the terse note in my diary: "En route—Deo gratias! Prompt departure." On July 1: "At sea—wunderbar—Deo gratias!"

Sharing a stateroom with Fathers Hill and Powers—Rome-bound to earn doctorates in canon law and dogmatic theology, respectively—I was on my way to Europe on the SS *Liberté*, a relatively small ship of the French Line. It had a little swimming pool and a little theater for movies. And it had a little chapel, in which we were able to offer daily Mass. Our Masses were attended by John Stacer and Alan Arias, New Orleans Province seminarians on their way to Europe to make their theology. The five of us Jesuits took our meals at the same table. On July 3, we Jesuits, along with other clergy, were invited to a cocktail party hosted by the assistant captain of the ship. On the fourth, the pop of a cork flying out of the neck of a bottle of champagne signaled the beginning of Fourth of July celebrations at our table.

"Wonderful last day", I entered in my diary on the fifth. Throughout my part of the trip, we had had nothing but cool, fog-shrouded weather, making for absolutely smooth sailing. In passing, I might mention that on board with us were the American actor Jimmy Stewart and the French philosopher Jacques Maritain, whose writings on art and beauty had by then become very much a part of my aesthetic life. Respecting his privacy, I did not make an effort to meet him, something I subsequently wished I had done.

On the morning of July 6, I disembarked at Plymouth. I was now in Europe, where, during the next five years, I was to find that virtually every aspect of my stay would contribute appreciably to my general intellectual and cultural—and less so, spiritual—broadening. Just being in Europe proved to be, in and of itself, already a true education. Much of what I experienced during my European sojourn served me as a remote preparation for classes I taught at the University of Alaska–Fairbanks. The humanities course "Unity in the Arts" and the courses in German civilization and culture, in particular, were greatly enriched by what I absorbed during my years in Europe.

At Plymouth, I boarded a train, with London my ultimate destination. On the way up to London, I stopped off to visit the Salisbury Cathedral and Stonehenge. In London, I stayed at the Mount Street Jesuit Residence, the home of some rather famous English Jesuits, among them the brilliant Martin C. D'Arcy and Thomas Roberts, retired archbishop of Bombay, whom I had met in Spokane the month before. One evening at supper, I found myself sitting between Fathers James Brodrick and Philip Caraman, whose lives of various Jesuit saints I had read. I offered and attended Masses in the Jesuit-staffed Church of the Immaculate Conception next to the Mount Street residence.

When I sailed for Europe, it was not yet determined where, after completing my tertianship, I would make my doctoral studies, or even in what field. Father Boileau had suggested the field of history. Sociology was considered. My natural bent and academic background, however, strongly inclined me toward philosophy. Father Nigro had tried to persuade me to get a degree in philosophy at the Gregorian University in Rome. I was rather opposed to getting a degree from there, reasoning that I would be better prepared for future work at the University of Alaska–Fairbanks, a state university, if I had a degree from some university less "parochial" than the Gregorian. I was strongly inclined from the outset to getting a doctorate in philosophy from some university in Germany or, as an alternate possibility, to getting a master's degree in some subject from Oxford University. Meanwhile, I was to think about place and field, pray over it, and scout out possibilities, then make a choice—subject to Father Provincial's approval, of course.

During my stay at Mount Street, I had occasion to speak at length with Father Joseph Corbishley, who had, for twelve years, been the master of Campion Hall, the residence of Jesuits teaching or studying at Oxford. He assured me that I could do nothing better by way of preparing for a future Newman chaplaincy at a state university than to go through some program at Oxford. Getting in at Oxford, however, was not automatic. They were overcrowded and could, therefore, be highly selective. Given my preference all along for some German university, I never even tried to get into

Oxford. My discussions with Father Corbishley were, nevertheless, of considerable value to me, as I continued to weigh the various possibilities prior to arriving at a decision as to where to do doctoral studies.

During my week in London, I was again a tourist very much on the go. At times, Brother George Banfield, a member of the Mount Street community and thoroughly familiar with London, especially Catholic London, was my tour guide. Treated in the late afternoon to a cup of tea and something to dunk in it, he felt amply rewarded for his guiding services. It gave him considerable satisfaction to be able to show me the little chapel in which Saint Thomas More regularly attended and served Mass. Being a great admirer of Saint Thomas More myself, this was a mini pilgrimage for me. Before my stay in London was over, I had occasion to see Paul Scofield in Robert Bolt's *A Man for All Seasons*, a stage play based on the life of Saint Thomas More, just opening in the Globe Theatre. It made quite an impression on me. I expected it to go far. It went on to become a major drama of its time and was made into a movie in 1966.

In London, I visited Westminster Abbey, Westminster Cathedral, and Tyburn, the place where many Jesuits were martyred. At the British Museum, I saw the Codex Sinaiticus and the Codex Alexandrinus, two ancient documents of interest to Scripture scholars, as well as the Magna Carta, the Rosetta Stone, and the Elgin Marbles. At the House of Parliament, I witnessed the "changing of the guard" routine. I saw the House of Lords in session. I visited Buckingham Palace, Windsor Castle, Eton, the Tower of London, and the London Bridge. I saw Saint James Place, where Saint Claude La Colombière lived during his time in London, 1676–1679. Less than two months later, at Paray-le-Monial, I was to offer Mass frequently at the altar enshrining his relics. At the Royal

Albert Hall, I attended a performance by the Bolshoi Ballet; at Covent Garden, a performance of Verdi's opera *Macbeth*. I treated Brother Banfield to the movie *Black Orpheus*.

Before I left London, I just had to make a trip, a quasi pilgrimage, to the hamlet of Stoke Poges, to see the church and the churchyard made famous by the poet Thomas Gray in his immortal poem "Elegy Written in a Country Churchyard". This was a poem I had had my Monroe High seniors memorize verbatim. At one time, I myself could recite virtually the whole of it.

In the early afternoon of July 13, I flew from London to Paris, where I had reservations for the weeks ahead in the *42, rue de Grenelle* Jesuit complex, a spacious building in which local Jesuits and Jesuits from all over the world were accorded gracious French hospitality. On July 29, in a joint letter to the Toussaints and Jesuit classmates, I could write: "Living at *rue de Grenelle* is quite pleasant, far more pleasant than I had anticipated. I'm very well satisfied with the setup here. I'm getting used to French food now. I hit upon a good thing, saying Mass every morning at a nearby convent of Carmelites. After Mass, the sisters have a better-than-par breakfast waiting, a good way to start the day. Walking to and from the Sorbonne and three hours of class makes a breakfast all the more welcome." The *Université de Paris—à La Sorbonne* was about a thirty-minute walk from the *rue de Grenelle* residence.

The Sorbonne, learning French there, was my reason for being in Paris. July 14 was Bastille Day, the French equivalent of our Fourth of July, a national holiday. That day, along with thousands of others, I visited Notre Dame Cathedral. The following day, I began attending classes at the Sorbonne. The method in vogue was the "Marchand Method", a manner of teaching students a given foreign language by using only that language and relying on much repetition. Our teacher, Madame Crahay, in all respects an excellent teacher, told us not even to *think* in English. Our class met six days a week, from nine in the morning until noon. There was homework, too. On Saturday mornings, we took a walk or trip to some place of interest, the while practicing our rudimentary French with Madame Crahay and fellow students from all around the globe.

In that July 29 letter quoted above, I was able to write also, "I'm very happy with the Sorbonne program. I enjoy it thoroughly and am making halting progress. The time I spent on French in Fairbanks is paying off now. But it is more difficult than I figured. The French *r* is the toughest. French is beautiful, if spoken well; sacrilege, if murdered! Paris is the place to learn French. It's a great city, living up to all expectations. I've really enjoyed my stay here so far." In learning French, I found having a radio in my room—something suggested to me by Father Nigro—of considerable help.

After I had studied French at the Sorbonne for six weeks and then taken both a written and an oral exam, that institution issued me an official certificate, dated August 27, 1960, attesting that I had studied French there from July 15 to August 27 and had passed successfully the two exams. I passed the written exam by earning eighteen points out of a possible twenty; the oral, by earning sixteen out of a possible twenty.

In the great city of Paris, the "City of Light", I again did a great deal of sight-seeing, gallery visiting, and theatergoing. Early on, I saw the city from the top of Notre Dame Cathedral. Twice later, I saw it from the top of the Eiffel Tower—once accompanied by my cousin Father Arno Gustin, O.S.B., who happened to be on a sabbatical in Europe at the time. I looked out over the city a number of times from the highest point in Paris, Montmartre—crowned by La Basilique du Sacré-Coeur. Halfway up the slopes of Montmartre, near the fountain of Saint Denis, I visited the little chapel in which, on August 15, 1534, Saint Ignatius and his six companions—among them Blessed Pierre Favre, who offered the Mass of the Assumption—bound themselves by vows of poverty and chastity. Alone and with fellow Jesuits, I visited the main churches in Paris and the famous La Sainte Chapelle, a "jewel box" built out of stained-glass windows to enshrine the Crown of Thorns and other relics of Our Lord's Passion. One day, along with fellow Oregon Province Jesuits Emmett Carroll and Anthony (Tony) Via—both in Europe at the time for theological studies—I made an excursion to Chartres to visit the most famous of all of France's cathedrals, the magnificent Gothic cathedral of Notre Dame.

Several times I went to the Louvre to have Leonardo da Vinci's *Mona Lisa* bless me with her smile. Under the Dôme des Invalides, I paid my respects to the remains of Napoléon Bonaparte, entombed in the crypt there. The royal palace at Versailles called for a visit, as did the various parks and gardens in and around Paris. I toured the UNESCO headquarters, along with many other places of interest in Paris.

At the Paris Opera, I took in, among other operas, Donizetti's *Lucia di Lammermoor*, Gounod's *Faust*, Bizet's *Les pêcheurs des perles*, and Puccini's *Tosca*—this last in company of Father Arno. I also attended some operas at the Opéra comique, among them Puccini's *Madama Butterfly* and Gounod's *Mireille*.

On July 22, I teamed up for some sight-seeing with Father William J. Loyens, who had just finished tertianship in Belgium and was soon to take my place at Monroe—before going on to be my fellow faculty member at the University of Alaska–Fairbanks, then general superior of the Alaska mission, then the provincial of the Oregon Province. Walking along the Champs Elysées from the Place de la Concorde on our way to the Arc de Triomphe, we were stopped by a street photographer, who offered to take our picture, for a price. We paid, posed walking full stride, had our picture taken, and received each a fine photo some time later. After doing the Arc de Triomphe, we took in the movie *La dolce vita*. To relax and, at the same time, to soak in French, I frequently went to an afternoon movie.

An exchange of places at the dinner table on August 15, 1960, seemingly a matter of minor importance at the moment, turned out to be a matter of major importance subsequently, to affect the whole of the rest of my life significantly. On that day, in the *rue de Grenelle* Jesuit residence, Jesuits from near and far had gathered on the feast of the Assumption of the Blessed Virgin Mary for a festive dinner. Seating was open. The man to my immediate right, a stranger, wanting to sit next to the man three places to my right, exchanged places with his neighbor. As a kindly Providence disposed, that placed Father J. Giles Milhaven, a member of the Maryland Province and still a total stranger to me, next to me. At the time, Oxford still seemed a real possibility as the place for my advanced degree work. At heart, however, I was still quite set on getting a doctorate in philosophy from some university in Germany. Following mutual introductions, Father Milhaven went on to tell me that he would, that fall, begin his final year of doctoral studies in philosophy at the Ludwig-Maximilians-Universität, München, under Dr. Helmut Kuhn. At the beginning of that dinner, I knew nothing about that university. By dinner's end, I was firmly convinced that Munich was the place, that philosophy was the field, and that Professor Kuhn was the man under whom I would be doing my doctoral studies. I subsequently informed Father Provincial McDonald of these developments. After discussing the matter with his committee on

graduate studies, he gave me the green light to make plans to
enter the University of Munich. I owe a lasting debt of gratitude to Father Milhaven for paving the way for me to do doctoral studies in philosophy in Munich under Professor Kuhn.

Before I left Fairbanks, Mrs. Erna Meier made contact with
Herr Anton Rosa, a friend in Switzerland, and told him about
my coming to Europe. On August 19, I wrote him that I
was scheduled to arrive in Zürich the evening of the twenty-
ninth. All went as planned. Herr Rosa and I had dinner
together and then took a walk before I retired for the night
in a rooming house. Before doing so, I noted in my diary:
"Arrived at Zürich after a most wonderful one-hour train ride
from Basel." Somehow, I felt more at home in Switzerland
than I had in Paris. The alpine countryside, the tempo of life,
the people, and the language all added up to what was closer
to what I might call my "native habitat". Thanks to having
listened at length to German language records while still in
Fairbanks, I was able to carry on a passable conversation in
High German with Herr Rosa.

During my short week in Switzerland, I spent some more
time with Herr Rosa and took some tours into the alpine high
country. One day, by rail, I went all the way up to the Jung-
fraujoch, a mountain saddle 11,333 feet above sea level, the
highest point in Europe reachable by rail. This elevation was
enough to make me mildly altitude-sick. On a day's outing
to Einsiedeln, I visited the famous Benedictine Abbey and saw
Das Grosse Welt Theater, a religious play by Calderón put on
by the townspeople. On September 4, I took the train to
Geneva. There, the following day, after Mass in Saint Joseph's
Church, I joined a group touring the World Health Organization complex. That evening, by train, I left Geneva on a
journey into the peace and quasi-medieval solitude of Paray-
le-Monial, France.

Chapter 11

Paray-le-Monial, France: 1960–1961

From Paray-le-Monial, on September 8, 1960, I wrote to Father Nigro:

> Here, more than ever, I find myself in a foreign land. Only one other American here. The majority are French or French-speaking. This is what I hoped for. In general, the tertians have been out of theology for several years. They are a fine group. My first, and continuing, impressions of Paray are very good. The house is comfortable and quiet, the table very good. All in all, I am very well satisfied. This hallowed village seems to be a good place for tertianship. I can use it. This place radiates peace and holiness. It is small but has about seventeen religious communities in it. Already I feel in retreat, such a contrast is the present order to that of the last two years and, especially, to that of the last three months. The retreat will begin in about two weeks. Your prayers, if you please!

To the Toussaints I wrote six months later, "Paray is often fogged in by fog, but it is always bathed in grace."

In Paray, home to 11,077 in 1968, I found myself in a rural area of France about an hour's train ride northwest of Lyons. The neighboring town, Charolles, is known to the world for the Charolais cattle raised there and exported widely abroad. Paray itself is known to the world as the place where the revelations of the Sacred Heart of Jesus to Saint Margaret Mary

111

Alacoque, a Sister of the Visitation, took place. Only Lourdes surpasses it as a site of pilgrimage in France. The centerpiece of Paray is the medieval Romanesque basilica of the Sacred Heart. The principal place of pilgrimage in Paray is the Visitation monastery, in which are the shrine of the revelations to Saint Margaret Mary, as well as her relics. I had a number of occasions to offer Mass in both the basilica and in the monastery, as well as to offer numerous Masses, hear confessions, and give Benedictions in other monasteries, convents, and schools in Paray.

My home during tertianship was La Maison Colombière, an old, stone, three-story building with a basement. By my time, it had central heating, hot water, and radiators. There were still fireplaces in the individual rooms, but the fireplaces were no longer used. All in all, the place was so poorly heated that most of the community generally wore overcoats around the house. I used sweat pants and sweat shirts as underclothes to keep me warm. There was a beautiful, devotional chapel at one end of the building dedicated to Blessed Claude La Colombière. He was to be declared a saint in 1992. An altar, at which I occasionally offered Mass, enshrined his relics. There was an enclosed courtyard behind the house, a quiet haven for prayer or for walks with a companion or two. The countryside, well suited for lengthy walks, was virtually out the back door of the house. The path along the canal near Paray, too, provided pleasant walking. A small woods an hour's walk from Paray served us well as a secluded place for an occasional picnic outing.

Of the twenty-four men making tertianship with me, two Frenchmen had served as missionaries in Africa—one in Chad, the other in Cameroon. A man from Belgium had spent time in the Central African Republic. Two fellow tertians were from Italy. Johannes Mühlsteiger was from Innsbruck, Austria.

When Johannes and I took walks alone, we spoke German. The other American was Emmett Holmes of the Detroit Province. He and I occasionally walked alone together; when we did, we spoke "Frenglish". All in all, I found my fellow tertians agreeable companions, tolerant enough of those of us who spoke French less than fluently.

When I began tertianship, I was already fairly certain of doing doctoral studies in Germany. Still, I wanted to get a decent grasp of spoken French. In that letter to Father Nigro cited above, I also wrote: "The other morning, I prayed the Lord to send me a French teacher. That night a Parisian tertian [Jean-Claude Guy] volunteered, on his own initiative, to help me. He seems to take pleasure in helping a foreigner and has done it before. How lucky can I be! I can get along reasonably well, but there is still much room for improvement. It is a pleasure to live in a foreign country when one can speak the language; it is miserable otherwise."

In reality, tertianship was not a good place for me to learn French. Making a thirty-day retreat, an eight-day retreat, and two three-day triduums in the course of ten months, all in silence, does little to foster fluency in the language of the place. In addition, during my tertianship, I spent a total of over two months at U.S. military posts in Germany.

My deficiencies in French led to some humorous incidents. One day the sacristan, Brother André Pacaud, a somewhat crusty individual, walked into the sacristy to find me bent over a sink full of soaking purificators. He asked me what I was doing. I told him I was washing the purificators, as he had asked me to do. "I told you to *bless* them, not to *wash* them!" he exploded in French. Given my limited understanding of French and his poor articulation, I mistook his *bénir* (to bless) for *baigner* (to wash). I had wondered why he had asked me to "wash" what were obviously still new purificators.

Tertianship constitutes the last stage of the formal Jesuit training process. Tertianship begins with a thirty-day retreat, as does the novitiate. While making his tertianship, a Jesuit studies in depth and hears conferences on the Constitutions of the Society of Jesus, engages in various apostolic works—called "experiments"—reflects on his life and call as a Jesuit, does much praying and meditating, resolves whatever conflicts or crises he may have in his spiritual life, and, in general, rekindles some of the religious fervor supposedly lost since his novitiate days. All this he does under the direction of an older, experienced Jesuit, known as the tertian instructor. I, having been blessed with a life quite free of conflicts and crises, had none to resolve. As for that novitiate fervor: My spiritual life has, from the outset, and up to the present, been marked neither by dramatic surges of fervor and growth nor by significant cooling-off periods. Beginning with novitiate days, and throughout the decades, there has been steady, measured, organic growth along the road to a degree of spiritual maturity. A more-or-less full maturity, it is hoped, will have been attained by the time my life's end is reached. Tertianship had no noticeable impact on my spiritual life. It seems less than a coincidence that my spiritual life as a Jesuit should resemble somewhat a successful crop planted and harvested by a North Dakota farmer.

We were blessed to have Père Jacques Goussault as our tertian instructor. In a letter from Paray to Father Nigro written on October 29, I described Père Goussault as "a most kind man, and a man of great common sense". On March 2, 1961, in a letter to the Toussaints, I was to write of him, "He looks very ascetical, sleeps little, works constantly, and lives on dry toast and nude noodles and other unspiced, tasteless things but explodes goodness into your face every time you see him." Père Goussault, born in 1905, died in the year 2004! Evidently, dry toast and nude noodles do not necessarily shorten a Frenchman's life.

Père Goussault assumed that we tertians were mature men, treated us as such, and did not impose himself upon us. During the thirty-day retreat, which began on September 22 and ended on October 26, he spoke to us only once per day for about thirty minutes but visited us in our rooms individually every three days to see how we were doing.

As early as September 12, I was writing letters to the U.S. military chaplains in Germany. On the day the thirty-day retreat ended, I wrote in my diary, "News—'Go to Munich!'" By November 25, I knew that I would be at the U.S. Army base in Kaiserslautern, Germany, helping the chaplain there, Father Martin Hoehn, during the Christmas–New Year's Day octave, then filling in for him during most of January 1961, while he was on leave.

I spent the night of December 21 in Paris. The following day, I arrived in Kaiserslautern and settled into a room in the bachelor officers' quarters. On the twenty-third and twenty-fourth, I heard many confessions. At the solemn High Midnight Mass, I was deacon and gave the sermon. On Christmas Day, I celebrated and preached at the 10:00 and 12:30 Masses. I had Christmas dinner with a certain Sergeant Conway and family. When not invited out, during my stay in Kaiserslautern, I ate at the officers' club. On the twenty-eighth, I made a trip to nearby Landstuhl. (I was to be there during the Lent of 1961.) Meanwhile, I offered Masses in the Kaiserslautern post chapel and in the smaller nearby Kapaun chapel. Ministry and social life among Americans rather quickly made Paray seem quite remote, almost unreal. The last words in my diary for that eventful year 1960: "Deo gratias!"

During the first week of the year 1961, I baptized an infant girl, had a sick call, began conducting the Miraculous Medal novena, heard the First Friday confessions, taught catechism to the eighth-graders, and held regular office hours. With several chaplains, on the tenth, I went to Frankfurt to take part in a day of recollection for chaplains. This was the first time I crossed the Rhine River.

Absenting myself from chaplain duties, I took the train to Munich on Wednesday, January 18. There I reconnected with Father Milhaven. We had exchanged a number of letters since our first meeting in Paris. He was now personally able to show me the Jesuit residence, where I hoped to live later that year, and the university, from which I hoped eventually to receive a doctorate in philosophy. The main reason for my trip to Munich, however, was to meet Professor Helmut Kuhn and discuss the matter of my doing doctoral work under his directorship. We had a somewhat short, but amicable, meeting. He agreed to accept me as a doctoral candidate. What a cause for gratitude and joy—and celebration! That evening, I attended a performance of Strauss' *Die Fledermaus*, an operetta quite familiar to me from records I had had in Fairbanks. The following day, I returned to Kaiserslautern to carry on with my duties as a substitute military chaplain. Four of us made a day's trip, on the twenty-third, to Heidelberg. In Fairbanks, my German class and I had often sung the song "Alt Heidelberg, du Feine". By now, Paray was really beginning to seem to me like little more than a memory out of the distant past. However, by the twenty-sixth, after spending a night in Paris, I was back at Paray.

My sojourn in Germany, while most satisfying and rewarding even from a purely natural standpoint, was technically, in tertianship terminology, an "experiment", part of the spiritual formation program. In my case, it was also financially rewarding. For my services in Kaiserslautern, Uncle Sam, in the person of the U.S. Army, gave me a generous, officially established honorarium, plus the privilege of shopping in the post exchanges, where one could "buy American" at very reasonable rates. The extra dollars came at about the right time. Before I left the Northwest, I visited Father Schultheis, then the financial officer of the Oregon Province, in Portland to talk about monies for my upcoming trip to Europe. He gave me four hundred dollars, with the words, "If you need more, ask for it—but remember you are a poor man." By the time I had first reached Paray in September 1960, after a long summer of traveling and touristing, I pretty well qualified as a "poor man". No longer so, when I returned there after my five weeks in Kaiserslautern!

On February 2, after three days in silence, prayer, and reflection, we renewed our vows. By February 17, I was back in Paris. This time I took in the Rodin Gallery and made a mini pilgrimage to the place where the Miraculous Medal was revealed by the Blessed Virgin Mary in a vision to Saint Catherine Labouré. For many years, my mother was an enthusiastic promoter of that devotion. I arrived at the thousand-bed U.S. Army hospital at Landstuhl on the twentieth to make my six-week "hospital experiment" by substituting for the chaplain, Father Jerome Sommer. During my stay at Landstuhl, I lived in his quarters. On March 2, I wrote the Toussaints: "I relax nicely in my quarters. Sometimes I serve up my own out-of-the-can meals. Sterno and electric cords do the trick nicely. That way I can get out of this black suit and also put to good use the ample record collection and the stereo that the chaplain put at my disposal." I ended that letter by telling Wilda, "Let your letters be long, newsy, friendly, and seasoned with wit and a touch of indiscretion." During my ten-month tertianship year, I very much missed Monroe and Fairbanks.

As substitute chaplain at the Landstuhl hospital, I offered the Masses, heard the confessions, visited the sick, heard their confessions, brought them Holy Communion, and anointed some. I heard confessions and offered Masses also at the nearby Vogelweh barracks. On March 7, I attended another day of recollection for U.S. military chaplains in Frankfurt. There were several side trips to Ramstein. With Father Fredric W. Schlatter—two years ahead of me at Bellarmine, one year ahead of me in the Society, and now also a tertian, on "experiment" in Pirmasens, Germany—I made a two-day trip in late March to Heidelberg, where we took in the sights and attended a performance of Verdi's opera *Un ballo in maschera*.

From March 25 to Easter Sunday, April 2, living in Kaiserslautern again, I was responsible for confessions and Masses at the Kapaun and Vogelweh chapels. After offering the two Easter Sunday Masses in the Kapaun chapel, I took the train to Freiburg im Breisgau, where I again joined up with Father Schlatter. There, on the third, we visited the old Gothic cathedral, saw Leo Fall's operetta *Madame Pompadour*, and spent the night. We spent the fourth in Lucerne, Switzerland; took the funicular to the top of Mount Pilatus on the fifth; and then went our separate ways. I spent that night in Lucerne, confident that I would have ample time to make it back, via Lyons, to Paray, where I was due the following day. Before I left Paray, Père Goussault had impressed upon all of us how important it was that we all be back there by the sixth of April. No excuses would be accepted. This was Easter Week, and I should have suspected that many people would be traveling. When I got to Lyons and tried to get a train for Paray, I was informed that all space was already taken. I spent the night with the Jesuits in Lyons. My feeble attempt to explain to Père Goussault the reason for my returning a day late fell on deaf ears. "*Oui, mon père, mais ...*" ("Yes, Father, but ...") he kept repeating, as I kept repeating my feeble reason for my overdue return. That night, at supper, I found myself on the floor in the middle of the refectory, with arms outstretched— "making the wings"—telling the whole community of my peccadillo. It was all I could do to suppress the smile of my insincerity.

The night of April 27 I was in Paris. The following day found me again at the Landstuhl hospital to replace Father Sommer for a time. On May 4, I helped with confessions at Ramstein. Three days later, I took the train to Strasbourg, France, where I planned to visit the famous cathedral, spend the night, then travel on to Paray. A train strike, however, kept me in Strasbourg an extra day. By the tenth, I was back at Paray.

On May 17, I arrived at Lamure-sur-Azergues, where I was met by Curé Henri DuLac, the pastor of the small, rural, grape-growing village of Cogny near Lyons. On the way to Cogny, we stopped off at Ars, famous for its onetime curé, Saint Jean-Baptiste Vianney. I fervently prayed the sainted curé to obtain for me the "grace of final perseverance and the grace to be a good priest". With equal fervor, I prayed him, too, for the gift of tongues—not necessarily for all of them, nor for the rest of my life, but just the gift of the French tongue—and that he grant it, if for no longer, then at least for the next five days. Well, as I soon learned, he proved to be no Holy Spirit. He did, however, see me through my do-or-die days in Cogny, and for that I was sincerely grateful to him.

As one of our tertianship "experiments", we were all assigned to various places to give a three-day retreat to early teenagers by way of preparing them to make their Solemn Communion. By midafternoon, Curé DuLac had me in Cogny. After showing me my room, he presented me to some twenty youngsters, to whom I was to give a retreat consisting of fourteen talks in all. My telling them, at the outset, *"Je suis d'Alaska"* impressed them. I had learned early on during my years in Europe always to introduce myself to Europeans as being from Alaska. To tell them I was an American would impress no one. So were hundreds of thousands of U.S. military personnel, students, and tourists in Europe at the time.

My May 18 diary entry reads: "First day of retreat—longest, hardest, sweatiest day of my priesthood." It was the French language. Having had only a week between Landstuhl and Cogny to work on the retreat, I was very poorly prepared to give it. Curé DuLac heard some of the talks I gave that opening day. After them, I asked him to tell me frankly if he thought I should go on. He assured me that, while my French was not all that perfect, I was making adequate sense to my young audience and that I should carry on. *"Moins pénible"*, I noted on the nineteenth. On that "less painful" day, in addition to giving some talks, I heard the confessions of the girls. The following day, I heard the confessions of the boys and the adults in addition to working on my sermon. On Sunday, the twenty-first, I noted: "Preached five times at Cogny. Received warm send-off to Paray-le-Monial." As Curé DuLac drove me to the train station, he had the kindness to assure me that, all in all, my days in Cogny were not without fruit and that Our Lord Himself had seen to that. Seldom in my life have I been more relaxed than I was on that train ride back to Paray. Paray never looked better to me than it did that day.

On June 9, the feast of the Sacred Heart, I took part in the solemn High Mass celebrated in the Basilica of the Sacred Heart and in the procession that followed. The following day, Père Goussault gave us our final conference. On the thirteenth, a group of us tertians made a bus pilgrimage to Ars. Our examination on the Institute of the Society of Jesus took place on the nineteenth. From June 24 to July 1, we made our eight-day retreat for the year 1961. On July 3, under the trees of Paray, we had a warmhearted, somewhat nostalgic departure party, as we were all set to head out in all directions the following day. As I was about to leave Paray-le-Monial—"a good place to get all detached and humbled up ... a good place to fatten the spirit by leaning the body ... a good place for French slugs, snails, moss, and mushrooms ... a place where, at times, I was bored almost to extinction", as I wrote to the Toussaints in several different letters—I was then, and ever after, deeply grateful to a kindly Providence, and to my superiors, for having seen fit so to arrange affairs that I made my tertianship there.

Chapter 12

The Summer of 1961

On July 4, 1961, in the company of two Belgian fellow tertians, Fathers Jean LaGros and Josèphe Snyders, I boarded the
train at Paray-le-Monial for the last time. It was Independence Day! I must confess that, not being a mystic, I had
found my ten-month year at Paray a long one. We arrived,
via Paris, in Brussels that evening. The following day, out of
Brussels, Father Snyders tour-guided me to Bruges and then
to Ghent, there to show me Jan Van Eyck's great *Ghent
Altarpiece*, also known as the *Altar of the Mystical Lamb*. The
forenoon of the sixth I spent seeing some of the highlights
of Brussels before going on to spend the afternoon and night
at Louvain. I went to Amsterdam, Holland, on the seventh,
walked around some, and took a boat ride on one of the
canals. The next day, I took a bus tour to The Hague and
Delft, famous for its ceramics, delftware. On the ninth, I visited Amsterdam's world-famous Rijks Museum.

I arrived in Cologne, Germany, on the tenth. There I had,
of course, to visit its Gothic cathedral and ascend the stee-
ple. I took a bus tour around the city. The following day, after
offering Mass in the cathedral, I enjoyed a day-long cruise
down the Rhine River from Cologne to Mainz, where I spent
the night. By train, I arrived in Munich on the thirteenth.
After reconnecting with Father Milhaven, I went on a bike
tour with him. I made the acquaintance of Father Paul F.

Conen, a Jesuit of the Detroit Province also doing doctoral studies in philosophy under Professor Kuhn. For the first of many times, I visited the *Haus der Kunst*, Munich's principal art gallery. I met Father Georg Schurhammer, S.J., widely known for his multivolume life of Saint Francis Xavier. Before leaving Munich, on the seventeenth, for Innsbruck, Austria, I had another reassuring talk with Professor Kuhn.

Innsbruck, with the Inn River flowing turbulently through the heart of it and alpine mountains all around it, I found *"magnifique!"*—according to the note in my diary. The first thing I did in Innsbruck was to buy myself a pair of sturdy hiking shoes. The surrounding hills and mountains were beckoning. My first hike took me to the nearby Jesuit villa, Zenzenhof. Back in Innsbruck, I took in a film version of Goethe's *Faust*. All the while I kept working on my German.

My main reason, however, for being in Innsbruck at this time was to attend the ordination to the priesthood of my fellow Oregonian, Thomas N. (Tom) Gallagher, in his theological studies in Innsbruck at the time. In the Jesuit church in Innsbruck, on July 26, with his parents and many others present, I saw him ordained a priest. The following morning, we attended his first Mass, celebrated at Zenzenhof. That evening, likewise at Zenzenhof, a big dinner was held for all the Americans from near and far. Excitement was added to the whole affair by a tremendous thunderstorm reverberating through the surrounding mountains.

On July 28, Mrs. Gallagher wrote a card to Dad and Mom:

Dear Folks:

Well, it's over now, and we are the happy parents of two priests. [Tom's brother, Richard, had been ordained shortly before him.] What a day! And your dear son was right with us a good part of the time. At the ordination and breakfast, of course, and then last evening at the big party (supper) at the villa. He sat at the same table with us. I know he is really getting a lot out of being over here. Louis seems in perfect health and looks so happy. It was a very happy time for us all.

From the time a sojourn in Europe first became a real possibility for me, Vienna was the city of my dreams. Strauss' waltzes and other Vienna-related music had been part of that summer school in German in Fairbanks. At the beginning of August 1961, those dreams were to become reality. For me, there was only one way to enter Vienna, and that was to enter it in style! That meant entering it after cruising down the famed Danube River on a fancy tourist boat from Linz.

On July 31, the feast of Saint Ignatius Loyola, after attending the solemn High Mass and dinner at the Jesuit complex in Innsbruck, I left Innsbruck on a train bound for Linz. The first thing I did upon my arrival there was to go to the boat dock, find out about departure times for Vienna, buy my ticket, and have them place my suitcase, with everything in it except my toothbrush, in a safety locker. I then did a little sight-seeing, had an early supper, and went to bed in a rooming house to get a good night's sleep. Departure time was scheduled for early the next morning.

On the morning of August 1, before leaving Linz, I phoned ahead to Jesuit headquarters in Vienna, informing them that I would arrive late that night and would appreciate it if someone were to meet me at the door and show me to my room. We left Linz on time for what turned out to be a full day of very pleasant cruising along a lengthy stretch of the Danube as it wound its way from the Black Forest in Germany down to the Black Sea past little villages, grape fields, and high hills topped with medieval castles and monasteries. Long after dark, on schedule, we arrived in Vienna. When I presented my claim ticket stub to the baggage handler, he glanced at it; then, to my great shock, he told me that my suitcase was back in Linz, in a safety storage locker! As it turned out, I had assumed, falsely, that the boat people would know my luggage was to be put on board to accompany me to Vienna.

What to do? It was approaching midnight. I had only the clothes on my back. At Jesuit headquarters, they were expecting me about this time. There was only one thing to do—go back to Linz and get my belongings. I took a taxi to the train station, checked the schedule to Linz, waited a couple of hours, then was on my way back to Linz. Very sheepishly, on the morning of the second, I rang the doorbell of the Jesuit residence next to the Universitätskirche at the Ignaz-Seipel-Platz. A sleepy-eyed brother answered the door. In halting German, I began to explain. In German that I understood perfectly well but pretended not to understand, he told me how he had to scold me for having kept him waiting up well beyond midnight. He called my bluff. I apologized. All was soon well between good Brother Karl Neumann and myself. Talk about entering Vienna "in style"!

That summer in Vienna—*Wien* to the Austrians and Germans—that had begun so ludicrously turned out to be one of the happiest, most fruitful summers of my whole life. By then, my German was quite good, so that, from the outset, I felt perfectly at home with and was accepted by the Jesuit community living at the Ignaz-Seipel-Platz in the heart of the city, virtually within the shadow of the Cathedral of Saint Stephen. I found the Austrian Jesuits a most congenial group, living life "at ease". From where I lived, I could easily walk to most of the other famous churches in Vienna, as well as to the opera, the theaters, the museums, the palaces, parliament buildings, parks and gardens, the Danube, and, most importantly, to the university. German studies at the university were my reason for being in Vienna in the first place.

On August 3, I began courses in German at the university. My momentary stumbling during the preliminary placement exam inclined the teacher to put me into the second-level class. However, after I assured him in passable German that I thought I could make the grade in the next-higher class, he moved me up. I attended classes faithfully, studied hard—when I studied—and practiced speaking the language with any and all. A little portable tape recorder proved to be a very helpful tool.

One day, a certain Dr. Karl Weber, a newspaper man due to travel soon to the United States, made it known at Jesuit headquarters that he was looking for someone who spoke English as his native language and who was working on his spoken German. His proposal was that he and his English-speaking partner would help one another in the language foreign to the other, conversing half the time in German and half the time in English. I happily teamed up with him, got good practice speaking German, and, at the same time, learned much about Vienna as we walked its streets and parks, drank its coffee, ate its Wiener schnitzels and its famous Sacher torte, and spoke its language, High German—but with a Viennese accent.

On August 18, as part of our course, I had to give a lecture in German to the class. "Alaska" was the magic word! The actual topic of the lecture, however, was "Die Kunst des Lehrers" (The Art of Teaching). Classes at the university came to an end on the twenty-ninth. Graded on the basis of pronunciation, grammar, vocabulary, conversation, written exercises, an essay, interpretation of literature, and lecturing, I was given 145 points out of a possible 160—the whole, summarized in two words: "*Sehr gut!*" For my "overall achievement", I was awarded the second prize, a book about Vienna.

Living with me in the Jesuit community that summer was a young Jesuit priest from sunny Sicily, Padre Felice Scalia. If anyone ever lived up to his first name, he did. While I was taking courses at the university, he was being tutored in German by Fräulein Katarina Inhauser. He spoke highly of her, introduced me to her, and, once I had finished the courses at the university, I, too, began taking tutorial lessons from her, September 6–15. Mostly we just conversed in German. One evening, we went to the Burgtheater for a performance. During the intermission, out of her gilded little handbag, she produced a tiny box of chocolates to share with me. I early on observed this to be a common practice with theatergoers and opera goers in Germany and Austria. Fräulein Inhauser knew the leading actress and, after the performance, introduced me to her.

As I had done in Paris, so in Vienna: I mixed the useful with the pleasant. I formally studied the language and, all the while, took in the sights, visited the major churches, attended theater and opera performances, went to the movies, visited the museums and galleries and the palaces and places of historical interest, heard the Vienna Boys' Choir sing, and watched the famous white stallions, the Lippizaner, being trained at the riding school. In the Prater, a sprawling amusement park in Vienna, I took a number of rides on "the giant wheel", from the top of which one could see most of the city. I also made a number of excursions out of Vienna: to the Vienna Woods, to the outlying vineyards that grow the grapes processed into the choice *Heuriger* wine, and to the medieval Cistercian abbey Heiligenkreuz—so named because a relic of the true Cross was venerated there. Often I had a companion; often I was alone.

In the course of that summer, I became a kind of tourist guide in my own right to Jesuits passing through Vienna. Prices for everything were remarkably reasonable. As in Paris,

I was occasionally called upon to offer a Mass now in this church or convent, now in that. Happily I obliged.

My first stay in Vienna came to an end on September 25, the morning after I had attended a grand performance of Wagner's opera *Die Meistersinger von Nürnberg*. Vienna, "the city of my dreams", did not disappoint. In fact, it lived up to, and surpassed, my expectations. I was to visit it again, both during that first sojourn in Europe and again on several subsequent trips to Europe.

On September 25, I arrived in Salzburg. That evening, I went to the marionette theater to watch puppets perform to the music of Mozart and Tchaikovsky. The following day, I was back in Innsbruck, where I took some hikes into the high country with Father Tom Gallagher. Then, it was Munich again, out of which I took a bus tour to Neuschwanstein and other castles in the Bavarian Alps. Thinking it would border on the unforgivable to be in Munich with the Oktoberfest in full swing without checking it out, I patronized one of the *Bierhallen*. Although Munich is famous for all that hopped-up stuff that made Milwaukee famous, I, for my part, left most of the beer drinking to others. As for pretzels, them I liked.

After the excitement of Paris, it was the peace and seclusion at Paray-le-Monial. After the excitement of Vienna, it was the peace and seclusion at Neuhausen, the novitiate of the Jesuit Upper German Province near Stuttgart, where I arrived on October 2 to immerse myself in a sea of nothing but German and things German. On the fifth, I more or less wasted the day touring Stuttgart. On the twelfth, on bikes, a novice and I took a day's trip to Tübingen to visit the renowned university there. Pope Benedict XVI and Father Hans Küng, the well-known Swiss theologian, were fellow faculty members there at one time. My two-week stay at Neuhausen came to an end on the sixteenth, when I left it for Munich.

Chapter 13

Doctoral Studies in Munich, Germany: October 1961–July 1965

On October 16, 1961, I arrived in Munich to take up residency in Ignatiushaus on Kaulbach Street, confident that that would be my home until I walked out of it with a doctorate in philosophy in hand. Ten days later, I wrote to the Toussaints,

I am in Munich, happily settled in my room, which will no doubt be home for about three years. I am now matriculated in philosophy, dogmatic theology, and psychology. All in all, I think I'll enjoy my stay here, but it will be work, too; and in about three years I'll be happy to triculate out again. This first semester will be the toughest, with everything so new. But, living in a Jesuit community, I have lots of generous people around me to give tips and advice. I like the community I'm living with—mostly Germans, but also four Americans, plus South Americans, Spaniards, and Cubans. The house is comfortable and very well situated; the food, German. I'm living in a remodeled wing and am very well satisfied with my room.

Ignatiushaus was indeed "very well situated". The University of Munich was but a five-minute walk out the back door; the *Englischer Garten*, a big, rambling park, a five-minute walk out the front door. A convent, where I frequently offered Mass,

was a twenty-minute walk away. The heart of downtown
Munich was about a thirty-minute walk from Ignatiushaus. To
be found in the heart of downtown Munich were the train station, the opera house, various theaters and movie houses, the
cathedral, the Jesuit Saint Michael's Church, and the Bürger-
saal Church, in the crypt of which were enshrined the relics
of Rupert Mayer, a beatified Munich Jesuit priest. Faced with
the daunting challenge of getting a doctorate in a foreign country and in a foreign language, I was to pay many a visit to the
shrine of Blessed Rupert Mayer to ask him to help me get that
doctorate. As events were to prove, he did not fail me.

Living with me in Ignatiushaus and pursuing doctoral
degrees at the university, in addition to Father Milhaven, were
also Fathers Richard Loftus and Norbert Rigali, members of
the California Province, whom I had first met at Mount Saint
Michael's. Father Loftus was doing doctoral studies in biology; Father Rigali (older brother of Justin Cardinal Rigali) was
doing doctoral studies in philosophy. Father Paul Conen, of
the Detroit Province, too, was living in Ignatiushaus and doing
doctoral studies in philosophy. The five of us had many an occasion to gather informally in one or another's room—sometimes
around a bottle of good Mosel wine, sometimes around several bottles of good Munich beer—to discuss, often in considerable depth, matters theological, philosophical, biological,
political, or whatever. Occasionally, some member of the Ignatiushaus community joined us. At times, we Americans had
to treat ourselves to a genuine American steak dinner at the
"Ma Schneiders" downtown restaurant. The Ignatiushaus superiors were most understanding of our mildly nonconformist
American ways. In fact, fully appreciating the academic pres-
sures we were under, they, indirectly, encouraged us in them.
They were equally indulgent with all the other foreign doctoral aspirants.

The typical doctoral candidate at the University of Munich needed to enroll for eight semesters. As a rule, fellow American Jesuits with my academic background, upon petitioning, were dispensed from three semesters of compulsory enrollment. I, being bold, and feeling I had nothing to lose, petitioned to be dispensed from *five* semesters. I based my case on the fact that I had, by then, earned two M.A. degrees and had some lesser achievements to my credit. To my surprise, my petition was granted. In an ideal order, therefore, assuming that I was able to take all the needed seminars and to produce an acceptable doctoral dissertation, I could have had, within only three semesters, my doctorate in hand. However, I was far from living in an ideal order.

The day I arrived in Munich, after I was settled in my room, Father Rigali took me on a bit of an orientation tour. Among other places, we visited the university. At the American consulate, I obtained the official papers authorizing my prolonged stay in Germany. A few days later, I registered with the German police department and received official identification papers. On the seventeenth, I enrolled at the university.

As I had done ever since leaving the Pacific Northwest, so in Munich, too, almost from the outset, I began to visit art galleries and places of interest, as well as to attend performances in theaters and in the opera house and go to movies of operas and dramas. However, I was not in Munich to "do the town".

By October 1961, after some two years of trying to arrive at key decisions relating to my getting a doctorate, I was certain that Munich was the place, that philosophy was my major field, and that Professor Kuhn was my director. I was certain, too, that dogmatic theology was to be one of my minors, with Dr. Michael Schmaus as my director. To get a doctorate at the University of Munich, one had to take seminars and pass examinations also in two minor fields of one's choosing. As for my second minor, I inclined at the outset toward rational psychology and, in fact, matriculated in that. However, I soon thought Italian might be a better choice—easier and more enjoyable. We had complete freedom regarding the two minors.

As I began degree work in Munich, one major question still remained for me to answer: On what subject should I write my dissertation? Even before I began that first semester in Munich, I had found myself often thinking about, anguishing over, and discussing with others the matter of a dissertation subject. True, there was no immediate urgency; still, it would have put my mind at ease considerably to know early on that I had a feasible dissertation subject, approved by my director. For a time, I considered doing my dissertation on the problem of evil as treated in Boethius' philosophical masterpiece, *De consolatione philosophiae.* I never even considered writing about some German philosopher or some German philosophy. For the most part, German philosophers and German philosophies had already been or were already being treated in depth—and were, in any case, best left to the natives.

On November 2, I bought myself a simple bicycle, a new one, not as a means of transportation, but for recreational outings. I was to enjoy many a bike tour to and around the outskirts of Munich. Bicycle trails laced the city and surroundings.

November 7 was a day of major importance for the Ignatiushaus community. On that day, Father Augustin Rösch died. He had been the rector of that community since 1956. But that was not the principal reason for his having been held in the highest esteem, both in Jesuit and in civic circles. During the Hitler years, he was the father provincial of the Upper German Province. As such, he constantly had hanging over him the real threat of being arrested and imprisoned. Toward the end of World War II, he was offered a hiding place in the garret of a private home. One winter day, a Nazi official noticed that one of the garret windows in that home was frosted up. Suspecting that someone was being hidden away there, he investigated, found Father Rösch, and led him off to prison. Father Rösch's life was spared only by the rather abrupt end of the war. After the war, for his having stood up to the Nazi party, he was elected to serve in the Bavarian legislature. In recognition of his bravery during the Hitler regime and for his service in the legislature, the state of Bavaria granted Jesuits virtually tuition-free attendance at the University of Munich. Father Rösch's funeral Mass and burial took place on November 10, at the Jesuit philosophate at Pullach, a short distance from Munich. I was present at that Mass and burial, along with many Jesuits—and Professor Kuhn.

That Professor Kuhn was present at that Mass and burial is significant. Jewish by birth, he had been received into the Church by Father Rösch. The two were close friends. During the latter 1930s and until the end of the war, Professor Kuhn, to escape the Nazi persecution of the Jews, was in the United States, first as a visiting professor at Emory University, then as such at the University of North Carolina. Fellow American Jesuits living at Ignatiushaus and doing doctoral work under him described him as "most friendly and helpful, especially to the clergy". The father minister of Ignatiushaus described him to me as *"mimosenhaft"* (highly sensitive, touchy).

The connections between Father Rösch and the university and Father Rösch and Professor Kuhn, while certainly major pluses in my favor as a doctoral candidate at the university under Professor Kuhn, did, at the same time, put me under a definite stress, albeit self-imposed. I felt I just owed it to both of those noble men to make a success of my doctoral aspirations. It was a clear case of noblesse oblige. Furthermore, inasmuch as other American Jesuits had completed doctoral studies under Professor Kuhn with a certain éclat, I did not want to be the first not to live up to his expectations— nor did I want to disappoint those in Alaska and Portland who had placed their confidence in me.

Seminars were what the Munich doctoral program was mainly all about. I had to earn three seminar certificates of participation in my major field and three in each of my minor fields. Attendance and active participation in the seminars were required. There were no examinations other than the comprehensive oral examinations that followed upon the completion of all the prescribed course work: a two-hour oral exam in the major field, and a one-hour oral exam in each of the two minor fields. Though one was free to attend, or not to attend, the lectures offered in one's chosen fields, one was well advised to do so. One was, of course, free to attend any lectures held at the university. I had occasion to attend lectures given by, among others, the eminent theologians Jesuit father Karl Rahner and Monsignor Romano Guardini. Admittedly, this borders on name-dropping; but it did mean something to me to see and hear in person men with whose books and articles I had been familiar for some years. While in theology at Alma College, I had translated Father Rahner's long article on the Sacred Heart of Jesus from German into English. In March 1973, I was to give a lecture on the theology of Father Rahner at the University of Alaska–Fairbanks. All in all, doctoral candidates were given a considerable amount of freedom and were presumed to be mature students by the time they reached that academic level.

One word in my diary summarizes my feelings for November 9, 1961: "Disappointed!" On that day, I learned that I was unable to get into Professor Kuhn's seminar. It was already filled up with carry-over students. (A spin on my new bike helped clear the head and pick up spirits.) I was, however, able to get into Professor Schmaus' seminar, and that was of some consolation. I was finally taking a concrete step toward that doctorate. The name Schmaus first became known to me when I was at Alma.

On November 12, I attended my first *Doktorandenkreis*, the first of many. This was a "circle" composed of the students doing doctoral work under Professor Kuhn and headed by him. The circle met every other week in the early evening during semesters at the university. Attendance was optional, though most of its members attended it faithfully. The basic format was that, for about thirty minutes, one of the more advanced doctoral candidates would read a part of his disser-tation to the group. A rather informal discussion on what had been read, normally led off by Professor Kuhn himself, would then follow. The discussions generally lasted about an hour. They were always quite cerebral, at times somewhat heated, but always amicable. To read and defend a part of one's dis-sertation at a *Doktorandenkreis*, too, was optional. When the logical time came for me to do so, I chose not to.

"Thinking very seriously about Italian as a minor", I wrote in my diary on November 18. On the twenty-seventh, I enrolled in the Berlitz Italian program offered in Munich. For the time being, that resolved the concern about my second minor. Meanwhile, I was still plagued by my concern over what subject to write on for my dissertation. On the twenty-fourth, I found myself in Innsbruck, talking about that con-cern with Jesuit father and professor of philosophy at Innsbruck Otto Muck. "The Definition of Unity in the Philosophy of Boethius" was discussed as a possible subject. At the Zenzen-hof villa, on the twenty-sixth, I joined the American Jesuits studying in Innsbruck as they enjoyed a Thanksgiving Day dinner—on a Sunday. I was back in Munich the following day, where, during subsequent days—again mixing the useful with the pleasant—I attended opera performances of *Lucia di Lammermoor*, *Boris Godunov*, and *Der Rosenkavalier*.

On December 8, I took the train from Munich to Stuttgart to help out the U.S. military chaplains serving at the Robinson, the Krabbenloch, and the Pattonville barracks on the outskirts of Stuttgart. I was to make many a trip to Stuttgart for weekend and holy-day ministrations at now this, now that of those three barracks. I taught catechism, heard confessions, and offered Masses. This pastoral ministry among Americans was a good counterbalance to my academic work.

I was, by this time, determined to go all out for Italian. The day after Christmas, I took the train out of Stuttgart for San Remo, Italy. My diary entry for the twenty-seventh reads, "First day in San Remo. *Sono perfettamente contento.* First visit to Berlitz school." The following day, I offered the Mass at the main altar of the Jesuit church in San Remo. While in San Remo, I took ten hours of Italian lessons at the Berlitz school. What made San Remo especially attractive to me was the fact that Father Daniel Fontana (see chapter 5) was stationed there. A native Italian, he was fluent also in English. In him—a short, most pleasant, likeable man—I had the perfect private tutor and personal guide.

On the last day of the year 1961, one of the most memorable years of my life, the captain of the USS *Quillback*, a submarine moored to the San Remo pier, approached Father Fontana in hopes of finding an English-speaking priest to offer a New Year's Eve Mass for the submarine's crew. Father Fontana suggested I offer the Mass. It was the chance of a lifetime for me to be able to offer Mass in a submarine. In the torpedo room, below the waterline, a makeshift altar was prepared. Crew members knelt in the narrow aisle to my left and right. When I said a *Dominus vobiscum*, I made only a quarter turn. A half turn would have had me praying the Lord to be with the torpedo immediately behind me. On Sunday, August 11, 1963, I was again to offer Mass in a submarine moored in San Remo, in the USS *Becuna*.

On January 4, Father Fontana and I made an all-day excursion by train to the principality of Monaco and to Nice, France. On the eighth, after visiting Cannes, we crossed over to the nearby Island of Lérins to tour the oldest monastery in western Europe, a monastery founded in the year 400 by Saint Honoratus. The island is, actually, better known because of Saint Vincent of Lérins.

By January 10, I was back in Munich for more Berlitz classes and the final weeks of lectures and seminars of that first semester at the university. On February 22, I completed my first seminar in dogmatic theology under Professor Schmaus and received my first certificate of participation in that minor. With that, I stood at "one down overall, eight to go!"

My overriding concern at that time, however, continued to be the matter of a dissertation subject. Neither Munich nor Innsbruck had been able to help me allay that concern. Maybe Rome could help me find a definitive answer.

On February 27, 1962, I arrived in Rome. The principal reason for making that trip, my first to the Eternal City, was to try to resolve, once and for all, the question of a subject for my doctoral dissertation. While in Rome and Italy, I had again, of course, also to mix the useful with the pleasant, to visit places both sacred and profane, and to attend various events. Doing doctoral work at Rome's Gregorian University were longtime classmates and close friends: Fathers Vince Beuzer, Dick Hill, Joe Powers, and Thomas (Tom) Royce.

Tony Via was now also in Rome, studying theology in preparation to being ordained a priest. In those fellow Jesuits, well acquainted with Rome by this time, I had the best of knowledgeable and willing guides. Now with one, now with another of them, I visited Rome's major basilicas and churches, museums and art galleries, places of special interest to Jesuits, places of historic interest, and famous fountains. I also attended several concerts and met and talked with many Jesuits.

Saint Peter's Basilica I had to explore from the very bottom to as high up as one could climb in the dome. None of the places of interest in Rome impressed me more than the *Scavi*, the catacombs under Saint Peter's. Down in these escavations, I felt myself transported back to the earliest days of the persecuted Christian Church. In Saint Peter's itself, on March 14, I saw Pope John XXIII during a general audience. A week before, I was within two yards of him, when he came up the aisle in Saint Sabina's Church. I saw him also when he visited the Jesuit church, the Gesù. In matters more mundane, I had myself a good swim in Rome's Olympic pool. On the last day of my stay in Rome, March 15, Father Beuzer and I visited Naples and the ancient city of Pompeii.

March 10 was the red-letter day of my days in Rome. By the end of that day, I could write, "Rome mission accomplished!" On that day, I had a lengthy discussion with Father Robert H. Taylor, a California Province Jesuit doing doctoral work in philosophy in Rome. In the course of that discussion, he brought to my attention the real feasibility of my doing—and recommended that I do—my dissertation on the subject of the moral philosophy of the Scottish philosopher Sir William David Ross, a man known to me then only as the translator of Aristotle's *Metaphysics*. It was immediately evident to me that this was just the kind of subject I was looking for. It was in English. It was presented by Ross in only one relatively small volume. There was enough supportive literature to enable me to produce a fleshed-out dissertation. Of critical importance was the fact that no one had ever treated it in a doctoral dissertation. In addition, moral philosophy had been of special interest to me ever since my days at Mount Saint Michael's. Had a kindly Providence come to my rescue? I sincerely prayed and hoped so; I hoped, as well, that Professor Kuhn would approve of my choice of Ross' moral philosophy as the subject of my dissertation.

With considerable relief, I left Rome on March 16 on a circuitous return trip to Munich. I spent the sixteenth to nineteenth in San Remo visiting again with Father Fontana. In Milan, I toured *Il Duomo*, the famous cathedral; and in the Church of Santa Maria delle Grazie, I viewed Leonardo da Vinci's still-more-famous fresco, the *Last Supper*. On the twenty-first, I arrived in Venice, where I toured the Piazza San Marco and visited the Basilica San Marco and the Rialto Bridge. I took a cruise on the Canale Grande. After the noise and the traffic-dodging of Rome, the peace, quiet, and utter lack of motorized vehicles in the heart of old Venice was a wonderful cure for frayed nerves. "Only one mishap in Venice", I wrote to the Toussaints on May 3 of that year. "I got badly sea-gulled as I romantically gazed at the Bridge of Sighs." Giving voice to my general anxiety, I ended that letter with, "I feel a heavy cloud of responsibility hanging over me. The Society is investing so much time and money in me that I feel I have to make good. So, your prayers, please!"

After Venice, it was Florence for four days. There, I visited that city's centerpiece, the cathedral Santa Maria del Fiore, famous for its baptistery doors. I took in the artwork in both the Uffizi and Pitti galleries and visited the shops lining the *Ponte Vecchio*, the old bridge crossing the Arno River. (My Benedictine cousin Father Arno Gustin had derived his religious name from that river.) Out of Florence, I visited the small town of Fiesole, whose villas and gardens are beautifully situated on a hill overlooking the Arno valley and the city of Florence. Out of Florence, too, on a bus tour, I visited also the walled-in medieval hill town of San Gimignano and the city of Siena.

By way of Innsbruck, I arrived back in Munich on March 28. That same day, I ordered Ross' books and, soon thereafter, other books related to his writings and the subject of moral philosophy in general. My first order of business now was to acquaint myself well with Ross' writings, so as to be able to make a persuasive case when I talked to Professor Kuhn about doing my dissertation on Ross' moral philosophy. I began intensive reading in that field.

When I stopped off at San Remo on the return trip from Rome to Munich, my intention was to spend a month there working some more on Italian, since, at that time, I still looked upon Italian as my second minor. However, waiting for me in San Remo was a letter from our prefect of studies, Father Leo B. Kaufmann. He wondered about the advisability of my making Italian my second minor. I thereupon reverted to my initial choice of psychology as my second minor.

From early May to the third week of July, my second term at the University of Munich was in progress. I attended Professor Kuhn's lectures, seminar, and *Doktorandenkreis* sessions. I attended Professor Schmaus' seminars. I made regular weekend trips to Stuttgart to minister to American military personnel stationed at the several different barracks there.

July 2, 1962, proved to be a day of major importance for me. My diary entry for that date: "Ross approved!" On that day, after listening to me briefly and after a moment of sputtering hesitation—and a comment about "that sober Scotsman"— Professor Kuhn, to my very great relief, gave his approval of

Ross, in general, as a dissertation subject with a *"Ja, ja—gut, gut!"*

Thereafter, and especially during the early months of 1963, I anguished over and painstakingly applied myself to the production of an outline for my dissertation. With joy of heart, I was able to write in my diary under the date of April 17, 1963: "Kuhn approved outline—Deo gratias!" The following day, I wrote to Father Provincial McDonald:

> Well, yesterday I saw Professor Kuhn, and things could hardly have gone better. I gave him a pretty well fleshed-out outline of what I plan will be the dissertation. He said to go ahead and write it and have it translated into German. Normally, he reads the English first and then says to have it translated. He does have a pretty good idea of what I will do and has approved it, so I feel confident, more or less for the first time, that things will really work out all right. Makes me feel kind of good after so much uncertainty. I estimate I will finish in August 1964.

To that, Father McDonald responded on May 15: "It was good to receive your encouraging progress report. The fathers in Fairbanks are naturally anxious to have you back with them, but it is important to finish your degree first."

One of the two Cuban Jesuits living with me in Ignatius-haus was Father Armando de la Torre, a most likeable individual. We soon became close friends and often took walks together or went to some performance or other. To him I was "Gringo". On July 2, he invited me to join him and some Latin American students at semester's end on their planned trip to Berlin. On the twentieth, I found myself on a flight headed for West Berlin. There, he and I were given rooms in the Jesuit residence. On the twenty-first, we took a bus tour around West Berlin and, through "Checkpoint Charlie", into East Berlin. By contrast to West Berlin, this was another world. On the twenty-third, on my own, I again went into East Berlin, to see some of the main attractions but also to visit the Jesuits there. Before I left, one of them gave me a crucifix to bring out to one of the Jesuits in West Berlin. I had been checked rather thoroughly by the East Berlin border guard on my way in, so smuggling a crucifix out could, I anticipated, be a bit risky. Having hidden it on me, I had "nothing to declare" on the way out and so was waved through without incident. One of the highlights of that Berlin trip was seeing the famous bust of the Egyptian queen Nefertiti in the Dahlem Museum in West Berlin.

Sometime in early June 1962, I received word from the Portland provincialate that I had been approved for final vows and that I was to take them on August 15. Accordingly, on that day, the feast of the Assumption of the Blessed Virgin Mary, in Ignatiushaus—after having made my annual eight-day retreat at Rottmanshöhe, the Jesuit retreat house on Starnberger Lake, a little south of Munich—I took my final vows, simple vows, but vows constituting me a formed spiritual coadjutor in the Society of Jesus. Final vows are also commonly referred to in Jesuit circles as "last vows". In my case, however, those 1962 vows were to turn out not to be my last vows. Although I had not passed the *ad gradum* exam at the end of my theological studies at Alma College—as already noted in chapter 7—I was to be raised, seventeen years later, to the ranks of the solemnly professed fathers of the Society of Jesus. On July 31, 1979, in Immaculate Conception Church, Fairbanks, I pronounced the three solemn vows of poverty, chastity, and obedience, plus the fourth solemn vow of special obedience to the pope "in regard to the missions". *Those* were my last vows.

On the evening of August 16, I took the train out of Munich with Oxford, England, as my final destination. My journey took me across Germany to Aachen, then across Belgium to the port city of Ostend. Traveling as I did, in an overheated compartment, because there was a mother with an infant in the same compartment, it turned out to be a long train ride. Hungry when I arrived in Ostend, I ordered myself some chicken for breakfast—a poor choice. The chicken was on the greasy side. It never made it to England. The crossing from Ostend to Dover was an exceptionally rough one. Before it was over, many of the passengers, myself included, and even some of the crew members, had made part of the crossing "by rail". I had held my own, till the domino effect claimed me, too, as a victim. That was the one time in my life when I was thoroughly seasick. But on to Oxford! From Dover, I took the train to London, and from there on up to Oxford, where I arrived in the late afternoon of the seventeenth.

At Oxford, I was warmly welcomed by the Jesuits into their Campion Hall community. With that began one of the most relaxed, pleasant, satisfying episodes of my life. By now, I had my Oxford mission clearly in focus; and I would know clearly when I had accomplished it. I was there to acquire books and other materials needed for the writing of my dissertation. Besides seeing to the acquisition of those materials, I was there, too, to discuss, in depth, dissertation-related materials with fellow Jesuits. Campion Hall, and Oxford, in general, positively crackled with intellectuality. By visiting its bookshops and spending long hours in its renowned Bodleian Library copying documents, I was able to amass what turned out to be around 80 percent of the materials I eventually needed.

Having allotted myself fully six weeks in Oxford, from August 17 to September 28, I had time enough to do things besides reading Ross-related materials. Father Beuzer chanced to be in Oxford at the same time. Together we took walks, visited many of Oxford's special attractions, and saw movies, among them *The Music Man*. We spent a day together in London. One day, with two other men staying at Campion Hall, I went on a day trip north to visit Stratford-upon-Avon and the bombed-out cathedral in Coventry. On my own, at Stratford-upon-Avon, I attended a superb performance of Shakespeare's *Macbeth*. In Oxford, I attended several operas, as well as the Gilbert and Sullivan operetta *Iolanthe*. Up to that time, I thought I liked Gilbert and Sullivan operettas. However, halfway through the performance of *Iolanthe*, it suddenly all seemed so utterly silly to me that I got up and walked out, never again to listen to a Gilbert and Sullivan note.

On September 28, I went to London. During my stay there, I visited the National and Tate galleries and Madame Tussaud's wax museum. I saw film versions of Shakespeare's *Richard III*, *Henry V*, and *Hamlet*—and *The Sound of Music*. I attended opera performances of Verdi's *La forza del destino* and of Puccini's *La bohème*.

On October 8, I left London for Dover. With some trepidation, recalling the misery I had experienced on my crossing of the channel from Ostend to Dover, I boarded the ferry to Calais, France. That crossing was as smooth as the previous one had been rough. Loaded down with books and optimism, I was back in Munich by the ninth.

November 8 triggered a major change in my life in Germany. On that day, I visited Father Paul Conen in Oberammergau, a picturesque village nestled in the foothills of the Bavarian Alps, a two-hour train ride south of Munich, known worldwide for its wood carvings, for its *Lüftlmalerei*—the paintings in color on the outside walls of homes and public buildings—and for the *Passion Play*, staged there, normally, every ten years. For about a week, Father Conen had been relaxing there in the *Hänsel-Gretel Kinderheim* and, at the same time, serving as a temporary priest. This home for orphans and children from broken homes was owned by the city of Munich and was staffed by twelve Niederbronner sisters, who had their motherhouse in Neumarkt, a small town near Nuremberg. The sisters were assisted by five hired young lay women called *Tanten* ("aunties"). There were eighty-two children, the majority preschoolers, in the *Heim* at the time. Understandably, they could never be left without the supervision of at least several sisters. This meant that the sisters could not all go to what was often the one and only morning Mass in the village church. They were, consequently, forever looking for a priest to offer morning Mass for them in their ornate little chapel, a room in the *Heim*. They were more than willing to give him room and board for that service.

As Father Conen and I were chatting away in the small parlor–dining room and time for the noon meal was approaching, Sister Gundharda, the guest hostess, came in to prepare the table. We told her not to bother, that we would eat at some restaurant in the village. She tried to persuade us to stay and said that it would be no trouble. But we would not be persuaded. She left, and a bit later, Sister Emmerana, the superior, a stout, persuasive woman, came in, sat down, and absolutely insisted that we stay for the noon meal. We relented. She left. During the meal, she came in again, sat down, and began to stress the importance of daily Mass for all the sisters and the impossibility of that for the reason given above. She pleaded with me that I seriously consider spending some time in Oberammergau, so that they could have daily Mass. I, then and there, assured her that I would give the matter serious thought and that I would almost certainly be back soon for a stay of some undetermined length. She understood, of course, that my Jesuit superiors would have to approve a lengthy stay. From what I had by then already seen of Oberammergau and heard from Father Conen about the sisters and the home, I came to a very quick conclusion that we were meant for one another.

On November 20, I returned to Oberammergau. Two days later, I wrote to Father Provincial McDonald from Ettalerstrasse 41, Oberammergau, Germany:

Possibly the above return address and this letter surprise you. I am here for four weeks, saying the morning Mass for the twelve sisters who staff the orphanage here, which cares for eighty-two children. The sisters are so eager to have a priest that they provide him with fine living accommodations and excellent food—all for nothing. Morning Mass is all they ask. After Mass, I am free to study or to enjoy the magnificent mountains that rise to the clouds from my doorstep. You probably do not know how much I love the wilds and a good shaggy winter. It is snowing heavily today. Wonderful atmosphere for body and soul! But I discipline myself and spend long hours daily working on my dissertation. I seem to have more time here than in Munich.

Now you may be wondering how I can be going to school and still be up here. I've had good fortune. My Gonzaga University transcript and a bit of salesmanship got me credit for five semesters of former studies, so, instead of having to enroll for eight semesters as is normal, or five as most foreigners have to, I have to enroll for only three. This is my last one now. That means going into Munich once a week, a two-hour train ride. It is yet too early to say when I should be done with my doctoral work. I am hoping to finish in about a year from the coming summer. That would be doing it faster than most of the others who are now working for the doctorate.

My health is good; my professor and I seem to be mutually satisfied. This all sounds rather optimistic, and it is meant to sound so; but there have been some very frustrating times, too, already, and there will be more probably. But with God's help, our prayers, hard work—and a little bit of my-fair-lady luck.... I spent the summer weeks in Oxford getting the material I need for the thesis. I have the books and articles with me here, so I can work without a library at my elbow.

Now for the purpose of this letter. If the sisters will have me permanently (and I think they'd be overjoyed not to have to be looking for someone continually), and if the superiors in Munich see no difficulty, what would be your advice? I should add that I am more than content in Ignatiushaus. Reasons for moving here would be primarily to help where help is badly needed without in any way hurting my work, which must, of course, always take precedence. Financially, I'd be way ahead, since here I get room and board, and that includes considerably more than the same in Ignatiushaus, where we now pay a $2.50 per diem. But, while money plays a role, I don't think it should change things essentially. Recreation is built into the life here; in Munich it must be sought and bought. But I'm afraid I'm trying to prejudice you. Since I need to know fairly soon whether your preference is that I stay permanently here or in Munich till work is done, I trust you. will answer reasonably soon, dear Father. I might add that moving here would not prevent me from spending an occasional few days or even weeks in Munich during "critical times". I hope you will feel perfectly free to advise me as to what to you seems best. I can honestly say that, at times, I've found the responsibility of making important decisions to weigh rather heavily upon me over here. The local superiors are always most kind and ready to advise, but so often they don't really know what my provincial would want. (Man, is it ever snowing!)

I still go to Stuttgart about every two weeks to help the army chaplain. I go on Saturday and return on Sunday. The trip nets about twenty-five dollars. But the more important feature of this work with the U.S. troops and families is that it gives good and necessary priestly work. I tend to be shy by nature (something not evident to many people), and this ministerial work is good for me. Now I have taken enough of your time. Sincerely in Christ . . ."

On November 27, Father McDonald wrote me his answer: "As for your staying in Oberammergau rather than in Munich, I have no objection if local Jesuit superiors have none. The only stipulation I would make is that you do not let more than six months go by without a sojourn of several weeks in one of our Jesuit houses. Otherwise, as long as you can study better and keep up your spiritual exercises in the new location, you may go ahead."

The Second Vatican Council was convened in Rome by Pope John XXIII on October 11, 1962. When I learned that Bishop Gleeson would be attending it, I made known to him that I would like to meet with him to inform him as to how my doctoral work was progressing and, in turn, to be informed by him as to how things stood with my likely future at the University of Alaska–Fairbanks. During the Council, we Jesuits not assigned to Rome were not to visit there without special permission. At first, therefore, I assumed Bishop Gleeson and I would meet somewhere other than in Rome. He, however, in his kindness and sensing my preference, invited me and, using the power of his purple, obtained permission from Jesuit superiors for me to visit him in Rome—he even paid for my round trip! This I did, "with great satisfaction", from November 29 to December 1. "We had a wonderful six-hour visit one day," I wrote the Toussaints on December 9, "then dinner together my last night there. I was again assured that they were looking to my return to work at the University of

Alaska." To Father Provincial I wrote, "The talk with Bishop Gleeson gives new urgency to my work. Optimism is mounting, but I am still cautious."

During that Rome visit, I spent time, too, with fellow Oregonians and with Father Taylor, who, earlier in the year, had so strongly recommended that I write my dissertation on the subject of Ross' ethical theory. Again, we had a very fruitful discussion on the general subject of English moral philosophy.

It was not long before I was warmly adopted into the *Kinderheim* family and was part of Oberammergau's parish and social life. I soon became acquainted with the pastor and the assistant pastor of the one and only parish in Oberammergau. During my two and a half years in Oberammergau, I was occasionally to help out in the parish church, generally by hearing the confessions of the children and by serving as subdeacon at solemn High Masses and solemn Benedictions and during Eucharistic processions in the village. As need arose at irregular intervals, I was to offer Masses also in the Oberammergau hospital. This was staffed by the same congregation of sisters as the *Kinderheim*.

On December 20, I heard the confessions of the children in the parish church, worked on my Christmas sermon, and packed for Stuttgart, where I arrived on the twenty-second. I spent the next two and a half weeks helping out the military chaplains, mostly by hearing confessions and offering Masses in the U.S. Army barracks on the outskirts of Stuttgart. On January 7, 1963, after attending a Professor Kuhn seminar in Munich that day, I was back in Oberammergau. The year 1962 had been a long one for me but a richly rewarding one in many ways.

As it turned out, I spent virtually the whole of 1963 in Oberammergau. Except for the final Kuhn and Schmaus seminars during the early part of the year, and the ongoing *Doktoran-denkreis* sessions, I had little occasion to go even to Munich. As for my second minor, psychology under Professor Philip Lersch, it was only a matter of buying and virtually memorizing the twelfth edition of his voluminous book *Aufbau der Person* (Structure of the person). Apart from offering an infrequent Mass at the Oberammergau NATO (SHAPE [Supreme Headquarters, Allied Powers, Europe]) school, I no longer offered Masses at military bases. So my only real commitment now—in addition, of course, to my academic work—was to offer the daily morning Mass for the sisters. Holding occasional Benediction services for them or offering an occasional Mass for the sisters staffing the Oberammergau hospital were hardly burdens. The same holds true for hearing the confessions of the children in the parish church and serving there occasionally as subdeacon. I did not hear the confessions of the sisters. A monk from the Benedictine monastery in nearby Ettal was their regular confessor—and mine. (A footnote: It was at the NATO school that the impact of the Second Vatican Council was first reflected in my life. During one of my Masses there, I read the opening prayer, for the first time, in English. Regarding that council, I took its teachings and mandates in stride and was neither a zealous promoter of its innovations nor a foot-dragger when it came to implementing them. I welcomed the use of the vernacular in the liturgies and the offering of Mass facing the congregation.)

My living conditions at Oberammergau were ideally suited to enable me to carry out my basic responsibilities. I lived in a small house right next to the big *Kinderheim* complex. I had one small room for a study, and another small room next to it for a bedroom. In the basement, I kept my bike. I was the only one in the house all day. At night, one of the sisters and two little girls slept upstairs. My meals were served in the main building, in the guest parlor right below the chapel. Sister Gundharda, in spite of her many other duties at the *Heim*, was assigned to see to all my needs. She served me my meals and the afternoon cake-and-coffee snacks. At first, she insisted on making my bed and cleaning my hiking boots. I soon got her over that. For two and a half years, she was wonderfully good to me. Sister Emmerana, the superior, also showed nothing less than maternal solicitude for me—as she did for all the sisters and children under her care. She would not let go by my birthday or name day, or Christmas or Easter, without bestowing on me gifts: gifts to eat, to drink, to wear. The cook, Sister Berga Maria, likewise tried her best to spoil me—and did so with some success. Quite often, I helped her out with the dishwashing.

As my Oberammergau days began to slip ever more rapidly by, I put in long hours at my desk, reading in depth dissertation-related books and articles and working on a dissertation outline. As to that outline, I was favored by a kindly Providence in a very special way. From January 8 to February 13, Father Taylor, taking a break from his philosophical studies in Rome, lived in the Oberammergau hospital and offered daily morning Mass for the sisters staffing it. The two of us spent a fair amount of time together, now enjoying a meal served by the sisters at the hospital, now taking a hike in the alpine foothills. Often, as we ate and hiked, we discussed philosophy and, specifically, my outline.

After my outline was finished, and approved on April 17, I began work on the dissertation itself. For short breaks from desk work and for some leg stretching, I went outside, when weather permitted, and paced back and forth, as I prayed the breviary. Sometimes, one of the little *Heim* boys, to the amusement of the sisters, would follow along behind me, pretending likewise to be praying the breviary. In winter, I got my short-term exercise by helping the house maintenance man keep the steps and walkways free of snow; in summer, I helped out with the mowing of the lawns.

The *Heim* children were divided into four groups, each group consisting of both girls and boys. Each group was cared for by a sister and an "auntie". The youngest group, two- to four-year-olds, was named the *Sonnenschein*. The second group, still preschoolers, was named the *Edelweiss*. The third and fourth groups, all of school age, were named *Immerfroh* (Always Happy) and *Rotkäppchen* (Little Red Riding Hood), respectively.

On December 9, 1962, I wrote to the Toussaints concerning the *Kinderheim* children: "There are some wonderful kids among them. Were I in a position to do so, I believe I'd go on quite an adopting spree. There is sadness here, as in all institutions of this kind, but also much fun and wonderful goodness, especially on the part of the twelve sisters."

On February 21, 1963, while I was having my noon meal, Sister Emmerana came in to talk to me about "*das Väterliche Element*" (the fatherly element). She had noticed how the kids were taking to me, and I to them. Coming from a big family myself and having spent time in a boarding school, I could readily relate to children and their natural yearnings for some kind of parental attention. While the sisters were like mothers to them, the fatherly element was lacking. Except for the comings and goings of the maintenance man, I was the only man connected with the *Kinderheim*. Sister Emmerana appreciated having me around not only for the daily morning Mass but also as one who presented to the children a kind of father figure.

One day, looking out my window, I saw the *Sonnenschein* group playing on the asphalted play area behind the *Heim*. I just had to join them. Opposite the *Heim* was a steep bank retained by a concrete wall about a foot wide and four feet high. One end of that wall had a slant to it before it leveled off at the top. It was a no-no, but one little fellow went up that slant and ran along the first stretch of that wall. Fearing he might fall and crash-land on the blacktop, I stretched out my arms to take hold of him and set him down. Without hesitation, he jumped into my arms. Meanwhile, others had seen his antics and had begun to imitate them. It was all I could do to keep up with them, to catch them, as they jumped into my arms, one after another, and set them safely down. It was jolly fun for the kids. For me, it was a wonderful example of childlike confidence in fatherly love and care.

The sister and auntie in charge of any given group always welcomed me to join them, whether for indoor games or for walks, hikes, bike tours, a game of Ping-Pong or shuttlecock, or just plain romping around. We could amuse ourselves at considerable length with a simple rubber ball. Occasionally, I did some TV watching with them. The figure skating contests were a must, as one of the star skaters was from southern Germany. During the heat of the summer, I went swimming with some of the older *Heim* kids in Oberammergau's Alpenbad. A number of times, one or other group, accompanied by a sister or two, and I went on an all-day bike tour to the Plansee, an alpine lake just across the border in Austria, for a swim.

The city of Munich was appreciative of the sisters and their services and generous with them. Several times during my years in Oberammergau, the city treated some of the sisters and aunties to marathon outings. I was invited along. One predawn to postmidnight drive took us all the way into northern Italy; another took us into the Bernina Alps in Switzerland, where we visited Saint Moritz and the biggest glacier in those Alps, the Morteratsch.

During my first winter in Oberammergau, the Alps received unusually heavy snowfalls. Behind the *Kinderheim*, there was an extensive cow pasture with several small hills. I frequently went sledding there with the smaller kids or skiing with the older ones. I had never been on skis previously. It so happened that, the year before I went to Oberammergau, there was a tall girl in the *Heim*. When she left, she donated her skis and ski boots to the *Heim*. Both skis and boots fitted me perfectly. Sister Iniga, the seamstress—no doubt anticipating that, as a beginner on skis, I would take many a pratfall—made me a pair of ski pants with a very ample seat. She had anticipated correctly. In spite of my rank amateur status as a skier, I spent many pleasant hours during that 1962–1963 winter, in the purest of air, on skis.

On February 22, 1963, I was out taking a solo walk on the snows behind the *Heim* when along came a figure dressed all in black. I stopped to greet him, then introduced myself. He did likewise. There I stood, alone, in the presence of the head man of the Archdiocese of Munich-Freising, square-jawed Julius Cardinal Doepfner! I was to meet him again the following July at a reception and dinner when he was in Oberammergau for confirmations. I was his subdeacon during the confirmation Mass.

February 26 was *Faschingstag*, the German equivalent of Shrove Tuesday or Mardi Gras. In the *Heim*, this was looked forward to, as were other days of importance, and it was celebrated with everything befitting the occasion. There were the costumes and disguises, the music and the dancing, and goodies in abundance to eat and drink. I was invited, of course, to take part in the festivities. In due time, I showed up in the big playroom, dressed, however, not in some disguise, but in my clerical suit, Roman collar and all. I told the assembled gang of sisters, aunties, and kids that, regretfully, I was being called away and had dropped by just to say "so long". "*Ach, nein, ach, nein, Herr Pater!*" they yelled, and begged me to stay and join them in the fun. After all, it was *Faschingstag*. But, in spite of their repeated "oh no's", moans, and entreaties, I begged for understanding and took my leave.

What they did not know, but what Sister Gundharda knew, was that, in the room next door to the big playroom, I had my own disguise: a striped pajama top, a big black hat with a red headband to hold it on my head, a big plume to stick into the headband, and a pair of wild socks. In the twinkle of an eye, I threw off the black suit coat, the collar, and my glasses, then rubbed on a black mustache, donned the pajama top, put on the hat and the headband, stuck in the plume, tucked the bottom of my pant legs into the tops of the socks, and danced in just as Sister Gundharda began to spin the recording of "*Der Vogelfänger bin ich, ja!*" (The Bird Catcher I Am, Oh Yes!), an aria from Mozart's opera *The Magic Flute*. The older ones in the audience knew immediately, of course, who it was dancing and hopping around to the strains of the aria. Not so the little ones. When the music stopped, I, gasping for breath and with a great flourish, doffed my hat, scattering out of it a shower of wrapped candies into the crowd of little ones. Ah yes! Life in Oberammergau could be serious at times, even on *Faschingstag*, especially for one anguishing over doctoral degree work.

On March 15, Sister Emmerana asked me to come to the parlor at a certain hour. There I found her and an American military couple, an army captain and his wife. They were hoping to adopt one of the small *Heim* boys. My role was that of interpreter. At one point in the interchange, Sister told me something in German. Promptly, I turned to the American couple to tell them what Sister had said, only—to my embarrassment, and their amusement—I did so in German. German was getting to be my vernacular.

On September 3, I was again asked to play the role of interpreter. On that day, a choral group from Strasbourg, France, on tour in Germany, was scheduled to put on a performance for the people of Oberammergau. Naturally, the songs were to be sung in French. The choral director asked his German host about an interpreter. No one in all of Oberammergau seemed to know French. At the last minute, I was called upon. Before each song, the choral director told me, in French, what the song was about. This I rendered into German. And so it went, song after song, throughout the concert. At the end, the director was applauded, the choral group was applauded, and I was applauded—and thanked, both by the French director and the German impresario. I had been in a win-win situation. The Germans heard French but did not understand it. The French heard German but did not understand it. I was in total control. Both sides assured me that I had made a good job of it.

During my years in Oberammergau, I heard the town referred to, at times, derisively, as *"das Kuhdorf!"*—"that cow village!" However, despite its humble origins as a rural farm village, it was not without a high level of culture. It was famous for its artistic wood carvings and for the *Passion Play*. It had very fine musical combos, choirs, and choral groups. On special feasts, a full orchestra and choir would perform a Haydn or Mozart Mass in the ornate Bavarian baroque church. It hosted performances of the highest quality. On March 28, in Oberammergau—continuing my custom of mixing the useful with the pleasant—I attended a superb performance by the renowned violinist Yehudi Menuhin.

Occasional trips to Munich, too, provided me with pleasant getaways from the books and dissertation writing. It was my good fortune to be in Oberammergau during the years that Josef Hamberger was the *Kaplan* (assistant pastor) in the parish there. He was a priest of about my age, played the violin well, sang well, had a natural appreciation of the fine arts, and, being from a small Bavarian alpine village, was at home in the mountains. Having many common interests, we soon became close, mutually compatible friends. Living alone in the old parish house, as he did, he routinely joined me for the noon meal at the *Kinderheim*. Our conversation topics ranged far and wide and often continued well beyond the end of the meal. The priestly companionship did both of us good. In addition to being assistant parish priest, Kaplan Hamberger was also the moderator of Oberammergau's Catholic youth group. For its members, he arranged many an outing. I was always invited along, and I gratefully accepted. On April 21, he, the Catholic youth group, and I, in a chartered bus, went to Munich to attend a performance of Shakespeare's *King Lear*. Another day, we took a trip to Munich to attend an opera. No royalty being present that evening, he and I were offered the seats in the royal box. We accepted. During the intermission, when the lights were on, he turned to me and, in a very dignified tone of voice, addressed me, in German, "Your Highness!" "Yes, Your Excellency?" I responded, likewise in a dignified tone of voice and in German, but with an affected foreign-sounding accent. Those five words turned many a head in our direction during that intermission!

The Bavarian Alps are a hiker's paradise. With Kaplan Hamberger, and often with priests visiting Oberammergau, and sometimes with sisters and *Heim* children, I took many a hike in them. There were wonderful hikes, in all directions, literally out the front door of the house in which I lived. Sometimes we took the bus to Garmisch-Partenkirchen to take the funicular to the top of the Zugspitze. This, at 9,718 feet, is Germany's highest peak. Those ascents were easy. An ascent of the nearby Alpspitz, by contrast, was a hard day's work but most rewarding. A number of times, I made solo climbs to the top of the Alpspitz, a peak in the same massif as the Zugspitze and virtually of the same elevation, but a far-more-dramatic mountain, ending, as it does, in the shape of a massive pyramid. A long, fairly level climb took me back in to the actual foot of the mountain; then, for a rather short stretch, I had to work my way, hand over hand, up a cable attached to a vertical cliff. After that, it was a long, steep climb over a relatively even surface to the peak. The view from there, on a clear day, well rewarded the long, fatiguing ascent.

One day, as I was nearing the summit of that most picturesque mountain, a dense cloud cover settled over the whole general area. Even though I knew I would have no view, I had to work my way to the very top, simply—because it was there. After a snack and a short rest, I began my descent. When I was only a short distance below the summit, I thought I heard a plaintive voice calling out, *"Hilfe! Hilfe!"* Having assumed that I was all alone at that elevation, I could, at first, not believe my ears. I listened carefully. True enough, what sounded like a girl's panicky voice was calling out for help. I told her to stay put but to keep calling. Slowly, I worked my way toward the voice. A bit later, shrouded in fog, there stood before me a trembling little girl. In the fog, she had become separated from her mother. I told her to follow me. She was too afraid even to take a single step and begged me not to leave her. After I had calmed her down and assured her that I would not leave her and that everything would be all right, I took first her right hand and placed it where she felt she had a secure hold, then her left foot, where she felt it securely planted, then the other hand likewise, and then the other foot likewise, and so on. Slowly, cautiously, we worked our way down to where one began to be able to see a short distance. All the while, she was calling out in hopes that an anxious mother would hear and find her. All this transpired in a relatively short time, of course; but, given the circumstances, it all seemed much longer. Soon, the little one was reunited with her greatly relieved, and grateful, mother. With *"Nichts zu danken!"* (about the equivalent of "Don't mention it—glad to do it!"), I accepted her expressions of gratitude. I introduced myself. They were from Munich. She thanked me again. The little girl gave me a bashful smile—and down the slopes of the Alpspitz into bright sunlight, we went our more secure ways.

On April 24, 1963, the eve of my thirty-seventh birthday, I noted in my diary: "Solid day at desk." About this time, similar expressions found their way into my diary: "Hard at it all day." "Hard day on 'knowledge of actual duty'." "Typing all day."

Early in 1963, Fathers Beuzer, Fontana, and I agreed to make our annual eight-day retreat together in August in Genoa, Italy, with Father Beuzer directing it. I arrived in San Remo on the seventh, Father Beuzer on the eleventh. The days were hot, but prolonged swims in the Mediterranean had their cooling effect. On the seventeenth, we arrived at the Villa San Ignazio, the retreat house overlooking Genoa. Finished with our retreat by the morning of the twenty-sixth, we each returned to our home bases.

From Oberammergau, on September 19, I wrote to the Toussaints:

The retreat was a success beyond expectations. Here, I daily worry and work away, sometimes with tangible results, sometimes with hair-whitening frustration. But, overall, there is measurable progress, and I'm reasonably hopeful. I must say, my circumstances here for doing what I am doing are really ideal. I have quiet and time unlike at any place else and the conditions that allow for hard work without having to worry about cracking up. The sisters worry about that and, therefore, see to it that I get the food and exercise I need. And the surroundings here are very conducive to mental refreshment. More-citified beings would go mad here, but I like a semi-out-of-doors atmosphere. And, then, with radio and records and bookwork, I find the time all too short to go mad in. And with the kids: eighty strong and dear! It was a genuine delight coming back after three weeks away and receiving the welcome the sisters and kids gave me.

Throughout the last quarter of the year 1963, I was preoccupied with the writing of my dissertation. By Christmas, I had the first four chapters roughed out. At the Christmas Midnight Mass, I was subdeacon. The Mass was celebrated by Bishop Rudolf J. M. Koppmann, O.M.I., a German, who was home for Christmas from Windhoek, South-West Africa (now Namibia). The year 1963 ended for me on a pious note with, in one word, a *Jahresschlussgottesdienst* (an end-of-the-year divine service) in the village church.

In many respects, the year 1964 paralleled that of 1963. Oberammergau continued to be my home base. There were the occasional trips into Munich, mainly for *Doktorandenkreis* sessions. During January and February 1964, I devoted most of my time to completing the writing of my dissertation. By March 4, I was able to entrust this into the hands of Herr N. Heuss, the man designated by Professor Kuhn to translate it into proper academic German. To my considerable frustration, it was to be close to a whole year before I finally had the entire translated dissertation back in my hands again. As things turned out, in retrospect, I saw the long wait as providential. It gained me additional time to read and somewhat digest a whole stack of books and articles by way of preparing myself for the final exams. I could not know just when these were to take place, but I knew for sure that the day for them would inevitably come.

Preparing for Professor Schmaus' and the Professor Lersch's one-hour final oral exams was, in one sense, relatively easy. All I had to do was read and virtually memorize their hefty tomes, Schmaus' *Katholische Dogmatik* and the twelfth edition of Lersch's *Aufbau der Person*. With the two-hour Professor Kuhn final oral exam, it was a different matter. In that case, all I had to do was—well, be prepared to be examined in all areas of philosophy: Greek, medieval, and modern. Knowing his leanings, however, I focused on the areas I knew to be of special interest to him, mainly the field of ethics and Aristotle.

On February 12, 1964, I wrote to Father Provincial McDonald:

> I really do not see how I can finish everything within the next five months. Time is running against me. And, physically, it would be quite a strain. I have been pushing pretty hard since I got down to the thesis itself, and, though my health has been good, I am beginning to feel the pressure. If I do not finish this summer, it will mean only that I did not finish ahead of schedule. The normal time for an American Jesuit is seven or eight semesters. I had hoped to do it in six, since I received credit for former seminar work and since my thesis subject ("The Theory of Right in the Philosophy of Sir W. D. Ross") is comparatively easy. But a dissertation simply does not write itself—especially in the presence of my very modest talents. In the course of the past years, I came to feel the advantage enjoyed by those who had occasion to teach philosophy during regency. In my case, ten years away from philosophy have made a difference. Such are my excuses.... If

I do not finish this summer, the sisters here will surely clap their hands and thank Divine Providence for providing them with a priest for yet another half year. I have charged them with praying only halfheartedly for my speedy success; and, only halfheartedly, have they denied the charge. They are grateful to have a priest and take excellent care of him. But for their unabated solicitude and the relaxing atmosphere of O-gau, I could never have accomplished what I have up to now. I am alone all day. The assistant priest usually takes his noon meal with me; and there is often a Jesuit in the village hospital, so my semihermitude is only semi-. Within the next few weeks, I will again spend several weeks in one of our Jesuit houses.

In reply, Father McDonald wrote, on the twenty-ninth: "The fathers in Alaska were hoping for your return next summer, but I am sure they will understand your reasons for thinking that this date may be unrealistic. It certainly would not be wise to overburden your health by undue haste. All I can advise is for you to find your proper pace and do your best."

To prepare for the final exams, I had so much reading to do that prudence dictated I rest my eyes and stretch my legs whenever and as long as thought necessary. Still, often, even on my walks, I had with me a pocketful of notes, generally definitions from Lersch's volume, which I tried to memorize. There were rainy days, when I walked with an umbrella in one hand and the Lersch volume, much of it underlined, in the other.

The break between the spring and summer semesters, when there were no *Doktorandenkreis* sessions to attend, and while Herr Heuss was working on the translation of my dissertation, was a good time for me to make my annual eight-day retreat. This I did at the Jesuit Zenzenhof villa near

Innsbruck, on March 10–17. That so-called villa was an old stone house. Those March days in the mountains were still wintry. The room I had during the retreat was furnished with a *Kachelofen*, a stove with ceramic tiles on the outside. Once that stove was thoroughly heated by the burning in it of some coal briquettes, it kept the room cozy warm for many hours. For that 1964 retreat, I used Father Karl Rahner's retreat notes.

While teaching at Monroe, I had Jerry Warner in my classes during his senior year. He went on to graduate from Gonzaga University and to become an officer in the U.S. Army. Now stationed in Fulda, Germany, he and his wife, Natalie, invited me, during the early part of 1964, to spend several days with them as their houseguest. On September 28, from southern Germany, I took a bus up "the Romantic Road"—stopping off at the picturesque, best-preserved, walled-in medieval town of Rothenburg ob der Tauber—to Fulda. I spent two days there, graciously hosted by the Warners and taking in the highlights of Fulda, principal among them the crypt in which Saint Boniface, "the Apostle of Germany", is buried. By the time I returned to Oberammergau, on October 4, I had made tourist stops also in Bamberg, Regensburg, and Passau. In Bamberg, I had as my guide Erika Künasch, a former *Heim* girl.

After attending a session of the Second Vatican Council in the fall of 1964, George T. Boileau—the coadjutor bishop of Fairbanks as of July 31, 1964—did some sight-seeing in Switzerland in the company of Jesuit brother Carl Wickart, who, after many years in Alaska, was visiting the land of his birth for the first time. The two had been together in Fairbanks for some years. On October 21, they arrived in Oberammergau in the new Volkswagen station wagon Bishop Boileau had had delivered to him in Rome. After visiting with me, they stayed overnight in the Oberammergau hospital as guests of the sisters. The following day, the three of us drove to Pirmasens to spend the night in U.S. Army barracks there. After another drive across a long stretch of Germany and through Luxembourg, interrupted from time to time for some sightseeing and eating, we arrived at the Chevetogne Benedictine monastery in Belgium. On the twenty-fourth, before we went on to take in the highlights of Bruges, we visited the family of Father Loyens in the village of Vlijtingen. We spent the night of the twenty-fifth in Brussels. Being from Alaska, Bishop Boileau was a hit wherever he appeared. I was assumed to be his personal secretary, an assumption, albeit a false one, I soon learned to let work in my favor. On the twenty-sixth, we drove the long Brussels–Paris stretch, stopping off along the way to visit the cathedral at Reims. That night we stayed in Paris. The following day, after some sight-seeing in Paris, we drove to Versailles to visit the mother and family members of another Alaskan Jesuit, Father René Astruc, and to spend the night there as guests of a group of sisters. We then enjoyed another day in Paris before returning for a second night in Versailles, where the sisters insisted on favoring us Alaskan missionaries with a second night's hospitality.

On the twenty-eighth, via Rouen, where we visited the cathedral, we drove to Lisieux. By the time we got there, the big basilica of the Little Flower, built to accommodate the many pilgrims visiting Lisieux to venerate Saint Thérèse, was closed for the night. However, a sister at the Carmelite convent insisted on having it opened just for us. She even provided a guide to show us through it. How could she do less? After all, were we not three missionaries from Alaska, a mission that had been entrusted to the patronage of Saint Thérèse? With all lights on, we were given a grand tour of the basilica. The next morning, both Bishop Boileau and I celebrated Mass at the altar enshrining the relics of Saint Thérèse. After the Masses and breakfast, the three of us drove on to Le Havre. There, final farewells said, Bishop Boileau and Brother Wickart boarded their ship and, with the Volkswagen also on board, sailed for the United States.

I, for my part, began to inquire about the train station. It so happened, however, that just then an American soldier was in Le Havre to claim his transshipped car. After mutual introductions, we were on our way in his car across northern France to Metz. At filling stations, I came in handy as an interpreter. From Metz, I took the train on to Oberammergau, where I arrived on the thirtieth—richer than when I left it. In country after country, Bishop Boileau had had dollars changed into the local currency. As we left the given country, with a "Here, you can use it", he gave me whatever in local currency had not been spent.

On December 17, I attended my last *Doktorandenkreis* session for the year 1964 and picked up twenty-five pages of my dissertation, now translated into German. It was a great disappointment to have less than the whole, given the fact that Herr Heuss had had, by then, the manuscript since the previous March 4. Nevertheless, it was something. As a one-time farm boy, I should have realized that, with both nature and man, certain things come to fruition only gradually, after the passage of a predetermined length of time.

Just as the year 1963 had ended, so did the year 1964. At the Christmas Midnight Mass, again celebrated by Bishop Koppmann, I was again subdeacon; and, on the thirty-first, there was another *Jahresschlussgottesdienst*.

By sometime in February 1965, I had the whole of my dissertation back from Herr Heuss, had proofread it, had touched it up, and had it in the hands of Professor Kuhn. On March 15, I received a card from him asking me to see him at his home on the eighteenth, *um 12 Uhr* (at twelve o'clock). Finally, the eagerly awaited day, but a day awaited not without a measurable degree of nervous anxiety, came. What would be his verdict regarding my dissertation, now finalized, as far as I could judge? I was up early that morning, having to take the train to Munich. I arrived there on schedule. Thinking I had enough time to make it to Professor Kuhn's home by noon on foot, I decided to walk. However, after walking a few blocks and then checking my map again, I saw that his place, on the far side of the Isar River dissecting Munich, was farther away than I had estimated. I boarded the next streetcar headed in my direction. This made more stops than I had anticipated. Glance after glance at my watch made me more and more anxious, so much so that I got off the streetcar and hailed a taxi. That got me to my destination much faster than I had expected. Knowing good Professor Kuhn, and knowing that to him twelve o'clock meant only one thing, noon sharp, I did not even consider knocking on his door before that precise hour. There was a little park near his home. I had just sat down on a bench in the park, when, lo and behold, whom should I catch out of the corner of my eye strolling along a little bit to the rear of me but one Herr Professor Helmut Kuhn and his wife. I pretended not to recognize them; they, in turn, had the courtesy to pretend not to recognize me.

Promptly at twelve o'clock, I rang the doorbell. Professor Kuhn graciously invited me in and, after introducing me to his wife, bade me have a chair. In short order, he told me the dissertation was quite acceptable. He raised only one question. It had to do with a quote from Aristotle. (I resolved that quibble by simply dropping the quote.) After a few minutes of small talk, he stood up. I did likewise. With a stiff handshake, and bowing my gratitude as I backed out the door with dissertation in hand, I took my leave. Walking on air, I went on to eat the best hamburger I ever ate in my whole life. Whether it was made of sawdust or prime beef, I did not notice. It was ordered and eaten in the U.S. Army commissary in Munich by one greatly relieved doctoral aspirant.

From March 20 to April 3, Elizabeth Hafeneder, a bank clerk and member of Oberammergau's Catholic youth group, and I worked long hours typing up the dissertation in keeping with university specifications. As a kindly Providence would have it, Elizabeth had a typewriter identical to mine and was an excellent typist. That enabled us to type away simultaneously. I did some of my share of the typing in my room at the *Heim*, and some of it in her parental home. Even though Elizabeth expected only token payment for her services, I felt she should receive what I considered a just recompense. When I was about to give her this, her mother would not hear of it, saying it would be more than Elizabeth earned at the bank in a month. Accordingly, I paid her somewhat less than I had originally intended but more than her mother had suggested. On April 6, I handed the finished typescript of my dissertation to Herr N. Wiedmann, Professor Kuhn's academic assistant, to pass on to Professor Kuhn. It was now a good time to make my annual retreat.

On April 7, I arrived in Vienna. About the first thing I had to do was to see what the *Wiener Staatsoper* had on its schedule—*Die Meistersinger von Nürnberg*, one of my very favorite operas! On the spot, I bought myself a ticket: orchestra, up front, center. It would be Easter Sunday. I would be out of retreat by then. Dissertation concerns were now behind me. (At the University of Munich, doctoral candidates did not defend their dissertations before a board of examiners.) There was cause for joy—and celebration! On the ninth, I spent the forenoon visiting with Fräulein Katarina Inhauser, who had been my tutor in September 1961. After making my retreat, from the tenth to the seventeenth, and spending close to four hours awash in Wagnerian opera on Easter Sunday the eighteenth, I returned to Oberammergau on the nineteenth.

On May 25, I was in Munich to attend my final *Doktoran-denkreis* session. It was led by Professor Kuhn and was on Aristotle's concept of God. After the session, in the semidarkness of that May evening, Herr Wiedmann, with his index finger, beckoned me aside. In a low voice, in German, he said, "I should not be telling you this, but I thought you might like to know. I saw the grade Herr Professor Kuhn gave you on your dissertation. It's magna cum laude." What those three little Latin words did for me! I, then and there, felt fairly sure that, even if I did poorly on the final oral exams, I would at least scrape by and fly out of Munich with doctorate in hand.

During most of June, I kept preparing for the final oral exams. For my name day, the feast of Saint Aloysius Gonzaga on the twenty-first, the sisters outdid themselves with kindness and gifts in my favor, among them a beautiful crucifix carved out of linden wood by an Oberammergau artist.

The days for the final exams—there were only oral exams— finally came. On June 23, a very hot day, I had the one-hour oral exam with Professor Schmaus. Having considered this the least important of the three exams, and having assumed that my general background in theology was an adequate enough preparation for at least a passing grade, I had spent relatively little time preparing for the Schmaus oral exam. If the truth be told, I had done little more than merely splash around in his big *Katholische Dogmatik*. While doing so, the chapter on Hindu theology caught my eye. Somewhat curious, I read it. To my disbelief, after asking me a few questions dealing with basic Catholic theology, he asked me about, of all things—Hindu theology! When he sensed I knew a little about that esoteric subject, he presumably took it for granted that I knew a lot about theology in general. Then and there, with a *"Schon gut!"* he extended his hand and called an end to the exam. One word in my diary summarizes my verdict on that exam: "Good!"

The exam in my other minor, rational psychology with Professor Lersch, took place two days later, on the twenty-fifth, another very hot day. This one-hour oral exam, too, must have gone well enough in my judgment, for a fervent "Deo gratias!" is noted in my diary for that day.

The two-hour comprehensive oral exam in my major field, philosophy, was scheduled for 10:00 A.M. on the twenty-eighth. By this late June date, the heat of summer and anxiety had me quite exhausted. I had a back room in Ignatiushaus that allowed for little air circulation, so I slept rather poorly in the stifling-hot room. In spite of my almost-woozy condition, the exam went quite well. I had almost exactly anticipated the areas Professor Kuhn would choose to discuss: moral philosophy and Aristotle. Being the gentleman that he was, he, no doubt, chose to give me a break by dwelling on what my dissertation was all about. At one point, I quoted and commented on something in Aristotle. To my confusion, he responded, "Where does Plato say that? Was it not Aristotle who said that?" At that moment, the *Protokolant*—a man the university has present during those final exams to take notes to make sure that the professor does not, on the one hand, crucify the one being examined nor, on the other hand, dismiss him with a top grade after a little small talk—broke in: "Excuse me, Herr Professor, but you misheard. Father Renner did say 'Aristotle'." All in all, the exam went well—to my great relief. By that evening, I was back in the relative cool of Oberammergau and ready for a good night's sleep.

On June 29, I took a refreshing swim in the Ammer River and relaxed. The thirtieth was uneventful, though again very hot.

July 1, 1965, was a milestone day in my life. It was another extremely hot day, but it was graduation day for several dozen of us getting doctoral degrees from the University of Munich. I took the morning train to Munich. By eleven o'clock, we graduates—with neither pomp nor musical circumstances whatever, and with neither caps nor gowns—had all drifted into one of the lecture halls at the university. As we were gradually assembling, a janitor was still emptying wastebaskets and straightening things up somewhat. Then, some dean, accompanied by an assistant carrying a box full of diplomas, came in and, at once, began reading a set formula giving the name of the one graduating, where the graduate was from, the title of the dissertation the graduate had submitted, and the grade received. One by one, each graduate, upon hearing his or her name, rose, stepped forward and, with a crisp handshake and a stiff bow, received that coveted scroll. No cameras clicked; no bulbs flashed. Eventually the philosophy majors had their turn—and I mine. In German, we heard: "Mr. Louis Lawrence Renner out of Alaska, U.S.A., having written the dissertation entitled 'The Theory of Right in the Philosophy of Sir W. D. Ross', graduates magna cum laude." There followed the standard applause from the assembled, the handing over of the diploma, the handshake, the bow. The whole graduation ceremony, so utterly devoid of festive trimmings of any kind, ended as simply as it had begun. But who cared? Having in hand that rolled-up, beribboned piece of paper with the official university seal and signatures duly affixed made all the difference. After the last diploma was handed out, we all simply got up and, again without further ado, went our separate ways.

Even after that graduation ritual, one still could not use the title of "Doctor". One needed first to have his dissertation printed and a certain number of copies of it delivered to the university. From the university, I took the streetcar downtown to a firm that printed dissertations, dropped mine off, paid to have ten copies printed, received a receipt, and was assured that, in due time, six copies would be delivered to the university and four sent to me. I then walked over to the train station and boarded the train for Oberammergau.

As is common in the alpine regions, days that begin hot and clear, as did my graduation day, frequently bring with them powerful afternoon or evening thunderstorms. So it was the afternoon of that July 1. A short distance out of Munich, there was a rapid buildup of dense clouds, and soon lightning and thunder flashed and clapped. Then the cooling rains began to pour down. The release of tension within nature brought with it a corresponding release of tension within me. I rarely in my whole life felt so utterly relaxed, so totally at ease, so grateful, as I did in that train rumbling along, Oberammergau-bound, through a now gently falling rain. When Libby Riddles arrived in Nome after winning the Iditarod Trail Sled Dog Race in 1985, the first woman to do so, she was asked, "How does it feel, Libby?" Her answer, "What I feel is, if I died right now, it'd be *okay*." That was my feeling that unforgettable July afternoon.

I spent July 2–3 doing the final packing and paying farewell visits to various people in Oberammergau. Tears flowed from both sides as I bade *auf Wiedersehen* to the different *Heim* groups and sisters. Sister Gundharda found it too difficult to say good-bye to me face-to-face. In a letter dated "Departure day, July 7, 1965", she wrote:

Dear Father Renner!

I find it very difficult to say good-bye to you. I cannot get myself to express orally my thanks to you as I would like to do and as I owe it to you; therefore these lines in writing. I sincerely ask God to reward you for everything, dear Father Renner. Your exemplary life will always remain in fondest remembrance. Your fine, elegant, reserved manner as a priest and as a guest have made a deep impression on me. I, by contrast, often paid too little attention to you. Please forgive me. With a wholly sincere heart, Sister Gundharda thanks you, dear Father Renner.

Early in the morning of July 4, Sister Gundharda walked with me to the train station, where, for the last time—for some years—I boarded the train for Munich. In Munich, I went directly to the airport and caught my flight to Amsterdam. After a wait of some hours there, I boarded a KLM jet for the flight to Anchorage, Alaska. As I was flying west, I recalled how, exactly five years earlier, to the day, fellow Jesuits and I were celebrating the Fourth of July on the SS *Liberté* as we were sailing east for Europe.

At no time in my life did I experience timelessness more than on that flight. Below us, we had a uniform sea of clouds. We were flying west with the sun. Hour after hour, this cast the same beam of light into my left-seat window. The drone of the jet remained constant. There was no sense of motion of any kind.

On that memorable flight, I crossed some major thresholds in my life: physical, social, academic, spiritual, and—above all—emotional. Eager as I was to see my family, last seen a little over five years earlier, I was, nevertheless, leaving much of my heart behind, especially in Oberammergau.

Chapter 14

Becoming a Faculty Member at the University of Alaska–Fairbanks: 1965

My KLM flight arrived in Anchorage on schedule. It was now past midafternoon, still the Fourth of July. Being scheduled to leave early the next morning for Fairbanks, I took a room for the night in a motel close to the airport. While I had dozed some during the flight, I was still very much in need of a good night's sleep. Around five that evening, I set my alarm to wake me up the next morning at six o'clock and then went to bed. It was still broad daylight. This was Alaska, where, at that time of year, the days last all night. After some restless tossing and turning, I finally fell asleep. Oh no! About thirty minutes later, promptly at 6:00 that same evening, the alarm sounded! That clock, I had failed to realize, had a time span of only twelve hours. I reset it for 6:00 and, after a while, was once more asleep. Again, oh no! Promptly at midnight, Fourth of July fireworks began to boom and shriek and light up the twilight sky.

As mentioned earlier, on February 9, 1959, Father Boileau wrote to Father Provincial Schultheis: "Should Father Renner come back to Alaska, it might be wise for him to have a doctorate in philosophy. This would give him knowledge and prestige, which he could use to great advantage with those public educators." When Father Boileau wrote those words, he was still viewing me as a future Newman Club chaplain. Bishop

Gleeson shared that view, as did I, when I first went to Europe. However, during the early 1960s, reconsiderations concerning the roles Jesuits in Alaska should play modified our view on my future role in Alaska. In 1961, Father Loyens began studies in anthropology that led to his earning a doctorate in cultural anthropology in 1966. In the course of those five years, seeing the Society's mission in Alaska—one of basic evangelization—through the eyes of an anthropologist, he shared his views and ideas with Father Boileau and Bishop Gleeson, and with Alaskan Jesuits, in general. Persuasively, he argued that the time had come for the Church and the Society to be an influential presence in higher education in Alaska, specifically at the University of Alaska–Fairbanks, because more and more Alaska Native graduates from the two Jesuit-run high schools, Copper Valley and Saint Mary's, along with Alaska Native graduates from other schools, were attending that university. He felt that priests, as priests and, at the same time, as professional educators, could be of special help to them, both as students and as young men and women living in a world of major cultural change. In his thinking, Father Loyens was in step with the principle of *aggiornamento* (updating) mandated by the Second Vatican Council, in session from 1962–1965. In light of this updated thinking in the Diocese of Fairbanks, as I was finishing doctoral work in 1965, the idea of having priests on the University of Alaska–Fairbanks faculty as regular staff members was an idea whose time had come. In addition to Father Loyens and me, two diocesan priests, Fathers Patrick S. Duffy and Wallace M. Olson, also were members of the university faculty during the 1960s and 1970s. Fathers Loyens and Olson taught in the Department of Anthropology. For a few years, Father Loyens headed that department. Father Duffy taught in the Department of Education and, for a short time, headed it.

Thus began my fifteen-year career at the University of Alaska–Fairbanks teaching—German! You may wonder how it happened that, after earning a doctorate in philosophy, I ended up teaching German. About a year before I had completed my doctoral work, the university needed a German teacher. Aware of my hopes of having a future with it, the university, in the person of Charles J. (Chuck) Keim, contacted Father Boileau about the possibility of my coming there already then to teach German. Wisely, however, it was decided that I should not leave Germany before I had the doctorate firmly in hand. The basic assumption on the part of the university and of the Jesuits was, from the outset, that I would eventually teach philosophy there. However, given the present need for a teacher of German, on the one hand, and no need for a teacher of philosophy, on the other, all agreed that I should begin my career at the university as a teacher of German. Later, if a position in the philosophy department were to open up, I could still move over into that department.

On July 5, I flew to Fairbanks, where, after I had offered Mass in Immaculate Conception Church, I had dinner and a lengthy talk with Bishop Gleeson about my future work at the University of Alaska–Fairbanks. Among other things, we talked about where I would live and what I would wear. Regarding the latter, "Of course," he volunteered right away, "you won't be wearing your Roman collar." As for lodging, he left that up to me.

The following day, I went to the university to renew acquaintances with Chuck Keim, now dean of the College of Arts and Letters. It was with him that Father Boileau and I were dealing regarding the matter of my taking a position at the university as a regular faculty member. During my two years as Newman Club chaplain at the university, 1958–1960, Chuck frequently served my Sunday morning Mass.

Betty was his wife. His daughter, Janet, attended Monroe when I taught there. During my latter years in Europe, Chuck and I exchanged a number of letters about my becoming a faculty member at the university. After he had somewhat briefed me on affairs at the university and matters concerning my position there, he introduced me first to Howard A. Cutler, vice-president of the university, then to Dr. Bruce R. Gordon, head of the Department of Linguistics and Foreign Languages. Dr. Gordon, in turn, introduced me to Charles H. (Charlie) Parr, who was to be my fellow German teacher. Meeting those principals early on did much to put me somewhat at ease as I faced a life wholly new to me in most major respects. Dean Keim, especially, did much to help allay my anxieties. Several times, during the course of our conversation, sensing my apprehensiveness, he said, reassuringly, "I'm not worried, Father."

On July 7, I arrived in Tacoma. After an initial visit with my family, I spent July 8–10 in Seattle, living at Seattle University, renewing acquaintances there, and visiting Seattle Prep and former Seattle Prep students. Among these latter was Patrick J. Geraghty Jr. It will be remembered that he and I co-founded the Orphean Club at Seattle Prep during the early 1950s and that he was the master of ceremonies at my first solemn High Mass, in Saint Patrick's Church in Tacoma, on June 23, 1957. Patrick was now an attorney-at-law. To him I took my doctoral diploma to have some photocopies made and officially notarized.

After Seattle, I was back in Tacoma to spend some more time with my family before going on for a leisurely vacation at the Nestucca villa. Among the men there was Steve Sundborg, whom I had last seen over five years earlier in Washington, D.C. On August 14, I officiated at the nuptial Mass at which my brother Len married Martha (Marty) Klee.

Soon thereafter, I returned to Fairbanks to get ready for the upcoming fall semester.

In Fairbanks, the first order of business for me was to find myself a suitable apartment within walking distance of the university and to get settled. The Tanana Village Apartments on College Road, offering one-bedroom efficiency apartments at a reasonable rate and just a fifteen-minute walk from the university, were the perfect answer to my need. The last six units of this thirty-six-unit apartment complex were just being readied for occupancy. I chose the end one, the one next to College Road. The management was still vacuuming up sawdust and hanging drapes as I moved in. The apartment was furnished with all the basics. The "bedroom" could be closed off from the rest of the apartment by a folding wall. I made bookshelves out of stained boards and cement blocks. The wall separating my apartment from the one next to it was made of cement blocks, as was my outside one. Before long, I had Allan "Bud" Neidhold panel this with knotty pine. (Bud's wife, Jane, had been an active member of the Newman Club at the university when I was its chaplain.) The knotty pine paneling gave the place a warmer feeling than the green-painted cement blocks had done and enabled me to put up pictures, as well as the wooden crucifix given me by the sisters when I left Oberammergau. On one side of the crucifix, I mounted an ornate, honey-colored German candle, and on the other side, a wooden plaque of Albrecht Dürer's praying hands. Visitors found this blend of art and religion of interest, a conversation piece. All in all, my apartment was considered so neat and attractive by the management that they showed it to prospective tenants checking out the Tanana Village Apartments.

On the cement-block "bedroom" wall I taped a big photo of Giotto's painting of Christ washing the feet of His disciples at the Last Supper. To the left of this stood my low chest of drawers. On top of this, I placed the coffee table to make an altar, on which, fully vested, I daily offered morning Mass. Occasionally, I was asked by people who knew of this practice of mine if I did not feel ill at ease offering Mass "all alone". The answer is simply that I have never felt myself all alone while at the altar. Firmly believing in the communion of saints and in the Mystical Body of Christ, I have felt, throughout my priestly life, a real sense of solidarity with the saints, with family, friends, and with all who have, in any way whatever, been part of my life. Spiritually, they have shared in my Masses, even if not physically present. During my university years, it was especially the university community that was present to me, even if only in a mystical sense, during those morning Masses.

(Nine years later, in June 1974, when I was on King Island—you'll hear about this in chapter 17—Mike Saclamana gave me the ivory crucifix off the tabernacle door in Christ the King Church with the words, "Here, I feel something like this should go to a person like you." Thereafter, until 1980, when I moved out of that apartment upon my leaving the university, it was before that crucifix that I daily offered Mass.)

One drawback to that apartment was the poor quality of its water. It was so discolored and vile-tasting that one hesitated to drink it. White items laundered in it came out yellowish. From 1967 to 1972, Richard and Gisela Dykema and their four children lived in the middle section of that same apartment complex. At first, Gisela, then Richard, too, was a member of my German classes. When their daughters, Carmen, the older, and Renee, started attending college, they likewise took German from me. For a time, Michael, the oldest of the four children, was my paper boy. Stephanie was the youngest. The customary Saturday ritual was for me to join

Richard and one or other of the kids on a drive out to Fox—a little fork-in-the-road community ten miles northeast of Fairbanks—to fill a bunch of jugs with crystal-clear spring water. This flowed even at the coldest of temperatures. Filling narrow-necked jugs with splashing, ice-cold water at roughly fifty-degree-below-zero temperatures was a chilling experience. That made Gisela's cinnamon rolls, fresh out of the oven, and a cup of steaming hot coffee back in the Dykema apartment all the more welcome. The same fare was welcome, too, after Richard, the kids, and I had had ourselves a skate on the university's hockey rink or a swim in its pool.

For over three decades, the Dykemas were a second family to me. With them, I went gold panning, picnicking, dipnetting for salmon, blueberry picking, and commercial salmon fishing. With them, in their vehicles, I traveled the highways and byways of most of northern Alaska's roads. With Richard, I went moose and sheep hunting. When, in 1972, they moved out into the woods off Henderson Road, I helped with the moving and helped clear the land of brush, scrub trees, and stumps. Several times, I helped Richard put up a wire fence to confine their German shepherds. These became my pets, too. They retrieved many a stick, a ball, a Frisbee thrown by me. I helped to transplant trees and to get Christmas trees. In the Dykema yard, I felled trees, sawed them up into stove-length pieces, and split and stacked these into many a multicord woodpile. I helped spade up their garden in the spring and helped dig up the potatoes in the fall. I shoveled tons of snow off their roof and out of their driveway. Countless times, after hearing Gisela's ever-welcome call ring out through the trees, "We can eat now!"—and after washing up and leading the blessing—I ate the best meal in town. A number of times, they hosted my German classes and my out-of-state visitors. Birthday and holiday gifts from them came my way with predictable regularity. When my parka needed cleaning, or mending, or a new ruff, Gisela saw to it. I attended the weddings of Carmen and Stephanie. When I was about to leave Alaska in the year 2002, Dykemas attended my going-away party. The last homes I visited before leaving Alaska were Dykema homes.

As for my laundry, that I sent out, except for the white shirts. Catherine Calvin—who lived only a couple of blocks from my apartment and was editor of the *Alaskan Shepherd* and head of the Diocese of Fairbanks' development office at the time—insisted on washing, starching, and ironing them. It was her way of showing appreciation for what I had done for her son, John, while he was a student of mine at Monroe. My first few years at the university were still white-shirt-and-tie years. Those white shirts, along with slacks and a sports jacket, made up my classroom attire.

My tie served me in unconventional ways as well. I frequently used recordings of German songs in my classes. One day, bending over the record player, I placed the end of my tie over the revolving record to free it of lint. Out of the back row, from a guy not in the know, came, "What's your wife gonna say about that?" Snickers came from different corners of the classroom from guys and gals who *were* in the know! Another time, Chuck Keim, presiding over a late-afternoon meeting of the faculty of the College of Arts and Letters, said, as the meeting began to get somewhat lengthy, "Well, I think we'd better call a halt to this, or your wives will start wondering what's keeping you." Looking in my direction, he added, "Isn't that right, Dr. Renner?" Again, snickers from various members of the assembled in the know! (Throughout my fifteen years on the teaching staff of the University of Alaska–Fairbanks, I neither vaunted nor made a secret of my priesthood. In general, it was never long before new students and new faculty members knew that I was a priest. Given the reputation Jesuits had as educators, Father Loyens, who began to teach at the university the year after I did, and I were seen by most people more as Jesuits than as priests. For us, as Jesuits, to be teaching at a state university was perfectly in keeping with the Jesuit principle of "finding God in all things".)

Another drawback to that Tanana Village apartment was that, during the first several years, before an overhead door was installed, the carport underneath the apartment was open. Therefore, the dwelling was not adequately insulated. The waterline tended to freeze up. One year, upon my return from a Christmas vacation in Tacoma, I found everything frozen solid. But, being a renter, all I needed to do was call the management. They came, they saw, they thawed. Promptly water began to pour out of cracked pipes. Soon stalactites of ice began to decorate the carport ceiling. For several days, I wore rubber overshoes as I squished around the apartment on a soggy carpet. Electric baseboard heat, however, kept the place adequately warm.

There was one winter woe I was spared. I did not have to worry about keeping a car operational at sub-zero temperatures. That was one of the real pluses to my living within easy walking distance of the university. I actually suffered less from the cold than people who had to struggle to get a cold car started, scraped free of frost, warmed up, and ready to roll—on partially flat tires. In my forty years in Alaska, I never suffered so much as a single frost nip. Early on, I learned to respect the cold and how to dress for it.

My housekeeping was utterly simple. Keeping the place clean was easy. Dust from the unpaved driveway and College Road immediately at the end of the driveway—still unpaved when I first moved into that apartment—was a bit of a problem during dry, hot spells, when the only way to keep the place tolerably cool was by opening windows or the door to the balcony that fronted to the driveway. The balcony served me no purpose other than as a parking place for the bike I bought soon after beginning my teaching career at the university. In the winter, it was too cold out on the balcony. In the summer, it was home for hordes of mosquitoes and layers of dust.

Living in that apartment was really country living. Immediately on the other side of College Road, there was a vast spread of tundra and taiga, a great place for a wilderness hike or for picking blueberries in season. There were also some rather large ponds in the area. One October, these were frozen over solid enough to enable me to get in some relaxing solo ice skating before the snows of winter came.

The little kitchen area of my apartment had all the basic necessities for cooking and storing food, fresh or canned. I did my own grocery shopping. There was Lindy's corner grocery about a ten-minute walk from my apartment. The College Post Office was conveniently located about halfway between Lindy's and my apartment. A Safeway store was several miles away in one direction, and the Hub Wholesale Grocery about the same distance in the opposite direction. Even in extremely cold weather, I did not hesitate to go shopping, sometimes more just to get out than because of urgent need. When making an "apple run" to Safeway in sub-zero temperatures, I wore two shirts. Between these, belt cinched tight, I would stuff—once out of sight of the checkout stands—my purchase of apples to keep them from freezing during my walk home.

On rare occasions, I ate in the university commons or cafeteria, simply joining the students or entertaining some as my guests. At times, I walked along the railroad tracks into Fairbanks to eat with the Jesuit community at Loyola Hall, or with the group at the bishop's residence. Contact with fellow Jesuits was important to me. Occasionally, friends, fellow faculty members, or married students invited me to their homes for a meal. They never expected me to reciprocate. A blessing at the beginning of the meal was all they asked; a compliment at the end paved the way to future invitations. For the most part, however, I did my eating in my apartment, doing my own cooking. This was a simple matter. A one-quart Pyrex porcelain CorningWare dish with a glass lid pretty much sufficed for all my cooking, and dining, needs. Everything desired for a given meal went into this to form a heavy stew, the base of which was usually a can of some kind of Campbell's soup. This was easy to heat, or reheat. There was no danger of burning it. I just had to keep it from bubbling over. In those pre-microwave-oven days, that was a good way to go. I never poisoned myself and never had a stomach problem or a weight problem. I spent little time doing dishes. Once through eating, I did the dish, and that was it. I have all my life been a slow eater. Eating alone enabled me to take my time. During my fifteen years in that apartment, I never had a TV set. I did, however, have an extensive record collection of classical music and of poetry and dramas in German, English, and Italian. I also had a radio. Few were the meals I ate in absolute silence. There were never leftovers to my meals.

During my years at the university, I fairly often invited members of my German classes to my apartment to practice chatting in German while socializing over cookies and ice cream with tea or coffee. Occasionally, we read some German drama. The lead role, if a male role, I always assigned to Dr. Wolf Hollerbach. His wife, Christa, and I took secondary major roles; students took the rest. It was all rather informal but taken seriously enough—a case of mixing the useful with the pleasant. For one of those evening sessions, Renata VanEnkevort, one of my German students (and the daughter of Mrs. Erna Meier, the cook at Loyola Hall, when I lived there) was present. Not having eaten dinner yet, she hoped to find some edible leftovers in my refrigerator. After a momentary glance inside, with a look of disgust on her face—and the comment to me, "You bachelor guys!"—she shut the door again, with a bang. There was simply nothing in that fridge for her to eat.

At this point, I feel I should introduce some key people in my life during my University of Alaska–Fairbanks days. First, the Hollerbachs. Wolf was from Cologne, Germany. His wife, Christa, too, was from Germany, a refugee from West Prussia. I first met them shortly before the fall 1965 semester began, at the Bruce Gordon home the evening they and their two preschool boys first arrived in Fairbanks from Ecuador, where Wolf had taught German and French. He was coming to the university to teach Spanish and French. Christa was a teacher of French and German. For a time, after their little girl was born and out of infancy, Christa taught French at the university. When I left the university in 1980, she took over the Latin program from me. On campus, in the Eielson Building, for a number of years, Wolf and I had our offices in the same room. Only a thin, low wall separated them. I was often a guest at the Hollerbach home, both as an individual and as a member of the foreign language department, when the Hollerbachs hosted department members or the annual fall picnic held for students majoring in foreign languages. The Hollerbachs and I soon became very close friends. Shortly before I left Alaska, they had me as their dinner guest. Both attended my farewell party on the afternoon of May 23, 2002. Among the tears that flowed that afternoon were Christa's. In February 10, 2005, the Hollerbachs sent a generous check toward the publication of my *Alaskana Catholica*. At that time, I learned, to my considerable sadness, that Wolf's health was in decline.

Dr. Bruce R. Gordon, my department head for the majority of my years in the Department of Linguistics and Foreign Languages (DLFL), and his wife, Jean, likewise became very close friends of mine. They were devout Methodists. Shortly after I had begun teaching at the university, I attended their daughter's wedding. Jean's father, a Methodist bishop, officiated. At the home of the Gordons, as at the home of the Hollerbachs, I was an occasional dinner guest. I was present there also when they hosted members of the DLFL for the annual fall picnic for foreign-language majors. After Bruce retired from the university, he made a full-time profession of his hobby as a photographer. He was so good at it that he never needed to advertise. The word of satisfied customers making the rounds was enough to give him more business than he could handle. However, he always found time to be of whatever photographic service I needed when I was editor of the *Alaskan Shepherd*. When Bruce was about to celebrate his eightieth birthday on March 13, 1996—Jean was deceased by then—Wolf and Christa invited him to celebrate it at their home and told him he was free to invite as guests whomsoever he wished. There was only one he wished to invite—me! Almost the same was true five years later. Bruce died on August 19, 2001. I attended the memorial service held for him in the First United Methodist Church in Fairbanks. Wolf delivered the eulogy. When Chuck Keim was dying of cancer in Tacoma, Bruce flew down to spend some time with him.

Charlie Parr and his wife, Karen, could not have been kinder to me, from the day we first met to the day of Karen's final hug at my May 2002 farewell party. Charlie and I were the two German teachers during the latter half of the 1960s. He was already on the staff when I began. From the outset, he was most understanding of my position as a beginning teacher on the college level at a state university. We worked together in close harmony until he went on to become the Arctic bibliographer in the Elmer E. Rasmuson Library at the university, then a state representative, and then a state senator. We continued to be close friends. The Parrs hosted me as their Thanksgiving Day dinner guest my first semester at the university. I was routinely invited to their annual Christmas parties. In turn, I helped them with stove wood during the years they were living in a tiny cabin while building their new home next to it. Charlie died in March 2000. I was present at the memorial service held for him. Bruce gave the eulogy.

Whereas Chuck Keim always addressed me as "Father" when we were alone and as "Doctor" in academic circles, I generally addressed him as "Chuck". Bruce, Wolf, Charlie, and I were, from the outset, on a mutual first-name basis. Keim, Gordon, Parr, Hollerbach, and Renner: a quintet of friends, blessed to have met in academe and to have known one another throughout much of their earthly lives. (May they all meet again in life eternal!)

In March 1965, from the provincial's office in Portland, I received an application form inviting me to apply for a position as a teacher of German at the University of Alaska–Fairbanks. Chuck Keim had given the form to Bishop Gleeson, who had sent it on to Portland, from where it was sent on to me in Oberammergau. Bishop Boileau, only several weeks before he died, unexpectedly, had initiated the process leading to my first contract with the university.

On March 13, I wrote to Chuck:

Though I have no very impressive credentials as a German scholar, I do feel myself well qualified to teach German and fully agree with what I take to be the plans agreed on by you and the bishop that I be hired as a teacher of German. No one need worry that German is merely a Trojan horse used to smuggle in a "papist proselytizer". I am convinced that the only feasible thing is for me to present myself on my academic credentials, unsponsored by the Church, ready to rise or fall on my own showing. I am hired; the responsibility of measuring up to the expectations of the university rests on me.

On April 20, I filled out a personal data form. In answer to certain questions, I wrote: "Interests: arts and letters, things of the Spirit. Hobbies: classical music, literature, languages, chess, outdoor activities (swimming, mountain climbing, hiking). I am interested in university teaching for reason of the above-mentioned interests and, especially, because my professional interests have been and are youth in its quest for truth, beauty, and goodness. I am interested in Alaska because that is where the pioneers are—on all levels of development. Alaska was my childhood dream, my home for two years, and where I plan to spend the rest of my days."

Even before receiving solicited letters of recommendation about me, Bruce Gordon, on April 23, wrote to me, when I was still in Oberammergau preparing for my final exams: "Dean Keim has given me the personal data form you completed, and I have received transcripts of your work at Gonzaga University, Seattle University, and Santa Clara University. It is my pleasure to offer you an assistant professorship in German for the academic year 1965–1966 at a salary of $9,675 for nine months of teaching. The normal fringe benefits are available."

In his April 27, 1965, letter of recommendation, Father Christopher J. McDonnell, S.J., principal of Seattle Prep when I taught there from 1951 to 1954, wrote to Dr. Gordon:

Father Renner has a fine head, a good pursuit of knowledge, and an excellent general background. Nor do I feel that he is lacking in attractive personal traits. I feel that in this latter field, his personality will appeal more to college teachers and students than it did to high school boys, though he had more than his share of success among these.... In his early years, he was inclined to being, if you permit, a culture vulture, cultivating the arts for culture's sake.... I can recommend him most sincerely, for he has all the equipment and is open to suggestions.

Two days later, Father Norbert Rigali, S.J., wrote:

Father Renner does work well with others; he is neither moody nor temperamental. He is extremely easy to get along with, an obliging person, perhaps at times too obliging in the sense that he seems on occasion to defer to others even when a situation would be better served by self-assertion.... I think that he would be a good teacher of German, as he seemed to me, when we were living together in Munich, to have a "feeling" and "relish" for that language. Although not brilliant or a genius, he is a very hard and conscientious worker who is capable of accomplishing much.

That same day, April 29, 1965, Father Lewis N. Doyle, S.J., principal of Monroe High when I taught there from 1958 to 1960, described me to Dr. Gordon:

I might begin by saying that I spent two happy and profitable years with Father Louis Renner at Monroe High School in Fairbanks. As a teacher at Monroe, he performed with excellence and enthusiasm and with depth and skill. The students who were fortunate enough to be in his classes worked hard and fruitfully under his guidance, and they liked him immensely.... But, to answer your questions more specifically. My opinion is that he is one of the three best teachers in my experience as an administrator. If he performs according to his past record, I have no doubt that he will be a solid and most dependable scholar. Yes, he does work well with others and has a pleasant, friendly personality, a good sense of humor, and a ready wit. . . . He does understand Alaska's problems and does aspire to contribute as best he can to Alaska's promising future. I'm convinced that Father Renner will prove a valuable addition to the university. . . . He definitely ranks high in my opinion.

The following day, Edward A. Merdes, an attorney and a devout Catholic, wrote:

I personally became acquainted with Dr. Renner prior to his doctorate studies, when he taught at Monroe High School. I spent many hours in conversation and in athletic competition with Dr. Renner. He and I, along with other friends, competed against one another in various athletic endeavors [basketball] on a fairly regular basis, and during the course of these contacts, I got to know him quite well, and we established a rather close friendship. Without qualification I can state that Dr. Renner's character is above reproach in all respects. He has an especially pleasing and friendly personality. I noticed this particularly under athletic stress and in competition, when he maintained his sense of humor at all times. . . . Dr. Renner, in my opinion, is a truly outstanding person both intellectually and personally.

On May 1, Edward Hagemann, S.J., my former spiritual father at Alma College, penned his evaluation of me to Dr. Gordon:

I knew Father Renner well during the four years, 1954–1958, in my capacity as student counselor. It is my opinion that Father Renner will make a splendid teacher. He is an excellent student and scholar, but I should not fancy him as a research scholar. He is too interested in people to devote much time to research. He works well with others and is not at all temperamental. In fact, he is quite self-sacrificing and gives himself to others and their interests. He is very easy to get along with, being pleasant and affable; here at Alma, he was quite well liked. He is quiet by disposition and does not get on the nerves or irritate people. He has his own opinions but is not stubborn or aggressive. You ask whether he is sufficiently self-motivated. I believe he is, although an occasional prodding would help. His Germanic background comes out here. While not a brilliant man, he is a good, steady worker dedicated to his work. I think that, in your words, he does have something of a venturesome spirit but in a Germanic rather than in a French way.

Voilà, a portrait of me, a chiaroscuro portrait, quite true to life, in my judgment, painted jointly by five "artists", who knew me well!

The confidence placed in me by the writers of those letters of recommendation, as well as that placed in me by Chuck Keim and Bishops Boileau and Gleeson, caused me to feel a tangible degree of pressure, albeit self-imposed, to make a success of this whole new venture. And a "new" venture it was in many respects! As one of the very first American Jesuits to be hired on as a regular, full-time faculty member by a state university, I was a pioneer. That, too, put pressure on me to live up to the expectations of many in high places. It was a challenge to be met—with God's grace, and to His greater honor and glory.

On May 13, 1965, I signed that $9,675 contract, my first with the University of Alaska–Fairbanks.

Chapter 15

University of Alaska–Fairbanks: September 1965–December 1971

On September 7, 1965, I was present when Dr. William R. Wood, president of the University of Alaska–Fairbanks, opened the academic year with a general faculty convocation. At this, "Dr. Louis Renner", among other new faculty members, was introduced to the assembled. Departmental meetings soon followed. By this time, I was happily settled in my office on the second floor of the Eielson Building—named for Carl Ben Eielson, America's foremost Arctic pilot—and another North Dakota boy! As mentioned in a previous chapter, Wolf Hollerbach and I had our offices in the same room. He had the back half, the window side; I, the hall side. A low wall with a door separated the two offices. Immediately across the hallway from my office was the big classroom in which, as Newman Club chaplain from 1958 to 1960, I had heard confessions, celebrated Mass, and held Newman Club meetings. This was now newly transformed into the foreign language laboratory. During my latter years at the university, a few doors down from my first office, I had a whole room for my office.

Classes got under way the second week of September. I was assigned two sections of beginning German, one of second-year German, and the third-year course. In 1965, the university still had a foreign language requirement for most students.

The two sections for beginners numbered about thirty-five students each; the section for second-year students, about twenty-five. In the third-year class, I had around fifteen. The classes for beginners met five days a week; the other two, three days a week. All this, translating into sixteen hours a week in the classroom, was considered a full load. We were expected to have a daily office hour as well as to serve as advisors to students. I always asked to have a maximum number of students assigned to me as their advisor. I preferred advising to committee work, though I did, at various times, and for various lengths of time, also serve on a fair number of different committees. During my career at the university, I was asked, at one time, to consider being dean of the College of Arts and Letters. At another, I was urged to serve as head of the Department of Linguistics and Foreign Languages. Not in the remotest did I even consider serving in either capacity. My focus was almost entirely on teaching and advising students. Having, throughout most of my years at the university, full teaching loads and full quotas of advisees, I was never under pressure to do research and publish. Nevertheless, as shall be seen, I was to do a considerable amount of this. In spite of the classroom, the advising, and the committee work, after five years of high school work, the university workload seemed to me relatively light.

Before the beginning of my first semester of teaching at the university, I had gone to a men's clothing store in Fairbanks and told the clerk who and what I was and what I was about to be. I told him to outfit me in sports clothes befitting me and currently in fashion. He understood. It was a nervous Dr. Renner, now all decked out in a white shirt and green tie to match his dark green sports jacket and gray slacks, that walked into the classroom to face his first University of Alaska–Fairbanks class of German students on opening day. Throughout my years of teaching, it was always with a certain degree of nervousness that I first faced a new group of students. However, after the first several meetings, I was totally relaxed.

I always made it a point to get to know the names of all my students within the first several days of meeting them in class. In keeping with the Jesuit tradition of *cura personalis alumnorum* (a personal concern for the students), I wanted my students to feel that I knew and cared for each one of them as a specific person. From the outset, too, I encouraged students to get to know one another, to be at ease with one another. I tried to create a relaxed classroom atmosphere, an air of informality. This was important in a foreign language program, for it made it easier for students to practice speaking German with one another. That my personal concern for students as individuals was not a wasted effort is clear from what one student wrote in her evaluation of me: "I feel you are one of the BETTER [*sic*] professors on campus. You view students as people, and you're sensitive to each student and his needs and problems."

Humor, too, helped create a favorable classroom atmosphere. The first day of class, I let my students know that I planned to be present every class day and that I asked no more of them than I asked of myself. I told them that, while they might eventually graduate *in absentia*, they, *in absentia*, could not be taught by me. I also told them that they should study hard from the outset, because then they would not be coming around at the end of the semester crying because they had failed the course. "The salt in your sweat", I reminded them, "is worth more than the salt in your tears." Half-seriously, I assured them that I was a reasonable man and that, therefore, if they were really sick, they would be excused. However, no matter how sick they might think themselves to be, they were to show up in class anyway, even if they had to be carried in on a stretcher. We would, then, take their temperature, check them over, and arrive at a diagnosis. If it was determined that they were truly sick, they would be excused. After all, I repeated, I was a reasonable man. They got the point. Attendance was good, except during some spells of extremely cold weather.

What kind of students did I have? As might be expected, in the course of fifteen years, a considerable variety. Some were real students; some were just teenagers fresh out of high school going to college. A few were Alaska Natives with weak academic backgrounds. Occasionally, I had fellow faculty members auditing a class by way of preparing themselves for a stay in Germany or Austria. To some, German came easy; to others, in spite of a sincere effort on their part, it never ceased to be a wholly foreign language. Many students took it just to fulfill the foreign language requirement. They could have taken some other foreign language but opted for German. Some majored in it. Susan McMahon switched from majoring in linguistics to majoring in German, went on to earn a master's degree in it, and then became, for many years, the head German teacher at Lathrop High School in Fairbanks. As of the year 2006, we were still exchanging letters and cards.

I always let students know exactly what they were expected to learn from day to day. My grading was rarely contested. I gave very few failing grades. Instead, I saw to it that even struggling students deserved at least a passing grade. Frequent quizzes let both teacher and student know just how each was doing.

I can honestly say that, basically, my relationship to virtually all of my students throughout my years at the university was that of a friend helping friends. I was there for them. They sensed that. The friendship was mutual, and, in some cases, lasting. As the third millennium began, I was still corresponding with several who were in my very first classes.

The previous chapter mentioned that I had been offered the German position with the option that, when there was an opening in the philosophy department, I could switch over to that department. However, almost from the day I first began teaching German, as a member of the Department of Linguistics and Foreign Languages (DLFL), it was immediately evident to me that German was what I wanted to teach and that the DLFL was the department of which I wanted to be a member. Accordingly, early on, I let it be known that, even if a position in the philosophy department should open up, I wished to stay on as a teacher of German and as a member of the DLFL. I loved teaching German, and I was perfectly at home in the DLFL. As with the DLFL, so with the university, in general, mutual relationships were most cordial and harmonious. I was accepted as "one of them". The fact of my being a priest was never an issue with anyone. Academic credentials and academic performance alone came into consideration, whether there was question of a contract, a pay raise, a promotion, or tenure.

From January to April 1966, Father Edward L. Murphy, S.J., of Boston College made a personal tour of Alaska at the request of Father Jules M. Convert, general superior of the Alaska mission at the time. In his "Report on Jesuit Missionary Work in Alaska", Father Murphy wrote:

At present there is one Jesuit [Renner] teaching at the university. Next scholastic year, there will be another Jesuit [Loyens] and possibly a diocesan priest [Olson]. It has been decided that the priests will appear on campus in secular dress, not as priests. The present father has his own apartment near campus with periodic association with ours [fellow Jesuits] in the

city. He is known as "Doctor", so there is not a direct apologetic for the Faith in their presence, nor do the fathers care
directly for Catholics on the campus. A father [James R. (Jim)
Laudwein] who teaches at Monroe High School, the parish
school, has charge of the Catholic students. While I am indeed
in favor of locating Jesuits in national universities, especially in mission countries, I do wonder about obscuring the
priesthood. The Church thus loses an apologetic in this area
of national life. The reason given for the priests having their
own apartments that are not on the campus is that anonym-
ity is thus preserved and the professors have a place for informal discussion with student groups that do not have the
Church label attached to them. I am unwilling to take any
firm position on this situation.

I consider Father Murphy's words "direct" and "directly"
well chosen. Not so the word "obscuring". We three priests
mentioned in his report certainly made no conscious effort to
obscure our priesthood. Father Loyens and I both had served
in Fairbanks and on the campus and were known to many
to be priests. While Father Laudwein was now the Newman
Club chaplain, I associated with the program, though in a
low-key sort of way. Ten years later, when the campus ministry program came into being under Paulist father James M.
Kolb, I related warmly to that. Soon after beginning at the
university, I took part in the informal religious discussions
held in the Presbyterian church at the foot of the campus hill.
For some years, a group of us faculty members of different
religious persuasions met to discuss different philosophies and
religions. They knew, of course, that I was a priest.

Regarding our dressing, or not dressing, as priests, university officials never said anything one way or another about that.
As far as they were concerned, it was simply a nonissue. The
only comment I ever heard about it—as mentioned in an

earlier chapter—was Bishop Gleeson's unsolicited remark to me some weeks before I began teaching at the university: "Of course, you won't be wearing your Roman collar." Possibly he and Chuck Keim had discussed the matter.

Once, asked by a man why I was teaching on a state university campus instead of doing "priestly work", I assured him that I considered the work I was doing on campus as, indeed, priestly work and that, if I were not considering it such, I would leave it immediately—adding that it was one of our Jesuit charisms "to find God in all things". I never saw my two roles, that as priest and that as university professor, militating one against the other. Rather, they blended harmoniously into one, with that of priest clearly, and by far, the more important role. I always considered myself first and foremost a priest, even if on campus I performed no direct priestly functions other than hearing an occasional confession in my office and doing some spiritual counseling. Several times during academic years, I also baptized children of fellow faculty members and of students. However, that was off campus, in Immaculate Conception Church or at a home Mass. Summers were something else again. When not traveling in Germany, or teaching a summer session at the university, or doing research work, I occasionally replaced pastors in various places around Alaska for longer or shorter periods of time. Then, of course, I carried out a regular priestly ministry.

Some years later, in the fall of 1974, Father William C. Dibb, S.J., pastor of Sacred Heart Cathedral in Fairbanks, wrote to me about my possibly helping out with the liturgies there. He also asked Father Loyens, general superior of Jesuits in Alaska, as of August 15, 1973, about his thoughts on the subject. On October 1, 1974, Father Loyens made them known to Father Dibb:

I gladly share with you the advice I give and the practice I was told to follow in my own case for the past eight years as professor at the university. I am vitally concerned that the men in other apostolates have the necessary time to adequately prepare their work and to execute their many tasks without being unduly overburdened and also that they have some time for themselves to recreate and to devote to their personal lives as Jesuits. Therefore, I tell them that their first responsibilities are to their assigned works and to themselves and their professional lives and that if they so desire and have the time, they are encouraged to help you in the parish in any way they wish and you approve. In short, they have to assess their time and talents, and then they make the decision as to whether they can help in the parish. After all, a man can do only so much if he is to be outstanding in his own area. This was the basis for my own conduct during the last eight years, and I found that, being busy all week, it was precisely the weekend that was left to me to attend meetings, prepare courses, correct tests, and try to get some relaxation. This left me little time to get involved in the parish directly.

Such sage thinking and advice, formulated nine years after I had begun teaching at the university, I had, in reality, been following from the time I first began my career there. My own response to Father Dibb's request for help at the cathedral I wrote on October 3:

After thinking about it and praying about it these past several days, I have come to the conclusion that it would be wiser for me not to commit myself in the matter of helping out in the parishes here. My apostolate at the university just about fills out my workweek. Saying Mass for the sisters on Sundays takes very little time and, more importantly, very little nervous energy. More and more, as I go along in my work at the university, people come to me to speak to me "as Father". So I do feel that I am part of the apostolic effort here, part of the team.... Regarding the reconciliation ceremonies, I will very likely be able to help out.

For some years, while teaching at the university, I routinely offered an eleven o'clock Sunday Mass in the convent chapel for the sisters staffing the Fairbanks Catholic schools. Sister Mildred Niehuser, S.P., with whom I had taught at Monroe, would pick me up at my apartment and drive me to their convent. After hearing confessions, I would offer Mass. Then, following a leisurely breakfast, I would walk the three miles along the railroad tracks back to my apartment. Those Sunday hours with the sisters were weekly highlights for me.

Not having spent a Christmas with my family since that of 1959, I asked for permission from superiors to spend Christmas 1965, my first Christmas since becoming a professor, with them. Permission was gladly granted. It was important for both the family and me that I spend that Christmas with them. During the previous summer, when I spent several weeks with them, after not having seen them for a little over five years, I was simply not myself. They noticed, and I subconsciously felt, that I was "out of sorts", somehow not the same son and brother they had known in 1960. By Christmas, however, I was my old self again, to them and to me.

On April 1, 1966, Charles J. Keim, dean of the College of Arts and Letters—addressing me as "Dear Professor Renner"—wrote to me:

I want you to know that both your department head and I have appreciated your contributions to the university this year. You have properly shaped dignity, maturity, erudition, humility, spunk, and deep conviction into an edifice labeled "excellent teacher and highly valued colleague". I am gratified that the unsought "feedback" I receive from students is that they, too, highly value your good teaching and deep concern for them as individuals. You are helping them to grow in the right direction as you are helping the university to grow. I hope that the salary increase in the enclosed contract proves more concretely than words that we appreciate your contributions.

On June 10, 1966, my department head, Bruce R. Gordon, wrote to Bishop Gleeson:

I simply want you to know what a fine job Dr. Renner has done this year. He has earned the respect and admiration of faculty and students alike, both for his scholarship and for his genuine interest in the students. Personally, I have been grateful for Dr. Renner's dependability, and because I had confidence in him, he was not supervised as closely as other new instructors normally are. In these days, when we frequently find, even among university faculty, persons who attract students by their defiance of accepted moral codes and all forms of authority, persons like Dr. Renner are particularly needed to counter these influences and to set an example for the students. I know that you and Dr. Renner have both carefully considered how he may best serve his Church. I hope that he may have a long and fruitful career in higher education. I can foresee that with experience he will become an outstanding teacher and will be a positive influence in the shaping of many young people.

At the end of the 1966 spring semester, with Father Joseph E. (Joe) Laudwein—twin brother of Father Jim Laudwein and just finishing his first year of teaching at Monroe—I flew to Juneau. We spent part of the day and the night there before taking the ferry to Ketchikan to do likewise, before flying on to the Seattle-Tacoma airport. In Juneau, while we were having a noonday lunch in Saint Ann's Hospital with Father David A. Melbourne, pastor of Juneau's Cathedral of the Nativity of the Blessed Virgin Mary, Father Melbourne mentioned, in passing, that he had not had a vacation in years. That noon, Juneau, enjoying a rare sunny day, looked most attractive to me. Wanting to see more of it, and wanting to give Father Melbourne a vacation break, I told him that I would ask superiors for permission to replace him during the month of July. Permission was granted. After visiting my family and others in the Northwest, I returned to Juneau to tend the cathedral parish and its dependent mission, Saint Paul the Apostle, in Mendenhall Valley. A number of times, I viewed the Mendenhall Glacier from close up and hiked along its flank. I toured the state capitol, the salmon canneries, and other points of interest. I did some marriage-related legwork for Bishop Dermot O'Flanagan. On the rare nonrainy days, I hiked to the top of Mount Roberts. I visited Douglas and the Shrine of Saint Thérèse. That month in Juneau was another classic example of mixing the useful with the pleasant.

On January 18, 1967, on a "supplementary personnel information" form, I listed, among other things, that I had given a talk and conducted a discussion entitled "The Individual and His Response to Authority" at the "Coffee House" meeting, that I was serving on the Committee for a Better Understanding of the Problems of Alaska Native Students, and that I was a member of the American Association of Teachers of German. I was soon to become a member also of the National Carl Schurz Association and of the American Council of Teachers of Foreign Languages, as well as the regional chairman for the National High School German Contest sponsored by this latter organization.

Regarding committees: During my fifteen years at the university, I served also on the Humanities Committee, on the Special Events Committee, on the Sabbatical Leave Committee, on the Dean's Ad Hoc Advisory Committee, on the Campus Evaluation Committee for the Fulbright Scholarship Program, and on the Grievance Committee. I was a charter member of this last and helped draw up its guidelines. Upon the urging of fellow faculty members, I served on it for a second term. I was also the proponent, the architect, of the university's Ad Hoc Interdisciplinary Seminars program— "an attempt to be responsive to student demands for 'more relevant' courses". In passing, I might mention here that, after listening for several years to student announcers on the university's radio station, KUAC, mispronounce and mutilate foreign language names and words, I proposed a one-credit-per-language course on the pronunciation of French, German, Italian, and Spanish. My proposal was implemented. For years I taught the German and Italian pronunciation courses. Italian, which at one time seemed a luxury acquisition, now proved to be of practical value.

On February 3, 1967, Dr. Gordon recommended that I be given a "modest" salary increase with my next contract on the basis that I was doing an "effective job" of advising students, adding, "in fact, it is in this latter area that Renner wins the affections of students by giving of himself generously and showing them his sincere interest in their problems and welfare." Commenting further on my contributions to the foreign languages program, he added, "The curriculum of German studies has been greatly improved through his leadership." He closed his recommendation with: "And he has performed more than his share of departmental chores. So far he has shown no inclination to publish, so his contribution will probably be made more in teaching than research. However, he not only keeps abreast of his field but constantly broadens his knowledge in other areas as well."

Dean Keim concurred with Dr. Gordon's evaluation of me, adding, "I am especially impressed by his interest in advising, and on several occasions I have had students request that he be their advisor. *He was listed in third place in the students' evaluation of faculty last spring* [Keim's emphasis]."

The summer of 1967 was a summer Fairbanks long remembered. It was the summer of the Great Flood. By mid-August, heavy rains had put much of the city of Fairbanks and surrounding areas under water. Both the Tanana and the Chena rivers overflowed their banks. On the fifteenth, Father Loyens, with me sitting next to him, drove away from our apartments, headed for the university campus—an ad hoc hilltop refuge for a great number of evacuees—as the waters were already flooding the driveway. I spent the next three days on campus, sleeping on the floor of my office during the night. When the waters began to recede, I helped Salvation Army personnel empty Lindy's grocery store and deliver the food to needy people in the higher off-campus areas. The flood put a premature end to the summer school sessions scheduled to end on August 18. Since July 10, I had been teaching a six-credit course in elementary German. Having a good idea, thanks to routine quizzes, of how each of my German students had done, I was able to turn in grades for them. Other faculty members, who had relied on final exams to determine grades, were not as fortunate. It was a soggy Fairbanks and a student body of reduced numbers that began the 1967–1968 academic year.

Anticipating the academic year 1968–1969, in a memorandum of recommendation to Dean Keim, Dr. Gordon (described as "a staunch Methodist"), in his evaluation of me, wrote:

> Dr. Renner's quiet manner and sympathetic attitude attract students to him, after which they quickly discover his honesty and kindliness. His competence in German is surpassed only by his character and convictions, which go far toward counteracting the influence of certain more dramatic, but less praiseworthy, members of the university community. He participates actively in all department affairs, cheerfully accepts whatever is requested of him, and makes valuable suggestions. Although he does not write for publication, he continually deepens his knowledge of German literature and civilization. By his example, and with the approval of his church, he is bringing a wholesome religious influence to the campus without a trace of proselytizing.

The summer of 1968 found me back in Germany again. The first thing I did, of course, was to pay a nostalgic visit to dear old Oberammergau. There, much was as when I left it three years previously; but much had also changed. Three years can make a significant difference, especially in the lives of little ones. Some of the children, members of the *Sonnenschein* group when I was first there, no longer recognized me, nor I them. A larger room now served as the chapel. I offered Mass in this in German instead of the traditional Latin. On one of the hills in the cow pasture, where I had skied and sledded with the *Heim* kids, there now stood a tourist hotel. The major change, however, as far as I was concerned, was that Sister Gundharda was now the sister superior—with a driver's license! With her at the wheel, we took drives to the monastery at Ettal and to the Plansee. Later that summer, at her new station near Nuremberg, I was to visit Sister Emmerana, who had been the superior when I was first in Oberammergau.

During the 1967–1968 academic year, Marjorie Shelby had been a student in one of my advanced German classes. Majoring in German, she had hopes of one day teaching it. I arranged for her—a devout member of her church and a Sunday school teacher in it—to spend a month living in the *Kinderheim*, working there for her room and board while, at the same time, getting much practice in spoken German. The sisters were very kind to her, treating her more like a guest than an employee. Everything worked out very well for her. Before, during, and after her stay in Oberammergau, she and I spent some time together touring parts of Germany and Austria. We took a cruise on the Rhine, spent a few days in the Lake Constance area, and visited the highlights of Munich and Nuremberg. Shortly before we left for Germany, I had dinner with her and her parents in their home on Koyukuk Street, the very house that was to become, in 1973, the residence of the priests staffing Sacred Heart Cathedral parish, and then, in 1992, the bishop's residence! I was to spend many an afternoon and evening in that house at priest gatherings hosted by Michael J. Kaniecki, S.J., bishop of Fairbanks.

My principal reason, however, for being in Germany—in addition to once again visiting Oberammergau—was to take a Goethe Institute course for foreign teachers of German and Germanistics. This I took, along with German teachers from a considerable number of different countries, from July 1 to August 10 in Nuremberg. Naturally, we all spoke German with one another but a German seasoned with the accents of our respective native languages. In Nuremberg, I lived in the Jesuit community. Various excursions and visits to museums and the Nuremberg opera were part of the course. There was no pressure to achieve anything in particular. The stamped document we received at the end of the course attested only to the fact that we had participated in it. During subsequent years, I was to attend several more such courses, one in Munich and one in Lübeck. Much of what I learned and gathered while taking Goethe Institute courses found its way into my German History and Civilization course, a third-year-level course I taught at regular intervals. Friends were made at the institutes. For some thirty years, I corresponded regularly with Sister Laetitia, a sister from Turnhout, Belgium. We met and became friends, correspondents, and mutual prayer partners at one of the Goethe Institutes. Participating in the courses bordered on "vacation with pay", for, by upgrading myself as a professional, I was, at the same time, giving cause for a salary increase. The courses were greatly enriching and, all the while, truly enjoyable. Yet another case of mixing the useful with the pleasant!

The year 1969 dawned cold. It was minus fifty-six on January 3, the day I wrote to Mom to assure her I would offer my Mass for her on her birthday, the sixth. "Dear Mom," I began my letter,

> I hope this thaws out before you grab it and freeze your hands on it. We came very close to setting an all-time-low record, but now it's warming up. I might even consider taking off one of these layers of wool. But I'm comfortable. I'm enjoying a holiday, as a matter of fact. I called off my classes for today. Too many students still not back from vacation, and many fearing to venture out at minus sixty. I bundle up and go for my usual walk. The waterlines have been frozen ever since I got back, but with some snow water I manage. Having had about the best vacation ever this holiday season and still surrounded by the many goodies and dear memories make it easy to put up with the little inconveniences of this "missionary" life.

During my university years, I spent most of my Christmases with my family. Always I returned to Fairbanks with a big box crammed full of edibles of all kinds. My universal favorite among them: borscht!

On May 1, 1969, university president William R. Wood wrote me: "I am pleased to approve your advancement in rank from assistant professor of German to associate professor of German, effective July 1, 1969." The promotion was recommended by Dr. Gordon, who saw my "value to lie principally in two important areas: teaching and counseling". In his memorandum, he commented also on my "quiet, relaxed attitude" and on my "teaching technique", which "substitutes sincerity and conviction for flair, and patience and kindness for the dramatic approach used effectively by others". It should be noted here that this was the time of the war in Vietnam and of the turmoil and many problems it brought to university campuses, the University of Alaska–Fairbanks campus not exempted. It is in light of that, I believe, that Dr. Gordon— before recommending a substantial salary increase—ended his memorandum, referring to me, with: "His religious background apparently has proven helpful in dealing with moral as well as academic problems, and students have great respect and admiration for him. We need more professors like Renner whose example and advice are both effective with students facing real problems."

This was a time, too, when a bit of good news did a religious superior good. Father John J. Kelley, my former teacher and football coach at Bellarmine, was now my father provincial. To him I sent the documents dealing with my promotion along with a cover letter written on May 20, 1969. "Feeling", I wrote, "that it does not hurt even a provincial to hear a little bit of good news from time to time, I thought you might be interested in knowing how things are going up here. The enclosed pages tell the story. Sorry to have to be my own trumpeter. Father Loyens, too, has been promoted. Our work seems to be going well. My fourth year at the university is at an end." By return mail, Father Kelley sent me his words of sincere congratulations.

Before I signed my first contract to teach at the University of Alaska–Fairbanks, I had made known to church and state that I wanted to serve at the university on its own terms, as any other regular faculty member: to receive contract renewals, merit increases, promotions, and tenure, all on the condition that I measured up to standards; and to be terminated if I did not.

In a letter dated November 14, 1969, Dr. Gordon proposed to Dean Keim that I be granted tenure. He gave as reasons for his proposal that I was "thorough, conscientious, and imaginative in the preparation and presentation of all course materials and particularly interested and effective in emphasizing to students the relationship between language and culture." He pointed out that, with "patience, understanding, and kindness", I gained "the confidence of shy students" and that I was "especially effective with Native students". That my evening class in beginning German, which included townspeople, was "large and popular" he attributed more to "the instructor's personality than to the scheduled hour". He mentioned my "professional ethics and high moral standard" and the "harmony" I contributed to the Department of Linguistics and Foreign Languages.

Being an honest man, as well as an accurate evaluator of me—a onetime North Dakota farm boy, who had had a chance to go to college as a Jesuit—Dr. Gordon did not hesitate to point out also my shortcomings. "Renner", he wrote further, has only two weaknesses of any significance. The first is his tendency to melt into the background and to undervalue his own opinions. As a consequence, he never shows real leadership and lacks a certain vigor in dealing with others or carrying out projects. The second, related to the first, is his habit of submitting to authority in any form. Undoubtedly this characteristic stems from his many years of Jesuit training. He has improved, however, during his years in an academic rather than a religious environment, and I believe we can expect further improvement in the future. I criticize these characteristics only in respect to his total job as university professor and member of the academic community. In some ways they are not weaknesses at all but assets in that they allow him to function more effectively with a certain type of student.... In summary: I recommend that Dr. Renner be given tenure.

On March 27, 1970, President Wood wrote to me, "I am privileged to offer you a tenured appointment effective July 1, 1970."

Father Convert, in his "Relator's Report" of May 12, 1970, wrote to Father General Arrupe in Rome about the Loyens-Renner presence on the University of Alaska–Fairbanks campus. "The experiment at the Alaska state university has, I believe, proven its usefulness and importance for a presence of the Church there. Even if the two fathers don't wear clerical dress, they are universally known as priests and enjoy the esteem and respect of faculty and students." After commenting on Father Loyens' "wide influence", especially on Native students, he went on to write, "Very different in temperament and the kind of influence his talents give him, I believe that Father Renner's academic excellence and quiet ways are also a great asset for the Church on campus. If he were not there, he certainly would not be in Alaska but teaching at one of our own universities among other Jesuit staff, where, most likely, his influence would not be what it is at the state university, since he would just be another Jesuit there."

This is the first, and only, time, to my knowledge, that the word "experiment" was used by anyone in connection with our presence on the faculty of the University of Alaska–Fairbanks. I have no reason to believe that Father Boileau or any other Jesuit superior or Bishop Gleeson ever looked upon it as an experiment, as a program to be monitored along certain guidelines and then confirmed or terminated, depending on positive or negative findings. We were assigned to this particular apostolate much as fellow Jesuits in Alaska were assigned to their respective apostolates.

The summer of 1971 found me again in Europe. I began that stay by making my retreat at the new Jesuit retreat house in Zug, Switzerland. On May 11, I wrote greetings to Dad and Mom from the famous monastery of Einsiedeln. A five-hour predawn hike with a Swiss father had brought me there. From June 28 to July 22, I attended a Goethe Institute in Munich. Again, some excursions were part of that. Among them: a flight to Berlin for a three-day stay, and a bus trip to the Czechoslovakian border. At the border, I daringly walked around behind one of the stone border markers just to be able to say, "Oh yes! I've been to Czechoslovakia." From August 2 to August 21, I attended a Goethe Institute in Lübeck, Germany. That was my first longer stay in northern Germany, and it was most rewarding. With the institute and on my own, I visited the major cities and attractions in that area, among them the North Frisian Islands, the Halligen. Having stood on top of Germany's highest mountain, the Zugspitze, and now having been at sea level on the northern German islands, I could honestly claim to having "done Germany from top to bottom".

"The North Dakota Kid", riding high in the saddle in front of the barn on Grandpa Renner's farm, ca. 1929.

The John J. Renner farm, three miles north of Flasher, North Dakota, my home from 1929-1937. Note the "straw barn" on the left!

Tacoma Parochial Champs of 1941

Here are the 1941 champions of the Tacoma Parochial Schools' Basketball league. They are the Sacred Heart squad of McKinley, Hill. The boys are, from left to right, Chuck Schuler, Jimmy Collins, Bill Cline, Louie Renner, Paul Robinson and Tom Creedican. Pat Schilley, another member, was absent when the picture was taken.

The main Bellarmine Preparatory School building as it appeared in the 1940s. Photo courtesy of Jesuit Oregon Province Archives/125.1.19.

Proudly sporting my first letter in varsity football, 1942.

The John J. Renner family, 1943. Back row, from left: Leonard, Louis, William, Richard, and Julie. Front row: Albert, Rosa Gustin Renner, John J. Renner, and Della.

Saint Francis Xavier Novitiate, Sheridan, Oregon, after it received its first coating of tar in October 1944. Photo by Tom Cohen/courtesy of Jesuit Oregon Province Archives/184.2.33.

With my sisters Julie and Della by the Novitiate guest house, on Vow Day, March 25, 1946. Photo by John J. Renner.

Aerial view of Mount Saint Michael's, the Jesuit philosophate on the northeastern outskirts of Spokane, Washington, as it appeared in 1948.

Aerial view of Seattle Preparatory School as it appeared in the early 1950s. The smaller building to its right is the gymnasium. To the school's left and at a lower elevation stands the Faculty Residence. Interlaken Boulevard runs between the two buildings. Lake Union is in the background. Photo courtesy of the Jesuit Oregon Province Archives/116.1.08.

Aerial view of Alma College, the Jesuit theologate, as it appeared in the mid-1950s. It was located in the Santa Cruz Hills near Los Gatos, California. Giant redwoods were prominent among the trees that surrounded it.

With a Mexican-American child—a member of Our Lady of Guadalupe parish, San Jose, California—whom I prepared for her First Holy Communion in 1956.

*The moment of ordination to the priesthood at the hands of Bishop
Bernard J. Topel, Bishop of Spokane, in Saint Aloysius Church,
Spokane, June 15, 1957.*

The official ordination photo, spring 1957.

In the Bellarmine Preparatory School cafeteria before the reception on the afternoon of my first Solemn High Mass, June 23, 1957. The Renner family, left to right: Albert, Della, Julie, Mom, Dad, "Father Louie", Bill, Dick, and Len. Photo by Robert Treleven.

With Monroe High School's Music Appreciation Club, 1959. Photo courtesy of Diocese of Fairbanks Archives.

Celebrating the Fourth of July 1960, on the S.S. Liberté, with, from left to right: Jesuit Fathers Joe Powers and Dick Hill, our waiter, and Jesuit seminarians Alan Arias and John Stacer. Photo by Georges Gratiet.

The Romanesque Church of Notre Dame—dating from the twelfth century—in Paray-le-Monial. I offered Mass in this a number of times.

The French village of Cogny, where I gave a retreat to young teenagers by way of preparing them for their Solemn Communion, May 18-21, 1961.

Ignatiushaus, my Munich home from October 1961 to November 1962.

Offering Mass for the crew of the U.S.S. Quillback, December 31, 1961.

The village of Oberammergau in the Bavarian Alps of southern
Germany. Mount Kofel towers over it.

The Hänsel-Gretel Kinderheim *in Oberammergau. The parlor/ dining room and the chapel were in the three-story building on the right. The chapel was on the second floor, extreme left; the parlor/dining room was beneath it.*

Disguised as Der Vogelfänger *(the bird-catcher) at the Fasching celebrations in the* Kinderheim *on February 26, 1963.*

Relaxing with Kaplan Joseph Hamberger, on Mount Laber, on July 21, 1963, after the Mass he just offered.

"Spring Street" in Garmisch-Partenkirchen, Bavaria, Southern Germany. The Alpspitz is the peak to the upper left. Photo used with permission from Fotoverlag Huber, Garmisch-Partenkirchen, Nr. 8132.

Resting while on a hike in the high country above Oberammergau with some of the Heim children and Sisters Gundharda and Berlindis (glasses), spring 1964.

Offering Mass in the Kinderheim *chapel for the Sisters, spring 1965.*

Entertaining some of my third-year German students in my apartment, 1966.

Aerial view of the University of Alaska-Fairbanks campus, ca. 1970.

On a September 1973 afternoon, in the backyard of the Bruce and Jean Gordon home, four members of the Department of Linguistics and Foreign Languages enjoy one another's company at the annual picnic held for foreign language majors. The four are Patricia Dietz, Guenther Matschke, Louis Renner, and Wolf Hollerbach. Photo by Bruce R. Gordon.

On the rocks on the leeside of King Island shortly after landing there on June 18, 1974.

Praying before the statue of Christ the King on King Island, June 23, 1974. The village of Ukivok is visible in the background. Photo by Hubert Kokuluk.

Offering Mass in the home of Dr. Joseph John Brenckle Jr.—Professor of Russian at the University of Alaska-Fairbanks—and wife Carol, at which I baptized their infant son, Joseph John III, on August 31, 1974. Photo by Paul H. McCarthy.

On Little Diomede Island with Michael Soolook Jr., June 1975. A stretched sealskin and walrus tusks form the backdrop. Photo by Sister Judy Tralnes, C.S.J.P.

Dipnetting for sockeye and king salmon in the Copper River down-stream from the small community of Chitina, September 1977. Photo by Gisela Dykema.

With the last group of fellow members of the Department of Linguistics and Foreign Languages—for the academic year 1979-1980—clockwise to my right: Martha Flora, Wolf Hollerbach, Sheila Cox (secretary), John Koo, Sylvia Navarro, Serge Lecomte, and Glenda Burbank. Photo by Jimmy Bedford.

Showing my newly published book, Pioneer Missionary, *to University of Alaska-Fairbanks student Annina Salvagno, October 1979.*
Photo by Ben Swan.

Professor of German, Emeritus as of May 11, 1980. Photo by Jimmy Bedford.

On September 20, 1971, I gave a presentation entitled "Campus Consensus" at a university faculty seminar. "The heating plant alone", my presentation began, "does not hold the University of Alaska together. A far-less-concrete and seldom-discussed factor", I went on, "is responsible for this. Our university is founded on the (at least implicit) conviction that there is a campus consensus, a campus philosophy." "Campus consensus" I defined as "that largely intangible body of principles, norms, standards, and criteria of judgment that, ultimately, determines what makes the best sense, what is acceptable to the academic community". I might have added, "and to the state legislature, and to the public at large, that see to the financial needs of the academic community". I charged the academic community with the task of "helping toward the discovery, the formation, and the articulation of an intelligent and reasonable campus consensus".

The presentation was well received. In addition to thanking me for it, Dr. Walter J. Mueller—the new dean of the College of Arts and Letters, replacing Dean Keim—wrote to me, "Your topic was thought-provoking and most appropriate for the initial seminar of the 1971–1972 academic year. It is a pleasure to place a copy of this memorandum in your personnel file." The mentioning of this terse memorandum may seem a trivial matter to note, but Dean Mueller, a Germanist, was by now also my fellow German teacher. When he, an unknown to students, first started his career at the university, most of the students about to begin their second year of German asked to get into my section. He was aware of this but took it in good spirits without a trace of envy or resentment. From the outset, our relationship was most cordial, one of mutual respect. We became and remained close friends. In his evaluation of me in the spring of 1974, he referred to me as a "superior member of our faculty" and added, "I have a profound admiration and appreciation of him as a human being and as a teacher, whose discipline I share." With pleasure on my part and gratitude on his, I served on the Dean's Ad Hoc Advisory Committee, which he headed, for some years. In April 2005, along with a most heartwarming letter, he sent a generous contribution to help finance the publication of my *Alaskana Catholica*.

By way of bringing this already somewhat lengthy chapter to a close, I cite in full my November 14, 1971, letter to Father Edmund W. Morton, S.J., provincial assistant for education. The letter, as a summary report of my six-and-a-half-year teaching apostolate at the university, was solicited by him. The letter begins:

Dear Ed: *Pax Christi!*
You asked for it. Here it is, for what it's worth: my "Apologia"—or maybe I should right off call it my "Brag", with apologies to Edmund Campion, especially if he is your patron. [St. Edmund Campion, while in prison and shortly before his martyrdom, wrote what he entitled his *Brag*. This he addressed to the Privy Council of the Queen of England.] I have been thinking for several days about your request for a report on my work at the University of Alaska. No matter what approach I take, it seems I will have to talk a lot about *my*self, *my* work, *my* ideas, *my* accomplishments. My task would be easier if I had specific questions to answer.

Further difficulty derives from the fact that we are here talking primarily about priestly work, an apostolate, Christian influence, spiritual values. How can one adequately assess these? I do not really know. For the most part, then, I will simply recount facts. They may serve as indicators of the success or lack of same in my professional and apostolic work, if indeed there is a difference between these in my life.

My priesthood, my apostolate, has for the last seven years been exercised in and through my work as teacher, counselor, and committee member at the University of Alaska. My visibly "priestly" work on campus is quite minimal and, I would add, even incidental. As Newman chaplain earlier, I regularly said Mass on campus. Now I say Mass in my apartment or for sisters in the area. It was once suggested to me that I say Mass and preach in a church on Sundays so that I do not get out of touch with my priesthood. Frankly, if I felt that that were necessary for the reason given, then I would leave my present work immediately. If I felt that my work at the university were anything less than the full exercise of my priesthood, I would leave this work. But no. The mystery of the Incarnation has given a new dimension to reality and to my understanding of reality. I believe that I can be 100 percent a priest in my present work, somewhat unconventional as it may seem to be in America. This kind of apostolate is not always obvious and easy and needs to be worked at more, possibly, than the more traditional ones. It calls for considerable reflection, reassessment, openness to guidance, inspiration, and discernment. However, I believe it is eminently worthwhile in that it makes the priesthood present in an area of profound influence on the young of our nation. I used to question my presence on the secular campus somewhat more in the beginning but now feel fairly confident that this is the place for me. External evidence for the confidence is the fact that two bishops, two provincials, and two mission superiors have encouraged me in my work.

I can honestly say that I have enjoyed the work immensely all along. It has been intellectually and spiritually satisfying and fulfilling. I had a good preparation going into it. I've had the time, the money, and the opportunity to grow professionally. My living conditions are ideally suited to my work. I have been left free to do my work at the university. Seldom have I been asked to "help out" in the parishes, and I

have resisted the temptation to do this on any big scale. I
see this as a matter of priorities, time, and talent. I am quite
clear about this. I have done some summer work in rural
Alaska and Juneau. But getting to know Alaska and the people actually helps me in the university work. This has the
priority, and all else has to be judged in the light of this.

My life is not very dramatic. It's a daily routine of teaching, preparing classes, correcting papers, holding office hours,
doing departmental chores, doing committee work, counseling students, and maintaining contact with fellow professors. We are given some choice in filling our "full professional
workload". I choose the classroom and counseling rather than
research and publishing. *Cura personalis alumno(a)rum* is my
inspiration. Somebody has to do committee work, but I try
to choose those committees where I, because of my Jesuit and
priestly training and experience, can make some special contribution, or committees that deal with students and very academic issues.

More concretely: I have been a member of the core advising program since its inception. This program helps to get
freshmen and new students off to a good start in their college work. I have always had a good load of advisees. I have
never taught as few as twelve hours, which is considered the
maximum teaching load. But I like to teach and have never
really felt overburdened. I have organized and moderated our
German Club.

Regarding committee work: After volunteering for the general committee called to look into difficulties Alaska Native
students have in their academic life, I was appointed to the
subcommittee charged with the drawing-up of a statement.
Last year I was elected by the University assembly to the
newly formed Grievance Committee, about the most delicate and time-consuming committee on campus. We drew up
the guidelines and handled two cases. This year I was again
elected to that committee. I served twice on the Sabbatical

Leave Committee. The Ad Hoc Interdisciplinary Seminar program was my idea. I've served on this committee and also on the "Peace Arts" committee.

I have been a member of the Christian Faculty Forum. At my suggestion, we discussed Cox' *Secular City*. The last three weeks, we took *America's* Rahner issue. I was asked to lead the discussions, and I did. In September I addressed the Arts and Letters Faculty Seminar on the topic of "Campus Consensus and Community". [In substance, this was published in the university's student paper, *Polar Star*.] I've even written letters to the editor of our school paper! (Said little Jack Horner: "What a good little boy am I!")

Teaching, counseling, committee work, and contact with fellow faculty all present opportunities to filter Christian wisdom, values, and approaches into the academic community. The label is lacking, but the reality is there. There is no question here, however, of proselytizing. One needs to be very clear about this. Such efforts would be a sneaky betrayal of the confidence one receives along with his professional position. Serious mistakes could be made along these lines.

How do the administration, colleagues, and students see me? (The "Brag" goes on!) When the time came, I was promoted to associate professor. When the time came, I received tenure. Pay raises reflect the administration's satisfaction with my work. Several times the department head asked me to represent him when he could not attend meetings. He asked me to represent the foreign languages department at the Northwest Foreign Language Conference [held in Boise, Idaho] last April. The dean asked me to help count votes when department heads were elected last spring. Relationships with colleagues could hardly be better. Student evaluations have been consistently favorable. I know, these are not ends in themselves, but I feel I can regard them as positive indicators that the work seems to be going well and is blessed. I could be deceived in this, and only investigation and discernment by less-prejudiced minds can come up with a fair objective evaluation.

Possibly I've written much that is not very relevant and left out much that is. But, as I said, I have no guidelines for this report. I can only hope that, in the main, I've given you what you wish, and I assure you that I'd be more than happy to answer any specific questions you may have, dear Ed!

If there was an echo to all this, it never reached me.

Chapter 16

University of Alaska–Fairbanks:
1972–1973

In early February 1972, the annual evaluations of faculty took place. As a member of the foreign language department's Peer Evaluation Committee, I drew up the criteria for the evaluations. Evaluating one's peers can be a sensitive matter. All in all, everything went smoothly. I, too, of course, was evaluated by my peers, as well as by my department head, Dr. Bruce Gordon, and my dean, Dr. Walter Mueller. Wrote Dr. Gordon:

> Dr. Renner is one of the best professors on the teaching faculty. Student ratings of him are uniformly high, and their comments indicate how much they appreciate a stimulating, understanding, and patient teacher. Comments such as "by far one of the best instructors I have had in seven years of college" and "an outstanding foreign language instructor in every respect" are typical. He carries a heavy teaching load, and his sections are always popular. Although he does not plan to publish, his scholarship is unquestioned.

Dean Mueller, among other comments, wrote that I was "easy to establish contact with", adding, "My only complaint is that he is too self-effacing." His rating of me: "Outstanding." Dr. Gordon's: "Very good." A year later, in their evaluations of me, both were still of the same opinion. My Jesuit training continued to make itself felt.

In early April 1972, I drew up a petition concerning a piece of land next to the Eielson Building. There was question of turning it into a parking lot. The petition read, "Not convinced that more parking spaces are needed on the Fairbanks campus; on the contrary, convinced that more green lungs (trees, grass, flowers) are badly needed in the core area of the campus, we, the undersigned, strongly protest that said piece of land be turned into yet another parking lot, and strongly urge that it be instead landscaped." Approximately one hundred students and faculty signed the petition. The piece of land remained unpaved.

I submitted, on April 29, 1972, the following letter to the editor of the *Fairbanks Daily News-Miner*:

Dear Editor:
It may be a lone voice, but I feel it must be raised. And it must be raised in public; for, after your article "UA to Expand on Parking" it concerns what is now a public matter.

It is admitted that "on-campus parking is more than ample now." Yet "this year's parking lot improvement and expansion program will include paving of the Ballaine lot and installation of an elevator" because "people don't want to walk."

As a UA faculty member who has seen colleagues terminated, courses eliminated, programs cut, workloads increased, and higher student fees discussed—all this for financial reasons—I, for one, seriously question the need at this time for this expansion program.

However desirable such improvements may be, I ask, is this the year—the year of "financial exigency", of an "austere budget"—for building an elevator so the "men to match my mountains", "men of the last frontier" [Alaskan slogans], may, true to the university's motto, go *ad summum* without having to walk up a flight of steps?

Not convinced that this improvement and expansion program rates the priority assigned to it, at least at this time, I hereby go on public record as one who opposes this program, for the present, and as one who is willing to continue walking up steps.

The Ballaine lot was paved; the elevator, never installed.

From July 24 to August 11, 1972, I taught a noncredit short course in introductory Latin for the university's Division of Statewide Services. Students had requested this. During the latter part of that August, I was in Nome for a week as substitute pastor for Father James E. Poole, S.J. That short stay led to the production of my article about the well known Catholic radio station. "KNOM Helps Make Men Free" was published in the December 1973–January 1974 issue of *Sign* magazine.

During the latter 1960s, the war in Vietnam was still raging. More and more, faculty and students at the University of Alaska–Fairbanks hoped for a speedy end to it. At the time, there were "war colleges" in the country, but no "peace colleges". In the spring of 1969, Charlie Parr, with my enthusiastic support—for the beatitude "Blessed are the peacemakers, for they shall be called children of God" had, all along, been my favorite beatitude—proposed that the university curriculum include a "Peace Arts Program". This would be a far cry from a peace college, but it would be a step in that direction. The program would consist of a series of interdisciplinary seminars. Believed to be the first of its kind in the nation, the program was designed to prepare students for a professional career in achieving and maintaining peace as members of the U.S. government or of some international organization. Students in the program were expected to study a foreign language and complete "basic core courses in comparative politics, international affairs, political geography, and the diplomatic history of the United States". The program was approved by the university administration. A Peace Arts Committee was formed. I was a charter member of this. The committee was chaired by Dean Mueller, who brought to the program his twenty-five years of experience in international relations. The committee saw to the contents and the coordinating of the seminars. Student response to the program was described, in a University press release, as "very strong". There were no funds in the university budget for the program. However, at the suggestion of Father Loyens, also a member of the committee, Father Bernard F. McMeel, general superior of Jesuits in Alaska, made a donation of one thousand dollars in their name toward the building-up of a basic library for the program.

"A Philosophical Foundation of Peace" was the title of the paper I presented at the Peace Arts Seminar held on September 20, 1972. I proposed to answer the basic question "What foundation for the edifice of worldwide peace is there, acceptable to all men, no matter what their differences may be, so long as they are reasonable men of good will?" The answer was, of course, "natural law." I made my case by quoting from the Declaration of Independence, from the United Nations General Assembly's "Declaration of Human Rights", from Pope John XXIII's *Pacem in terris*, and from Aristotle's *Rhetoric*. Cicero and Sophocles, too, had their say. "As modern warfare becomes ever more total and devastating," I concluded, "peace becomes ever more a desperate imperative." It was a lengthy presentation, followed by a lively discussion. Given my philosophical background, with emphasis on ethics, I was in my element here.

Concerning me as a member of the Peace Arts Committee, Dean Mueller, in a memorandum dated January 25, 1973, wrote: "Dr. Renner has played a key role on the Peace Arts Committee, helping to establish the curriculum we now have for a major in this program. He has contributed many useful ideas and given our discussions a sense of perspective as we felt our way along unknown terrain. He has made many valuable contributions to the discussions of individual papers. His sense of organization and unflagging cooperation were but a small measure of the man."

By September 1972, the historian in me was beginning to stir. On the fifteenth, I wrote to Steve Sundborg in Rome, "Steve, the Society of Jesus is approaching the century mark of its presence in Alaska. By 1987, a solid history of our work here should be produced." My hope was that Steve would be able to trace down, in various archives in Rome, materials relating to Jesuit missionary activity in Alaska. He did not disappoint. John E. (Jake) Morton, studying theology in Toronto at the time, too, rendered me invaluable service along these same lines by inventorying, copying, and sending me materials in the Jesuit French-Canadian archives in Saint Jérôme, Quebec.

At this time, I was corresponding also with Father Wilfred P. Schoenberg, S.J., historian and head of the Jesuit Oregon Province Archives—then still housed in the Crosby Library at Gonzaga University—about "a possible history of the Society in Alaska", concluding, however, with, "I know I'm not the man to do it." Time was to prove otherwise.

On October 15, 1972, I addressed a lengthy letter to "Jesuits in Alaska—past and present". In that letter, I solicited "memoirs, recollections, and reflections" with a view to helping someone write "a history of the Jesuits in Alaska on the occasion of their centenary in Alaska, 1987". The letter was written also "to remind us that we, too, in our day, and in our way, were making history, and that someday a historiographer would be grateful for documentation concerning the period of our Alaskan passing". The focus was, admittedly, still only on a centenary history of Jesuits in Alaska. Father McMeel wrote a joint letter to the Alaskan Jesuits, giving in it "all encouragement" to me in this project and asking all the men to cooperate with me in any way they could.

Late in June 1973, I made the Better World Retreat in Portland. This was a rather novel, onetime experience. I let it count for my annual retreat. I then spent some weeks at Gonzaga, doing research in the Jesuit Oregon Province Archives, laying the groundwork for what I was calling "the King Island project". While in Spokane, I was interviewed by Father Clement J. McNaspy, S.J. To his lead-off question, "Louie, you've survived some time in Alaska; do you really like it?" I answered, "Yes! And, during my time in Alaska, I've survived two bishops, two provincials, and two religious superiors; and, I might add, two university presidents and two deans."

In the Bellarmine student chapel, on August 18, 1973, I offered a Mass of thanksgiving for Dad and Mom, who were celebrating their golden wedding anniversary that year. It was a grand, joyous affair for all my immediate family and for many relatives and friends. Betty Creedican was there to play the organ. I offered Masses of thanksgiving for Dad and Mom again in 1983 and 1988, the years they celebrated their sixtieth and sixty-fifth wedding anniversaries. Those two Masses were offered in the McMillan home—the home of my sister, Julie, and her husband, Duncan McMillan—in the big front living room looking out on Horsehead Bay on Puget Sound. Again, in addition to members of my immediate family, there were many relatives and friends present. The Masses were offered on an improvised altar set up before the fireplace. They were less formal than the one in the Bellarmine student chapel had been; but they were, nonetheless, devotional and festive. Relaxed picnics followed both of them.

As the academic year 1973–1974 gradually unfolded, King Island loomed ever larger on my horizon.

Chapter 17

University of Alaska–Fairbanks: 1974–1975

During my novitiate days, I had already exchanged letters with Father Bellarmine Lafortune, S.J., missionary to the King Island Eskimos. As mentioned in the preceding chapter, I spent a week in Nome during August 1972, substituting for Father Poole as pastor of Saint Joseph's parish there. In the Nome rectory, I came upon a photocopy of Father Lafortune's house diary, entitled "History of the Mission of King Island". I read this with the greatest of interest and began thinking about possibly editing it for publication or writing a life of Father Lafortune.

"More than of any other country," Father Lafortune wrote in that diary, "it can be said of this place that 'one has to see it to know it.' No amount of writing or talking or picture-taking will ever give to people the real idea of this place." Those two sentences kept haunting me. I felt it imperative to make a trip to the island to get some "real idea" of the place before I undertook to write about Father Lafortune.

Preoccupied as I was with preparations for my prospective trip to King Island in June, the spring 1974 semester passed quickly. Father Poole gave me much valuable advice as I prepared for this major venture. His putting me in contact with Mike Saclamana, who accepted to have me make the trip with him and his family in his skin boat, took care

224

of my one most critical concern: It was by no means easy for a white man to find a place in a Native skin boat about to make the annual trip to King Island. Space was a problem. Another serious obstacle to overcome—or to be overlooked by the Natives—was the fact that the white man was just that, a white man and not an Eskimo. The trip was regarded as exclusively an Eskimo affair and jealously kept as such. However, when it was learned that I was planning to write the life of Father Lafortune and needed, therefore, to see first-hand the setting of his long apostolate to the King Island Eskimos, I was graciously welcomed by Mike Saclamana to join his party.

On May 22, 1974, via Kotzebue, I flew to Nome. That evening, after I had introduced myself to the KNOM volunteers and made myself at home in the parish rectory, a simple matter, I walked to King Island Village, about a mile east of Nome. There, down on the beach, I met Mike Saclamana for the first time. He was just in the process of oiling the wooden frame of his twenty-four-foot skin boat with walrus blubber. After we had chatted a little while, I asked him, "About when might we leave for King Island?" "In a few days", was his answer. He then told me to go up to his house to meet his wife, Marie, and the other women there. Marie, Barbara Kokuluk (Mike's mother-in-law), and other women, wives and mothers of crew members, were just putting the final stitches to the four split walrus hides needed to cover the frame of Mike's boat.

The next few days were foggy. Using his own version of the idiom, Mike told me, "We have to play it by the ear." Hopes were high that we would leave on the twenty-eighth. That evening, however, Mike phoned me, saying, "It will be some days yet; lots of ice over there." On the thirtieth, I visited Arthur Nagozruk Sr., the first schoolteacher on King

Island. On June 5 I noted in my diary, "At noon: overcast, cold wind, choppy." In the evening, Mike told me, "It all depends on the weather now. As soon as it clears up." After we had had some days of seventy-five degrees above, it was only thirty-four degrees and overcast on June 6. "Fog clouds, choppy sea, cold wind" greeted us on the seventh.

On the evening of the seventh, as I was in the King Island Hall watching the King Island Dancers perform, I was called out and asked to go to the hospital, where Peter Seeganna was dying. I got there just as he expired. I gave him conditional absolution and the last anointing. Now, of course, we could not leave before the funeral Mass and burial. June 9 was Trinity Sunday. The Rosary was prayed for Peter on Monday evening. The following day—a windy, rainy day—at 3:00 P.M., I concelebrated at the funeral Mass offered by Father Harold J. Greif, S.J., who had returned to Nome on June 3. Burial in the Nome cemetery followed the Mass.

For the next few days, Mike was away from Nome, out at Cape Woolley, to where he had trucked his two skin boats with crew. Frank Ellanna's and Edward Muktoyuk's boats, with crew and passengers, were already at Cape Woolley. In the early afternoon of June 15, Mike phoned to tell me that there was a possibility that the Coast Guard icebreaker, the *Burton Island*, might be able to take us out to King Island. At 11:00 that evening, he phoned again to tell me that we would go on Monday morning, the seventeenth.

My diary entry for Monday, June 17, 1974:

Up early. Shower. Mass. Breakfast. At 10:30 we leave on the *Burton Island* launch for the cutter [anchored some distance off shore]. Arrive at *Burton Island* at 10:45. Fill out liability forms. We are fifteen. Sea has whitecaps. At 2:30 we are off Sledge Island. Water looks too rough for skin boats! At about 3:15 I am called up by Captain Moore. Will try to bring men and boats out in *Burton Island* launch. Looks grim! I urge people to pray. We should be off Woolley at about 4:00 P.M. About 4:30 we hear an announcement that a helicopter would go in to tell people the plan. More optimistic. Sea still choppy at 5:00 P.M. Lots of sun. At 5:45 we have a fine stroganoff dinner. Now 7:00 P.M. Sea calmer. Helicopters are away, making contact. A Walt Disney movie shown for the kids. I must write to Captain Moore and crew and thank them for great kindness to us. New optimism. 7:40 announcement: "King Islanders shoving off. Four boats heavily loaded coming. Expected to arrive in ninety minutes." *Deo gratias!* Around 9:00, Mike's two boats come bucking along. Sea very rough. Some time later, Ed Muktoyuk comes along. Frank Ellanna still way out. Around 10:20 Ed Muktoyuk goes to tow Frank in. Frank's boat seems to be dead in the water. Shortly after Ed leaves, a dense fog rolls in. Looks bad. Now 10:45. Fog horn blowing. Elderly ladies show concern. Around 11:00 the two boats arrive. Wet. Too much water in boat. I've been chilly all evening. At midnight last boat coming on board. Breezy, dusky fog, very poor visibility. Many shivering as they come on board. I'm tired but relaxed and grateful. We should soon offer a Mass of thanksgiving. What the immediate plans here are, I don't know. Kids are tired. All were well fed. Boat rolling. It is now midnight.

The following day, I logged:

At 1:45 A.M. we are pounding and rolling and foghorning our way toward King Island. Fairly dark and cold. Yawning but can't doze off. Deck kind of hard. Moved into mess and dozed on floor during movie. Dozed in chair till 4:00. Still fog. At 4:30 word goes out to wake all, to be ready for arrival at King Island around 5:00. At 5:45 we circle King Island to see how close in we can get. At 7:00 A.M. we are on the lee side, fairly calm. Slit of silvery sun through fog. About 7:10 began unloading with Frank Ellanna's boat. Breakfast at 8:30. Mike's boats are going over the side about now, 8:30–9:00. Have had a fantastic appetite. Find it hard to get and stay warm. At 10:30 A.M. all safely on King Island. Sitting on lee side. Real calm on this side. Tired but relaxed. Boats are ferrying people and things around to village. 2:30: Now I realize a bit the exhausting labor involved in landing at the foot of the village in rough surf and in unloading and dragging boats out of the knee-deep, foaming surf. And then everything up the steep cliff. Everybody helps. With enough manpower, muscle, and well-timed "hooooo-UKE's", the umiaks ease their way up on the rocks.

After helping others move gear up to their respective houses, I moved my own up to the priest's house at the top of the village. It was now 5:45 P.M. It took me some time to make the place habitable and to get settled in. "Am so grateful for everything", I continued that day's diary entry. "So elated. Hope we stay a good ten days. Need a good meal. Snickers bars not enough." On my little Sterno stove, I boiled myself a thick soup. It was now 9:40 in the evening, not dark, but so cold that "my breath comes out a white cloud." I made my meal "a candlelight occasion." The warmth the two candles produced was more psychological than physical.

I was now more than ready for a good night's sleep. Fortunately, I found in the priest's quarters a big sleeping bag. On it in big black letters were printed the words B. HUBBARD ARCTIC EXPEDITION. It was a fortuitous find, for the sleeping bag I had brought with me would not have been adequate, given the raw, damp cold. Comfortably bedded down in the two sleeping bags, as I was, and with the sound of the surf at the foot of the village the only sound, I still had trouble falling asleep. I could still feel the boat rocking. The staccato of Iñupiaq Eskimo kept ringing in my ears. And I was overtired—and overeager to explore the village and the island. Nevertheless, I was fairly refreshed when I woke up around 8:00 on Wednesday morning, the nineteenth, to the sounds of the pounding surface and the screeching of thousands of birds of many kinds. The day began with "heavy seas, fog, some drizzle". However, I was soon exploring the village, chatting with people, and hiking to the top of the island, all the while exposing roll after roll of black-and-white film.

The big event for that Wednesday, for all the people and me, was, of course, a Mass of thanksgiving. We had all been too busy and tired the day of our arrival for this. In the afternoon, at 5:15, I rang the rusted, but still resonant, old church bell long and loud. To the young, the bell's call to Mass was a new sound. To the old, it had a familiar, nostalgic ring, one evoking memories of bygone village and church celebrations, of sad burials, of hunters lost out on fog-shrouded ice floes. Slowly, young and old made their way up through the maze of houses to the weather-beaten old church dominating the village below it. This was to be the first Mass on the island in fourteen years, and, in keeping with the wishes of the older people, it was to be offered in Latin, the way they remembered the last Masses they had attended on the island.

"In nomine Patris . . .", I began the Mass. Having no server, I was about to answer the prayers myself, when, out of the front pew, without hesitation and in perfect Latin, the proper response came. Ursula Ellanna had not forgotten. As I was unvesting, Mike Saclamana came forward to invite me to his place for a reindeer stew dinner. After that Mass in that cold church—so cold that I had trouble reading the missal through the clouds of my own condensing breath—his invitation was most welcome. Outside the church, fourteen-year-old Gilbert Taxac was waiting to ask me, "What kind of talk was

that?" "Latin", I told him. "Where do they talk *that?*" he wanted to know. By 1974 my Mass Latin had become somewhat rusty. Ursula told me I had made several mistakes. This I already knew.

Later that Wednesday evening, the weather turned still foggier and colder. The rusting oil stove in the priest's quarters had been standing there cold for more than a decade now. I did not give it a thought. Around nine o'clock, however, I heard a noise outside on the roof. Shortly afterward, Mike came in to tell me that he and others were concerned about my health in those cold quarters and that they hoped to get the stove going "to take off the chill". That night I wrote in my diary: "11:10: Mike and his crew got my oil stove fixed up and going great guns." The chill was off.

On Thursday and Friday, I did much exploring of the village and the island, to the frequent click of my camera. "My nose is getting sore from photography", I noted in my diary. By the time I left King Island, I had exposed over thirty rolls of film: color, black-and-white, and slide. Fortunately, all the exposures produced fine results. Early on, I assured the people that I would take no artifacts, that I would take only photos. One of the photos shows a murre's egg at the foot of the Christ the King statue standing on a ridge above the village. Murres invariably lay their eggs on little ledges on the steep cliffs ringing the island. When I told the people about that egg, they were amazed and could only assume that a murre had laid it there. There was a feather next to the egg. One of the boys volunteered that the egg got there "by a miracle".

Saturday the twenty-second dawned clear but frosty. Many murre eggs were gathered that day. Hiking across the top of the island, I saw, to my surprise, a white fox. He seemed rabid; he did not spook. I kept my distance. That Saturday evening, I again offered Mass in the church—as opposed to the little chapel attached to the priest's quarters. This Mass was in English, and, since it was attended mainly by children, I had them come close to the altar. On Sunday morning, beginning at 10:00, I again offered Mass in the church, and in English. All attended this Mass.

While we were still in Nome, King Islanders expressed to me their concern for the island's church and some of its fixtures. Of special concern to them was the solid ivory crucifix on the tabernacle door. It had been carved by one of the King Island men in one piece out of a walrus tusk over forty years earlier. After that Sunday Mass, unprompted, Mike brought me that crucifix with the words, "Here, I feel something like this should go to a person like you." As mentioned in an earlier chapter, I offered daily Mass before that crucifix in my apartment from 1974 to 1980. At a later date, someone in Nome asked that the crucifix be returned to Nome. I happily returned it.

After that Sunday Mass, Mike told me, "We were gonna leave today." That came as a surprise to me. The day was bright and sunny, but a very strong wind was blowing out of the northeast. Mike, eyeing for some time the heavy swell and choppy seas, decided to wait for better travel conditions. One boat did leave; another left but returned and waited for a while before leaving again. By this time, I had done about everything I felt I needed and wanted to do on the island and was ready to leave, though in no hurry to do so. I was now alone with the extended Saclamana family and was happily part of it. That Sunday afternoon, I joined them for a climb up to the statue and for a very pleasant, relaxing picnic near it. Bathed as it was with the light of a sun just then putting in its longest days of the year, and covered with a dense carpet of lush green vegetation brightened by a great variety of wildflowers in bloom, and with the skies overhead filled with the screeching and whirring of myriads of birds of all kinds, King Island—nature immediate, raw, and wild—was now fully alive. That June 23 picnic was anything but a Sunday afternoon picnic in the park. I ended that day on top of the island, shivering in the face of an unabated north wind and taking pictures of the setting sun, virtually a midnight sun. By around 1:45 the morning of Monday the twenty-fourth, after a postmidnight snack—and with a heart filled with gratitude for the previous day's blessings—I was happy to snuggle down in the two sleeping bags for what I thought might be my last sleep on King Island. Despite the roof-rattling wind, I was soon fast asleep.

Later that morning, at 8:20, I was up. In my diary, I noted: "Wind seems stronger than ever. Mighty gale blowing. Sea covered with whitecaps. Blue sky." In the afternoon, the wind blew the top off the stovepipe. But I did not let the wind keep me from further exploring the village. For some time, one of the semisubterranean men's houses held my attention. "Kind of spooky", I noted in my diary.

During my days on the island, I picked and pressed wildflower specimens. One of the last things I did, while still on the island, was to put all these into an old paperback book. Four of these specimens were happily welcomed by the curator of the herbarium at the University of Alaska–Fairbanks.

Tuesday, June 25, dawned "windy as ever". Shortly before noon, Mike dropped in for a lengthy, very pleasant visit. He said nothing about a possible departure time. We were playing everything "by the ear". It all depended on the weather now. I did some preliminary packing, just in case. At 5:30 P.M., I wrote: "Wind still real strong." By that time, I was "ready for Nome and home".

When I got up on Wednesday the twenty-sixth, I found the day cloudless, the sea much calmer. In a skin boat, the men went off to the back side of the island to gather eggs.

They came back with 828 by actual count. In the early afternoon, I found two cans of soup in my quarters. Some soul, kind and anonymous, sensed that I was getting low on food. The previous day, I was invited to wild-bird-and-macaroni soup. The people were more than good to me. My self-prepared meals consisted mainly of various kinds of dried soup mixes—enhanced with different kinds of seeds, flakes, and bouillon cubes—boiled on my little Sterno stove. The smell of glowing Sterno remained ever after one of my favorite smells, evoking memories of those cozy King Island meals eaten at all hours of day and night and by the warmth and light of burning candles.

At 1:40 P.M. that Wednesday, I wrote in my diary: "Beautiful corona around sun! Milky canopy covering almost whole sky. It's a silvery, shimmering sea. . . . It's a miracle the way so many crawl around these rocks and rickety stairs and houses without serious injury." We were truly fortunate and grateful to God that there were no accidents of any kind. At 2:30: "Willie Kokuluk just puffed in to tell me, 'Get ready to leave for Nome!'" I began final packing in a hurry. By 6:30 that evening, we were well under way in Mike's bigger boat, towing his smaller one. We were nineteen in the boat, loaded to the gunwales. Having a tailwind, we were comfortably warm. As we were leaving, I led the people in some prayers, thanking God for the good stay on the island and asking Him for a safe crossing.

As we motored steadily toward the mainland, the island began to lose its sharp contours, to flatten out, to become ever smaller, a sinking blue rock in the distance, before it disappeared altogether. When we were about three hours into our thirty-six-mile crossing, it began to drizzle. Under a sheet of plastic and a space blanket, we kept dry. By 10 P.M., after a pause to refuel, we had Cape Woolley well in sight. At 11:20,

I wrote: "We have been under way five hours and are paralleling the shoreline between Capes Douglas and Woolley. Beautiful orange sunset. An airplane just flew over. Very picturesque skyscape. Oh, for color film!" Never in my life did I wish more for color film. My last roll was long since exposed. Right at midnight, the motors fell silent. Shortly thereafter, we were all safely ashore. People that had made the crossing before us gave us a warm welcome—as did clouds of mosquitoes. From Ursula Ellanna, I received a piece of salmon and a cup of hot tea. By shortly after 3:00 A.M.—it was now Thursday morning, June 27—on the back of Mike's overloaded pickup truck, along with several others, I was rolling along on the Teller highway headed for Nome, where we arrived at 5:25. In the early afternoon, shortly before I boarded a Wien plane for the Nome-to-Fairbanks flight, Mike phoned me to say good-bye and added, "Welcome aboard anytime, Father!" In a mid-July letter to me, Father Poole wrote: "I was very pleased, Louie, with your visit up here, and just, in general, with the wonderful impression you made with everyone. It was a wonderful thing to run into when I came home. You are most welcome up this way anytime."

On April 27, 1949, I had written to Father Thomas P. Cunningham, S.J., on King Island at the time, about my possibly spending my regency period there, during the years 1951–1954, to learn the Eskimo language. Jesuit fathers Paul C. O'Connor and Bernard R. Hubbard both thought it an excellent idea. In higher Jesuit echelons, however, it was an idea whose time had not yet come. Frankly, in light of how my life unfolded subsequently, I am grateful to a kindly Providence for sending me to Seattle Prep for regency rather than to King Island. Now, finally, after that long week there in June 1974, King Island, an island that had been on the horizon of my dreams for over a quarter of a century, was to me a concrete reality. I now knew what Father Lafortune meant when, referring to King Island, he wrote in the King Island diary, "one has to see it to know it."

After my King Island sojourn and a few days in Fairbanks, I flew to Spokane to do research on King Island and Father Lafortune in the archives there. I then spent a short time in Tacoma visiting my family before returning to Fairbanks.

My trip to King Island resulted in two published articles: "The Eskimos Return to King Island" [1] and "Return to King Island". [2] Two other articles of mine appeared in print about this same time: "A Footnote to Stefansson's *The Friendly Arctic*" [3] and "Julius Jetté: Distinguished Scholar in Alaska". [4]

In early September 1974, when Guenther Matschke, my fellow German teacher at the University of Alaska–Fairbanks, asked me if I wanted to join him on a weekend sheep hunt in the Jarvis Creek area of the Alaska Range some one hundred miles south of Fairbanks, I thought to myself, "Well, why not? Why not one last outing before settling down in earnest to another year of teaching?" I was never a rifle hunter, but I was always fond of the out-of-doors; and, armed with a camera, I always found something to shoot. The time of year was ideal, early September, when Alaska's tundra, trees, and bushes are ablaze with all the colors of autumn. A trophy-size Dall ram was his hope. On the second day of our three-day hunt, we came across a number of legal-size rams, but a trophy-size alone would do. Such a ram eluded him. Nevertheless, we both enjoyed a very pleasant outing. With our cameras, we had a successful hunt. My

1. *Catholic Digest* 39, no. 5 (March 1975): 46–55.
2. *Alaska Magazine* 41, no. 7 (July 1975): 6–8.
3. *Alaska Journal* 4, no. 4 (Autumn 1974): 203–4.
4. *Alaska Journal* 5, no. 4 (Autumn 1975): 239–47.

written account of it, my first sheep hunt, appeared in *Selected Alaska Hunting & Fishing Tales* in 1976. It bore the title, "Stalking the Stalker".[5]

My second, and only other, sheep hunt—almost over before it began—was quite a different venture. During my forty years in Alaska, there was only one time when the cold came close to doing me in. It was not some extremely low winter temperature that threatened to chill me to death but hypothermia resulting from being soaked to the skin and exposed to high winds. The month was August, and it was while I was on another sheep hunt, in the very same area in which that first one took place.

On August 13, 1976, the day after that ill-fated venture, in a letter to my niece Kathleen Renner I wrote a somewhat detailed account of my ordeal by water and wind.

It was 2:37 in the morning. We were fourteen miles into the high country. Outside my dripping tent, fully dressed, standing in the semidarkness, was Richard Dykema. "We've got to get out of here as soon as possible. I've been watching that rock in the creek, and it's going under pretty fast. If we don't go soon, we'll never get across the river."

"Okay, I'll get dressed. Wait for me in your tent!"

"I'll wait for you right here." He didn't want me to roll over again. I did get dressed right away. In about twenty minutes, we were making our way toward the Jarvis. We forded the newly filled rivulets with no difficulty. The main channels of the Jarvis were running high and fast. I had gone in partway the day before, and was, frankly, somewhat anxious.

It was raining all the while and had been raining since the afternoon of the day before. I was pretty wet and on the cool

5. *Selected Alaska Hunting & Fishing Tales*, vol. 4 (Anchorage: Alaska Northwest Publishing Company, 1976).

side, so the fording of the river was not a cold experience. After we got across the main channels of the river, we both had that "We've-got-it-made!" feeling.

On down the side of the river we went, getting soaked again and again as we went through dripping brush. All of a sudden, our hearts and spirits sank. A little creek that we had crossed just the day before, a side creek to the Jarvis, so insignificant that we had forgotten about it, was now a raging torrent, worse than the main river itself. Up along its right bank we went, hoping to find a place where we could ford it. Rather desperate, yet cautious and cool-headed enough, we came to a spot where we thought we could safely cross it. In he went. When I thought he already had a solid footing on the far side, I went in after him, grabbing for his outstretched hand. Got it, moved in deeper, lost footing, and down we both went, rifle completely submerged, water over our shoulders. But we were across. My teeth were really beginning to chatter now. We moved fast to keep warm, keeping eyes peeled especially for bears.

When we got to the point on the river where the trail back to the highway takes off, Richard said, "I've got to dry out the rifle." I dreaded the thought of any stops. But it had to be done. Having read enough about hypothermia, I knew that I was already in the uncontrollable shivering stages of it. Starting a fire would have been most difficult in the wind and rain and with all the wood soggy. He gave me the rifle, since, to keep halfway warm, I needed and wanted a faster pace than he could keep with the rifle. I felt an urgency to keep going. As long as I did, I didn't feel overly chilly.

We were now about two-thirds of the way back to the road and close to what I considered an insignificant little creek. I looked forward to reaching it, knowing that once across it, we would be getting close to a dry car. Alas, even at some distance from the creek, Richard said, "Just listen to that!"

Bad sounds. The sight of the creek, swollen and swifter
than any of the waters we had crossed up to this point,
depressed me totally. Up along the right bank we went, looking for a crossing place. Brush along the creek was so dense
that we had to go higher up on the ridge above the creek.
The wind and rain were straight into our faces now. After a
short while, I knew I had to get out of this. I was again shivering, and no pace kept me warm enough. I told Richard we
just had to get down into the brush, where there were some
spruce trees, and get a fire started. Don't think I wasn't praying at this time.

As luck, or God's goodness, would have it, just at the place
where we hoped to make a fire, we found a spot narrow but
very deep and swift. On the opposite bank was an alder bush
leaning over our way. We went in. I held on to his left hand.
With his right he was able to grab the tip of the bush. I
moved in after him a bit more. He got a firm hold of the
bush and dragged me after him. We crawled out soaked but
relieved at the thought that the last hurdle was finally crossed.
We were both getting tired, after eight hours of steady going
in soaked clothes. Tired and hungry, we reached the car,
changed into dry clothes, turned the heat on to full, and
headed homeward.

We stopped at Delta Junction so that Richard could phone
Gisela and assure her that we were all right. In a café, we
had coffee and something hot to eat. At the table next to us
sat a state trooper and a Fish and Game Department officer.
We overheard talk such as "hunters still back in there", "people worried and calling", and "keeping an eye on things".
Helicopters were mentioned. The rain was still coming down,
and more was forecast. The rivers and creeks could only rise.

In that same letter to Kathleen—about to begin her sophomore year at Gonzaga University—I wrote,

Why do we go on such expeditions? In part, I suppose, because we are fools; in part, too, to get out into the peace of the wilds.... The weather could have been nice, too. Even on this trip, there were real high points of scenery and lazy moments at river's side, campfires, coffee, food, dozing in the sun. It's a gamble. Frequently on this outing all we could do was to tough it out. You get to see yourself in a new light. When I got home yesterday, after a shower and shave, I said a Mass of thanksgiving. There were times on that trip when things looked rather dire. Especially when the cold got to me, and I prayed. We made it, and I was only too thankful. I learned from certain mistakes I made. Mostly, I should have had woolen, rather than cotton, clothes. Wool, even when wet, insulates.

On May 7, 1975, Robert L. Whelan, S.J., bishop of Fairbanks, phoned me. Before we hung up, it was decided that I would accompany Sisters Marie Teresa Boulet, O.P., and Judy Tralnes, C.S.J.P., to Little Diomede Island, where they were to begin teaching catechism around the middle of June. Father Greif, regular visitor to the island, would be out of Alaska on business and spending time with his seriously ill brother. It seemed essential that a priest accompany the sisters, at least for a while. I was more than eager to make the trip. The island and its people had fascinated me ever since I first heard about them. Moreover, for me personally, this would be a "field trip", enabling me to do research related to my writing of the life of Father Lafortune during my upcoming year of sabbatical leave. Father Lafortune was the first to instruct the Little Diomeders in the Catholic Faith.

The two Diomede Islands, Big Diomede Island and Little Diomede Island, lie just below the Arctic Circle and are situated almost exactly in the middle of fifty-seven-mile-wide Bering Strait. For countless ages, they had been stepping-stones between Siberia and Alaska, between Asia and America. The distance between the two islands is a scant three miles. The international date line and the U.S.S.R.-U.S. boundary line, as of 1975, still ran midway between the two islands.

Little Diomede Island, an immense granite rock rising abruptly out of the icy blue-green waters of Bering Strait to a plateau 1,308 feet above sea level, is about two miles long and a bit over a mile wide. The flanks of the island are nearly perpendicular cliffs on all sides except for a section of the southwest side, where a massive rockslide has created a gentler slope. At the foot of this is the island's only landing place, a narrow, three-hundred-foot-long beach of wave-worn boulders. Even this area is covered by breakers in stormy weather. The southwest side of the island is the only habitable site, and it is here that the village of Ignaluk has stood since prehistoric times.

The mainland Eskimos call the Diomeders "the people of the open water", the "open water" being the ever-shifting leads in the ever-moving ice fields that choke up Bering Strait from October to July. The islanders consider themselves the *Iñupiat*, literally, "the genuine people". It was to further catechize these people that the two sisters and I were sent by Bishop Whelan to Little Diomede.

On Tuesday, June 10, Sister Marie Teresa and I flew from Fairbanks to Nome, where we met Sister Judy, coming from Tacoma, the following day. Immediately, KNOM radio sent out a "hotline message" to Diomede announcing our presence in Nome and our hopes of getting to the island at the first opportunity. The very next day, the twelfth, we were informed by telephone: "Boats leaving Diomede for Wales." Things were happening faster than we had expected. In a great hurry, we did some last-minute shopping and packing. A plane was chartered for us.

At 4:45 P.M., on Thursday the twelfth, in a Cessna Sky-wagon 207, we took off from sunny, windy Nome for the Eskimo village of Wales at the westernmost extremity of the North American continent. About forty-five minutes into the flight, as we approached Bering Strait, we came into some light fog but not enough to discourage our young pilot from taking us down to see seals basking by their breathing holes in the ice fields. "Watch him jump!" he yelled above the roar of the motor as we zoomed down toward a dozing seal. "There he goes! There's another one!" And again, down we dove to what seemed only a few yards above the whitish-green ice. While I enjoyed the excitement, my stomach seemed less eager for it. From the back of the cabin, I heard what seemed like hastily mumbled prayers. "Take 'er up!" I told him.

The fog then began to thicken noticeably. The pilot himself showed some anxiety. We were now flying below the fog cover, just barely above the rotten ice and along the coastline cliffs. "No Wales today", I thought to myself. Then the pilot took her up, up above the fog. "Back there in that fog bank is the landing strip", he yelled to me a bit later. I took his word for it, as I had seen nothing but dense, luminous fog.

We next made several wide circles; then, after several swoops down toward the landing strip, we made the final plunge through a momentary hole in the fog bank and scooted along the narrow runway between high mounds of snow. After we stopped, I said to the pilot, "You must know this landing strip very well, to dare to land under these conditions." "I fly it often; otherwise, I would never have come down. No way!" Immediately after we and our gear were out of the plane, he took off again, leaving us standing on the runway, quite alone and wondering, "Where do we go from here?"

Some minutes later, out of the silence and fog, came three snow machines towing sleds. Roy Okpealuk, one of the few

Catholics in Wales, introduced himself. (Wales, at the time, was a stronghold of the Seventh-Day Adventists, "the Saturday People", as the Natives referred to them.) We loaded our gear on the sleds and took our places behind the drivers of the machines, and then we were off. Those "Eskimo taxis" gave us quite a ride over the slushy, bumpy trail leading to the village of Wales. The village was still buried roof-deep by unusually late and heavy snows.

In Wales, we learned that the Diomede boats had already left for Diomede. We now had no idea how long we might be in Wales. We were wondering where we might spend the night when Pat Ongtowasruk, mayor of Wales, came along, introduced himself, and offered to let us sleep in the community hall. This was but the first of many kindnesses shown us by the people of Wales. Before the evening was over, we had accepted two different invitations to tea and turned down two. By 11:30, I was stretched out on the floor in the community hall in my sleeping bag—with no idea what the morrow might bring.

Early the next morning, Friday the thirteenth, around 8:10, while I was still in my sleeping bag, I heard heavy footsteps outside. A moment later, into the community hall strode two tall Diomeders. Strapped to their hips were long hunting knives. With their faces blackened by the glare of the sun and ice, and their heavy clothes blood-bespattered from walrus hunting on their way over, they looked rather ferocious. But then I recognized one as Pat Omiak, whom I had met in Nome several years earlier. The other one was Sam Soolook. I was glad to see them and quickly roused the sisters.

Soon we were packed. After breakfast with Roy and Helen Okpealuk, we made the trip on sleds towed by snow machines across the shore-fast ice out to the water's edge. Again, it was a bumpy, slushy ride, as the ice had puddles on it and was beginning to crack up. Tom Menadelook's skin boat, an open dory about thirty feet long made of walrus hide stretched over a wooden frame, was still hauled out on the ice. Around it lay about twenty sets of walrus tusks. Crew members had spent the night sleeping out. There was frost that night. My admiration for the hardiness of those Diomeders grew considerably.

We dragged Tom's boat to the edge of the ice, pushed it into the water, loaded tusks and gear in, then boarded. In the distance, some twenty-five miles out, lay Little Diomede Island, visible on a clear day but not this day. Bering Strait lay under a blanket of fog. With great care, compass readings were taken before the motor began to purr for the three-hour crossing to Diomede.

I picked myself a few inches of thwart (board) to sit on and, facing the stern, rested my back against the iron curve of a fifty-five-gallon oil drum. The sisters, wrapped around their Dramamine pills and bundled up in parkas, sat opposite me on the "grub box". Skin boat accommodations are simple. You sit on a board or on gear. You eat and drink what you brought along. When that tea that warmed you so nicely a short while ago wants out, they pass you a tin can if you are a man; if you are a woman, you take it to the bow while the men face the stern.

As soon as we were under way, the canvas spray hood was put up. This helps keep the wind and spray out when the seas are rough. Our crossing was bouncy but quite tolerable. While a skin boat is no luxury liner, it is ideally adapted to its purpose, being sturdy yet not rigid. Leaning against the oil drum, I could feel the boat bend and yield as it was pushed along through the heavy seas by the powerful outboard. When a skin boat hits an ice floe or a boulder, it merely bounces off. A puncture hole is readily patched with a piece of walrus hide.

The first two hours of our crossing were uneventful. Though I was dressed four-ply, the damp cold gradually seeped into my very bones. Hunched up against the oil drum, cramped and stiff, I tried to doze. Sister Judy had come well prepared for the trip. Sister Marie Teresa, too, seemed adequately insulated against the cold, outfitted, as she now was, with my heavy wool socks, a Diomeder's bunny boots, Pat's sealskin mitts, and a fur parka loaned her by Lena Sereadlook in Wales.

Just as the trip was beginning to get boring, we came into an ice field, with numerous walrus popping up around us. A few shots were fired but no kills. The excitement, along with the sun starting to break through the fog, warmed us. And by now, the Diomedes were well in sight. A sense of exhilaration came over us. Around 3:30 P.M., we pulled up to the shore-fast ice in front of Diomede Village. The whole village, it seemed, dogs included, came down to meet the boat. We hardly needed to introduce ourselves. The "hotline message" had announced our coming. We were warmly welcomed. This was surely due to the great and well-deserved popularity enjoyed on Diomede by Father Greif and the Little Sisters of Jesus. On my third day on the island, one of the boys, honest to be sure but no respecter of egos, called to me: "Wish you Father Greif!" "Why?" I asked. "Father Greif lot funner" [*sic*], he answered.

Since the Little Sisters were in Nome for the summer, the two catechists stayed in their house. The priest's quarters up in the church had been rented out to Department of Fish and Game personnel, so I spent my first night on Diomede on the floor in the back of the church. The next day, I was offered the use of a small nine-by-nine-by-seven-foot house. This house, still almost entirely buried in snow, had not been lived in for several years. With a snow shovel, I got it dug out. After clearing the place of what, according to my diary, was "a big mess", I set up a kerosene stove and began to thaw the place out. For several days and nights, the heat of the stove, melting the inch-thick crust of hoarfrost on the inside walls, turned the place into a Turkish steam bath. Slowly the frost began to disappear, leaving water on the floor a half inch deep. Rubber overshoes kept my feet dry. After much sopping up and wiping, I finally had the floor so clean that I was able to wash out some clothes in the soft frost-melt water that kept drowning the floor. The sisters found my make-do home laundry rather amusing; but to me, every drop of water was precious, since the only source of water was snow, carried in and melted on a stove burning limited, expensive kerosene. When, at length, I had the place more or less dried out, I became very fond of it despite its rather primitive furnishings: the kerosene stove, a Coleman lantern, a wooden bunk, a little table and chair, and the slop bucket, also known as the "honey bucket".

On our first Sunday on the island, June 15, we awoke to a violent wind driving snow flurries out of the south. Mass was held in the armory, as this was heated. After the Gospel, the sisters explained their proposed catechism program. This was to begin the following Wednesday morning. School had just ended the day of our arrival on the island, and we felt the children should have a few days of complete freedom.

Pack ice was still clogging up the water between the two islands when that Sunday's storm hit. I took my meals with the sisters. (To compensate them for sharing their meals with me, I helped with the grocery bill, helped with the dishes, provided clean snow to be melted for water, and emptied their slop bucket.) As we ate dinner that Sunday evening, we gazed through the big, west-facing window and watched, fascinated, as wind and wave broke up gigantic ice pans and swept massive chunks of ice northward into the Arctic Ocean.

Among the most pleasant memories of my stay on Little Diomede are the tasty meals shared with the sisters as we watched the ever-changing scenes right outside our window. There were the graceful gulls in flight; the hunters parading up from the boats carrying rifles and walrus tusks; and the women, sometimes with babies belted to their backs, bent over seal or walrus hides, trimming off slabs of blubber with their fan-shaped ulus, or hanging strips of meat on poles to dry. Occasionally, we could see the head of either a seal or a walrus suddenly pop up out of the water in front of us. A scant three miles across Bering Strait, Big Diomede presented a constantly changing face as sun and fog alternately illumined or shrouded it. Here we sat, a mile and a half from Siberian waters, where democratic freedom ended and Soviet Communism began. Before our eyes hung the Iron Curtain, invisible yet very real, that then divided two worlds. It had not always been so. Before 1917, there had been, for all practical purposes, no border between Russian Siberia and Alaska. With the international date line running between the two islands, when looking across to Big Diomede, we were looking into tomorrow.

Sometimes before, sometimes after, the evening meals, in the sisters' front room, we had Mass. Generally, some of the villagers, especially kids, attended these. Once, at the end of a presupper Mass, I spontaneously dismissed the "congregation" with, "The Mass is ended. Go in peace—*and let the sisters eat in peace!*" The little ones were relentless visitors at all hours of day and night and no matter what the weather. While the sisters did welcome them and turn their visits into informal catechism sessions, they did, nevertheless, also need some time to themselves.

Promptly enough, Wednesday rolled around, and with it, the first day of catechism. "Well, how did it go?" I asked the sisters that evening before supper. "Oh, Father!"—and, right away, I could tell things had not gone exactly as planned. We were near the Arctic Circle, near the border of the Land of the Midnight Sun. The longest days of the year were upon us. The kids did not differentiate between night and day. The parents were eager to have their children taught. The sisters were more than adequately prepared to do the teaching. Somehow, however, the small fry were unable to concentrate long enough to put together a decent Sign of the Cross, while the next-older age group could not stay awake. They had been "playing out", in Diomede jargon, till as late as 2:00 in the morning. Boys from seven to twelve had been out "birding", climbing among the rocks above the village trapping and netting birds for the soup kettle. Classes were switched to the afternoon. Successful efforts were made to bridge the generation and the cultural gaps. Before long, real catechizing was taking place. While the program never did turn into a model minor seminary program, it was, under the circumstances, thanks to the dedication the sisters brought to it, an adequate program.

During my three-week stay on the island, there was only one truly beautiful, warm, cloudless, windless day and several marginal ones. On those good days, I climbed to the top of the island and explored it from end to end. Often I looked across to Big Diomede and on into Siberia, snapping pictures as I went. A number of times, I visited the burial sites on the slope above the village. I visited the people in their homes.

Thanks to a kindly Providence, Fred Bruemmer, a writer and the foremost photographer of the Arctic regions, especially the Canadian ones, happened to be on Little Diomede the whole time I was there. We had many a lengthy conversation, ate meals together with the sisters, and became close friends. For years after, we remained faithful correspondents. His books, autographed to me by name, have ever since graced my bookshelves. On Little Diomede, I met also John Bockstoce, a recognized authority on the Arctic, especially on Arctic whaling. Knowing him and reading his books, too, enriched my life.

As the month of June was rapidly coming to a close, I began thinking more and more about when and how I might get back to the mainland, to Fairbanks. When traveling in that part of the world, where the unpredictable weather ultimately, and solely, determines goings and comings, one might as well leave his watch at home and simply take along a calendar. Systematic planning and to-the-minute scheduling are simply wasted effort.

From June 25 to July 2, I made an eight-day retreat. I noted in my diary that there were "many distractions". Nevertheless, I let it count for my annual retreat.

On the morning of July 2, at around 6:30, while I was still soundly asleep, suspecting nothing, I suddenly heard a banging on my door, then, "Boat for Wales in half an hour!" During the night, the weather had, somewhat suddenly, turned favorable for a crossing. In a great hurry, I packed, emptied the slop bucket, ran down to the boat landing, and, with my duffle bag, jumped into Tom Menadelook's skin boat. Fred was already on board. Almost exactly three hours later, we were in Wales. (The sisters left Little Diomede several weeks later.) The weather in Nome being unsuitable for flying, we spent the day and night in Wales. Preferring the quiet of my little pup tent to the inevitable noise in the community hall, I tented that night. By 10:58 A.M. the following day, we were airborne, headed for Nome. A short hour later, we were in

Nome, where we were fortunate enough to find seats on a flight scheduled to leave in the afternoon for Fairbanks. We arrived there in the later afternoon. After living on the rocks of Little Diomede between the waves and the birds for three weeks, I found Fairbanks, momentarily, a whole new world.

My trip to Little Diomede was written up in a published article: "Catechizing the Vikings of Bering Strait".[6]

6. *Eskimo*, 32nd year, n.s., no. 10 (Fall/Winter 1975–1976): 5–20.

Chapter 18

Final Years at the University of Alaska–Fairbanks: 1975–1979

What today is the University of Alaska–Fairbanks was founded, in 1917, as a land-grant college with the name of "Alaska Agricultural College and School of Mines". Over the decades, it went on to attain international status as a center for scientific research and study. Scholars from all over the world came to do research and get degrees at its institutes. It became renowned especially for its Geophysical Institute and Institute of Marine Science. While it took pride in its strength in the area of the sciences, it had an inferiority complex in regard to the area of the arts and humanities. Aware of its weakness in those areas, it struggled constantly to overcome it by introducing new courses and programs and strengthening old ones.

By the year 1974, I had been at the University of Alaska–Fairbanks for almost ten years and was, therefore, long since eligible for a year of sabbatical leave. Wanting to devote all my academic time to what I labeled my "King Island–Father Lafortune project", I applied for sabbatical leave for the academic year 1974–1975. However, I was then asked by Dr. Wolf Hollerbach, architect of the humanities program, to teach a two-hundred-level, three-credit humanities course entitled "Unity in the Arts". This would be a new course for me, a course offered by the university for the first time. I was expected to offer it, along with my routine German courses, during the spring semester of 1975. It was left to me to create the course as I saw fit. Although my general training as a Jesuit and my extensive exposure to the fine arts during my time as moderator of the Orphean Club and my years in Europe had given me a good general background for teaching the kind of course here in question, I felt, nevertheless, that I would need a considerable amount of time to create it to my satisfaction. I requested, therefore, to be assigned to teach only a half load of German courses during the fall semester of 1974, at half salary, leaving me time to create the new humanities course. My request was granted.

A posted flyer announced the course, in part, as follows:

While the course is not primarily a course in the history of art, you will, nevertheless, be confronted with the history of art. And while the course is not primarily a course in the philosophy of art (aesthetics), you will, nevertheless, be philosophizing about art and beauty. And while the course is not primarily a course in art appreciation, you will, nevertheless, it is hoped, come to an understanding of the role played by the arts in the life of man and to a gentleperson's appreciation of them.

Together with your teacher, Dr. Louis L. Renner, you will investigate the principles that underlie the various arts and integrate them into a meaningful, organic whole.

The method will be Socratic. All students will be expected to be active ingredients in the discussions.

Humanities 201 will apply the pedagogical principle of "exemplary teaching". That is, it will focus on certain works and periods of art and show how the principles of unity in the arts are applied in these specific cases, in such a way that a student will be able to apply these same principles to other works and periods.

That "Unity in the Arts" course was a new venture for students and teacher alike, pretty much created as we went along. About twenty-five signed up for it, almost double the number that had signed up for a similar course the previous year. They came from various backgrounds and with various academic interests and expectations. What students taking the course thought of it, I left to them to say. Their evaluations of it and its teacher as the course was nearing its end created the following chiaroscuro mosaic:

> The teacher is excellent both as a person and an instructor, but the course was worthless. An entire B.S. course. The better you can sit around and B.S., the better your grade.
>
> This course was much more interesting and informative than I had ever hoped. It should be taught every semester, with an emphasis on making it as interesting and helpful as it was this semester.
>
> An interesting, provocative course. Dr. Renner is excellently suited for teaching such a diverse subject.
>
> I like this type of course structure because it stimulates thinking rather than memorization. After all, that's what being a human is all about.
>
> I would recommend more reading, of a broader range of criticism, aesthetics, artists on art.
>
> I enjoyed the course, but I feel that if at all possible we should have more than one instructor for a more rounded look at the material presented.
>
> Amazed at instructor's knowledge.
>
> Hope to see the program expanded.
>
> I found this course to be absolutely fantastic. Dr. Renner is the perfect professor for this course. It is such an interesting and valuable class that it seems like it would be a perfect mandatory class for everyone.

Renner is a very good instructor. There are few of his intellect at this institution. The class could have been better if Renner had lectured more instead of allowing B.S. sessions. The very idea that someone thought there was unity in the arts prompted me to take the course. I like Renner's idea that there are objective standards in art.

I feel that this is one of the few classes in which individual feelings are freely expressed and the creative intelligence is put to work. *Thinking* is stimulated, and I have learned so much from the instructor and class members. I feel this class is necessary for a well-rounded education and is a very valuable class.

This course stimulated me to evaluate my attitudes and ideas about art, to formulate some philosophy and collate my knowledge, so I found it very interesting. The discussions were very vague and general because there were so many people who were not *thinking* about the subject.

Well, Dr. Renner is a fine man, but why encourage empty questions—"What is beauty?" People could go on for weeks. And too many Latin and German words on the board.

Being a biology student, I found myself rather lost in the beginning. My methods of thinking and participating in class weren't adjusted to this type of class. Later, however, I started to learn how to perceive the class and how to understand what was being dealt with. Now I find that I am enjoying the class and mourn my lack of artistic background. I do feel that my background has been broadened by the class and that my interest in the arts has been spurred.

I enjoyed the course very much. But I wonder if, since I am an artist, and think about art constantly, whether the nonart people, the people in the sciences, got as much out of it. A frequent comment I heard from fellow students is that the class was, at times, boring. I disagree. The class required the student to think and to exercise his mind. In this class, I felt more thinking was taking place.

I was asked to teach the course again the following year but declined. I wanted to take a sabbatical in order to get on with my King Island–Father Lafortune project. Sabbatical leave, at two-thirds of full salary, was granted me, as well as to six others out of over two dozen applicants, for the academic year 1975–1976. It is interesting to reflect that, while granting so few sabbatical leaves, given so many applicants, a state university should have seen fit to grant one to a Jesuit priest proposing to write the life of a Jesuit missionary priest.

On July 3, 1975, the day I returned to Fairbanks after my stay on Little Diomede Island, the *Fairbanks Daily News-Miner* carried an article announcing the promotions of forty-eight University of Alaska faculty members. My name was among those promoted to a full professorship, effective as of July 1, 1975.

My promotion did not escape the attention of my one-time dean—and onetime altar boy, during the years 1958–1960. On letterhead printed with "From the Desk of C. J. Keim", I read a truly heartwarming note, dated July 3, 1975, and addressed to "Dr. Louis Renner, Professor of German". The handwritten note read: "Father, I was very pleased to read about your promotion to professor. This is a well-earned advancement, and when I read about it I recalled at once how one day when you were saying Mass in Eielson 218, and I was serving, you said, 'I'm going to go on to school. One day I'd like to teach here.' Congratulations! Chuck Keim."

After my sojourn on Little Diomede, I spent some time doing research in the archives at Gonzaga, then some time with my family in Tacoma. During some of my years at the university, when visiting my family in Tacoma in the summer, I—in the company of Dad and Mom, and Julie and her girls, Kristin and Angie—would spend a few days at the Iron Springs Resort on the Washington coast. There we took lengthy walks along the beach, swam in the motel pool, played card games in the evening, and, with relish, ate to full satisfaction. After one sumptuous evening meal during our 1975 ocean stay, I sat back with the remark, "You know what? I now really feel like a full professor." Admittedly, this was not a great play on words, but it did make Dad and Mom feel good, and that was the intent. I always made known to them my little accomplishments, triumphs, and honors received. It enabled them to answer meaningfully, and with a certain degree of parental pride, questions put to them such as "How is Father Louie in Alaska doing?" or "What do you hear from your son in Alaska?"

In December 1975, during my sabbatical leave, I was in Tacoma. While there, in addition to visiting my family, I celebrated, in Holy Cross Church, on the twenty-seventh, the nuptial Mass at which my niece Cheryl Renner and Brian J. Partridge were married. (I was to officiate, subsequently, at the weddings of three more close relatives. On August 31, 1985, in Saint Joseph's Church in Seattle, I offered the Mass at which my niece Kathleen Renner married Reimer Douglas; on April 16, 1988, in Shrine of Saint Joseph Church in Saint Louis, Missouri, the one at which my nephew Michael (Mike) Renner married Karen Offner; and, on February 11, 1989, in Saint Gabriel's Church in Port Orchard, Washington, the one at which my nephew Mark Renner married Shelley Shellgren. While in Saint Louis, I had, naturally, to see the city from the top of the Gateway Arch.)

On March 14, 1976, I was again in the Alaskan Arctic, at Barrow, to offer the Sunday Mass. (By then, I had already

seen Barrow, as a tourist, in mid-May 1968.) I was to fly to
Barrow a few more times for Sunday Mass. Later that month,
in Anchorage, I attended the meeting of the Alaska Anthro-
pological Society, of which I was, by now, a member. It was
my working so closely with Native students at the university and associating so closely with Father Loyens and Gisela
Dykema, both professional anthropologists, that prompted me
to join that society. I was, at this time, also a member of the
Alaska Historical Society. During most of April and the first
half of May 1976, I was in Germany. That was my last trip
abroad.

While doing research for the Father Lafortune biography,
I also pieced together the story of the Alaska mission's first
airplane, the *Marquette Missionary*, and the story of the freezing to death of Father Frederick Ruppert, S.J. Those efforts
resulted in the publication of "The Beginnings of Missionary Aviation in the Arctic: The '*Marquette Missionary*'",[1] and
of "Fr. Frederick Ruppert, SJ: Martyr of Charity".[2]

On August 3, 1976, I signed a contract to teach a full load
of German during the academic year 1976–1977. That same
day, referring to my Lafortune-related research, I wrote to
Father Clifford A. Carroll, S.J., Oregon Province archivist:
"Surely no 'writer' has had more generous, prompt, kindly
support for his project than I have had for mine. You and
the archivist at Saint-Jérôme, Canada, Father Joseph Cos-
sette, S.J., could hardly be more cooperative. I am fortunate
indeed."

I was indeed blessed, and grateful, to have the full and
enthusiastic support of those two competent archivists. And
I was likewise singularly blessed to have also the expertise of

1. *Eskimo*, 33rd year, n.s., no. 11 (Spring–Summer 1976): 8–19.
2. *Eskimo*, 34th year, n.s., no. 14 (Fall–Winter 1977–1978): 11–22.

Dorothy Jean Ray, anthropologist, ethnohistorian, and noted authority on matters relating to the Seward Peninsula area, making her home, with her husband, Verne Ray, in Port Townsend, Washington. The title page of my life of Father Lafortune lists me as author but immediately adds, "In collaboration with Dorothy Jean Ray". It was a kindly Providence that first put me in touch with her. Not being able to find a copy of her book *Artists of the Tundra and the Sea*, I wrote to her personally on April 15, 1975. She sent me her last copy. With that began a correspondence, a collaboration, and a cherished friendship that was to last over three decades. As of the early half of the year 2006, we were still carrying on a steady correspondence.

By the end of the summer 1976, I had the manuscript of my life of Father Lafortune finished to the point where I thought it ready to be submitted to some editor or publisher. Very wisely, in retrospect, I sent it to Dorothy Jean. She judged it to be "very valuable material, history at its purest", a publishable work, but one that still needed a considerable amount of editorial attention. This she gave it—for a fee far below one she could very legitimately have charged. She lavished no less care on it than she did on her own works.

"For some time already," I began my October 9, 1976, letter to Dorothy Jean, "my fingers have been hovering over the keys. How to begin this, what I feel will be one of the most important letters of my letter-writing days?" I was about to respond to her letter to me written six days previously. In that letter, she had informed me that she was willing to be recognized as my collaborator and as one who had done extensive editing of my text. In her November 14 letter to me, she wrote, "I had hoped to be able to take care of questions, etc., by mail, but there are so many things to discuss that it would be best if you could come here for a day or

two while on your holidays. You are more than welcome to
stay overnight here—plenty of room, and tons of potatoes,
beets, and carrots." (It is an understatement to describe Dorothy Jean Ray as an "avid gardener".)

Though I was again back to teaching German full time,
I had Christmas vacation to look forward to. I spent the
twenty-second and part of the twenty-third of December in
Port Townsend going over my manuscript in depth with Dorothy Jean. I had written the Lafortune story primarily along
chronological lines. She improved it greatly by rearranging
the material somewhat more along topical lines, without, at
the same time, doing violence to the basic chronological order.
After my stay in Port Townsend, we were able to attend to
all further details readily by mail. By March 1977, the manuscript was ready for a final typing. By early May, it had been
submitted to the University of Washington Press in Seattle.
On October 31, I wrote to Dorothy Jean, "No word from
Naomi [Naomi B. Pascal, editor at UW Press] yet. I wonder if I will have the courage to open the letter when it
arrives." By the beginning of December, I had word from the
UW Press. The word was negative. They did not consider the
life of a Catholic missionary priest something in keeping with
their press policy.

About this time, Dr. Robert A. Frederick, executive director of the Alaska Historical Commission, hearing that I had
a manuscript ready for publication, contacted me. On December 13, 1977, I mailed him a copy of the Father Lafortune
manuscript. His reaction was positive; but, understandably, the
decision to publish or not to publish did not rest with him
alone. In his preface to the book, he was to write: "Funding
for publication was provided through the Gifts-in-Matching
Program of the National Endowment for the Humanities
administered by the Alaska Humanities Forum, a state-based

activity of the NEH. The Alaska Society of Jesus and the Alaska Historical Commission contributed equally to the Endowment's matched gift. Finally, the Alaska Historical Society acted as fiscal agent to Binford & Mort, Publishers." Dr. Frederick went on to add, "It is anticipated that Renner's *Pioneer Missionary to the Bering Strait Eskimos: Bellarmine Lafortune, S.J.*, will be the first in a series on the theme *Alaska's History and the Humanities*".

As might be expected, the various parties involved naturally wanted assurance that they were backing a book that would be worthy of their support and serve well as the first of the anticipated series. The final decision to accept, or not accept, for publication the Lafortune manuscript rested with Gary H. Holthaus, executive director of the Alaska Humanities Forum. He submitted the manuscript to different readers. The readers supported publication but recommended further editing of the manuscript. The final professional editing was entrusted to George W. Sundborg Sr. (see chapter 10), onetime editor of the Juneau paper and author of several books. Meanwhile, I continued to teach.

* * *

He referred to me as "my professor". He was a member of my elementary German class during the academic year 1975–1976, when I was on sabbatical leave and was teaching half time. Although he himself did not ice skate, during the winter of that academic year, when the whole class went skating on the university ice rink, he enjoyed standing on the sidelines, watching his professor and his classmates skate to the strains of Strauss waltzes and German songs, stopping for hot chocolate and cookies only while records were being changed. He thought it great that his professor should be out there skating with his students. He was from India, a Hindu, and belonged to a high caste. He did not know what exactly to make of me, a Roman Catholic Jesuit priest, but something about me intrigued him and made him admire me. He was a doctor of medicine, specializing in ophthalmology and dermatology. Our relationship, which began as one of student to teacher, went on to become also one of doctor to patient, then also one of friend to friend, and one of host to guest. A number of Sunday afternoons, he entertained fellow students and me in his apartment. His name was a long one: Sharadkumar Dicksheet.

One day, Dr. Dicksheet noticed that my eyelids were inflamed. The following day, after class, he himself gave me the medicine that solved the problem. Soon thereafter, I saw him about my need for a new pair of glasses. An eye examination called for bifocals. He gave me the prescription, then phoned the optometrist on the first floor of the building in which both had their offices: "I'm sending my professor down for a new pair of glasses." Then he added, with emphasis, "And it won't cost him anything!" He hung up, turned to me, and said, "I do him favors, too."

As an afterthought to that eye examination, I described an incident to him, one that had befallen me one day in Oberammergau. When I got through, he just looked at his office nurse and said, "There you have it—from an educated man, a textbook description of a migraine headache." So it was a migraine headache, the first of many that were to afflict me at irregular intervals ever thereafter—without, however, seriously incapacitating me.

On the Fairbanks Memorial Hospital medical report, dated August 5, 1976, we find: "Patient: Renner, Louis L. Surgeon: Dr. Dicksheet. Clinical Data: Growth, right cheek, growing two years. Diagnosis: Basal cell, carcinoma, cheek."

The growth in question was removed on August 3 under local anesthetic in Dr. Dicksheet's in-office operating room. He absorbed the noninsured cost—his gift to me. On August 21, I noted on the bottom of the medical report: "All healed nicely. No cause for anxiety, nor is there any—at least on my part. In any case: *Fiat voluntas Dei!* At this time nobody but the doctor and staff and I know about this being carcinoma." While there was no reason for making a secret of this medical footnote to my life, it remained such until the noting of it here in this autobiography.

While my Lafortune project was far from finished at the time, the academic year 1976–1977 found me back teaching German full time, on four different levels. As that academic year wore on, I began to yearn more and more for outdoor activity. On March 8, 1977, I wrote to Dorothy Jean Ray, "It'll be a pleasure to turn over that first spadeful of dirt in the Dykemas' potato patch, a good break from the word and pen. I have several articles warming up."

During the summers of the better part of the 1970s, I spent longer periods of time in the Jesuit Oregon Province Archives doing research on a variety of subjects. Among the articles that "warmed up" and were published are the following: "The Jesuits and the Yupik Eskimo Language of Southwestern Alaska",[3] "Three Grand Alaskans",[4] "Father Francis M. Monroe, S.J.: 'The Alaskan Hercules', and Saint Francis Xavier Mission of Eagle",[5] "A Chronicle: The Catholic Church on the Seward Peninsula",[6] "Farming at Holy Cross Mission",[7] and "Fr. Aloysius Robaut, S.J.: Pioneer Missionary in Alaska".[8]

3. *Alaska Journal* 8, no. 1 (Winter 1978): 70–81.
4. *Alaska Magazine* 44, no. 12 (December 1978): 96.
5. *Alaska Magazine* 45, no. 4 (April 1979): A18–25.
6. Pt. 1, *Nome Nugget*, August 3, 1979, 5; pt. 2, ibid., August 7, 1979, 4–5.
7. *Alaska Journal* 9, no. 1 (Winter 1979): 32–37.
8. *Eskimo*, 37th year, n.s., no. 20 (Fall–Winter 1980–1981), 5–16.

As noted much earlier, my family moved to Tacoma, Washington, from North Dakota in July 1937. Almost exactly forty years later, I was to see the state of my birth again for the last time. On June 19, 1977, Dad and Mom, and Julie and her little girls, Kristin and Angie, arrived in Spokane from Tacoma. There, around noon, I joined them for the drive to North Dakota. After several nights in motels along the way, we arrived in Mandan. There, Julie, the girls, and I made the Seven Seas Motel our home base. Dad and Mom stayed with Aunt Anna Gustin. Out of Mandan, we visited the state capitol in Bismarck, the city of my birth. We took nostalgic drives to Saint Anthony, Fallon, and Flasher. In the Flasher cemetery, we shed a few tears at the grave of little Delores Marie, mentioned in chapter 1. Toward the end of our stay, there was a rather large reunion, with many relatives present. On the return trip west, we stopped off to visit the picturesque Badlands in western North Dakota. Leaving the others to continue their trip home, I stayed behind at the Saint Ignatius mission in Montana, to make my annual eight-day retreat. During that retreat, I spent long hours in the old mission church praying and admiring the newly restored frescoes. I also took some wilderness hikes in the Mission Range. After my retreat, Father Joseph L. Obersinner, S.J. (a classmate of mine), and I drove to Spokane. By sometime after mid-July, I was back in Fairbanks. On July 27, 1977, I signed a contract for the academic year 1977–1978. My full salary for the period was $34,663.20. It was those added twenty cents that really put the smile on my face.

On February 7, 1977, my department head as of the previous year, Korean-born Dr. John H. Koo, had been handed a petition that read: "The undersigned request a beginning course in Latin (three credits) to be offered for fall semester 1977 and, with his agreement, to be taught by Dr. Louis

Renner. The following people agree to enroll in this proposed course if it is offered." Twenty-four signed the petition. It went on to people in higher administration, who proved to be wholly in support of a Latin program. Larry J. Scoles, one of my German students, had taken it upon himself to initiate the petition.

Having taught Latin at Seattle Prep for three years, I did not think teaching beginning Latin at the university would overload me. Without hesitation, I agreed to teach what was labeled Latin 393, a two-credit course, during the academic year 1977–1978. This was the first time in fifteen years that Latin was offered at the university. On August 12, 1977, I wrote to Dorothy Jean, "These days I'm busy cramming Latin. It's coming back without much difficulty. I look forward to teaching it again." By September 8, I was able to write to Father Cliff Carroll, "School's under way here; forty-nine in my Latin class!" A few dropped out; but, even during the spring semester, most were still with the program, so much so that they wanted to move on into second-year Latin. Saddled with a full load of German, as I was, I was unable to teach second-year Latin. Another teacher was found. I did, for a time, however, offer an evening class for advanced Latin students. For some years, the Latin program was carried on by Christa Hollerbach.

As mentioned already in an earlier chapter, in 1972, I solicited "memoirs, recollections, and reflections" from fellow Alaskan Jesuits with a view to helping someone write a history of the Jesuits in Alaska on the occasion of their century of service there, 1887–1987. By 1978, I had come to the conclusion that what was really needed was some kind of a general, comprehensive history of the Catholic Church in Alaska. Accordingly, on February 6, 1978, I addressed a letter, accompanied by a form to be filled out, to a considerable number of priests—diocesan and religious—as well as to some sisters and brothers who were serving, or who had served, in Alaska. The letter read in part:

> The work in question here is to include biographical sketches of priests, sisters, and brothers who have served in Alaska, as well as brief histories of all the establishments the Church has had in Alaska. I appeal to you, the living, priests, sisters, and brothers, to help me. Regarding your own life and service of the Church in Alaska, you are the best and ultimate authorities. I look to you for an exact, absolutely correct, account of your role in the Church's apostolic mission in Alaska. You are receiving here a form to be filled out or to be used as a guideline in providing me with the *minimum* essential information. You are encouraged to add anything you consider significant. If in doubt, add it. Use additional pages, if necessary. Above all, be exact. Your promptness will be greatly appreciated.

In addition to calling for basic biographical data, the form asked recipients to "indicate in chronological order all the places and dates and capacities of service in Alaska." It went on, "Please also indicate anything worthy of special note, e.g.: the founding or building by you of parishes, churches, stations, schools, hospitals, radio stations, social programs, and the like." It sought information about service on boards and committees—local, diocesan, and national—and about service in the military and National Guard. It asked, "Were/ are you a pilot, a licensed ham radio operator (if so, call number _____), or a postmaster?" People were asked to date and sign the form. The fairly generous response to this appeal proved to be of major help to me when I eventually put together *Alaskana Catholica*.

From June 10 to the end of July 1978, I was in Spokane doing more research in the Jesuit Oregon Province Archives.

Among other researching, I gathered a good deal of original material for an article on the "Stickdance". For various reasons, among them the sensitivity of the subject at the time, I put off further work on that subject. It was a good thing I did so as will be seen in a later chapter.

That summer, in addition to doing my own research, I again helped Sister Carol Louise Hiller, O.P., with hers, as I had done four years previously, when she spent several weeks doing Gleeson-related research in the Jesuit Oregon Province Archives. Her book *Gleeson, the Last Vicar Apostolic of All of Alaska: The First Bishop of Fairbanks*, with a foreword by me, was published in 2004. With Father James C. Spils, S.J., doing the driving, she and I made a trip to Lewiston, Idaho, to see where Bishop Gleeson had served when he was still Father Gleeson. In her book, in the acknowledgments, Sister wrote: "For Father [Clifford A.] Carroll's warm welcome I am indebted to Father Louis L. Renner, S.J., who introduced me there as well as to numerous other people and places. In addition to introductions, Father Renner has given direction, help with research, encouragement, and multiple readings of the manuscript. He has exhibited great patience. Many times he has introduced laughter in place of imminent tears."

By early August 1978, after some time with my family in Tacoma, I was back in Fairbanks getting ready for the academic year 1978–1979. That same month, in addition to doing some successful dipnetting, as a member of the Dykema party, for sockeye and silver salmon in the Copper River below Chitina, I attended a conference in Anchorage on the theme "The Church in Alaska's Past". Various denominations participated. Papers read at the conference were subsequently published. I read one entitled "Catholic Pioneer Missionary Activity in Alaska and Archival Resources Relevant Thereto".

Concerning that conference and my role in it, I wrote to Dorothy Jean on August 28,

> Believe me, reading this was an ordeal for me. I find it very difficult to get up before a group—the first time, that is. After that initial appearance, I spoke up several times with no trouble. Anyway, it is now behind me. I was told it was a fine paper. I feel it did make a genuine contribution to the conference. I received word about my role in it only about a week before the conference began. But, all in all, it was as worthwhile as it was exhausting. On Friday we began at 8:00 A.M. and ended at 10:00 P.M.! I'm still reeling a bit. And this morning we begin at the university.

Ending that letter on a less serious note, I wrote, "May your peat and pen be equally productive! And may your compositions prosper no less than your compost! A beautiful vocation, being a writer and a gardener! I garden at the Dykemas and love it." By this time, Dorothy Jean, along with her husband, Verne, and I were kidding-cousin close friends. At the same time, I had the highest esteem for her both as a professional scholar and as a person. She, in turn, ending a May 3, 1977, letter to me, wrote, "In the inscription to you in my new book, the word 'gratitude' refers only to the fact that it is nice that you are on this earth."

As the fall 1978 semester drew to a close, I wrote to Dorothy Jean: "Just now I hear 'thirty-below chill factor'. It's been snowing since yesterday. But with all the calories the *Fraus* and *Fräuleins* in my German classes are giving me for Christmas, I should withstand much colder temperatures. They're too good to me! The mood for Christmas is right. And today was the last class day, so there is time to get into it. How quickly the semester passed! I must be getting old. It was a good semester." As I wrote that, I was not aware that I was to have only three more semesters at the university.

The first indication that my years at the university might soon be coming to an end appears in the form of a note on my calendar for January 13, 1979: "Frank raised the question of my taking over the Alaskan Shepherd [a direct-mail fundraising program]." For March 4, 1979, the note read, "Long talk with Bishop Whelan about my taking over Alaskan Shepherd." For March 9, "Spoke on phone with Fallert about the Alaskan Shepherd." For March 23, "Long talk with Anable about taking over Alaskan Shepherd."

At this time, Father Francis E. (Frank) Mueller was my local superior; Father Francis J. (Frank) Fallert, my general superior; and Father Edmund A. (Ed) Anable, head of the Alaskan Shepherd program. By 1979, Father Anable had been in charge of the program for many years. Born in 1903 and being, therefore, well along in years, he told Bishop Whelan, "Look, Bishop, I'm not getting any younger. We'd better think about a replacement for me." Father Mueller suggested me, urging that I knew Alaska and had demonstrated some writing ability. Bishop Whelan, too, saw me as a logical choice to take over the program. I myself—though I was perfectly content with my university work and had found my years there up to that point "truly happy, satisfying years"—having a good idea of what the job entailed, declared myself totally willing to take it on, "confident", as I told Father Anable, "that the same kindly Providence that had guided my life so happily up to then would continue to so guide it along this new path." Father Fallert, likewise, saw the logic of it all but made it known that he wanted me to put in yet one final year at the university. And thus it was agreed to the satisfaction of all concerned.

The spring 1979 semester was more or less a routine one. From May 22 to July 15, I was again at Gonzaga, doing research in the archives. During the second week of July, I made my annual retreat. On the fifteenth, I flew to Tacoma to spend time with my family. I was with Len and family at the ocean from the twenty-second to the twenty-fourth. By the twenty-seventh, I was back in Fairbanks. Three days later, I signed my final contract with the university, that for the academic year 1979–1980. My full salary for the period was $36,363.60. And on the following day, the thirty-first, the feast of Saint Ignatius, I took the four solemn vows that constituted me a solemnly professed father of the Society of Jesus (as recorded already in chapter 13). I was now, in every way, ready to experience all the excitement that the publication of *Pioneer Missionary* was to bring with it, as well as to embark upon the academic year that would bring to a close my career as a faculty member at the University of Alaska–Fairbanks.

But first a word regarding those solemn vows. By the 1970s, admittance to solemn profession by the taking of the four solemn vows was no longer based almost exclusively on whether or not one had passed the *ad gradum* exam. Other criteria were now taken into consideration. Among them: "a suitable knowledge of theology", "the overall religious and apostolic ability of a man", "proof of the candidate's high level of learning", "noteworthy talent in governing or preaching or writing", "proficiency in literature or the sciences", "reception of higher academic degrees", and "teaching successfully at an advanced level". On the basis of these criteria, Father Loyens—now the father provincial of the Oregon Province— invited me to consider requesting to be admitted to solemn profession. After considering and praying over the matter, I formally requested to be considered for solemn profession. He and his consultors looked favorably upon my request and recommended to Father General that my request for solemn profession be granted. Happily, he granted it.

August 1979 began for me with a blueberry-picking outing with the Dykemas and ended with a successful salmon dipnetting outing with them. Out of the Copper River, below Chitina, we dipnetted three limits (that is, we each caught the maximum allowed amount)—over three dozen silvers and sockeyes. On the tenth and eleventh, Father Frank Mueller and I hiked two-thirds of the Pinnell Trail, a wilderness trail northeast of Fairbanks. Assuming that the last third of the trail would be as tedious and boring as the first two-thirds had been, we decided to skip it.

Classes began on September 6. While *Pioneer Missionary*–related activities were a major distraction during that fall 1979 semester, teaching German was again what the semester was all about. The semester went by very quickly. However, before it was over, word was out that I was in my last academic year at the university. As already mentioned, the first of the Lafortune books arrived on October 3.

Wednesday, October 3, 1979 was a red-letter day for me. On that day, I noted on my calendar, "Ten copies of Lafortune arrived." Finally, the concrete results of my sabbatical leave, my Lafortune project, lay on my desk. Especially heartwarming was the congratulations received from my students. Some of them bought the book—leading me to ask myself, "Hey, how can you flunk someone who bought your book?"

"Wow, it's really kind of heady", I began my October 29, 1979, letter to Dorothy Jean,

> seeing the book for the first time (October 3), having the bishop phone me his high praise and order twenty-five copies for friends and benefactors, being interviewed and photographed twice in two days last week, being asked (just now!)

by one of the local radio stations to be on their talk show (I declined, as I am a lousy speaker), being scheduled for another interview and photo session next week, and receiving letters from various readers high in their praise of the book. And then your letter! Frankly, it all makes me feel rather humble, since I know full well that what we have here is the result of a dedicated team effort. Nobody will ever really know just how much the book is indebted to you.

On November 4, I wrote to Dad and Mom:

While details are still fresh in my tired mind, let me tell you a bit about the autograph party that took place yesterday afternoon at Alaska House. It was a roaring success, or failure, depending upon how you look at it. The Parrs (Charlie and I taught German together for a number of years) had ordered fifty copies of the book, thinking that that number would be more than enough. Well, halfway through the party, these were all gone. I still had thirteen in my apartment, which I had Father Mueller pick up. They were soon gone. Four at the bishop's, soon gone. Twenty-eight more copies were paid for before the 1:00–5:00 party was over. Success or failure? Let's call it a success.

At times I really had to concentrate as I autographed copies of the book, with people talking and asking me questions. I didn't want to mess up somebody's $12.50 book. Am aware of only one mess-up. I wrote 1971. But a little loop and the lost eight years were found.

A good number of book buyers were former and present students. The chancellor of the university was there. Former Nome people, acquaintances of Father Lafortune, wildlife people, Fairbanks friends were there. The timing seems to have been good. People were buying Christmas presents.

A real highlight for me was the King Island lady who, with deep emotion, pointed out a picture of her father in the book and thanked me for telling the story of her people. I thanked HER! Without the King Islanders, we'd have quite a different book, if a book at all.

One of my former students brought a loaf of gift-wrapped bread. It was, I admit it, an exciting, thrilling afternoon. This coming week, I will be interviewed on the university radio station and for *Now in the North*. After that, things should quiet down, I hope—not!

On November 6, Karen McPherson interviewed me for Alaska Public Radio. On November 27, after having listened to the taped interview, Dorothy Jean wrote me: "I hope that you will get the tape transcribed, because some of your comments were very perceptive. I don't know why you would shun the talk shows, because you did just splendidly on this tape. I thought that Ms. McPherson's questions were quite good. I thought that your answers about our collaboration were excellent. The interview as a whole is great, especially because of your lucid answers. Many thanks for letting me hear the tape."

My North Dakota farm-boy shyness did not qualify me very well for talk shows. But, before the year 1979 was out, I appeared on another talk show, in Tacoma, on December 28, on "Dick Week's Call-In Show", broadcast over Radio KMO. One of the callers wanted to know if I was the Renner who had been her paper boy. When she told me where she lived, I answered, "Yes. I'm your man! I was your boy!" And two days later, it was yet another autograph party, one hosted by Bill and Bernice (my brother and his wife) at their Tacoma home. On my calendar for that day, I rated the party, "Super success!"

That *Pioneer Missionary* is more than a simple biography of a dedicated missionary priest is attested to by the following quotations from various reviews of the book:

> The historian, the ethnographer, and the ordinary reader alike will each find abundant material in the life of this pioneer missionary among the people of Bering Strait (from 1903 to 1947) to capture his interest and satisfy his curiosity. The text is very readable and flows along with generous quotes from Lafortune's personal letters, mission diaries, and reports. The author's ability to weave these selections into his own lucid style makes for a smooth-flowing narrative.
>
> Father Renner's scholarly and definitive work is not only a transparent biography of Father Lafortune but the first general history ever written of the Catholic Church in Northwest Alaska.
>
> This is a book of hope and love and great poignancy.

On December 12, I addressed a joint memo to the chancellor, to my dean, and to my department head: "I wish to inform you of my intent to retire at the end of this academic year, 1979–1980. I have found my fifteen years at the University of Alaska to be very satisfying."

The December 1979 issue of the university's publication, *Now in the North*, carried a feature article, basically a book review, entitled "Bellarmine Lafortune—Pioneering Missionary", by Jon M. Nielson, a teacher of history at the university. The article began:

> After twenty years in the classroom, Dr. Louis L. Renner, S.J., has announced his retirement from the University of Alaska. A distinguished humanist, Jesuit scholar, and member of the foreign language department since 1965, Renner, perhaps above all, will be remembered by his students

and colleagues as a dedicated teacher who honored by example the Jesuit motto, *cura personalis alumnorum*, "a personal concern for students". Renner recalls, "My fifteen years at the University of Alaska have been truly happy, satisfying years. Already they seem like a dream, so quickly have they passed. This coming May will seem like little more than the end of a fine summer day."

Chapter 19

Two Years on a Broad Threshold of Life: 1980 and 1981

I knew it had been rumored. Still, it came as a surprise to me when I was informed officially that it was so. In a letter dated April 11, 1980, Chancellor Howard A. Cutler wrote to me:

> Dear Louis,
> President Jay Barton has extended me the privilege of informing you of your appointment to the honored position of professor emeritus. President Barton made the appointment with the support of recommendations from the College of Arts and Sciences, the campus Promotion Committee and the chancellor.
> "President Barton and I join in extending to you congratulations for this well-earned honor.

On May 5, along with fellow emeriti H. Theodore Ryberg and Arnold A. Griese, I was interviewed by Mildred Matthews, host of KFAR-TV's "Our Town" program. The videotape of the program was aired on the thirteenth and seventeenth. I was the first to be interviewed. In answer to one of her questions, "What's going to be happening next year that will involve the title 'professor emeritus' that's been given you?" I responded: "This coming year, I will actually be on sabbatical leave in Spokane doing some more research in the Oregon Province Archives. After that, I will be in Fairbanks, and I hope to maintain my ties with the

274

university. If I publish in the future, I would also then identify myself as an emeritus professor of the university. It's been
very good to me."

Two day later, the members of my second-year German class
surprised me with a cake-and-punch party, and with a gift
that has, ever since, been one of my most cherished temporal possessions: a watercolor depiction of the village on King
Island by noted Alaskan artist Nancy Taylor Stonington.

Sunday, May 11, 1980, was a threshold day in my life. On
that day, along with many others led by the university's mace-
bearing marshal, to the strains of Sir Edward Elgar's "Pomp
and Circumstance", I marched into the Patty Gymnasium on
the University of Alaska–Fairbanks campus. With a smaller,
select group, I took my place on the stage. The cap-and-
gown trappings I was wearing were no longer mine. They had
once been mine; but, not even thinking about the possibility of being granted emeritus status, and not intending to be
present for the commencement doings of that day, I had sold
them. I had to borrow them back for the occasion.

The moment came for my name to be called out, for me
to walk to center stage to accept from the hands of President Jay Barton a framed, beribboned, sealed, and duly signed
document, tangible evidence that the university, on the occasion of its fifty-fifth commencement ceremonies, was conferring upon me "professor of German, emeritus" status.

The document read:

WHEREAS Dr. Louis L. Renner has served the University of
Alaska for 15 years from 1965 to 1980 as a distinguished
scholar and devoted teacher; and

WHEREAS Dr. Renner, through a commitment to his students, has consistently provided quality instruction and given
generously of his time for counseling; and

WHEREAS Dr. Renner's devotion to teaching has been paralleled by sustained research endeavors; and

WHEREAS Dr. Renner has sought to inspire his students of German, Latin, semantics and Italian and thereby make them a credit to the University; now

THEREFORE BE IT RESOLVED that the faculty of the University of Alaska at Fairbanks hereby expresses its appreciation to Dr. Louis L. Renner for his contribution to both the State of Alaska and its University; and

BE IT FURTHER RESOLVED that the President of the University, in recognition of the valuable services rendered by Dr. Renner and as evidence of the University's desire that his identification with the University be maintained, hereby appoints Dr. Louis L. Renner Professor of German, Emeritus; and

BE IT FURTHER RESOLVED that this resolution be appropriately engrossed, signed by the Chancellor and the President as further evidence of the esteem and respect in which they hold Dr. Louis L. Renner, and conveyed to Dr. Renner on this day of May 11, 1980.

The following day, I wrote to Dad and Mom about the previous day's events and told them that I had been packing and would be out of my "hate-to-leave-it apartment of many happy memories" by the time my letter reached them. I made the move to the bishop's residence/chancery building on Peger Road, across the parking lot from Sacred Heart Cathedral, on May 14. Getting settled in and readjusted to community life was a simple matter. I knew well all the members of the community, having had frequent contact with them. That community consisted of Bishops Gleeson and Whelan; Fathers Anable, George Carroll, and Frank Mueller; and Brother George Feltes. After fifteen years of living alone, doing my own shopping, cooking, and housekeeping, I found community life, in general, and the evening community meals, in particular, a pleasant change. I soon became well acquainted with the Alaskan Shepherd staff and was introduced to the basics of the new job facing me. It was agreed, however, that, for the time being, Father Anable would continue on as head of the program, with me as his understudy. By this time, it had been decided, too, that I would spend the last part of 1980 and the first part of 1981 on a mini sabbatical at Gonzaga "to recharge my theological and spiritual batteries". However, I was in no hurry to get on with that sabbatical. The Chilkoot Trail had yet to be hiked, church construction at Healy had yet to be engaged in, and firewood had yet to be split at Kaltag.

The first Jesuit missionaries to enter Alaska did so by way of the Chilkoot Trail. As a historian of Jesuit missionary activity in Alaska, I needed one day to walk in their footsteps. The opportunity to do so came at the end of June 1980. On the twenty-first, Father Frank Mueller and I drove to Tok, where we spent the night before driving on to Haines. There we were overnight guests of Father James P. Ryan, pastor of Haines' Sacred Heart parish. On the twenty-third, we took the ferry to Skagway, where we were joined by Father Richard D. (Dick) Tero, pastor of Saint Mary's parish in Kodiak; George Cusick; and several others. By the evening of that day, we were well up the Chilkoot Trail, at Sheep Camp, where, in our separate tents, we spent the night. The following day, we were up and over the summit, into British Columbia, Canada. I was the first one up and over. As I was resting in a simple lean-to plywood shelter, waiting for the others to catch up with me, Father Frank arrived. By this time, George, who was handicapped, was lagging considerably behind the party. Father Frank asked me, "Do you think you could go back up and over and down and carry George's pack up? I don't think he'll make it otherwise."

It was a cloudless day. The sun's rays, reflected off the snow-field, made it really hot. Leaving my pack at the shelter, I went back up and over the summit and, sliding on the seat of my pants, was down near the foot of the American side in no time. George was grateful to see me. I took his pack and went up with it. Near the top of the pass, the trail was almost vertical. Just short of the rim of the summit, I set his pack down, leaving him the satisfaction of carrying it up the final pitch and over.

Later that evening, I caught up with Father Frank at Lake Lindeman, where we tented for the night. The other members of our party, having set themselves a slower pace, were a good distance behind us. Intending to do some visiting in Canada's Yukon Territory, we had pressed ahead rather steadily. From Lake Lindeman, we hiked on to Lake Bennett, where we caught the train back to Skagway. After a hot shower, a hot meal, and a good night's sleep in a real bed, we were ready for the drive from Skagway to Whitehorse. There we visited the Oblate Fathers and spent the night. On the twenty-seventh and twenty-eighth, at Elsa, we were guests of Father Henk Huijbers, O.M.I., and his dog, Fluffy, half wolf and half German Shepherd. At Elsa, in the bowels of the earth, we visited the silver mine. The following day, with Father Henk as our guide, we visited the mines at Keno Hill and Calumet. By the late afternoon of the twenty-ninth, we were in Dawson, guests of Father Marcel Bobillier, O.M.I. With him as guide, we toured the Klondike goldfields. Before leaving Dawson, we prayed at the burial site of Father William H. Judge, S.J. This occasioned another article by me: "The Saint of Dawson".[1] The last day of June saw us back in Fairbanks.

---

1. *North/Nord* 30, no. 1 (Spring 1983): 38–43.

During July and the first few days of August, I did a fair amount of work on what became a published article some five years later: "Francis A. Barnum, S.J.: Pioneer Alaskan Missionary and Linguist".[2]

I can still see it, crudely scratched with a nail in the corner of the newly poured concrete slab: "AMDG 8/5/80".[3] In the afternoon of that day, August 5, 1980, in the company of Father Paul B. Mueller, classmate of mine since novitiate days, I had arrived at Healy, then still little more than a budding community on the Parks Highway some ten miles north of Denali National Park and Preserve, more commonly known as McKinley Park. I was there to help him and his select crew build a new church.

Michael (Mike) Murphy, a twenty-seven-year-old family man, though not a parishioner, had agreed to serve as construction foreman at half of what would have been a reasonable full salary. He had been at the construction site long enough already to see it cleared, the ground prepared, and the slab poured. A man with wide experience in the building trade, Mike had with him as core crew members semiskilled construction workers Tony and Paul Mueller, brothers, twenty-four and twenty years old respectively, and nephews of Fathers Paul and Frank, likewise brothers. The "Mueller boys", or simply "the boys", as we generally referred to the two, had driven up from Waldport, Oregon, in a pickup camper. Father Frank was to spend some days at the site in early September to help get the walls up. Volunteers, mainly from nearby Clear Air Force Base and from the parish-to-be, were to come and go.

The boys lived at the site: Tony in the pickup camper, and Paul in a small borrowed house trailer, which served also

2. *Alaska History* 1, no. 2 (Fall/Winter 1985–1986): 19–41.
3. AMDG stands for the Latin "Ad Majorem Dei Gloriam", the Jesuit motto "For the Greater Glory of God".

as our tool shed, cook shack, warm-up hut—and card room. John McDonald—"old John" to us, a retired professional wildlife photographer from Minnesota and helper with the building project, whenever the weather was unfavorable for photography—slept in the back of his 1965 Ford sedan. Father Paul, when at Healy, stayed with the Gale Weatherell family. As my living quarters, for a total of roughly six weeks, I had the little orange backpacker's tent that had served me so often and so well on wilderness hikes and that I now pitched in a grove of spruce trees near the building site.

On August 12, I wrote to Dad and Mom,

Last week I was at Healy helping build a church for the area. Spent four ten-hour days driving many, many nails, carrying and stacking lumber and Sheetrock, shoveling and hauling gravel [by wheelbarrow], digging a seventy-two-inch-deep hole for the oil tank and a trench through the tundra, and, on my knees, tarring around the foundation. If people spend as much time in that church on their knees as I spent outside on mine, there will be some holy people around. They were hard days, believe me. I hammered and shoveled and sawed off a few pounds, but I felt good and found lots of satisfaction in what I did—building a church, building the Church. The scenery there is great, being in the foothills of Mount McKinley. I slept in my tent. Though there was already a touch of autumn in the air and the alpine tundra was taking on color, I was more than warm enough. And the tundra moss and pad made my bed comfortable as home. Keeping clean was harder. When I returned here, I could with all honesty tell them I was the dirtiest Jesuit in the world.

At that time, there was, as yet, no water at the site. Wet tundra moss had to suffice for a washup.

On the thirty-first, while again in Fairbanks with Tony to get a load of lumber, I wrote to Dorothy Jean:

> Want to hear the bare grisly details about a grizzly bear? Earlier this month, a sow [adult female bear] with a pair of two-year-old cubs raided our fridge, which was standing behind a small trailer. She ripped the handle off and knocked the thing over. On that same raid, she also took the side off someone's house trailer and killed a dog. That dog killing cost her her life. The owner of the dog, to keep her from teaching her impressionable offspring any more bad manners, and "in defense of life and property", shot her dead. She was old and had bad teeth and bad breath; there was little fat on her. Apparently she was rather desperate, with winter coming on.

Phyllis Stickle, a Healy parishioner, who generally served us our evening meals, meals prepared from groceries supplied her by Father Paul and from vegetables out of her garden, was given a goodly share of that grizzly. One evening, she served us grizzly-bear burgers as the main entrée. I ate mine with good appetite—and with a certain degree of smugness as I reflected how preferable it was to be the diner and not the dinner.

During that September, I was at Healy for all but the three days I spent in Fairbanks. My tent was a poor man's home away from home. But, with a tarp over the top, it kept the rain out; and, zipped up, it kept the mosquitoes out—but not the squirrels. One day, upon returning to it after a hard day's work on a meager diet, what do I find right inside the front entrance? A pile of finely shredded paper! A squirrel, which had for some weeks been busily engaged in caching spruce cones for the winter in its nearby midden, had somehow gotten into my tent and, except for some hard-boiled eggs, had wiped my edibles out completely. Gone was my whole supply of candy bars, Triscuits, and dried fruit. Retaliate? How could I, against a merely provident squirrel foraging in his own territory? A cast-iron pot with a heavy lid solved my squirrel problem.

Concerning eating accommodations: Breakfast was a matter of personal choice. The boys, as often as not, after playing cards far into the night, got up too late to eat anything. Old John began all his days with hotcakes. My first few days at Healy, I took the easy way out, brewing up a packet or two of instant oatmeal. I soon learned, however, that this did not give me quite the energy I needed for a long forenoon on the gravel or Sheetrock pile. Boiled eggs worked better. For lunch, too, we were generally on our own, though sometimes we went to the Totem Pole Café for some burger of choice. Father Paul paid for most of these. He was generous enough in providing food for us, but we were easily satisfied and tended to neglect the eating part. Often we settled for bread and peanut butter, sometimes spread on with a wood chisel for lack of something better at hand. The evening meals we most often took at the Stickles' place, where, after feeding seven of her own, Phyllis always had a plentiful, tasty meal on the table for us. We came as we were—a dirty, tired, hungry gang of church builders. After a long day of hard work outdoors, very often in the wind and rain or snow, it was a real pleasure to sit down to a leisurely meal in a warm, friendly atmosphere.

One day (I was looking especially grubby that day after shoveling ground back into the trench to cover the pipe leading to the leach box), I mentioned to old John that I usually read for a while in my tent at night. "What, and by what light?" he wanted to know. I told him I had a little flashlight and added, "John, I may look like a bum, but don't forget, I'm still a priest with the Divine Office to say." When it was very late, or I was too tired, I skipped it, confident that the Lord would understand. Generally, however, I said it, and with a certain relish, as I lay there on the spongy carpet of tundra vegetation, the spruce trees smelling of Christmas, the night still but for the patter of rain on the tent or, a few times, the doleful, drawn-out "hoooooot" of a nearby horned owl. But those still nights were the exception.

August and much of September 1980 were unusually raw, windy, and wet, even according to the locals. On September 1, the Healy area had the earliest snowfall of the season since the 1920s. On the morning of the fourth, it was only nineteen above. Ice crystals, frozen condensation from my breathing, sparkled on the tent ceiling in the shine of my flashlight. One morning, later that month, I stuck my head out of my tent to see three inches of snow on the ground. In my two sleeping bags, I was perfectly warm. Putting on frozen boots in the morning, however, was a chore. Almost daily we saw great wedges of honking geese and raucous cranes flying overhead, headed south to their winter quarters. Such weather was anything but favorable for church construction in the wilds of Alaska. However, as on slab-pouring day, so on the equally critical roof-tarring day, a kindly Providence saw fit to grant us favorable weather. By the fourth week of September, we had the building closed in and ready for the winter.

It was with mixed feelings that I struck my tent on Sunday, September 28, and returned to Fairbanks. In spite of hard work, often in rather nasty weather, I had enjoyed the time at Healy immensely. I had made new friends, had lived and worked in an area of rare natural beauty, and had, more or less, lived through three seasons in the course of two months. With the many quality photos I had taken and the notes I had scribbled into a kind of day-to-day diary, I had enough material to enable me to fill two issues of the *Alaskan Shepherd*. All in all, it was again a case of mixing the useful with the pleasant.

On October 2, in Fairbanks, a three-day diocese-wide meeting of priests, sisters, brothers, and representative lay people came to an end. The morning of the third dawned crisp and frosty, with ground fog. At 7:40 A.M., in a twin-engine Beechcraft, a "Twin Bonanza", with Father James A. (Jim) Sebesta, S.J., pastor of Kaltag, at the controls, we took off for Nulato. Up front, Father Charles A. (Charlie) Bartles, S.J., was wedged in between Father Jim and me, who had the choice window seat—because I had the camera! Strapped in behind us were Sisters Dolores Pardini, S.N.D., and Dolores Steiner, S.N.D.; Brother Jakes; and Father George S. Endal, S.J.

Forty-five minutes into the flight found us droning along above a solid cloud cover in the bright morning sun. To the south, only the summit of Mount McKinley was visible, a lonely isle in a vast sea of clouds. A short while later, to get a direct visual bearing on our first destination, Nulato, we plunged steeply down through the churning clouds, guided by radio contact, toward the all-weather field of Galena. We "shot the approach" to Galena, then flew on below the heavy overcast, skimming along the Yukon, Nulato-bound. At 9:45, we touched down on the airstrip on the bluff above Nulato. Moments later, Eddie Hildebrand, alerted by "Indian telegram", was there with his pickup to drive Father Charlie and me down to the village. The rest continued on to their respective destinations.

It was a personal thrill for me to be, finally, at Nulato, the oldest permanent Catholic mission in northern Alaska. I had visited many of the other Alaskan missions but never Nulato, a village steeped in history both sacred and secular. While at Nulato, I investigated and photographed the grave site of a victim of the notorious "Nulato Massacre" of 1851, British naval lieutenant John J. Barnard. This resulted in my published article "The Memory of a Brave Man: The Grave of Lieut. John J. Barnard".[4] One day, during my stay at Nulato, Father Charlie and I, in his skiff, propelled by a powerful outboard, took a trip up to Koyukuk—my first visit to that village.

On the sixth, Father Jim came to Nulato to fly me to Kaltag, where my "mission" was to split and stack stovewood in the porches of the church and of Sister Dolores Pardini's house. At the time, stove oil on the Yukon cost around three dollars a gallon. Wood was plentiful. Greeting me at Kaltag was a big pile of spruce logs next to the church. In the course of a week, a crew of four of us—Brother Jakes, Fathers Jim and Theodore E. (Ted) Kestler, and me—were gradually to transform that pile of logs into pieces of wood small enough to fit into the fireboxes of the various mission stoves. Brother Jakes and Father Jim manned the chainsaws, cutting the logs into stove-length rounds. Father Ted and I swung the splitting mauls. Driving wedges and splitting rounds down to size, even kindling, was one of my specialties. I had had much practice doing that at the Dykema home after their move into a wooded area a twenty-minute drive out of Fairbanks. Frankly, for me, splitting and stacking stovewood was not work. It was one of my most satisfying forms of exercise, especially on a cold day under trees ablaze with all the colors of autumn.

Somewhat tired at the end of my first short day at Kaltag, at 10:45 that night, after having done justice to a dinner centered around moose meat and having concelebrated at

4. *Alaska Journal* 15, no. 2 (Spring 1985): 16–21.

an evening Mass, I tossed a sponge pad on the church floor, crawled into my two sleeping bags, and was soon fast asleep. Toward morning, I needed to step out under a starry sky. It was still dark, the night frosty and breezy, but across the northern sky was draped a brilliant aurora, a delicate intermingling of color, motion, and cold light. Through this luminous curtain, myriads of trembling stars could be seen. Though again filled with a sense of awe and wonderment at the sight of the northern lights, as I had been so many times before, I was soon driven back into my down-filled sleeping bags by the predawn cold.

Tuesday the seventh dawned sharp and clear. Again, we spent the better part of the day on the woodpile. Around three o'clock on Wednesday afternoon, some lazy snowflakes began tumbling out of the gray overcast. It was time to begin the tedious task of stacking stove-size pieces into the front porch of the church. Things went well enough until some kids— they must have been first-graders on their way home from school—stopped by and offered to help. The work was dusty and somewhat dangerous for little kids, as I was stacking the wood pretty high by now. Kindly, but firmly, I tried to decline their offer of help. They insisted. So—reasoning to myself that maybe one should not, after all, discourage willing young workers—I let them "help". But what had been a difficult job soon became "mission impossible". I gave up stacking and went back to splitting, thinking to myself that one of the Creator's better jokes played on adults was to have created kids that insist on "helping" before they are able to help, but then, suddenly, as soon as they are able to help, absolutely refuse to do so.

On Sunday morning, the twelfth, I offered Mass before a relatively small crowd but in a church filled with the homey smell and crackling sound of burning spruce. During Mass, we sang the song "Peace Is Flowing Like a River". Behind the church and down the steep bank, the mighty Yukon was flowing by, majestically, timelessly, peacefully.

After that Mass, Edgar Kalland and his wife, Virginia, invited me to their cabin for a four-square breakfast. After it, Edgar showed me his parents' marriage certificate and his baptismal certificate: precious old documents with true calligraphy, drawn up and signed by Father Aloysius Ragaru, S.J., who had entered Alaska via the Chilkoot Trail in 1887. He showed me also the medal he had received for his part in the famous sled dog relay that carried diphtheria serum to Nome in 1925—an event that lives on in today's Iditarod Trail Sled Dog Race. He told me much about his long life along the Yukon. The impromptu interview resulted in a published article, "Edgar Kalland: Dog Musher and Boat Captain".[5]

Several times late that Sunday night and early Monday morning, I was awakened by the rumbling, swooshing sounds made by avalanches off the roof. Heavy, wet snow had continued to fall. That snowfall, the season's first, transformed Kaltag into a whole new world. Chained-up dogs took on new life. Snow machines began to zoom through the village. Kids snowballed their way to and from school. Having spent some hours at the airfield sweeping snow off the Twin Bonanza and clearing a strip for takeoff, Father Jim and I left Kaltag at 4:00 P.M. After bucking strong headwinds much of the way, we were on the ground in Fairbanks by 6:35.

My two-village outing, in addition to having been very enjoyable for me personally, also provided me with photos and material for the two articles mentioned above, plus enough for "The Kaltag Drum Festival"[6] and two issues of the *Alaskan Shepherd.*

5. *Alaska Native News* 1, no. 4 (February 1983): 16–19.
6. *Alaska* 10 (September 1982–August 1983): 62.

Regarding my account of my days at Kaltag that appeared
in an issue of the *Alaskan Shepherd*, a certain Margaret B.
McGee saw fit to write from New York City on May 26,
1982, to Bishop Whelan, addressing him as "Sir": "Father
Renner's flowing narrative and clear, concise style, his humor
and sensitive awareness of nature's beauties give me a veritable *tour* to our northernmost outpost. I should like him to
know how much I appreciate his writing."

By the twenty-eighth of October, I was at Gonzaga to begin
my mini sabbatical. At Immaculate Heart Retreat Center on
the outskirts of Spokane—along with Fathers Fallert, Michael
Kaniecki, Arthur Lopilato, and Sebesta—I made my annual
retreat on November 11–18. As mentioned earlier, my sabbatical was meant to help me "recharge my theological and
spiritual batteries". The retreat helped considerably with the
latter part of the objective. As to the recharging of my *theological* batteries, that was, for the time being, left on hold.
Digesting into publishable articles what I had experienced at
Healy, Nulato, and Kaltag I considered the first order of business. Before leaving Gonzaga, I was also to prepare articles
on Saint Thérèse, Saint Ignatius, and Saint Francis Xavier.
They were published subsequently in three issues of the *Alaskan Shepherd*.

Back in Spokane, after spending the last ten days of December 1980 in Tacoma visiting my family, I was ready to
recharge, to a major degree, my theological batteries. This I
did by auditing, during the spring semester 1981, Father
Vince Beuzer's course on the Gospel of Saint John and Father
Armand Nigro's course on the spiritual life. But, even more
than those two courses, it was G. Ernest Wright's slender volume, *God Who Acts*, recommended to me by Father Vince,
that made my sabbatical, from a theological-update standpoint, truly significant for me. I was immediately able to

relate to Wright's God—primarily the God of the Old Testament—for I had, by then, in my personal life, often and in a very striking way, experienced the intervention, the action, of a kind, providential God.

In the course of that same spring semester, I spent many long hours in the Jesuit Oregon Province Archives. This time, the focus was on Father Thomas P. (Tom) Cunningham, S.J. Father Tom and I had exchanged rather lengthy letters in the 1940s. In Fairbanks, in 1959, I had attended his funeral. By March 16, I was able to write to Father Fallert, "My gathering of Tom Cunningham materials for a book-length life of Father Tom has gone well beyond expectations." *"Father Tom" of the Arctic* was published by Binford & Mort in 1985. While doing the Cunningham-related research, I came to know about, and to be intrigued by, Charles Olaranna, the chief of the King Island Eskimos. This resulted in another published article: "Charles Olaranna: Chief of the King Islanders".[7]

I found my half-year stay at Gonzaga leisurely and enjoyable. Nevertheless, throughout the whole of it, my heart was in Alaska. I could hardly wait to return. By April 24, I was back in Fairbanks.

At the time, Father Anable was still with the Alaskan Shepherd work and was willing to carry on with it. Rita Johnson—who, it will be remembered, was on the Monroe High faculty when I taught at Monroe twenty years earlier and whose son, Jerry (my student), had given me driving lessons—was the top staff member after Father Anable. Very competently she helped keep the whole program running smoothly. Though I was somewhat concerned about gradually "learning the ropes", I was in no immediate hurry to

7. *Alaska Journal* 13, no. 2 (Spring 1983): 14–23.

take over the whole program. Consequently, I was able to devote most of my time to more personal pursuits.

My first major adventure of 1981 was to take me along the shores of Norton Sound, west of Nome. Anticipating that I was about to leave Fairbanks for Nome, Dorothy Jean wrote to me on June 17: "This is sort of an emergency. My reason for writing is to have you take a photograph of the buildings and surroundings at the mouth of the Sinuk River for my proposed article on the Methodist orphanage at Sinuk. But don't go to extra lengths for the photos." Two days later, I wrote her, "It will be a pleasure and a challenge for me to get you pictures of the buildings at the mouth of the Sinuk." And a challenge it proved to be!

On June 21, a Sunday, shortly before noon, after a flight from Fairbanks, I was on the ground at Nome. The following day, I offered Mass, did some visiting, bought a sport-fishing license, and had a talk with Carl Grauvogel of the Alaska Department of Fish and Game, whom I knew already from our days together on Little Diomede Island in 1975. Realizing that there were moose and grizzly bears on the Seward Peninsula, I wanted to learn from him what risks I might be facing on my hike to the mouth of the Sinuk River, twenty-six miles northwest of Nome. While assuring me that it was not too likely that I would meet up with a grizzly, he nevertheless advised: "Don't run. If you do, he'll think you're prey and run you down. You can't outrun him. You might throw him articles of clothing, one at a time, as you back away from him. When he gets the smell of man, he may not like what he smells and take off. Or back into water. There are no trees out there to climb."

Nome and the surrounding area during the third week of June knows no darkness, only a trace of twilight around midnight. On Monday evening, I left Nome. My plan was to hike along the Nome-Teller Road till I came to the Sinuk River bridge, cross it, then follow the river down to where it entered the Bering Sea. That would bring me to Sinuk, where I expected to find the old Methodist orphanage that I hoped to photograph. It would be a trek of some forty miles, but I was under no time constraints whatever. And I looked forward to being alone with nature and its Maker. During the latter part of June, the Seward Peninsula is a paradise of wildflowers and birds of countless kinds.

From my diary:

Monday, June 22, 1981: Left Nome at 8:30 P.M. Mostly blue sky. Sweated during the early part of the hike. Traffic passed me; none offered me a ride, nor did I hitchhike. Made seven and a quarter miles by 11:00. Sunset Creek by midnight. Had a midnight snack of three Mars bars and cold water. Snow patches along the way. Ideal weather for hike. Cool to cold from dusk to dawn.

Tuesday, June 23, 1981: Penny River at about 1 A.M. Averaged almost exactly three miles per hour. Beautiful clear water in rivers and creeks. Mosquitoes not too bad. Sometime after midnight a fat half moon appeared in the sky, a companion along the long, but not lonesome, road. Many wildflowers and birds of various kinds along the way. Melodious, haunting loon calls heard. Snacked at Arctic Creek, at mile 17, from 2:30–2:45 A.M. 3:35 A.M. at Sinuk River, at mile $19\frac{1}{2}$, exactly seven hours after leaving Nome. Fatigued, but elated at sunrise at 3:00 A.M. Virtually cloudless, windless up to now, 9:22 A.M. What wind there was during the night was at my back. That helped the mileage. It was a relief to get off the hard, at times monotonous, rocky road and head down the river over the spongy, fragrant tundra. The sound of the river was music. At times, going through brush was work. It was cold, feet-soaked going. Frost in spots, ice on quiet ponds. It's great to have this vast vacancy all to myself! 9:22, a bit more wind and a few more clouds as I lay myself down for some shut-eye after a breakfast of soup mix and Snickers and dried apples. No sign of man ever having passed here. Dozed for about forty minutes. At 10:35 I bestir my leaden corpse. Want to get to Sinuk to take advantage of good weather for picture taking.... Drying out footgear after fording for a stretch. Tough going along the river. Much disagreeable brush-breaking. Mosquitoes real bad in spite of strong breeze. "When will I hit the mouth?" I ask myself at 1:25. I left camp #1 at 11:25.... It is now exactly 8:35 P.M. and exactly twenty-four hours since I left Saint Joseph's rectory. I'm in my tent, about to begin supper of tea, corned beef, cheese, and crackers. Today's hiking has been the toughest I've ever done—punishment for both man and boots! I pushed on in hopes of reaching Sinuk for photos while sun was high. The mouth seemed never to want to come—always another bend in the river, another hillock to cross over. It was 5:40 P.M. when I first saw the Bering Sea still a good distance off. It's a great relief to be in tent away from mosquitoes. At 9:03 wind is down, birds in evening song. I will soon be asleep. Cloudless now.

To ease the tedium and fatigue of that long afternoon's plodding on and on with, at first, the imminently expected sight of the Bering Sea deluding me, then the mouth of the river seemingly being forever still around the next bend, I was inspired to start counting, in chronological order, beginning with my earliest youth, all the major blessings in my life that I had to be grateful for. Doing this not only shortened the seemingly endless miles by keeping my mind off my weariness but, at the same time, filled me with a profound sense of gratitude, which, in turn, buoyed up my spirits greatly, elated me, made my legs seem lighter, my stride longer.

From my diary:

Wednesday, June 24, 1981: Up at 6:30 A.M. after excellent sleep. Cool night, but now cloudless, very light breeze, lots of bird sounds. At 8:15 packing, making ready for departure from camp #3. All systems go! Mosquito intensity: seven, by actual count, per half minute per one square inch of wrist flesh exposed. It is now 10:20 A.M., cloudless, sounds only of surf, breeze, birds. All the struggles of yesterday are being rewarded one-thousand-fold. I'm sitting on a silvery old driftwood log near ruins of Methodist Mission at mouth of Sinuk River. Lots of driftwood. An ideal setting for an establishment. A flat plateau with hills rising a little ways back. This A.M. I finished shooting a roll of thirty-six #64 slides. Pix include shots of one remaining mission building and the ruins of another. Some pix will show mouth of Sinuk and Sledge Island. Ideal weather, ideal place! Difficulty of getting here makes being here sheer bliss. Left Sinuk exactly at noon. Now 3:35 P.M. Just finished leisurely lunch of freeze-dried beef stroganoff, followed by some halvah. Walk along beach for most part easy, especially on wet sand of receding tide. No mosquitoes along beach. Now everything is tops.

But I was in for a very rude awakening. The river I had followed down from the Nome-Teller Road was not the Sinuk River but Cripple Creek. The bridge I had crossed and thought to be the one crossing the Sinuk River was the Cripple Creek bridge, still quite some distance before the Sinuk bridge. The sign at the Cripple Creek bridge had been vandalized beyond recognition. However, after carefully studying my detailed terrain map, I had satisfied myself that it was the Sinuk that I had crossed. It was as I was walking along the beach, thinking that I was now on the far side of the Sinuk, well on my way northwest to Cape Woolley, where

I had hoped to meet and visit with King Island friends, that I discovered I still had a considerable distance to go even to reach the mouth of the Sinuk. The photos I had taken were not of the old Methodist Mission at all. How did I discover my mistake, out in that maritime wilderness, where chances of meeting another soul were exceedingly slim?

Back to my diary! It is still Wednesday, June 24, 1981.

!!!! Now 5:20 P.M. At five o'clock I met two fellows on three-wheelers headed for Nome. I learned from them that I had come down *Cripple* Creek, NOT SINUK! However, I feel physically in top condition, have food aplenty, feel I can safely press on to Sinuk for photos. BIG QUESTION = getting across Sinuk? "Build a raft!" the two guys suggested. On to Sinuk, then I'll take it from there! ... 9:30 P.M. In my tent having canned salmon and tea. It is safe to say there is no one within twenty miles of me. Last three hours were difficult, going into wind. To sleep around 10:00 P.M.

Thursday, June 25, 1981: Up at 5:15 A.M. Slight breeze, cloudless, slept fitfully. Chilly at first. Tent ceiling wet. Major decision today at Sinuk. Some fog banks. Will strike camp right away, then stop later for breakfast. Left camp opposite Sledge Island at 6:15 A.M. Saw walrus carcass on beach. At 6:45 I hit Sinuk mouth. Waded in up to shoulders. Can't ford. Too risky, with wind. Took several photos of buildings on far side. Breezy, fog clouds rolling in. Fished and caught one flatfish before losing lure. At 8:35 A.M. I started to head back toward Nome. 12:30 P.M. now. Just finishing lunch at mouth of Quartz Creek. Solid overcast of fog. Strong breeze out of west driving toward Nome. I got those slide pix of Sinuk just in time. I plan now to push on to Penny River and spend night there. ... Kept going after Penny, driven by wind. At 6:20 P.M. it began to rain. I pitched tent and was ready to crawl into sleeping bag, but rain came through, so I set out for Nome at about mile #6. Arrived in Nome at 11 P.M.

Those were the toughest six miles of the whole Sinuk-Nome stretch—loose gravel and sand, high surf, but strong wind drove me on. 11:45 now, sitting in clean bed. I must have hiked about eighty miles altogether. End of Thursday June 25, 1981.

By the twenty-seventh, I was back in Fairbanks. On August 2, Father Frank Mueller and I flew to Anchorage, where we spent the night. The following day, we flew on to Bethel, where Father Richard D. (Dick) Case, S.J., met us and flew us on to Alakanuk. From there, future Eskimo deacon Emmanuel Stanislaus took us in his boat, by way of Sheldon Point (officially Nunam Iqua since the year 2000), to Akulurak, the site of the old Saint Mary's mission. Spending the better part of two days there leisurely examining the old ruins and "artifacts" and meditating at length in the mission cemetery bordered on a pilgrimage for us. Of special interest to me, of course, was the grave of Jesuit father Julius Jetté, the subject of an article of mine mentioned already in an earlier chapter. On the fifth, James Afcan, in his boat, brought us to Sheldon Point, from where Dominic Andrews, in his boat, brought us to Alakanuk. On the sixth, we flew from Alakanuk to Mountain Village, where we stayed the night as guests of Father Bert Mead, S.J., pastor of Mountain Village. The following day, Father Bert drove us in the mission's beat-up old Scout over the rocky road to the Saint Mary's mission on the Andreafsky River, where, along with most of the other Alaskan Jesuits, we made our annual retreat, from the eleventh to the eighteenth. Father Nigro was the director. This was the first of a long series of retreats made by the Jesuits in Alaska as a group. To Father Cliff Carroll, I described it as "a period of much grace for us all". By the nineteenth, I was back in Fairbanks. While at Saint

Mary's, I took many photos and gathered enough material for a number of articles that appeared in issues of the *Alaskan Shepherd*.

On September 1, I officially became head of the Alaskan Shepherd fundraising program and editor of the *Alaskan Shepherd*. When it was first determined that I would take on this new assignment, I was encouraged by Bishop Whelan and others to get out into the field often for photos and live, current-interest material. I needed little encouragement to do this. On September 9, I flew to Kaltag, again with Father Jim Sebesta, for another stint of laying in a supply of firewood for the winter ahead. For a good week, I was to be engaged in one of my favorite pastimes, swinging an ax—and, all the while, enjoying a mid-September autumn at its finest. The birches and aspens were simply aglow with fall colors, the days still warm and sunny, the mosquitoes gone. However, there was still "a fly in the ointment". Rather, it was a gnat. According to notes in my diary: "Gnats frightful", "Gnats horrible", and "The gnats are turning paradise into hell." People kept complaining, "Too much gnats, Faahder! Too much gnats!" Owing to a gnat bite, one of Sister Dolores Pardini's eyes was swollen shut.

On the fifteenth and sixteenth, Father Jim, his friends Jim and Janice Mino, and I were on a successful, a "dream", moose hunt on a slough off the Yukon River below Kaltag. Jim Mino, with one shot, dropped a young bull in a patch of grass not far from where our boat was anchored. By the nineteenth, I was back in Fairbanks. Photos taken on that Kaltag outing subsequently appeared in issues of the *Alaskan Shepherd* and some, in color, in the *Alaskan Shepherd* calendar.

November found me spending long hours in my Alaskan Shepherd office writing articles and attending to mail. I also assisted one of my former German students with her paper on Father Bernard Hubbard. Seldom did a year pass after I left the university and before I left Alaska without my guiding some university student through some writing project. Teachers in the Northern Studies Program, as well as teachers in the Departments of History and Anthropology, routinely sent students to me, confident that I would willingly help them with projects related to Catholic missionary activity in Alaska. I found much personal satisfaction in working with the university and its students in this way. I took my emeritus status as more than merely honorary. Thanksgiving Day I again spent with the Dykema family. Rare was the Thanksgiving Day during most of our years together in Alaska that I did not spend with them. Watching the football game, then taking the dog for a walk with Richard, then enjoying a traditional dinner with all the trimmings— followed by a slide show or home movie—was the general routine.

On December 8, 1981, Bishop Whelan asked me whether I would consider going to Alakanuk for the Christmas season. "Think it over, and let me know!" Well, it took me little thinking, about three seconds, before I told him, "Sure, I'll go."

On Monday, December 21, at noon, Father Anable drove me to the airport. Snow was falling at takeoff time. We arrived in Anchorage on schedule. Around 5:50 P.M., a little later than scheduled, we left in a jammed Wien jet for Bethel. Word was that we might not be able to land in Bethel because of "strong surface winds". Airborne, we heard over the intercom, "Keep seatbelts fastened, turbulence all the way." However, we were able to land at Bethel. There Father Henry G. Hargreaves, S.J., pastor of the Bethel mission, met me and drove me to the mission, where he had a hot supper waiting for me. In spite of a "strong wind whistling around the house all night", I had myself a decent sleep. I woke up early, wondering to myself, "Will I get to Alakanuk today?"

From my diary:

Tuesday, December 22, 1981: Early at airport. Lobby full of patiently waiting Eskimos. From clerk at counter we hear: "Flight delayed ... soon ... visibility ... maybe ... awaiting word ... all depends ... if ... when we find out ... on hold." I pray, say Rosary, read, and read some more, and bless my literacy. Minutes of delay stretch into hours. Finally airborne. At 11:00 A.M. between Bethel and Saint Mary's on a Wien twin-propeller airplane. On third try power-land at Saint Mary's. Snow-laden ground-level jet stream, windsock straight out. Returned to Bethel in P.M. So much for schedule made out to the minute by travel agent! Walk to Hangar Lake. Concelebrated at 5:15. Dinner at 6:00 with six stranded Nelson Islanders and two other guests. Will I go tomorrow? About twelve people spending night here.

Wednesday, December 23, 1981: Up at 6:00. Whatever does the day have in store for me? 8:05 A.M. to airport. I'm no. 1 on standby. "Gonna try again?" the common question. 9:37: I'm on! About 10:00, leave Bethel for Saint Mary's, then Mountain Village. White-knuckle landing there after two aborted attempts—gale-force crosswinds. Next we land at Emmonak. Finally, after nine different takeoffs, I'm on ground at Alakanuk.

Two School Sisters of Notre Dame, Rose Andre (Rosie) Beck and Michael Marie Laux, met me at the Alakanuk airstrip on a snow machine and brought me to their house for lunch and a briefing. That afternoon, I heard the confessions of many. Having sinned in Central Yup'ik Eskimo, they confessed in Central Yup'ik Eskimo, not a word of which I understood. However, assuming that the Lord understood, I gave a standardized penance, asked for an expression of sorrow, and gave absolution. In the pre–Vatican II days, they confessed in Eskimo, were given a penance in English, and were absolved in Latin. Absolution was now given in English. While I heard confessions, the sisters and women parishioners scrubbed and started to decorate the church. We had dinner together at 6:15 and a well-attended Mass at 7:15. Word had gotten around fast that "a father" had come. After Mass, I heard more confessions.

On the morning of the twenty-fourth, Christmas Eve, I got up at 6:45, offered an unattended Mass, then had myself a simple breakfast. It was my choice to prepare my own breakfasts and lunches. In the morning twilight, I took a stroll through the village. Back at the church, I plucked several big icicles off the eaves. These I put into the water barrel next to the oil stove in the priest's quarters to create more water for drinking, washing, baptizing, and whatever. The church had no indoor plumbing. In the afternoon and in the evening of that Christmas Eve, I was again in the confessional, a tiny, closed-in "box" in the corner of the church. With stove oil costing three dollars a gallon, the church was kept on the cool side. However, with my snowmobile suit—topped off with the customary purple stole—over the rest of my clothes and with felt-lined boots on my feet, I was warm enough. By 8:15 P.M., I had spent a total of six hours in the confessional. My throat was hoarse. A leisurely supper with the sisters, however, improved matters. After hearing more confessions, I was able to relax for a short while.

By 10:15, over an hour before the Midnight Mass was scheduled to begin, there were already around twenty people in the church. Then, in colorful parkas and bulky boots, on snow machines, on sleds pulled by snow machines, and on foot, they kept coming from all corners of the stretched-out village until the church was filled to overflowing. Services began at 11:30 with carols and the blessing of the crèche. The readings and

Gospel were heard first in English, then in Eskimo. My homily, given a few sentences at a time, was interpreted into Eskimo by Xavier Joseph, a young man fluent in both Eskimo and English. Most went to Communion. After Mass, amidst billowing clouds of steam rolling out of the church, there was much "Merry Christmas!" wishing. Many people thanked me for bringing them the Christmas Mass. The sisters then invited me over for cinnamon rolls and tea. Gratefully, I accepted. In my diary, I noted, "Clear, starlit night, slight breeze, exactly zero degrees. To bed at 2:00 A.M."

On Christmas Day morning, at 10:00, just as it was beginning to get light, we celebrated the Mass at Dawn. A rather small, quiet, sleepy-eyed group was in attendance. After Mass, the sisters and I ate a hasty brunch, loaded the sled, and bundled up for the almost twelve-mile trip downriver to Sheldon Point. Knowing that the generator there was not working, we were in a hurry to arrive while we still had daylight enough to open and warm the church and call the people to confession and Mass. John Buster volunteered to guide us. With Sister Michael Marie and John on his machine and Sister Rosie and me on hers pulling a loaded sled, we snarled out of Alakanuk at 12:30.

Shortly after we left Alakanuk, John lost the trail. For some time, we wallowed along through the deep, loose snow in the alder thickets. Instead of us following a trail, a trail followed us. After a while, we came to the main branch of the mighty Yukon, now a winter highway paved over with rough ice and wind-hardened snowdrifts. It took an all-out effort on my part simply to hang on as that eardrum-numbing mechanical jackrabbit, our Polaris Cobra 440 snow machine, seemingly out of control, ricocheted along what was anything but a smooth trail. To ease my ride, I tried my luck by standing on the back of the sled we were towing. For a short while, this seemed the better way to go. Then we hit a big bump and were momentarily airborne. When the sled came down, I lost my footing and grip and soloed headlong into the drifted snow. My chest, the camera hanging on it, and the snow, all three, absorbed their fair share of the jolt. I picked myself up, dug the snow out from under my collar, wondered about the condition of the camera—and savored the sudden blissful silence as Sister Rosie roared off, trailing a plume of blue smoke. After a few minutes, having felt something missing, namely me, she was back. I now got on behind her again and, hanging on with both hands more tightly than ever, so rode on into Sheldon Point. By the time we got there, at 1:50, we had spent twice the normal time on the trail. Communications between the two villages being out, the Sheldon Point people did not know we were coming.

Within an hour, we had the "rectory"—a ten-year-old multipurpose house—and the church open, the oil stoves going, and word of our presence out to the people. Still dressed for the trail, I began hearing confessions in the icy entryway of the thirty-year-old church, a building constructed out of lumber salvaged when the mission at Saint Mary's in Akulurak was torn down. With confessions over by 4:10, I vested for Mass. When I stepped into the church, my glasses immediately fogged up so badly that I had difficulty reading the prayers for the blessing of the crib. For some time now, the stove had been putting out enough Btus—and noxious fumes—to melt the frost on the walls and windows and turn the small church into a steam bath. Outside, it was already quite dark. Candles and a hissing Coleman lantern illumined the altar area.

We were barely into the first scriptural reading when a little lad started running circles around the altar. I made two grabs for him but missed. Seeing that my misses only made the game more exciting for him, I let him be. Nobody in the congregation made a move to retrieve him. It is not the Eskimo way. Throughout much of my homily, I also fought a losing battle with a squalling infant. Then, during the first part of the Eucharist Prayer, I met with a distraction I had never before encountered. The church was so crowded that six little boys were seated so close to the altar that their knees touched it. Then, one of them—must have been about five years old—with elbows propped on the front edge of the altar, chin resting on closed fists, beaming a broad smile, stared me in the eyes. So far, so good. But then, in a low voice, he started telling me what he got for Christmas, not realizing that at that moment I was speaking to the Lord about serious matters. I kept my composure, smiled back, and carried on with the sacred liturgy. It was all one grand, joyous family celebration—and meant to be just that! I myself was all atingle with the spirit of that holy Christmas Day. That Mass, celebrated so far west, well west of Hawaii, and so late in the day, was, without doubt, the last one celebrated anywhere in the world that Christmas. The schoolteachers, a young couple with two little girls, treated the sisters and me to a relaxing, family-style Christmas Day dinner.

The three of us spent the afternoon of the twenty-sixth visiting homes. The sisters, with candy for the kids, began at one end; I, with the new 1982 *Alaskan Shepherd* calendars, began at the other. Around 5:00 P.M., we met in the rectory. While preparing dinner, Sister Rosie went to the storm porch to bring in dried salmon strips she had left there. In the dark, she reached into the box—to find, not salmon strips, but a furry ball. A puppy had smelled them out, snacked, and bedded down for a snooze. Luckily, we had enough other food along. Light to prepare it by presented more of a problem. Before the meal was on the table, our good two-mantle Coleman lantern was on the floor, the ceiling hook having given way. Matches were going fast as we tried to get first one, then the other of our backup lanterns going. No luck. I went to the church and got the candles off the altar. By soft candlelight, we got the meal on the table, ate, and yawned our way through vespers. Outside, a howling blizzard was chasing itself around the house. Our chances of returning to Alakanuk the next day looked bleak.

By Sunday morning, the twenty-seventh, the wind had turned into a real howler. At times, the church, about sixty yards from the rectory, was barely visible through the ground-level jet stream blizzard. Still, we had hopes of returning to Alakanuk, where we had Mass scheduled for 4:00 P.M. that day. So, just in case we might be on the trail, after all, I got myself all "caloried up" with a hearty breakfast—Christmas chocolates, courtesy of the sisters, included!

"I don't think we'll go today", Sister Rosie told me at around 10:00 A.M. However, after Mass, she was able to tell me that Tom Prince, postmaster and mayor of Sheldon Point, had volunteered to guide us back to Alakanuk. We made the trip without incident, even though it snowed and blew the whole time. When we got there, Tom told us that much of the time he himself could not see the trail. It was his total familiarity with that flat, trackless, white wilderness (for years he had hauled freight in the Yukon Delta area by dogteam) and a kind of instinct that had guided him. The people of Alakanuk were surprised to see us back.

On Monday, we snow-machined upriver to Emmonak to pick up a tank of propane. The sisters wanted also to pay a Christmas visit to the two sisters there, Mary Beck and Donna Mae Straub. Sisters Rosie and Mary were twins. All four belonged to the same congregation.

While we were in Emmonak, Eskimo deacon candidate Emmanuel Stanislaus, on his own initiative, made the rounds in Alakanuk to see what shut-ins might wish to receive Holy Communion. The next day, he took me, riding on the back of his snow machine, to various homes. As we were bouncing along through the village, with the Blessed Sacrament in my shirt pocket, I got to wondering; so I said to the Lord, "I bet you're finding this ride bumpier than the one on the back of the donkey on the flight into Egypt." He would not bet.

New Year's Eve was the stormiest of all my days at Alakanuk. A stiff, snow-driving wind blew most of the day. Still, I went about the village blessing homes. New Year's Day dawned cloudless, twenty degrees above, a slight breeze, a ghostly aurora hanging in the northern sky. Attendance at the ten o'clock Mass was only fair. Midnight fireworks had taken their toll.

January 2 turned out to be a fairly tame day. I celebrated Mass at 11:00. The plane came at 12:30. Only four takeoffs and eleven hours later, I was back in Fairbanks. My last scribble in my Alakanuk diary: "Most consoling of all my priestly Christmas seasons. *Deo gratias!*"

Chapter 20

Twenty-five Years a Priest: 1982

The New Year of Our Lord 1982 was to prove to be another eventful year for me. In my small, windowless office in the basement of the chancery building—an office often turned into a world-class concert hall or grand opera house by classical music—I began the year by getting caught up somewhat on a backlog of mail and by putting into publishable form an account of my Alakanuk sojourn. In my diary, I had all the raw material needed for an article. My camera, no worse for the incident mentioned in the previous chapter, had produced more than enough photos to illustrate it. "An Alaskan Christmas West of Hawaii" appeared in the November–December 1982 issue of the *Alaskan Shepherd*. Under the title "A Christmas Diary from Alaska", it was reprinted in *Extension Magazine* that same year.[1] Shortly after the *Alaskan Shepherd* issue was out, Bishop Whelan received a letter reading, "Greetings from a staunch Protestant! I read the *Alaskan Shepherd* from end to end. The human interest stories are great, the last one especially, "Christmas West of Hawaii". God bless you, even if He wouldn't take your bet on the bumpy ride." From a man in Chicago, the "Honorable Bishop Whelan" received a letter reading: "Should you be in contact with Father Renner, please convey to him for me my heartfelt congratulations on his masterpiece Christmas travelogue titled 'An

1. *Extension Magazine* 77, no. 6 (December 1982): 5–11.

Alaskan Christmas West of Hawaii'. Few, if any, could match his most interesting Yuletime story." A lady, an author in her own right, wrote to Bishop Whelan from Little Rock, Arkansas: "Father Renner's 'Alaska Christmas West of Hawaii' was the acme of delight—and as a story brimming with the true spirit of Christmas, I rate it alongside Dickens' *Christmas Carol*. I especially loved his recounting his experiences with the small fry attending the Christmas afternoon Mass at Sheldon Point, and visualized the scene."

From the first to the fourteenth of June, I was again at Kaltag for another working vacation on the woodpile. It was a good break from mostly office work and resembled my previous Kaltag ventures. A highlight of this particular outing was the afternoon Father Jim Sebesta, Jesuit seminarian Mark A. Hoelsken, and I flew to Huslia to visit people there. While at Huslia, we had a lengthy prayer session and evening meal in the home of Harry and Rose Ambrose, both regarded as the "true pillars" of Huslia's Catholic community. In the absence of a priest, they routinely conducted prayer services. Their concern for the local Catholic community was wonderful to see, a beautiful example, in miniature, of what had been advocated by the Second Vatican Council, namely, a greater role for the laity in the Church. It was also a sign that Jesuits in Alaska were achieving some success in carrying out their mission in Alaska as formulated in their mission statement: "We, the Jesuits of Alaska, state as our purpose the animating and enabling of peoples in Alaska to become a truly indigenous Church." Inculturation, so stressed by Father General Pedro Arrupe, was, again in miniature, taking place here.

In the last chapter, Eskimo deacon candidate Emmanuel Stanislaus was mentioned. It was especially the Eskimo Deacon Program that responded, in a major way, to the call for lay involvement in the Church, to the call for the inculturation, the indigenization, of the Good News, the Gospel. True, the Eskimo deacons were clerics, not laymen. Nevertheless, as Native Alaskans, in many cases bilingual and bicultural, they were ideally suited to bring about the inculturation of the Gospel. The Eskimo Deacon Program, begun in 1970, was soon to flourish and become the backbone of rural Native ministry in the Yukon-Kuskokwim Delta. Alvin F. Owletuk, of Marshall, the first Eskimo deacon, was ordained to the diaconate on February 8, 1975. While my contact with the Eskimo deacons was quite limited, I did get to know enough about a number of them to be able to write articles about them in the *Alaskan Shepherd*. I also wrote up the early history of the program in my article "Diocese of Fairbanks, Alaska: The Eskimo Diaconate Program", which appeared in two installments.[2] Part 2 has the story of Deacon Michael Nayagak, the "patron saint" of the program. This edifying story was so well received that it appeared in five different publications—and in three languages: English, French, and Italian.

The first part of July 1982 saw me involved again in a church-building project, this time at Chevak, a Central Yup'ik Eskimo village on the Ninglikfak River near the Bering Sea coast. That twelve-day spell of work and relaxation provided me with many photos and the raw material for another article. "Digging in at Chevak" was printed in an issue of the *Alaskan Shepherd* and was reprinted in *Extension Magazine*.[3] Excursions to various Native villages, in addition to providing me with material for *Alaskan Shepherd* articles, were for me also of significant educational value. On them, I came to know better both the geography of Alaska and the culture of its Native people.

2. Pt. 1, *Eskimo*, 50th year, n.s., no. 45 (Spring/Summer 1993): 3–19; pt. 2, ibid., no. 46 (Fall/Winter 1993): 3–13.

3. *Extension Magazine* 77, no. 8 (March 1983): 5–10.

The year 1982 was a milestone year for me and for the whole Oregon Province. It was the year my ordination class and I celebrated our silver jubilee as priests, and the year the province celebrated its golden jubilee as a province. On July 22, I flew to Missoula, Montana, to meet, visit, and celebrate with fellow silver jubilarians. During our four days together, we visited the Saint Ignatius mission and Glacier National Park and concelebrated a Mass of thanksgiving in Missoula's Saint Francis Xavier Church. On the twenty-sixth, I arrived in Spokane. The next day, with most of its members present, the province solemnly celebrated the fiftieth anniversary of its founding. The day following, many gathered in the cemetery at Mount Saint Michael's for a memorial Mass. On the thirty-first, after many had concelebrated at the Mass for the feast of Saint Ignatius, Jesuit fathers John McDonald and Peter Henriot, both "Tacoma boys", and I drove to Tacoma.

In Tacoma, it was again a series of pleasant days with my family, with good visiting, eating, and card playing. On Friday, August 6, at 3:30 in the afternoon, in Saint Charles Borromeo Church in Tacoma, with all the family and many relatives—among them my two cousin priests, Fathers Arno Gustin, O.S.B., and Clement N. Gustin, O.S.C.—and friends present, as well as a number of fellow Jesuits, I offered a Mass of thanksgiving for twenty-five years of priesthood. A reception and dinner in the school hall followed the Mass. The next day, in the Church of the Visitation in Tacoma, I concelebrated with Father Arno as he offered a Mass of thanksgiving for Mr. and Mrs. Nicholas J. (Nick) Gustin, who were celebrating their fiftieth wedding anniversary. Nick, Father Arno's brother, was my first cousin; Emelia (née Renner), his wife, was my aunt. Again, it was one grand, extended family affair. On Sunday, we had a Renner family picnic at the home of my sister Julie and her husband, Duncan McMillan, on Horsehead Bay across the Narrows from Tacoma.

By Monday, August 9, I was back in Fairbanks, filled with many wonderful memories, and faced with much catch-up desk work. However, I did find time to attend the Tanana Valley Fair, a major annual mid-August event in Fairbanks. My main reason for attending the fair was to meet, greet, and chat with friends. I found time also to split more birch rounds at the Dykemas', to go blueberry picking with them, and to further pamper the little chokecherry saplings I had planted near the chancery building when I first moved in there.

My note in the calendar square for September 19 reads: "Great day in Denali National Park with Dykemas. Saw moose, caribou, foxes, a grizzly, and sheep." Not being a driver, I was blessed to have the wonderful friends, friends with tastes similar to mine, that I had in the Dykemas. We traveled many miles together. They rendered me many services; in turn, I rendered them many. Never did one party feel it owed the other anything and needed to repay. Mutual services were all wholly spontaneous, as in a family.

On Thursday, September 30, my ax and I flew to Galena, where Father Charlie Bartles needed to lay in a supply of stovewood for the winter. I was more than eager to help him. However, the stovewood had to wait for the time being. Cooling in his shed was a recently dropped moose that needed first to be sawed and cut up, packaged, and put aside for the winter. The meat was to be divided more or less equally among the missions of Galena, Nulato, and Kaltag. On Friday, Father Ted Kestler, the man entrusted with the pastoral care of Nulato and Kaltag, came to Galena in his boat. In it, he and I, with the quartered moose on board, motored downriver to Nulato, while Father Charlie flew down in his plane. At Nulato, Sisters Dolores Steiner and Dolores Pardini, stationed at Nulato and Kaltag, respectively, awaited us with sharpened knives. With Father Charlie, a skilled butcher, overseeing the whole process, the five of us got to work immediately. By Saturday afternoon, we had the moose sawed and cut up and wrapped into meal-size portions ready for the deep freeze. Father Charlie flew back up to Galena in his plane; I flew up commercially.

On Sunday, October 3, Father Charlie and I concelebrated Mass, then "made a driftwood log run". For the next five days, we gathered, sawed up, and split stovewood. Father Charlie manned the chainsaw; I swung the ax. Keeping cool was no problem, for it was precisely during that week that the Yukon started to freeze over. One morning, there was a narrow trim of ice along the bank. Steadily, this kept growing, until it was out to where one of the season's last fish wheels was still in place. As the wheel kept slowly turning, dipping, dripping, gradually a chandelier of ever-lengthening translucent icicles began to grace it. A photo of it found its way to the October 1984 page of the *Alaskan Shepherd* calendar. (In addition to putting out six issues of the *Alaskan Shepherd* as head of the Alaskan Shepherd fundraising program, I also produced an annual calendar with pictures in color accompanied by meaty captions.) On October 8, I returned to Fairbanks. I was in Barrow for the Saturday and Sunday Masses the weekend of the twenty-third and twenty-fourth.

Shortly after the middle of November, I started to make a series of health-related notes in the squares of my calendar: "Sore ribs ... grippe ... herpes zoster eruption! ... miserable as a dog ... feverish ... didn't do much of anything, some football ... Dr. Lundquist confirms herpes ... Did little because of shingles misery." It was a classic textbook case of shingles. I had them around the right midriff. For several

days, they pretty well laid me up. I took only two painkill-
ers, not wanting to get addicted to them. To keep my mind
off my misery, I began again to do limited work in my office
and to lead a more-or-less regular life. Slowly, the pain ebbed.
By February 13, 1983, I was able to write Dorothy Jean, "I'm
just about down to my last shingle."

During the last long week of 1982 and the first two days
of 1983, I was again in Tacoma, spending the nights at Bellarmine, as usual, and most of the days with Dad and Mom.
Much as I personally enjoyed visiting the immediate family,
as Dad and Mom were getting older, I wanted to spend more
time with them for their sakes. During their later years, I also
phoned them more often, especially Dad, after Mom died. As
it turned out, the Christmas of 1982 was the last one I was
to spend with any members of the family.

Chapter 21

Three Highly Eventful Years: 1983–1985

The year 1983 began on the cold side. On January 10, I noted, "Minus forty-seven, heavy ice fog!" During the first three months of that year, I spent a good part of my in-office time working on my biography of Father Tom Cunningham. As mentioned in an earlier chapter, this was published in 1985. On March 19–20 I was in Barrow for the Saturday and Sunday Masses. In my homily, I talked about Saint Joseph, how his whole life was one of total confidence and loving trust in Divine Providence. I was to be in Barrow again on June 4–5 for the feast of Corpus Christi. On March 26, in response to Bishop Whelan's request for input concerning "the process that will bring a coadjutor bishop to the Fairbanks diocese", I stated my firm conviction that the coadjutor bishop should still be, but for the last time, a member of a religious order or congregation because the clergy of the diocese were still, and would be for some time longer, mostly religious. I concluded, "The one man I would recommend very strongly is Father Michael J. Kaniecki. I consider him an excellent choice for the office of bishop in this diocese." At this time Father Kaniecki, to be ordained a bishop thirteen months later, was general superior of Jesuits in Alaska and pastor of Holy Cross and its dependent stations. To most, he was commonly known simply as "Father Mike".

Again, the Yukon was calling. On Monday, March 28, 1983, I left Fairbanks at 5:00 P.M. on a Wien jet for Anchorage. Some three hours later, I was airborne on another Wien plane; this one headed for Aniak, where I arrived at 9:00. There Father Mike, in his Cessna 180 Skywagon, met me. Normally, he did not fly at night. However, by that Holy Week night, a prolonged wind out of the north had swept the skies clear as crystal, and the Easter moon, full to capacity, pouring its soft, silvery light down on the snow-clad landscape, was turning the night into day. Our flight to Holy Cross took us across the Kuskokwim River, still wholly in hibernation, due north into the teeth of a stiff wind, across a landscape of ice and snow. Thirty minutes later, we crossed the mighty Yukon and landed at Holy Cross. After securing the plane, with Father Mike on his vintage snow machine and me standing on the ends of the sled runners behind, we roared off over the rough, icy road leading to the village. At the mission, Sister Marie Teresa—who, it may be remembered, was with Sister Judy Tralnes and me on Little Diomede Island in 1975—had a choice of hot beverages and a warm welcome awaiting us.

On Wednesday, Father Mike left for his Kuskokwim stations, Aniak and Kalskag. Before Holy Week activities became preoccupying, I took advantage of the lull to visit the village cemetery, then to climb and take the first of several hikes along the high bluff that rims the village of Holy Cross on the north and west. It was a crisp, clear day. Snow crystals sparkled in the sun like diamonds. In the stands of spruce, alder, birch, and aspen, the shaded air smelled cold and clean, a treat for lungs that had wintered in dead, polluted city air. As I moved along over the firm, snow-packed trail—pondering, distractedly, the mysteries and solemn rites of Holy Week—I kept a wary eye out for possible trouble in the form of a bear.

Moose, fox, and rabbit tracks there were in abundance, but no sign of bear.

Holy Thursday, too, dawned clear, but windy and just two degrees above. The village paths and roads, most of them on a slant, were glazed, owing to the thawing by day and the freezing by night of the remainder of the winter's snowpack. They were so slippery that, to accommodate especially the older people, we scheduled services earlier than originally intended. For traction, some people wore old socks over their footgear. I was offered crampons; but, too proud to be seen wearing them, I turned them down and took my chances—and my tumbles.

Sitting in the sacristy hearing confessions before the Holy Thursday services, I heard a soft giggle unlike anything I had ever heard before. Later, Sister Marie Teresa told me it came from a six-month-old infant. So mirthful and contagious was that giggle, that soon the whole congregation was infected by it and convulsed with suppressed laughter. It took a bit for all to sober up for the beginning of the Mass of the Lord's Supper. This was fairly well attended by a cross-section crowd.

The spare, austere Good Friday services began at 3:00 P.M. Quite a few children were present but not many adults. All came forward to venerate the Cross. Most received Communion.

On Saturday, Father Mike came over to Holy Cross to pick up Sister Marie Teresa for the Saturday and Easter Sunday services at Aniak and Kalskag. He had been alone the previous two days. Sister Judy Tralnes—in her fourth year as a teacher in the Holy Cross school—back from a teachers' meeting in Anchorage by then, was to be my helper.

On Holy Saturday, while I was hearing confessions, Sister Judy, with one of the parish women and several girls, cleaned and readied the church for the Vigil services. From Anchorage, she had brought two potted live Easter lilies to go with the lilies from storage, the kind that never need water, only an occasional dusting. The live lilies she put in front of the altar. Saint Joseph and Our Lady had to be satisfied with the plastic ones. The bouquet next to Our Lady's statue was to cause me some anxiety just before the Vigil service. The statue was located up front, right where the bell rope came into the church. In the process of ringing the bell, I knocked over the tall, slender vase holding the plastic lilies. Down came lilies, vase, and all the ballast—rice, beans, corn, pebbles. The contents of that vase simply exploded all over the carpet. The first people were due to arrive any minute. Frantically, on my knees, I began to scrape together cereal and rocks in an attempt to restore vase and lilies to their original condition and position. But those perennial lilies were long-stemmed and top-heavy and wanted to keep falling over. Time was running out, so, in desperation, I wedged part of that bouquet behind the statue and part behind a hot-water pipe coming down just there. Soon the lilies began to droop. However, while I was vesting for Mass, Sister Judy's touch was able, somehow, to make everything look quite natural again.

"This is the day that the Lord has made!" we sang on Easter Sunday morning. "Let us rejoice and be glad!" The day dawned warm, twenty degrees. Later the thermometer soared into the forties. The trails began to go soft. The church was full for the eleven o'clock Mass. Everything went well. At the presentation of the gifts, some of the little ones brought forward their "rice bowls", heavy with the coin of Lenten sacrifice. Most all went to Communion. Easter greetings and double "Alleluias!" ended those paschal solemnities.

On Monday afternoon, April 4, Father Mike flew me back to Aniak in good time to see the church and living quarters there and to catch my flight to Bethel. From there, I jetted to Anchorage and on to Fairbanks. An account of that pastoral outing appeared in the *Alaskan Shepherd* and was reprinted in *Extension Magazine,* under the title of "Alleluia, Bush Country".[1]

On May 6, 1983, I ended a letter to Dorothy Jean, "A little secret I share—for the time being—only with you. I was asked by our father provincial [Father Thomas R. Royce] whether I'd consider taking over as Oregon Province archivist. My present inclination is negative. Several other men would be well qualified and would vacate positions that could be more readily filled than my present one."

By now, I had spent many long hours in the Jesuit Oregon Province Archives, was fairly well acquainted with their contents, and personally had contributed many valuable materials to them. Around 1980, archivist Father Clifford Carroll, born in 1906, suggested to Superiors that they would do well to look around for someone to replace him. My name was the first to come up. Father Royce asked me to consider seriously being Father Carroll's replacement. I had, by then, been on the Alaska mission for a total of twenty years and on the Alaskan Shepherd assignment for almost three.

On May 14, I wrote Father Royce:

Somehow I feel this is, and will remain, one of the most important letters I have ever penned, or will ever pen, my name to. It is written after much thought and prayer. I have not discussed the matter with anyone, though I did mention to Father Kaniecki that you raised the question of my possibly taking over as Oregon Province archivist. I suppose I could just let the whole matter simmer on the back burner of my mind, but that is not my nature. So, I will here put in writing the various considerations that occur to me—and, in between the lines, manifest my discerning conscience.

1. *Extension Magazine* 78, no. 9 (March/April 1984): 15–18.

Twenty-five years ago this summer I first set foot on this blessed soil of Alaska. Three years ago today I moved into the 1316 Peger Road residence, ready to take on the Alaskan Shepherd work on the assumption that this would be my last major life's work. I love Alaska. I love this present apostolate.

Some years ago already, Father Schoenberg asked me if I would consider taking over as Oregon Province archivist. Seemed like a way-out thought then. Now you ask me.

I think I could grow into the job and do it adequately. If this seems to be the will of God for me, I would like to understudy Father Carroll and have time to ease into the job. I would do well to visit some major archives. If these last two points are conceded, then my move south should not be too far off.

I am going on fifty-eight. If the Oregon Province Archives are to be my next apostolate, I would like to think that they will be my last major one—assuming that I measure up to expectations. I would not want to leave Alaska for just some years. I am speaking humanly here, not conditioning my obedience. If I were asked to leave this Alaskan Shepherd job, I would like to think that I am leaving it for good. The Oregon Province Archives and the Alaskan Sheperd jobs cannot be slipped into and out of all that simply. Both are my kind of apostolates and the kind to which I can bring total dedication more readily, if I see them as fairly long-range.

Several observations: It is no secret that within the not-too-distant future the Diocese of Fairbanks will most likely be headed by a new bishop. Will he want an Alaskan Shepherd operation? There is every reason to think that he should, but time alone will tell. I do not see an obvious successor to myself in this job, but prejudice in this matter surely clouds my vision.

In sum: All in all, and honestly, I feel myself fairly indifferent to staying on here or moving on to the Oregon Province Archives job. I do, however—again, without conditioning my obedience—feel I should let you know that I would not like this matter to drag on all too long, my nature being what it is, the nature of this job being what it is, Father Carroll's age being what it is.

Somehow I see myself as approaching the last major fork along the path of my active apostolic life. *Oremus....*

I might mention here that one day, before this archivist matter had come up and before he had any inkling that he might be the future bishop of Fairbanks, Father Mike Kaniecki, then my major mission superior, dropped into my office for some small talk. At one point, speculating about my future as head of the Alaskan Shepherd fundraising program, I remarked, "I suppose the next bishop, whoever he might be, will want this program to go on." To that, Father Mike said, "He'd be crazy if he didn't."

An answer to my letter to Father Royce was not long in coming. On May 18, he wrote:

Thank you very much for your letter of May 14. I see this now as an invitation to investigate further this possibility of your shifting to the archives as a real apostolate, perhaps the last of your career. I do not consider the decision coming immediately, but the considerations that you bring up certainly help us to proceed to a decision. Before I move any further with regard to you, I will write Father Kaniecki, and I am sure I will get an immediate reaction from him. This is an important consideration insofar as I certainly do not wish to cause an injury to the Alaskan apostolate that would be impossible to heal.

Thank you for telling me how you feel yourself and the necessity of not letting this drag on. I will do my best to come to some resolution as quickly as possible. I know that you're a good Jesuit who will tackle the jobs that you are given, but I want also to see what is the best way to work it out for all concerned. In the meantime we'll keep praying, Louie, for all the graces we need to do our various jobs and ask the Lord to help us accomplish what He wants in our lives.

By May 24, Father Royce had written to Father Kaniecki and had gotten an "immediate reaction" from him. On that same day, Father Kaniecki phoned me concerning his thinking on the subject of my becoming archivist. He felt strongly that I should stay with the Alaskan Shepherd job. To Father Kaniecki I wrote that same May 24 day—sending him copies of the letters Father Royce and I had exchanged:

Enclosed are two letters that fill you in on the subject of my possibly taking over as Oregon Province archivist. My letter of May 14 to Father Provincial states my position on the subject about as honestly as I can state it. Were I to write that letter today, I would write pretty much what I have written there.

I must add, however, that after the brief conversation we just had on the phone, I feel kind of "reborn", as if a sentencing has been lifted. That tells me something about myself: Alaska has me "hooked". I entered the province for Alaska. I want to give it my all. I am speaking humanly now, as Louie Renner feels. Father Renner, S.J., has stated his case in the letter to the provincial.

This Oregon Province Archives matter has been a time of deep spiritual considerations and prayer for me, a time of grace, a time of mixed emotions, a time of interior peace. For all this I am grateful. In sum: concerning the Oregon Province Archives position as it affects me, I leave the matter willingly and confidently in the hands of superiors. *Fiat voluntas Dei!* I pray. I await. My mind is more at ease.

On June 14, I wrote to Father Royce:

A month ago today I wrote you concerning my possibly taking over as Oregon Province archivist. It has been a tough
month for me. Just now I talked with Bishop Whelan, and
he suggested I write you my present thinking on this subject. I have given the matter thought and prayer.

Since my letter of May 14, several considerations have come
up that prompt me now to inform you that I would like no
longer to be considered for the Oregon Province Archives
position—all this being understood within the framework of
Jesuit obedience, of course.

Following your directive to "prayerfully read some sections of readings from the Constitutions", I reread the part
on mission service. From this, I conclude that a man should
be withdrawn from the missions only for very serious reasons. You know this, of course, but—I guess what I want to
say is that I should not give you encouragement to yank me
out. As you know [Father Royce and I had been fellow nov-
ices], I entered the Society with hopes of serving in Alaska.
This August it will be twenty-five years that I have been up
here, happy years, all of them. I would like to continue on
here. I feel I should be left here. But all this within the
framework of Jesuit obedience.

The very day I was writing that letter, Father Royce was
writing one to me. "This is to inform you", it began,

that we discussed the archives at our last consultors' meeting, and the general conclusions were that we would not
ask you to return to the province as yet. Father Cliff Carroll seems to be in pretty good shape and wants to continue.

Your work in Alaska is certainly important, and we do not
wish to disturb it now. I would hope that the commitment

you made to Alaska can be kept for some years to come. Thank you for your great indifference and willingness.

Assuming that the whole matter of my taking over, or not taking over, as archivist was now resolved and was a dead issue, and that I would not be yanked out of Alaska after all, I wrote to Father Royce on June 16:

This is to thank you very sincerely for your letter of June 14 and for the news it brings me and the kind words you have for me. All are much appreciated and gratefully received. My mind is at peace.

I am renewing my dedication to the Alaska mission almost as if I were just assigned to it. Much good has come to me during recent weeks thanks to the Oregon Province Archives matter. The archives will continue to receive my full support in the future, as they have in the past.

A flash ahead! On the evening of April 30, 1984, after a rehearsal for the services at which Father Kaniecki was to be ordained a bishop the following day, Father Royce and I happened to meet on the deck of the chancery building. In the course of some small talk, I said, "I suppose the archive matter is settled by now." "Ohhhh no it isn't! It's still very much up in the air!" he shot back. That came as a surprise, and as a bit of a shock, to me. So there was still the possibility that I might be called out of Alaska to serve as Oregon Province archivist! The import of those three little words in Father Royce's letter cited above, "as yet" and "now", had not registered with me.

The matter was definitively laid to rest when Father Neill R. Meany, approached by Father Royce about taking over the Alaskan Shepherd work in order to free me to be archivist, said (not suspecting that his answer would backfire), "Sure! I have always been interested in the archives." "You *have*!" Father Royce came back. "You're *it*!" On May 22, 1984, Father Royce phoned me the good news that Father Meany was the new archivist. And so, for years, Father Meany was Jesuit Oregon Province archivist, and I the happy head of the Alaskan Shepherd fundraising program.

My letter of June 25, 1983, to Dorothy Jean ends with, "There's a Ruby in my life!" At the very time I was seriously being considered for the archives position, I was also seriously being considered as the one to take over the pastoral care of Ruby. In its early days, Ruby, on the middle Yukon, was a white man's mining camp; but, by the 1980s, it had been, for many decades already, a predominantly Koyukon Athabaskan Indian village. The question of my taking on Ruby was raised for the first time by Bishop Whelan on May 24, 1983. In my June 14 letter to Father Royce, I wrote: "Bishop Whelan has been hoping all along that I would take care of the Ruby parish, going there about twice a month. I told him I was willing, as long as this additional duty was compatible with my present work and physical and spiritual energies. As of today, I am committed to Ruby, beginning in August."

During the early part of July 1983, Brother Feltes, born in 1898, took sick to the point of needing to spend some time in the hospital. When he returned to the Jesuit residence, I cared for him in a limited way, mainly by carrying his meals to him and by bringing him to the chapel, where we had Mass together. On July 19, I saw him to his seat on an Alaska Airlines plane for his flight south to California. By that time, we had become close friends. Until close to the end of his long life (he died in 1993), we exchanged letters at regular intervals. Brother Feltes was the first Jesuit ever to fly an airplane. My article "To Fly and to Fix" tells his story.[2]

On Friday morning, July 29, 1983, I saw Ruby—"the Gem of the Yukon"—for the first time. Father Thomas W. Fisk, S.J., whom I was replacing, met me and, at an afternoon cookie and tea party on the grass behind the church, introduced me to a fair number of the Ruby parishioners. Nora Kangas invited us to dinner that evening. Her husband, Al, was out at his gold mine. For almost two decades, I always felt myself a welcome guest at the Nora and Al Kangas home and table.

I spent the better part of Saturday with a paintbrush in my right hand. During the forenoon, I was on the roof of the church giving the big cross a new coat of white paint. This was a somewhat tricky operation for a man with only two arms and two hands. The roof, rather steep-pitched, was topped off with slippery sheet metal. Straddling the ridge of the roof bowleggedly, with my left arm wrapped around the cross and my left hand holding the paint bucket, I wielded the paintbrush with my right. Getting the upper two-thirds of the cross painted was not too much of a problem. The lower third, however, presented quite a challenge. Somehow, I managed to hang on and get the job done without getting white paint all over me. After the cross-painting job, I had an easy time of it in the afternoon. Standing on a ladder, I painted red the outside walls of the new addition to the living quarters in back of the church. One of the pluses of being up on the roof for some time, besides getting the cross painted, was that it gave me, a newcomer in the village, a high profile. Since the church was on the main road running through Ruby, many Rubyites saw me on the roof

2. *Company* 2, no. 3 (April 1985): 18–19.

of the church. To the question "Who was that guy up there on the roof of the church painting the cross?" they received the answer "Oh, that was Father Lou, our new Ruby priest." To most of the people in Ruby, I was always to be simply "Father Lou".

Sunday, the thirty-first, was the feast of Saint Ignatius. Concelebrating with Father Fisk, I offered my first Mass—of many—in Ruby. On Monday, around noon, we flew to Fairbanks. That flight turned out to be the roughest flight I was ever on. The whole plane load, including the pilot and me, became quite airsick before it was over. During my forty years in Alaska, that was the only time I experienced airsickness. However, by the evening of that day, Father Fisk and I, along with most of the Alaskan Jesuits, were at Holy Spirit Retreat House in Anchorage ready to begin our annual retreat, an event we Alaskan Jesuits always looked forward to.

A tragic death in Ruby necessitated my being back there sooner than I had anticipated. A young man had ended his life by his own hand. I flew there on Tuesday, August 16. The following day, while we were waiting for the body to be returned to Ruby from Fairbanks, where it had been taken for an autopsy, I painted the window frames of the church. The body arrived on the eighteenth. That afternoon, we had a Rosary and wake in the community hall. The funeral Mass and burial took place on Friday.

The last five days of September saw me at Kaltag again, helping Father Kestler and Brother Jakes lay in a winter's supply of stovewood. That was anything but a pleasant outing. It rained heavily the whole time. It turned out to be a case of mixing the useful with the—*un*pleasant. I spent the weekend in Ruby before returning to Fairbanks. On October 5, I wrote to Dorothy Jean, "Ruby is getting to be a routine, and I like it more all the time."

Not considering myself a "natural" for pastoral ministry in the bush, and having some misgivings about the quality of my Ruby ministry, I was heartened by what I read in a letter written to me on November 29, 1983, by my general superior, Father Kaniecki: "I had a nice visit with Tom Fisk when I was in Toronto the first part of this month. He is doing well but surely misses the folks in Ruby. However, he is so very, very pleased with the excellent job that you are doing there. I take it that the feedback from the locals is very favorable toward you. That's really great! Keep up the fine work."

From Friday the twenty-third to Monday the twenty-sixth of December, I was in Ruby for my first Christmas there. My account of that Christmas appeared in an issue of the *Alaskan Shepherd* under the title "A Ruby White Christmas". Under the title of "A Ruby Christmas", it was reprinted in *Alaska Magazine*.[3] Without a title, it appears in *Alaskana Catholica*. It is reproduced here.

It is early Friday morning, December 23rd. Seven of us, passengers ticketed on the last scheduled pre-Christmas flight to Ruby, are crowded into the small bush air service office on the east ramp of the Fairbanks airport. Heavy snows continue to bury Alaska's interior. Chances of our making it to Ruby for Christmas look bleak. However, the flight is still "on hold," so we continue to nurse die-hard hopes. The other six live in Ruby. I am the pastor of St. Peter's parish there, and the people expect me for Christmas. We pass the time making small talk, reading, dozing.

Finally, at 10:48, the pilot decides to "give it a try." According to weather reports, things look a bit better downriver. We are not given much hope, but invited to board. We

3. *Alaska Magazine* 54, no. 12 (December 1988): 24–26, 44–45.

spring into action. In the pale light of the sub-Arctic dawn, leaning into the driving snow, we single-file our way to the twin-engine Chieftain parked by the hangar and climb in. Our pilot makes the usual comments about seatbelts, smoking, fire extinguishers, survival gear. We taxi out to the runway, are given clearance for takeoff, are airborne.

Through the solid, snow-filled cloud cover we bore our way upward, onward, westward, Ruby-bound. From time to time, we break briefly through the overcast and cruise along above a sea of swirling clouds. A half-hearted winter sun sheds a soft pinkish light on the cloudscape beneath us. Headwinds slow our progress.

We are 90 minutes into our flight and should be on the ground at Ruby by now. However, we have over-flown Ruby and are headed for Galena. "So much for Ruby!" I think to myself, resigned. But, our pilot knows what he is doing. He "shoots the approach" to the all-weather field at Galena, plunges down through the cloud cover, makes a 180-degree turn, and doubles back upriver, skimming low along the Yukon through pelting snow. We circle and land. Great sighs of relief!

A pickup truck drives up. We transfer luggage and mail. Two join the driver in the cab; the rest of us pile in back for the 2-mile drive down to the village. In the church, Peter Captain, thoughtful as always, has the new electric oil stove going, "just in case." Church and attached priest's quarters are nice and warm.

It is now mid-afternoon. I phone people and ask them to spread the word that I made it. I grab my plastic water jugs to get water at the village Laundromat. On the way, I drop in at the Trading Post, more to be seen than to buy. People are surprised to see me and ask, "When you come? Gonna be church tonight?"

Back in my quarters, I boil the kettle on the wood stove and, with a pint of tea, wash down some pilot bread and dried salmon, as I sort through a pile of accumulated mail, mostly bulk-rate fire-starter stuff.

I shovel my way to the outhouse and the bell tower. Back inside, I hear a commotion in the church. Two young men have brought in a Christmas tree and are setting it up. We admire the tree, exchange comments about the weather, and jokingly weigh the possibilities of a white Christmas. I offer tea. They decline and go, leaving behind little pools of snow-melt and spruce-scented air smelling of Christmas.

The phone rings. Nora Kangas invites me to a moose stew dinner, and I accept. At 7 o'clock, I ring the bell for the 7:30 Mass. An avalanche of snow off the bell hits me in the neck. The bell's peal is muted by all the snow, but the village canine chorus hears and answers with its well-rehearsed howling. It is close to 8 by the time the last, of the few, drift in. Mass is in my quarters. The service is intimate, devotional.

After Mass, we have tea, then decorate the tree with tinsel and ornaments from Christmases past. This year, for the first time, the people will see lights on the tree in St. Peter's Church. This we owe to Peter, who only yesterday put in an outlet up front.

Before we break up, we discuss the matter of the time for the Midnight Mass. Mothers with little children might prefer an earlier hour. We come to no conclusion, decide to think about it, to ask around. They go.

The place has cooled down, but I decide to leave the furnace off. It's up against the foot of my bunk bed, and, when that gun-fired, hot-air hurricane—with its sucking, roaring, blowing—blasts into life, deepest sleep is rudely interrupted. I pay the Lord a brief visit in the church, retreat into my down-filled sleeping bag, read a little, soon am fast asleep.

It's 9 o'clock, Christmas Eve morning, but still dark, when I wake up. I start a fire in the wood stove, make a short visit in the cold church, snack a breakfast, then settle back to meditate on the mystery of Christmas. The tea kettle simmers; the fire, a warm companion, pops and crackles, contented. I nod off.

Confessions are scheduled for 3 to 5 this afternoon. We need heat in the church. I flip the switch to "On." No reaction! I go out and check the oil. Plenty. Dusk is already settling. The mercury continues to drop. This furnace is beyond my campfire skills. I phone Peter. "B'right up!" he chirps.

He comes with his tools, whistling. He flips a switch here, presses a button there. No reaction. With wrenches and screwdrivers, he begins the autopsy. He suspects a plugged nozzle. To get at this vital part, he has to disassemble the very heart of our new heating machine. Plying his tools with the skill of a surgeon, he soon has the floor littered with assorted pieces of metal.

His diagnosis is correct. A grain too tiny to identify has choked out life. He blows out the nozzle and reassembles everything. I assist by directing the beam of the flashlight to where needed. He presses buttons; I throw the switch. The furnace roars into life. We smile and are grateful. He paper-towels up oil, wipes his hands, then gathers his tools. I offer tea, but he is in a hurry. I thank him again, then ask when we should have Midnight Mass. "At midnight, it's the custom!" I mention the matter of mothers with small children. "At midnight; it's the custom!" he repeats. That settles it. I phone the word around and post signs.

Hardly is Peter gone when the first, of the few, come for confession.

I prepare myself a simple Christmas Eve supper, a can of clam chowder and crackers. For dessert, I put a badly bruised banana out of its misery. It is now 6:40, the sky clear, cloudless, star-studded, the wind of the afternoon little more than a whisper, the mercury at 3 below. I go out to clear the front steps of the church and to shovel out again the paths to the outhouse and the bell tower. A thick fog is drifting up the

Yukon valley. I pass the early evening hours listening to Handel's *Messiah*, reading, reflecting, nodding off.

As early as 11:08, the first, of the many, announce their arrival in the church entry by stomping snow off their boots. At 11:30, I go out to ring the bell, a mere formality tonight, but it adds a festive note to village life. Inside, the people begin singing carols. Well before midnight, the little church is packed. I hear a few last-minute confessions in my quarters, then vest.

It is midnight. I go unto the altar of God. I greet the people: "May the grace and the peace of Christ, the Prince of Peace, Whose birthday we celebrate on this holy night, be with you all!" We pray, we sing, we hear readings about "the kindness and love of God, Our Savior," about angels and shepherds, about good news, peace, and joy. Bread and wine are brought forward, offered up, made holy. Many go to Communion. I wish all a joyous Christmas, bless them, dismiss them. On foot and on snow machines, they scurry off into the night.

After Mass, I notice some gift-wrapped packages under the tree. I leave them there. I snack on fruitcake and tea, unwind, turn in. Sleep comes without an effort.

On Christmas Day morning, we have Mass at 11:00. The crowd is small, yawns a lot. After Mass, we gather in my quarters for tea and cookies. When all have gone, I bring in the presents, open them, and am happy to get wool socks, a velour shirt, and jarred salmon strips. As I lunch leisurely, my thoughts turn to parents, brothers, and sisters in faraway places, to Christmases of other years.

Katie Kangas has invited me to Christmas dinner. From experience I know that, when Katie invites, it pays to come prepared. No appetizer like a brisk, winter walk.

It is now midafternoon, minus seven. The fog has lifted. Every spruce needle, every birch, every willow twig is furred with frost. I move through a world of bluish crystal as I climb the steep path leading to the cemetery on the bluff overlooking the village. After plowing my way among the graves and praying for the dead, I see down below a snow machine trail leading out across the river. I go down and follow it.

Gradually, I leave the village and its sounds behind. The trail parallels the far bank for a mile before heading up into the mouth of the Melozi River. The cold gets more intense. A lone raven in the crown of a spruce tree calls out into the frozen stillness. Isolated stars begin to pop through the pale-blue sky. It's time I headed back.

Later, in front of Ivan and me and their three little girls, Katie spreads out a turkey dinner with all the trimmings. We ask God to bless the food, and then we enjoy the feast. Afterwards, I romp with the kids and help them play with their toys.

I step out into the night air. It is laced with the smell of burning spruce and birch. No clouds, no moon, no northern lights. Myriads of stars spangling the black velvet sky above shine to their best advantage. It is now minus twenty-one, but, all "caloried up" as I am, the night feels almost balmy.

This is a night made for cabin-hopping. Behind every door I knock on, I find an unusually warm welcome. Tea, fruitcake, cookies, candy are pressed upon me. Kids show me their gifts. I admire a doll here, a windup robot there. The night wears on. My visits become shorter. Finally, with a last "Thank you!" and a last "Merry Christmas!" I head home. Somewhat weary, but soul-satisfied, I enter the church, pray a brief spell, and thank the good Lord for inventing Christmas. I turn off the furnace, slip into the sleeping bag, stretch out, relax—soon wake up in dreamland.

Next thing I know, it's Monday, no longer early, 33 below. Frost ferns adorn the window panes. The outhouse door creaks, groans on its frosty hinges. I'm scheduled to return to Fairbanks today. Will I make it? Small planes don't fly when it gets to be about 40 below. I get ready, just in case, and snuggle down in my sleeping bag for some reading. Soon I hear the plane buzz the village. The pickup is already outside, honking.

Two teachers and I board the Cessna 207. The pilot adjusts his headset, glances back to see that we are buckled in, turns the key. The engine coughs and catches. We begin to taxi. Full power, and in the dense, brittle-cold air, the 207 roars into the cloudless sky like a homesick angel.

A vast, empty white world slips beneath us as we drone across the 200-plus wilderness miles that separate Ruby from Fairbanks. At 1:09 in the afternoon, we taxi up to the hangar on the east ramp. Our pilot chops the power. The plane shudders momentarily as the propeller jerks to a stop. Silence, except for the clicks of rapidly cooling metal. Our pilot logs the flight on his clipboard. We unbuckle, stretch, climb out, and wait for our rides into town. My first Ruby Christmas is history.

The year 1984 was to bring with it for me some events of major significance. There would be, of course, also the routine Alaskan Shepherd–related work, the trips to Ruby about every third week, the gatherings of priests every third Thursday of the month, the fairly frequent walks to Fairbanks Memorial Hospital to visit the sick (mostly people from Ruby), the Saturday afternoon opera broadcasts to listen to, the welcome changes from the desk to the Dykemas' garden or woodpile, the occasional lunches out with the Alaskan Shepherd staff to celebrate the birthday of one or other, the work on personal writing projects, the never-ending letter writing, the limited hours before the TV set watching some professional sports game, the receiving of visitors in my office, and many more matters of lesser importance.

On December 7, 1983, Father Poole had written to me, asking me to write a one-hundred-page book about the radio station he had founded. I agreed. Accordingly, after spending five days in Tacoma visiting my family, I spent January 3–5, 1984, in Spokane researching KNOM- and Father Poole–related materials in the archives. My 150-page book *The KNOM/Father Jim Poole Story* was published by Binford & Mort in 1985.

Once again, a sad event called me to Ruby at an unexpected time. I flew there on the eighth of February to bury the younger brother of the man I had buried on August 19 the previous year. The burial took place on the thirteenth. This man had fallen victim to an unexpected extreme cold spell that caught him between two of his trapping camps. His brother, also on the trail between the two trapping camps, was somewhat more fortunate. He survived but lost both hands and both feet from freezing. I was to visit him often in the Fairbanks hospital.

To Dad and Mom I wrote on February 15, "The grief that that poor family has suffered is beyond imagining. Many visitors from all along the Yukon were present for this sad occasion. But it was not only grief and sadness. There was also much caring and sharing manifested. And God bless the Olympic Games! Watching them helped pass some of the time and divert the mind for short moments from the almost overwhelming grief that rested over the whole village. As time goes on and I get to know the people better, their joys and sorrows become more and more also mine." Sister Patricia Ann Miller, O.P., then serving in Ruby, was of great support to me during that time of general sorrow.

Given the great amount of travel by air I did in bush Alaska, I met up with few "incidents". On March 9, however, I did meet up with a minor one. On the way to Ruby, we made a stop in Tanana. Boarding in Fairbanks, I took the last seat on the right, opposite the door. In Tanana, a little boy was placed across the aisle from me in the seat just ahead of the door. Shortly after takeoff, that rear door dropped open. Concerned that the little fellow might get sucked out, I leaned over and grabbed hold of his arm and, at the same time, tapping the shoulder of the guy ahead of us, I drew his attention to the open door. A relay of shoulder-tapping alerted the pilot. We made a wide circle and landed. The door secured, we were on our way again, Ruby-bound.

It was my good fortune to be in Ruby the second weekend of March 1984, just as the front runners of the Iditarod Trail Sled Dog Race—among them two of the four men from Ruby running the race that year—were coming in. At Ruby, the racers hit the Yukon for the first time. The first musher to reach the Ruby checkpoint always received a seven-course gourmet meal prepared by the chef from Anchorage's Regal Alaskan Hotel, as well as a cash prize. The media was there in full force. Sunday the eleventh was a cloudless, mild day, a cameraman's delight. At 10:55, I went out the back door again to ring the second bell for the eleven o'clock Mass. I then went in to vest. Hardly back in my quarters, I heard a hesitant rap on the door. I opened it. There stood a media man with a yard-long fuzzy microphone. "Could you please ring the bell again? I'd like to record it", he hesitatingly asked. I was happy to oblige. After I had vested for Mass, but before I began the liturgy, I told the congregation why I had rerung the bell. Smiles of approval! This was a most memorable, festive day for Ruby. That afternoon, I counted thirteen small planes parked on the river ice below the village.

With the race and its runners on the minds and on the lips of all the Rubyites, I took occasion, in my homily, to comment on race-related texts in Sacred Scripture. I reminded the people that we were all running a race, the race of life;

that we were not running it in vain; and that we had to per-
severe in it, had to finish it, had to reach its goal, had to
keep the faith, if we hoped to receive its reward, the crown
of unfading glory, the crown of eternal life. I reminded them
further that, in the race we were running, we were compet-
ing only with ourselves and that it was a once-in-a-lifetime
race, ours to win or to lose—a win-all, lose-all race.

As my scheduled "direct" Fairbanks-to-Ruby flight had
taken me to Ruby by way of Tanana, so my scheduled "direct"
Ruby-to-Fairbanks flight took me downriver for a landing in
Galena, then back upriver again and on to Fairbanks. During my years in Alaska, few flights to the bush went as scheduled. Departure delays and reroutings were the norm rather
than the exception. I learned early on to expect them and to
be prepared for them. I never considered myself ready for bush
travel until I had an easily accessible shirt, jacket, or parka
pocket full of throwaway reading material and crossword puz-
zles. Such items helped shorten what, at times, were hours
of waiting, or hours of flight over a sea of clouds.

On Monday, March 12, less than twenty-four hours after
I had returned to Fairbanks, I found myself once again airborne, this time en route to Saint Mary's, there to participate in a four-day meeting as a member of a diocese-wide
planning committee that had for its theme "Pulled by Our
Vision, Not Pushed by Our Crises". I took many photos. Of
these, a good number were used to illustrate "Mapping Our
Way", the printed brochure summarizing "three years of work
by the Long-Range-Planning Task Force of the Fairbanks diocese". At the meeting, I gave a slide presentation on the history of the Catholic Church in northern Alaska. Regarding
it, I wrote to Dorothy Jean on April 3: "My slide presentation seemed well received. I showed three of Ruby with the
comment that I was favoring Ruby a bit because the pastor

of Ruby and I are good friends. Some chuckled; some didn't."
I had, by that time, given many slide presentations, mainly
at the University of Alaska–Fairbanks to my German classes
on German-related topics. After my King Island trip, I gave
presentations about it to on-campus groups, as well as to
groups in Tacoma and Spokane. Being by nature a shy man,
I found it much easier to give slide shows than to give talks,
lectures, sermons, and homilies.

On Tuesday morning, as Father Kaniecki and I were walking from one of the mission buildings, where we had spent
the night, up to the community hall for another meeting and
were making small talk, I casually said, "I suppose one of
these days we'll find out who the new bishop is." Tapping
me on the shoulder and pointing to himself, he said, "Louie,
I'm it. Bob will announce it at the beginning of this meeting." And this Bishop Robert L. (Bob) Whelan did!

Soon after that meeting, it was made public that Father
Kaniecki would be ordained a bishop on May 1 and that the
Diocese of Fairbanks and the city of Fairbanks would, the fol-
lowing day, host Pope John Paul II and President Ronald
Reagan. Attending that Saint Mary's meeting was, among
many others, George Sundborg Jr., son of Mary and George
Sundborg Sr. and brother of Steve Sundborg. (As mentioned
in an earlier chapter, Mary and George and Steve were my
hosts in Washington, D.C., in 1960.) It was further made
public that George Jr. would be one of the co-chairmen, John
Hajdukovich being the other, of the Papal Visit Executive
Committee. Father Francis W. (Frank) McGuigan, S.J., was
to be the chief coordinator of the whole affair.

On March 18, I was on the roof of the Dykema house
shoveling off snow. The day following, as a member of the
Papal Visit Executive Committee, I took part in the first, of
many, breakfast meetings. Soon, a prebreakfast concelebrated

Mass began to be part of those meetings. My role, described officially as "diocesan media coordinator", was mainly to assist George Sundborg Sr.—called up from Seattle to be the committee's link to the media—to produce press releases, and to attend to publicity. Before Father Kaniecki moved to Fairbanks, I served also as his man there. Gradually, the committee grew and subcommittees were formed as the whole event became far more complex than any of us had ever imagined. With an episcopal ordination about to take place, and a pope and a president, along with a host of other dignitaries of church and of state, about to come to town, there were countless details that needed attention. It was a busy, exciting time for all concerned. Nevertheless, my Alaskan Shepherd–related work had to go on as usual. And there were the regular trips to Ruby. On April 19–23, I was there for the Holy Week and Easter Sunday services. By that time, there was already much thawing and melting and therefore lots of mud in the village— devout mud, judging by how much of it went to church that Holy Week and Easter.

On May 1, at the Mass during which Father Kaniecki was ordained a bishop, Father Jim Sebesta and I, as his assistant priests, had high-profile, even if merely honorary, roles. Throughout the ceremonies, we flanked him: Father Jim on his left, I on his right.

May 2, 1984, was a day without rival in the history of the city of Fairbanks. My laconic diary entry for the day reads, "Went to airport around 7:30 A.M. Saw Pope John Paul II and President Reagan. Everything seems to have gone all right. Cold, drizzle, was chilly." Sometime before May 2, I was told that, as a member of the executive committee from the outset, I would be given one of those VIP tickets that would clear me to be part of that elite group that would be allowed close to the pope and the president. Somehow, I was overlooked when the VIP tickets were handed out. At first, I considered myself lucky to get even a general-admissions ticket—and that, at the last minute. Soon, however, I saw that not getting that VIP ticket was actually a blessing in disguise; for, instead of being a member of a relatively small group of dignitaries surrounded by a ring of secret service men, I was part of a crowd of several thousand, free to come and go, to meet and greet friends and acquaintances, to enjoy the general excitement, to snap pictures at will.

At this time, I was still working on what was published in 1985—as mentioned above—under the title of *The KNOM/ Father Jim Poole Story*. For some years, I had been contemplating a "pilgrimage" to the closed Pilgrim Hot Springs mission and a hike to the summit of the Seward Peninsula's highest peak, 4,714-foot-high Mount Osborn, the crowning cap of the Kigluaik Mountains north of Nome, known also as the Sawtooth Range because of their jagged peaks. Given the need, admittedly rather slight, to do "research and fieldwork" for the KNOM/Poole story, I now had a plausible pretext for a trip to Nome. Via Kotzebue, I flew to Nome in the forenoon of June 28 in a Harold's Air Service twin-engine propeller plane. As we flew through, not over, the Kigluaik Mountains, I was rather sobered by what I saw. Far from being merely the high, somewhat bald, hills I had imagined them to be, they were real mountains, topped off by sharp peaks and big fields of snow.

Father Poole met me at the Nome airfield, drove me to station KNOM, and gave me a room in Gleeson Hall, one of the old bungalows housing volunteers working at the station. Next, he, Tom Busch—KNOM's general manager—and I sat down to lunch and to talk about the book I was in the process of writing. In the course of our conversation, I mentioned, in passing, that I would like to climb Mount

Osborn, then hike into Pilgrim Springs. It was a clear day. "This weather could change anytime", Tom said. "You'd better go for it while it lasts." By 4:30 that afternoon, thanks to my having accepted his spontaneous offer to drive me there, I found myself standing on the bridge spanning the Grand Central River and searching the irregular horizon at the far end of the river valley for the summit of Mount Osborn. There he stood, old Oz, my destination, back in about twelve miles, a little up and to the left. With the Grand Central having its source on Mount Osborn, there was little danger of my getting lost.

To some, 4:30 P.M. may seem like rather late in the day for one to be starting on a hike into the mountains. Elsewhere, maybe, but at that far-northern latitude and extreme western longitude, and with double daylight saving time in effect, it was, by actual sun time, little more than early afternoon. There was no wind; and the sun in the limpid blue subarctic sky above, having, at the moment, nothing more important to do, was blazing light and heat down upon me in superabundance. I shrugged into my backpack, crossed the bridge, and, paralleling the left bank of the river, began the gradual ascent of the valley over terrain that was alternately barren, brushy, soggy, and rocky. Mosquito repellent, Muskol, reduced the cloud of mosquitoes accompanying me to little more than a sight and a sound. I was now also in grizzly bear country—without a gun. In brushy stretches, I whistled snatches of many things to make my presence known. As it turned out, I saw no sign of bears on that hike. What the area, somewhat to my surprise, lacked in birdlife, it more than made up for in wildflowers. In endless profusion and variety, they bloomed to gladden the eye, to brighten and relieve the general austerity of that region. Some seemed to live on air alone, seemingly having only rock for soil.

I had set myself a steady, but leisurely, pace and paused only to photograph flowers, scan my surroundings for wildlife, or simply contemplate that vast, solitary wilderness. Still, given the heat of the late afternoon and the heavy pack, it took little exertion for me to get dehydrated. Fortunately, crystal-clear, refreshing snowmelt water was tumbling, gurgling, streaming all about me, irresistibly there for the dipping.

After a four-hour trek, I was well into the valley of Oz. The going on the other side of the river now looked somewhat easier; so I took off my boots and socks, waded into the knee-deep stream, and picked and shivered my way over its rocky bottom to the opposite side. Even at that time of year and day, the Grand Central was fordable all along its course.

When my watch was about to tick 10:00 P.M., I came to where the creek heading in Glacier Lake flows into the Grand Central. This presented an ideal campsite. By now, my boots and pack were getting rather heavy. I pitched my tent for the night. I was now, more or less, at the base of the Osborn massif.

The evening was calm, cloudless; the mosquitoes, mildly merciful. I snacked outside my tent, all the while studying the mountain panorama before me, trying to determine what might be the most feasible approach to the summit of Osborn. My eyes told me plenty; my memory of what I had seen earlier in the day, as we flew through the heart of these mountains, helped fill in the rest of the picture. By the time I turned in for the night, I had come to the conclusion that I had already pressed my luck far enough—hiking alone in that wild country—and that to continue on up, to climb around up there alone, would be foolhardy. I closed my eyes, resigned to the thought that I would have to content myself with exploring only the lower elevations.

The next day, Friday, June 29, dawned cloudless. Though I had had a short night's sleep, I felt refreshed and saw my immediate world in a new light. I decided it really would not be too risky, after all, if I just sort of nibbled my way up to one of the lower ridges. However, climb one, and the next one beckons and draws irresistibly. Up and ever up I clambered. My immediate goal was a big patch of shade up and to my left. There was, that morning, not a whisper of a breeze, and the powerful June sun on the dark talus made the ascent fiercely hot. The bandana I was using to keep the salt brine out of my eyes got so saturated that I had to wring it out from time to time. I never did catch up with that elusive shade. The sun kept erasing it as I kept edging toward it.

At one point, just as I was nearing the crest of a ridge, a pleasant surprise greeted my eyes. The going now resembled ladder climbing. Glancing up, looking for the next handhold, I saw before me—only inches from my face, and stretched across the boulders—a great, silvery cobweb gleaming in the morning sun. Its builder and sole occupant sat fat and contented at its central crossroads.

"Go for it!" they had urged me in Nome. "Go for it!" I now urged myself. "It" was now the very summit of old Oz himself. Although it was not in sight yet, I felt it was within reach. Several peaks that earlier appeared to be the summit were, by this time, well below me. I knew where the true summit had to be, up and to the right, at the end of that sharp rim just above me. I climbed resolutely onward, upward, pausing only to catch my breath, to wipe my brow, to take in the majestic scenery all around me, and to expose film.

At almost exactly noon, clock time, I surmounted a last, near-vertical wall, and, somewhat abruptly, there I was, standing on a tiny flat spot atop Mount Osborn. I sat down and, for a while, in solitary splendor, lunched, admired the few hardy flowers sharing the summit with me, and let my eyes roam out over the sea of peaks undulating off to the southwest. The short sleep the night before, the morning climb, the warm sun, and the lunch made my head heavy. I took my boots off, and, using my pack for a pillow, stretched out, yawned, and dozed off. Only inches from my feet was a sheer drop-off of nearly a thousand feet. I snoozed where sleepwalkers should fear to tread.

After a short, but refreshing, nap, I woke up a bit chilled. The slight breeze that had meanwhile begun to stir was bringing up to me cool air exhaled by the Seward Peninsula's only glacier immediately below me. Overhead, seemingly out of nowhere, wads of billowing clouds were forming. The sun was now no longer the sole master of the midday sky. It was time I headed down.

Before starting down, I lectured myself—out loud!—on the need for extreme caution. One false step on that steep pile of loose boulders could easily have spoiled what up to then had been a very rewarding day. Ever so slowly, I worked my way off the summit, along the great rim running southward. At regular intervals, I crept up to the rim's edge to peer over and take pictures of the still-icebound lake and awe-inspiring panorama below. Then I inched slowly backward and downward again.

When I got down and over to the long, narrow snowfield, I discovered an easier, faster way of descending than backing down on all fours. On the soles of my boots, I literally skied down the steep upper stretches of crusted snow. Farther down, on the gentler grades, I sat on my bottom and glissaded, being careful all the while not to lose control. Only the boulders at the bottom would have stopped me. Altitude gained so laboriously in the course of hours I lost in minutes. The speedy descent, and the fun of it all, more than compensated me for the temporary discomfort of a wet bottom.

It was by now midafternoon. I was down in the lower elevations again and felt secure, on easy street, relaxed. Once again, wildflowers were everywhere. I just kept slow-pokin' along, stopping often to admire them, to photograph them— and to take on water. The climb up had left me severely dehydrated. In the late afternoon, I reached my next destination, Glacier Lake. This calm, alpine mirror was still partially ice-covered, but the open part reflected to perfection the surrounding peaks. The stillness, the serenity of it all, was but the calm before the storm that was to overtake me some hours later.

When I was about to exit that immense, secluded amphitheater that the upper part of the Grand Central River valley is, I should have crossed the river to continue on out as I had come in. Had I done so, I would not have found myself slogging through a soggy, swampy, mosquito-infested jungle of alders and willows. To make matters worse, what earlier had been a sky splotched only with patches of clouds was now a solid overcast pouring down its surplus water unstintingly upon me. I had watched as the mountains gathered that rainstorm, and I had been on the lookout for a suitable campsite, but the rain overtook me before I could find one. Soaked from head to foot anyway, I decided to press on, straight ahead, with water squishing in my boots, onward through brush, swamps, and side creeks to the road to walk myself dry.

Just as I hit the road, a car happened along. The occupants stopped and offered me a ride. I didn't even take time to empty my boots. They drove me north on the Taylor Highway, to where the road into the Pilgrim Hot Springs mission forks off, then down to the end of that. This road was just in the process of being put in. It still had about two miles to go before it would reach the mission. A small jeep was parked at the end of the road. I climbed in and dozed from about 11:30 P.M., Friday, June 29, till 7:10 the next morning. Those final two miles to the mission proved to be rather tough going. The trail consisted of two ruts chewed into the tundra by an all-terrain vehicle. At the mission, I met the owner of the jeep, visited with him, and had him show me where the cemetery was. I wanted especially to visit the grave of Father Ruppert, about whom I had written an article. On my own, I visited the various mission buildings and grounds and took some photos. After we had had brunch together, he brought me out to the road on a cart pulled by a tractor. I made my way up to the Taylor Highway and hiked along this till I came to Crater Creek. I followed this up a little way, then pitched my tent and, according to my diary, "spent an excellent night there". On Sunday, July 1, I returned to the Taylor Highway. After I had walked this a good stretch, an Eskimo couple came along in a pickup and invited me to hop in back; and so, with their dog for a companion, I rode into Nome. I got there about 3:15 that afternoon. I celebrated Mass at 6:00.

I spent a good part of Monday in the KNOM studio observing announcers on the air. At 5:30, following the five o'clock Mass, I was on my way out of Nome, as a companion to Father Thomas A. (Tom) Carlin, S.J., pastor of the Nome parish, as he drove a woman, upon her pleading, out the Nome-Council Highway to her home in Council. It turned out to be a wonderful drive through raw wilderness. Along the way, we saw abandoned gold dredges, the rusting relics of the Council City and Solomon River Railroad, and even a grizzly bear. On the return trip, Father Tom stopped to do some fishing off the Solomon River bridge. It was now already past midnight, Tuesday, July 3. Near Nome, we saw three moose browsing together. By 3:30 P.M., that Tuesday, I was back in Fairbanks, with my "research and fieldwork" for the KNOM/Father Poole book well accomplished. Payment for my article "Hiking in the Land of Oz"[4] covered the costs of the trip.

In a letter dated July 5, 1984, Father Provincial Royce asked me, "Could you come to a special meeting at Gonzaga University on Monday, July 30, 1984, at 9:30 A.M.?" From 9:30 to 11:15 that morning, I was part of a group that discussed, at length, the matter of renovating Bea House on the campus of Gonzaga University, so as to make it a fit home for older, incapacitated, semiretired members of the Oregon Province, and how to raise the estimated five hundred thousand dollars needed for the renovation. Soon after that meeting, I drafted a special appeal letter addressed to the Alaskan Shepherd benefactors. The letter, over the signature of Bishop Whelan, appeared in an issue of the *Alaskan Shepherd*. It brought in around one hundred thirty thousand dollars.

On August 9, I made, among other notes in my diary, the simple notation, "At 8:30 A.M., concelebrated Mass for staff." This was the first Mass offered in the chancery building chapel for the members of the chancery staff. Thereafter, till I left Alaska in June 2002, on virtually every Thursday morning, I took part in those Masses, now as principal celebrant, now as concelebrant with the bishop or with another priest on the chancery staff. Homilies were always a part of those Masses. A simple breakfast, prepared by a staff member taking his or her turn, always followed the day's Mass. Those Thursday morning Masses and breakfasts did much to create a pleasant, familial spirit in the chancery.

4. *Alaska Outdoors* 8, no. 2 (March–April 1985): 66–71.

In Anchorage, at Holy Spirit Retreat House (known as Holy Spirit Center as of the year 1999), located in the foot-hills of the Chugach Mountains and overlooking Anchorage, my fellow Alaskan Jesuits and I made our annual retreat on August 16–23. Those retreats at Holy Spirit, harmonious blends of nature and grace, were annual high points for me for almost two decades.

On the weekend of September 1–2, Father Frank Mueller and I made a round trip up the James Dalton Highway to Dietrich Camp, near which we tented for the night. This was my only crossing and recrossing of the sole bridge spanning the Yukon River in Alaska.

On September 21–24, I was in Nome to attend Diocesan Planning Committee meetings but mainly to give the com-mittee members a slide presentation on the history of the Cath-olic Church in the Seward Peninsula area. Just one month later, I gave a Mission Sunday slide presentation in Sacred Heart Cathedral in Fairbanks; and, on December 12, I gave one on King Island to a class at Lathrop High School in Fairbanks.

Christmas at Ruby—with a penance liturgy, the Masses, two baptisms, and two First Communions—was for me the grand finale for the year 1984.

As early as January 1984, the word "Stickdance" began to appear in my diary. I was considering doing a major article on the subject of the Stickdance—a time-honored, sacred mor-tuary feast for the dead celebrated at irregular intervals alter-nately in the Koyukon Athabaskan Indian villages of Nulato and Kaltag. But I hesitated, since this was still a rather sen-sitive subject among some Jesuits in Alaska. However, in April 1985, I had my first opportunity actually to witness the whole ceremony. On the tenth, Bishop Kaniecki (pilot), Rita John-son, Morva Hoover—both Alaskan Shepherd staff members—and I flew to Kaltag. For four days, from the tenth to the thirteenth, we attended all the Stickdance ceremonies, observing them in all their details, and taking many photographs. The days were bright and sunny, the village still, for the most part, buried in the clean snows of winter. Many people I knew were in attendance. It was, in all respects, a most enjoyable, productive outing for me. My article "The Koyukon Athapaskan Stickdance and the Changed Attitude of the Jesuit Missionaries toward It" was published in *Alaska History*.[5]

The previous February, on the eighteenth, Dorothy Kamen-Kaye, a researcher in the field of ethnobotany at Harvard University, wrote to me, upon the recommendation of Dorothy Jean Ray, for help with her research "about the use of fungus as dried, reduced to ash, and combined with tobacco for chewing by Alaska Natives". The fungi in question were the kind growing on old, dead birch trees. "Specifically," she went on to add, "what I need is a sample of the fungus sold in Chevak and some of the fungi collected at Kaltag." How fortunate for her that I was to be in Kaltag so soon, something she could not have known when she wrote me! It was a simple matter for me to pick some fungi off old birch trees and send them to her. Also, from one of the users, I was able to get a sample of some ready-for-the-mouth "chew", as the Natives call it. The fungi, reduced to ashes, are mixed with the tobacco "to give it a bite". I interviewed several of the Kaltag women on the subject and sent the results of my interviews on to Dr. Kamen-Kaye. In her letter of thanks to Dorothy Jean for recommending me to her, she referred to me—only an instrument in the hands of a kindly Providence—as "that dear, wonderful Father Renner".

On April 18 and the following two days, I spent time with two Sisters of Saint Ann, Sisters Margaret Cantwell and

5. *Alaska History* 8, no. 1 (Spring 1993): 1–13.

M. George Edmond, discussing their manuscript history of the Sisters of Saint Ann in Alaska and in the Yukon Territory, Canada. I had given them some help with the production of it. Authored by Sister Margaret, in collaboration with Sister M. George, the book, entitled *North to Share*, was published in 1992. I was acknowledged in the book as one who "gave constructive criticism and assisted with Jesuit documentation". Sister Margaret inscribed her gift copy of the book to me: "For Father Louis L. Renner, S.J., whose encouragement, research assistance, prayer, and example helped to bring *North to Share* to completion, a grateful Sister Margaret gives thanks!" At the end of that three-day session, the sisters handed me a check in the amount of $500. Two days later, I put a check in the amount of $250 in the mail to them to help them with publication expenses. As will be seen, when I was in the process of writing *Alaskana Catholica*, Sister Margaret was to give me invaluable editorial assistance.

On September 24, I was at the University of Alaska–Fairbanks for the dedication of a new section of the Rasmuson Library. The principal speaker on that occasion was Alfons Cardinal Stickler, S.D.B, head of the Vatican Library and Archives. The following day, he and I sat across the corner of the table in the chancery dining room, lunching and chatting with one another, now in English, now in Viennese German.

Throughout the year 1985, I spent much time readying for publication *"Father Tom" of the Arctic* and *The KNOM/Father Jim Poole Story*. On October 15, three copies of the KNOM/Poole book reached me; and, exactly a month later, I picked up a shipment of the Cunningham book at the Alaska Airlines freight office. One reporter interviewed me on November 18, another on November 20. An autograph party took place at the Village Book Shop on the twenty-third. In my diary I noted a one-word summary of it: "Success!"

On November 17, it was my privilege to be the principal celebrant, with Father Anable concelebrating, of a Mass in the new home of Rita Johnson. The privilege of blessing the new home was Father Anable's. Together with Rita and some of her family, we enjoyed a simple meal after the sacred ceremonies.

On December 17, I gave a slide presentation to the urban deacon candidates entitled "The History of the Catholic Church in Northern Alaska". Another Ruby white Christmas more or less ended for me the year 1985.

Chapter 22

The Latter Half of the 1980s: 1986–1989

On March 24, 1986, in a letter to Dorothy Jean Ray, I commented: "It's been on the quiet side around here." The month before, I had written her that, other than producing copy for the *Alaskan Shepherd*, I was not into any writing. Her reaction to that was: "Since you have no writing projects under way, why don't you begin to write a history of the Catholic Church in Alaska? You are the *only* qualified person to do so." My answer to her question, given in that March 24 letter to her, was: "You ask why I don't begin to write a history of the Catholic Church in Alaska. One is surely needed; the materials are there; it's high time. However, much as I wouldn't mind giving it a try, I just do not have the time at present with the Shepherd job and Ruby. I would need to spend longer periods of time in Spokane. Your confidence in my ability to produce something worthwhile is really heartening. I shall wait and see."

In 1986, Easter Sunday fell on March 30. On Holy Thursday, Bishop Kaniecki, on his flight to Kaltag, dropped me off at Ruby for the Holy Week and Easter Sunday services. "That was in the Cessna 207," I wrote to Dorothy Jean on April 15, "a cold, cold airplane! I trotted the two miles down to the village and still was not warm. On the flight back I wrapped the engine cover around me. We were both dressed for the cold, but still it got to us."

349

During the middle of the afternoon on Easter Sunday, as I was relaxing, the phone rang. It was Dominican sister Patricia Ann Miller calling from Galena. "Can you come down to offer an evening Mass here? We'll charter a plane to get you." "Sure," I told her, "no problem." A military chaplain from Elmendorf Air Force Base in Anchorage had been scheduled to be in Galena for the Holy Week and Easter Sunday services. However, fallout ashes from erupting Mount Saint Augustine kept planes grounded in Anchorage. At the Galena airfield, sister met me in the pickup and drove me to the church. We had dinner, then I celebrated Mass for a packed church. A reception followed.

In that same April 15 letter to Dorothy Jean cited above, I added:

> Incidentally, ashes almost kept me grounded in Ruby that Easter Sunday afternoon. I had decided to carry the stove ashes out before leaving for Galena. I dump them behind the outhouse. There is a low stump by the outhouse. I was wearing slippers with smooth soles. Just when I got to the outhouse with a pan full of ashes, I hit a very slick spot. Out went my feet; up went my feet; up went the ashes. Down came I, and down came the ashes. Fortunately, I hit that stump with only the upper part of my left hip. Bad bruises for about a week. Had I hit with the tailbone, it could have been really bad.

By 1986, I had, for over a decade, often stood, for endless hours, on the banks of the Copper River just below the diehard town of Chitina, dipnetting for salmon. Staring at the roiling, boiling river, I was entranced as I watched it gallop past and disappear around the next bend. In my daydreams, I saw myself Huckleberry Finning my way down it on a makeshift raft of logs lashed together by spruce roots.

But along came a better way. In midwinter, Father Frank Mueller and I received a letter from Father Dick Tero—now pastor of Saint Patrick's parish in Anchorage and a veteran runner of many rivers—inviting us to join him and several of his friends on a float trip down the Copper. It may be remembered that, in 1980, we had hiked the Chilkoot Trail with him. Enthusiastically, we accepted his invitation.

On Sunday, June 8, Father Frank and I drove from Fairbanks to Glennallen, where we met Father Dick and fellow rafters: state archaeologist Doug Gibson and his German-born wife, Isolde, from Eagle River; Phil Barnes, outdoorsman and skiing coach from Palmer; and Dr. John Crowley, clinical psychologist and English specialist from Cordova. After hamburgers, apple pie, and coffee, we took off, traveling down the Richardson Highway to the Edgerton Highway, then down that to Chitina, where we arrived in the late afternoon.

Our put-in point was across and just above the bridge spanning the Copper at Chitina. By early evening, we had the three rafts inflated, rigged, and loaded. We put on waterproof clothes, topped them off with life jackets, and pushed off. Dr. John and Father Frank were in Father Dick's small raft. Phil was with the Gibsons in their fifteen-foot Avon. I was with Father Dick in his fourteen-foot Scout. The June sun, still high in the sky, was turning the surface of the Copper into a brilliant sheet of crinkled gold as our rafts were caught by the powerful current and swept swiftly under the bridge, past a throng of dipnetters and on downriver toward our first night's designated campsite at Taral, a onetime Athabaskan Indian village but, by 1986, nothing more than a name on the map.

Taral proved to be an ideal camping place. A clear-water stream flowed in there; firewood was in abundance; the tent sites were comfortable; and, mercifully, the location sheltered us from the stiff winds blowing upriver out of the Gulf of Alaska. After some hot campfire chili and Isolde's German apple cake, we did some exploring but found little of interest. We turned in early to be well rested for the following day, our first full day on the river.

Monday dawned crisp and mostly sunny. Excitement mounted as, shortly after putting in, we were funneled into Wood Canyon. "Now we're cookin'!" said Father Dick as we hurtled through the high-walled scenic rock canyon, the narrowest and swiftest stretch of the whole river. Vertical cliffs rose up on either side. Waterfalls seemed to tumble out of the sky. Swirling, slurping eddies boiled left and right. A few times, only quick bursts of rowing and paddling kept our rafts from being dashed against jagged, rocky outcroppings. No matter how one might run the Copper River, Wood Canyon will always be a highlight.

Below the canyon, we pulled out on the right bank, near the mouth of the Uranatina River, for a midmorning break. Across the river, 7,287-foot Spirit Mountain sparkled blue and white under the bright sun. A gentle breeze stirred the air. We were in high spirits, in no hurry. Concerns and cares of everyday life were now remote. Only the river, the weather, and our wilderness surroundings were of concern to us.

Time to push off again. The mouth of the Tiekel River, where we planned to spend our second night, was still about an eight-hour float downriver. As the day wore on, wind streaming up the Copper River valley freshened to near-gale force. Soon we found ourselves engulfed in a blizzard of glacial silt swept off sandbanks and gravel bars. Staying in the main current became difficult. Often, only vigorous rowing saved us from being driven into shallows and stranded. This did happen several times. Wading and pushing—and a few water-filled boots—were the price paid to get floating again.

We reached the mouth of the Tiekel by early evening, finding there shelter from the wind, as well as good tent sites. Under the large, roofed screen tent Father Dick had brought along, we set up the portable kitchen he had built. This was a big wooden chest that held everything needed for the preparation of meals, along with an assortment of tools and other useful items. Set up on removable legs, its lid serving as a work counter, this chest was most practical. It enabled the cook to stand upright while preparing a meal. In the raft, the chest served as the rowing seat.

After a leisurely meal centered around two salmon given us by a generous dipnetter at Taral, and camp chores taken care of, we sat on logs and folding chairs around the campfire listening to Father Dick tell us about the history of the area. But it was not long before we sought our tents in the alders and were lulled to sleep by the Tiekel's final rush.

Below the Tiekel outlet, the Copper widens into a braided section. Even with a careful reading of the river, it is easy here to be drawn down a secondary channel into slower water, where the wind is likely to drive a sluggish raft into shallows. For hours, these were the conditions we faced. The day wore on, and we were not making the hoped-for progress. To speed our crossing of one long, wide, windswept stretch, Dr. John cranked up Father Dick's four-horsepower outboard motor mounted on the small raft and took the two big rafts in tow, beelining the whole party down and across to a promontory on the left bank. Here we made our third camp, naming it "Mass Point Camp".

After we had pitched our tents, Father Dick spread out a blue ground cloth, on which we all sat while he led us in the celebration of the Holy Mass. The rustle of the wind in the alders, the whine of mosquitoes, the rushing waters of the Copper, and the slap of a beaver's tail provided the music.

After the Mass, I did some exploring. Below the bank on which we were camped, I observed a bear's recent passing was recorded in the wet sand. A bald eagle's nest crowned a lonely cottonwood halfway around the cove sheltering our camp. Then hamburgers on the grill, with trimmings beyond trimmings, capped a long, but soul-satisfying, day. That night, June 10–11, as we lay secure in our tents, we had the one and only real rain during our outing.

When we awoke to what was to be the longest and most interesting day of the whole excursion, we found the morning air washed clean and fresh, with only a few fog clouds hanging around. We were off to an early start but not without first having been treated by Isolde to an Austrian specialty, *Kaiserschmarren,* a kind of fluffy pancake grilled to a crisp, golden brown on both sides, then broken up and smothered with applesauce. Our river rafting, with its loading and unloading, setting up and striking of camps, rowing and paddling, and just keeping warm, made for powerful appetites.

Cautiously we eased the rafts out of our quiet cove. Immediately we were scooped up by the main current and, in the fastest spurt of our entire ninety-five-mile float trip, shot around Mass Point and on our way. Ahead and downstream lay the debouchments of the Bremner and Wernicke rivers. At this point, the waters of those two major tributaries from the east turn the Copper River into a broad, lakelike expanse of water. Below this, the Copper again narrows as it begins to funnel through Baird Canyon.

A short distance above Baird Canyon, we landed to take a break and enjoy the warm sun. Sandy beach, sunshine, and the calm air prompted the remark, "Just like Hawaii!" But a glance in any direction quickly dispelled any illusions about our being in Hawaii. We were now in the very heart of the Chugach Mountains.

Before shoving off, we agreed to pull out again above the Abercrombie Rapids, to walk ahead to check them out. Several times during the previous days, with a detectable tone of apprehension in his voice, Father Dick had mentioned those treacherous rapids.

Once again we were "cookin'" as we were swept along by the Copper's powerful waters, where it pours through Baird Canyon. Soon the river broadened out again for some miles, as if to rest and regroup before racing, in a wild rush, over and around the boulders along the stretch noted on maps as "Abercrombie Rapids".

Given all the advance billing those rapids had received, I—on my first float trip—felt a mounting mix of apprehension and excitement as we approached that almost-legendary terror of the Copper River. I expected Father Dick to pull out momentarily to reconnoiter ahead on foot. We sped past a series of large boulders lining the right bank and then around one almost in midstream. The water was fast all right, but its surface remained mostly unbroken. Any moment now, I thought to myself, we will land and walk downstream to check out the heart of the rapids. At about that point, Father Dick, with oar blades out of the water, leaned toward me and said, "Well, that wasn't much." "What wasn't much?" I asked. "The Abercrombie Rapids." Only then did I realize, somewhat relieved and, at the same time, somewhat disappointed, that we had just run the dreaded rapids. Unseasonably high water had tamed them.

After running the rapids, we were near the foot of Miles Glacier and the upriver end of six-mile-long Miles Lake. Here there was no longer a perceptible current. A moderate, drizzle-laden wind blew out of the south. We needed to go south by west. It was now late in the afternoon. Rowing rubber rafts against the wind would be impossible. It was precisely for the Miles Lake crossing that Father Dick had brought along the outboard motor. Slowly, but steadily, it powered the little raft, with the two big ones in tow, across the lake, past the face of Miles Glacier, and on to the southern shore just above the Million Dollar Bridge.

At a brief powwow held above the bridge, it was decided that each raft should now proceed on its own downstream to a point past the bridge, where we would again haul out to discuss our next move. This was done, and there we met a Fish and Game Department employee. She told us that good camping was to be had on the left bank not far below Childs Glacier.

We shoved off. The powerful outflow from Miles Lake shot us straight toward the face of the majestic, forty-square-mile Childs Glacier, then took us around a gentle curve to the left. When we were midway abreast of the four-mile-wide glacier face, a chunk of moderate size calved off, sending huge ripples across our path.

Not far below the Childs, on the left bank, we found a sandy beach just where a stream mingled its clear water with that of the silt-laden, gray Copper River. This turned out to be our best campsite yet, providing us with everything we needed, plus splendid scenery in all directions. At the foot of snow-capped Mount O'Neel, bathed now in the late evening sun, the Childs was still in full view, calving off icebergs at irregular intervals to flow in stately fashion past our doorstep.

We were fairly near the Gulf of Alaska now and had taken for granted that there would be rain from there on in. However, we were pleasantly surprised when Thursday dawned almost cloudless, with a breeze out of the north. We basked in the warm early morning sun as we breakfasted leisurely.

By the time we had struck camp and gotten under way, the downriver wind had picked up to a stiff and steady blow. With a well-defined current under us, and a willow-bending wind on our backs, we fairly sailed along.

The Copper, as it enters its broad delta, becomes multi-braided. For our final haul-out point, we had chosen the bridge at mile 27 on the Copper River Highway. To make sure we would not miss that bridge, it was impressed upon us at the Million Dollar Bridge that we had always to keep to the right. Throughout the last twenty miles of our float trip, we fought to keep to the right.

Our last lunch break found us sitting on a slate-gray gravel bar under a cloudless sky. In the channel in front of us, dusky Canada geese, ducks, harbor seals, and sea otters were disporting themselves. By that time, we had seen also moose, grizzly bears, terns, and many bald eagles. Across from where we sat, foothills of the Chugach Mountains rose from the banks of the Copper River to elevations of over four thousand feet. At frequent intervals, we heard sounds resembling the rumble of distant thunder. Thousands of feet up, we saw minor avalanches of ice, snow, and boulders, triggered by the hot weather, come roaring down ravines. A grand, powerful spectacle. But again, it was time to push on.

A few minutes after 4:00 P.M., our rendezvous time, we pulled into an eddy at the mile 27 bridge. Just as we had the rafts disassembled and deflated, Dr. John's wife, Dolores, and Father Robert Rietcheck, C.Ss.R., pastor of Cordova, arrived in a pickup and a borrowed van, respectively. We crammed most of our gear onto and into the pickup to be hauled onto the Cordova-Valdez ferry and then back to Chitina. In Cordova, hot showers and a multicourse dinner centered around fresh halibut put the finishing touches to a grand wilderness experience. My illustrated article recounting it, "Conquering the Copper River" (not my title!), in *Alaska Magazine*,[1] more than paid for Father Frank's and my

1. *Alaska Magazine* 52, no. 12 (December 1986): 32–35, 53–55.

part of it. By Friday, June 13, the two of us were back in Fairbanks.

After only two full days in Fairbanks, I found myself, rather unexpectedly, in Ruby. I flew there on the morning of Monday the sixteenth to offer the Mass of Christian Burial and to conduct the graveside services for Madeline Pitka Notti, an Athabaskan Indian elder born in 1905 who had died on the twelfth, as we were spending our last day on the Copper River.

Although it was still early forenoon when I arrived in Ruby, I could tell we were in for a brow-mopping hot day. At the community hall, I found some people sitting outside in the shade. Some were inside, sitting in small groups and visiting in subdued voices. Others, in silent prayer and reflection, sat by the open casket that rested on a raised platform. Burning candles and flowers were placed around it. There were flowers also on the casket itself. Tables in the hall were loaded with an abundance of food for the many people, Rubyites and visitors, who had taken part in the Sunday-to-Monday wake. Overhead, the ceiling fan was whirling with a low, steady hum, not to drive down the warm air as in winter, but merely to keep the air in the hall moving. The heat of the powerful mid-June sun, the burning candles, and the assembled people made it oppressively hot in the almost airtight hall, a structure of big, close-fitted logs. People from upriver and downriver, from villages, towns, and cities, by riverboat and bush plane, relatives, friends, and acquaintances, had come to honor by their presence the departed Madeline and to support and console her immediate family.

Members of Madeline's family thought that 1:00 P.M. would be a good hour for the funeral Mass. Shortly after noon, the hall was swept and the benches and chairs rearranged. Between the casket and two food tables, a round table was cleared and covered with a white cloth. On this make-do altar, flowers were set and everything readied for Mass.

By 1:00 o'clock, the hall was packed. Just then, yet another boat was seen rounding the bluff at the downriver end of the village. We delayed the services another ten minutes. Meanwhile, a trio of guitarists led the people in songs. "I am weak, but Thou art strong ... Just a closer walk with Thee ... Hold to God's unchanging hand", they sang. I then lit the altar candles and put on white vestments topped off with a green stole, the colors of joy and hope. Fellow Oregonian Jesuit father Brad Reynolds—happening just then to be on the middle Yukon on assignment for *National Geographic*—prepared to concelebrate by putting on alb and stole.

The first reading was about how "the souls of the just are in the hands of the Lord." The psalm reminded us that the Lord is our Shepherd. I read from the holy Gospel according to John about Jesus being "the resurrection and the life". For a homily, I spoke about hope and paschal joys. This was an upbeat, joyous occasion. Regarding Madeline, I had only to repeat what people had told me about her: namely, that she was loved by everyone, made people feel important and good, befriended outsiders easily, and was admired especially for the way she raised her family and for being a devout Catholic all her life.

Near the end of the Mass, as I was wiping out the chalice, a little girl came up and whispered something to me. Not at first catching what she said, I had her repeat. "Can I have juice?" she wanted to know. On the table right next to the improvised altar, there was still some food, including a few cans of fruit juice. Of course she could have juice. It was now really hot in the hall.

Immediately after the customary services were over, six men carried the casket out of the hall, down through the village, and on up the steep path leading to the cemetery on the bluff overlooking the village and the Yukon. Right behind them, another man carried the big cross that was to be placed at the head of the grave. Most of the people, myself included, set out right away for the cemetery. There was no formal procession. Heat waves were rippling off the dusty village road. Graveside ceremonies were held up for a short while to allow the older people to make the climb. Early arrivals sat in the shade of spruce and birch trees. A guitarist led them in familiar songs.

The burial service began with the blessing of the newly dug grave. The agreeable smell of the fresh, damp earth was accentuated by the heat of the day. As I read the prayers, sprinkled holy water, and said the last "Eternal rest grant unto her", I was reminded of the burial service (mentioned in an earlier chapter) held on February 13, 1984, only a few yards from this one, when we buried a young man who had frozen to death while on his trapline. That service took place in the dead of winter, in hip-deep snow, at minus seventeen, and with a stiff wind blowing. Instead of sprinkling holy water that day, I was spattering holy slush. We hurried that one. Madeline's burial service was much more leisurely. After the men had seen to it that the cross stood perfectly upright and that the mound was tamped smooth, the women put the final touches to the grave by arranging bouquets of flowers on it. Elsewhere in the cemetery, people sat in the shade, chatting. Some moved about, tidying up the graves of dear departed ones. To one side sat a group of elderly women, singing traditional songs in their native Athabaskan tongue. A squirrel amused the little ones. The subarctic tundra was alive, in full bloom, the air heavy with the scent of spruce, Labrador tea, and wild roses. Occasionally, one caught a whiff of the smoke of a distant upriver forest fire. Except for the mosquitoes, the Ruby cemetery was a pleasant place to be that June day, the day we buried Madeline.

Late in October 1986, I received a letter from Father Charles E. O'Neill, S.J., a member of the staff of the Jesuit Historical Institute in Rome. He wrote, "Reading your curriculum vitae, and reflecting on your knowledge of languages and talent for writing, I'm wondering whether you could ever get away for a sabbatical in Rome. A year? A semester? We are understaffed here." It was an attractive proposition. However, committed to the Alaskan Shepherd work and the Ruby ministry, as I was, I had to decline.

On October 31, a Friday, I flew to Ruby. That evening, I attended a Halloween party in the community hall. The following day, All Saints Day, the people of Ruby put on a surprise appreciation dinner "for Father Renner, for all of the times he has flown out here just to be with our village and serve Mass. We just want to show him how much we *appreciate* having a priest." At the dinner, they gave me a Walkman, so that I could listen to tapes of classical music while on the long walks I took without fail when in Ruby. There was also a cash gift—and many kind words. At the Sunday Mass, I baptized Jonathan Kangas, son of Ivan and Katie. About half of all the meals I ate "out", while serving the people of Ruby, I ate at the home of Ivan and Katie.

During December 1986, I spent long hours with Dr. Lawrence D. Kaplan, a member of the Alaska Native Language Center at the University of Alaska–Fairbanks. I had made available to him the extensive collection of King Island photos taken by Father Bernard Hubbard that was then still in the Alaskan Shepherd office. Together we selected almost eighty to illustrate the book *King Island Tales*, which he was in the process of readying for the press. It was published in 1988 jointly by the Alaska Native Language Center and the University of Alaska

Press. I wrote the foreword to the book. Nine of the photos I took while on King Island are included in the book. In his preface, Dr. Kaplan wrote, "Father Louis Renner read the manuscript at several stages and offered invaluable advice."

For Christmas 1986, I was again in Ruby. This was to be my last Christmas in Ruby—for a few years!

As the year 1987 dawned, so also dawned the one hundredth anniversary of pioneer Jesuit missionary service in Alaska. It was also a year that was to bring with it several major changes in my personal life. Among other events marking that centennial was the premier performance, on Palm Sunday, April 12, at the University of Alaska–Fairbanks, of Alaskan Jesuit father Normand A. (Norm) Pepin's oratorio on the Passion of Jesus, "Obedient unto Death", by the Fairbanks Choral Society.

On April 15, Father Jim Sebesta informed me that, as of August 1, I was no longer to have charge of the Ruby parish; I was, instead, to be visiting priest to Tanana, an Athabaskan Indian village upriver from Ruby, flying there every other weekend. From the sixteenth to the twentieth, I was in Ruby for the Holy Week and Easter services for the last time—for a few years!

"Getting to Ruby", I wrote my brother Bill on April 24 from Fairbanks,

was touch and go. Heavy snow showers kept us bush-planing low over the treetops and zigzagging along the rivers. Very poor visibility. At Ruby, we bounced down the runway before roaring back up again for another try, a successful one. Tail winds, crosswinds were the problem. But I survived the white-knuckle landing fine, and we had all the services.

The two sisters were there and orchestrated everything very well.

We had good crowds for both the Holy Thursday and the Good Friday services and a very good crowd for the Easter Vigil. We had a new paschal candle, a three-footer, a first of its kind. We had no stand for it, so we wedged it into a coffee can filled with nails, nuts, and bolts, and wrapped in foil. When the people, especially the kids, saw that candle, their eyes really opened up. I explained the symbolism of the candle and the role it plays at baptismal and burial services. We had the baptism of a little boy. Easter Sunday Mass, too, was well attended. I returned here on Monday.

On May 9, I was in Ruby. By then word was out that I would be leaving the priestly care of Ruby for that of Tanana. It was a quiet Saturday morning. I heard someone come into the church, then move forward, then knock on the door of my quarters. "Come in!" I invited. In came Johnny May, black fisherman's cap on his head, as always. I greeted him and gestured to him to have a chair. Without a word, he sat down. I offered him a cup of tea. A negative shake of his head. Mutual silence. Then he reached into his pocket, pulled out a crisp one-hundred-dollar bill and handed it to me. "For the church", I assumed. "For *you*! Hear you're gonna leave us." "Well, uh, thank you!" I said. More silence. End of Act I! Again, he reached into his pocket, pulled out another crisp one-hundred-dollar bill and handed it to me. "For the *church*!" "For *you*! Hear you're gonna leave us." End of Act II! Three more identical such acts were to complete this little one-hundred-dollar-bill, two-man drama!

Johnny May was a man of few words, but he had a kind and generous heart. He was a bachelor, past middle age. Although his shadow rarely darkened the doorway of the church, he was always kind and courteous to me. I was humbled by his generosity to me. To some, he seemed a bit odd.

During World War II, he was a gunner on bombers flying raids over Germany. The war left its mark on him. He had never known parents. His earliest years he had spent in an orphanage run by sisters. They were very kind to him, and he never forgot. His kindness to me reflected the kindness shown him by those sisters. I visited him in the Fairbanks hospital during his last sickness. There he died, unexpectedly, after receiving the last rites from Bishop Kaniecki. Whenever I was in Ruby, I made it a special point to visit his grave and pray for him.

Sometime during the year 1986, members of the Oregon Province were asked to write a brief article—to be printed in *Laborers in His Harvest*, a kind of in-house Oregon Province publication—on the subject of having a personal spiritual director. "It is, I know," I wrote in my article,

> somewhat anomalous for a Jesuit not to have a spiritual director. How come, then, I have not had one over the decades? Mostly, I think, it's because of my natural disposition. I have always been a rather private person. Being of a philosophical bent, I have always done a lot of reflecting on how God has acted in my life, both in my more personal spiritual life and in my apostolic life. By reflecting on and analyzing past experiences, prayerfully and according to the rules for the discernment of spirits given by Ignatius, I experience the guidance of Divine Providence. From my North Dakota farmboy beginnings to the present, a kindly Providence has guided and orchestrated my whole life, mysteriously, but reassuringly. In such a way of proceeding there is, I admit, room for self-delusion. More-or-less regular confessions, and colloquies and manifestations of conscience with superiors, have, however, provided safeguards.

The article appeared in the May 1987 issue of *Laborers*.

On June 17, I moved out of the bishop's residence/chancery building into the northeast corner room on the second floor of our new Jesuit House. This was located on North Kobuk Street, in the woods, about a five-minute walk to the west of the chancery and Sacred Heart Cathedral. On three sides, it was surrounded by a dense stand of trees; on the fourth, it faced the broad back of a hardware store. I loved that house and its setting. The fifteen years I was to spend in it were to match the fifteen years I had spent in my Tanana Village Apartment.

By the time I moved into Jesuit House, I had spent many an hour in it staining new, raw doors. About this same time, too, I devoted a considerable amount of time tracing down and lining up in alphabetical order the names of all the Jesuits, close to three hundred, who had served for, more or less, at least a year in Alaska during the century of the Jesuit presence there. It was not until March 22, 1989, however, that the bronze plaque with a listing of the names in relief was backed and surrounded by a wooden frame and, finally, mounted on the wall in the foyer of Jesuit House. When the Jesuits moved out of Jesuit House in 2002 and the Diocese of Fairbanks took it over, the plaque was taken down and remounted on the inside front wall of the lobby of the old, historic Immaculate Conception Church in Fairbanks.

On June 21, I offered my last regular Sunday Mass in Ruby. A simple farewell party followed the Mass.

Saint Mary's Mission High School closed in May 1987. On that occasion, the National Catholic Education Association asked me to write an article about the school. I produced the article in August of that year. Under the title "A 'Bright Era' in Alaskan Education", it was published six months later in *Momentum*.[2]

---

2. *Momentum*, vol. XVIV [*sic*], no. 1 (February 1988): 16–17.

On August 28, Father Jim Sebesta flew me to Tanana. I was anything but eased into the Tanana ministry. To Dorothy Jean I wrote on September 15:

> Well, the pastor of Tanana got his feet wet—all the way up to his ears! After that weekend, everything else should seem relatively easy. We had a wedding there Saturday afternoon, followed by a potlatch and wedding dance. Sister Maria thought we might have one or two for the Sunday 11:00 A.M. Mass. We had eighteen. The body of an Eskimo, Samuel Mogg Jr., with Little Diomede and Nome connections, was brought to the church at 4:00 P.M. On Sunday evening at 7:00, we had a wake in the church. The two of us spent the night under the same roof. Monday at 1:00 P.M., we had the funeral Mass, followed by burial in the Tanana cemetery. This cemetery is rather picturesque in that the graves are scattered in and among the trees, hardly visible from the air.
>
> Sister Maria Clarys, an Ursuline from Belgium, was a wonderful help. Sister Monique [Vaernewyck] was still away on vacation. She, too, is an Ursuline from Belgium, an artist. The two spent some years at the Saint Mary's mission and now four at Tanana. They are most essential to the Tanana ministry.
>
> Two media people from New York interviewed and audiotaped me for ninety minutes last week and are coming back for more. I told them they could do better than interviewing *me*, but they insisted I had important things to tell them about the ministry of the Church in Alaska, about the Native people, etc.

The two were Helen Thorington and Regine Beyer of New Radio at Performing Arts, headquartered in Brooklyn, New York.

Regarding my bimonthly visits to Tanana: As a rule, I flew there on Saturdays in the early afternoon. After a short visit with the two sisters, to get briefed on what was happening in town, I did some visiting around, before taking a walk. At 5:00 P.M., seated at a little table with only a stole by way of vestments, I offered Mass for the sisters in their home. We then had a leisurely dinner together. Early on Sunday mornings, I took a walk up to Mission Hill, a round-trip walk of about two hours. Sunday Mass was at 11:00. This was generally followed by a cookies-and-tea session in the church basement for those who cared to attend. After this, I had lunch, after which I routinely brought Communion to and visited with people in the Elders Home. Normally, I flew back to Fairbanks on Sunday afternoons. This continued to be the basic pattern throughout my five years as visiting priest to Tanana.

"Normally" in the above context has to be understood very loosely. As was the case with my trips to Ruby, so with my trips to Tanana. Only occasionally did everything go as planned and scheduled. Diary entries such as the following are common:

> Blowing snow. No planes. Overnight at Tanana.... Zero-zero visibility; therefore we turned back. No go to Tanana! ... Medevac. So we turned back. Left Tanana again at 6:15 P.M. ... Overnight in Tanana because of rainstorms.... Return via Rampart.... Returned via Minto.... Weathered out.... Stopped at Manley on return trip.... Snowstorm; therefore no flight.... *Zum kotzen* [the equivalent, in vulgar German, for about "enough to make you throw up"] rough at Squaw Crossing.

Concerning Squaw Crossing—an official geographic place name—I was to write to Dorothy Jean on December 5, 1988,

> Well, "Squaw Crossing" took on new meaning for me the other day. This area, near the confluence of the Tanana and Yukon rivers—the home of the winds, according to Athabaskan

folklore—is notorious for rough, turbulent winds making for "bumpy" bush plane flights. I've flown over this spot many times, but last Saturday was the first time the crossing was so rough that I hit my head on the ceiling of the plane. So far so good. As we continued to be tossed around, the little kid next to me, who had just emptied a bottle of milk, fairly erupted—all over his mother and down the left side of my parka, pocket included! I gave my parka three scrubbings, then rubbed it down with imitation vanilla. The blend of odors is now sufferable.

A most pleasant Thanksgiving Day for me to recall was that of November 26, 1987. Along with Wolf and Christa Hollerbach, I was invited by Jean and Bruce Gordon to their home. From 1:30 in the afternoon to 8:00 in the evening, we five very close friends were together for leisurely conversation and plentiful dining. I had, by then, been away from the University of Alaska–Fairbanks for over seven years; Bruce, for longer. We five, however, had continued to foster our mutual, treasured friendship during the intervening years. It was a solid minus twenty that night; but, so aglow was I with the warmth of our friendship and the fine food that I was able to walk home in perfect comfort with my parka hanging loosely from my shoulders.

On December 9, as historian for the Diocese of Fairbanks, I was asked to join Bishop Kaniecki and Dr. William R. Wood—president of the University of Alaska–Fairbanks when I first began teaching there in 1965 and now executive director of Festival Fairbanks, a nonprofit community services organization—in the chancery building. Our business was to discuss the creation of a forty-by-thirty-six-inch plaque that would commemorate succinctly, in bronze, the "Pioneer Missionaries of Interior Alaska". The plaque was to be mounted on a big boulder in Golden Heart Plaza in downtown Fairbanks. Two days later, in the Westmark Hotel coffee shop, Dr. Wood and I met again, now joined by Dr. William S. Schneider, the curator of oral history at the university, and Reverend Scott Fisher, an Episcopal priest, to discuss further—over a Belgian waffles breakfast—the makeup of the proposed plaque. After this meeting, Dr. Wood bowed out. More meetings followed. Present at these, in addition to Reverend Fisher, Dr. Schneider, and me, were now also Reverend Richard K. Heacock Jr. of the Methodist Church and Dixon Jones, a freelance Fairbanks artist responsible for the final layout of the plaque. By March 3, 1988, our product was ready to be sent to the foundry. My specific contribution to the whole project was the providing of basic historical data regarding Catholic pioneer missionary activity along the Yukon River. This became part of the "Select Chronology of Pioneer Activity in Interior Alaska" that accompanies the portraits in bronze of four select pioneer missionaries. To represent the Catholic missionaries, I chose a portrait of Father Julius Jetté, S.J., and a quote by him to go next to his portrait. The quote reads, "To understand the Natives, I have only to treat them as I would be treated myself."

On March 4, 1988, without prior warning, I was asked by Father Jim Sebesta, then Alaska mission superior, to consider switching to a new assignment, that of spiritual director to the KNOM radio staff. I had only pleasant memories of all my days in Nome. As mentioned in an earlier chapter, I had written a book about KNOM. This proposed assignment was wholly attractive to me. However, ultimately we both agreed that my Alaskan Shepherd work and the Tanana ministry were of greater service to the Diocese of Fairbanks.

From the Jesuit Curia in Rome, Father John J. O'Callaghan, S.J., wrote to me on May 5: "I am turning to you once again, as one of my tried and true—and hopefully long-suffering—translators for the yearbook of the Society. You have been so good in the past about acceding to my requests that I make bold to ask you once again this year." He sent me another article to translate from German into English, something I was only too happy to do. Rendering my fellow Jesuits this little service, if nothing else, helped keep my German from getting rusty.

On June 8, I found myself, unexpectedly, in Ruby again, there to officiate at the funeral Mass and burial rite of Peter Demoski. Referring to that event, I wrote to Dorothy Jean from Fairbanks:

> "Precious memories", they kept singing as they lowered him down, lowered down Peter "Precious" Demoski, lowered him down in the Ruby cemetery, last June 8. He had drowned a year earlier, but his body was found only this spring. He was one of seven to drown in that boating accident. One body is still missing. He was buried next to graves bearing the names of his parents, both bearing the same date, both drowned thirty years earlier. But their graves are empty. The bodies of his parents were never found. I was asked to come to Ruby to perform the burial rite. Never had I seen the community hall so filled to overflowing. Mostly they were strangers, members of the families of other victims. "Precious memories, how they linger", they kept singing.

In that same letter to Dorothy Jean, I continued: "The Fourth of July I spent in Tanana. Was supposed to return to here on the third, but heavy smoke from forest fires made flying conditions so poor that the plane that was supposed to pick me up had to return to Fairbanks. No flights on the Fourth. It was eighty-eight above that Fourth. I took a long morning walk and spent a lot of time shooting baskets on the outdoor court next to the school, next to the church. Found my shooting-eye was still pretty good." That outdoor basketball court was one of my Tanana fringe benefits.

On October 8, I took part in a pro-life march. Four days later, I was in my room in Jesuit House when, at 4:05 in the afternoon, my phone rang. Answering it, I heard, "Father Louie, this is Della. Mom died!" While in the kitchen preparing dinner for Dad and herself, unexpectedly, suddenly, she dropped dead to the floor. A heart attack ended her life at eighty-four years. Her prayers were answered. She had told me more than once that she prayed often to die before Dad did and prayed that she would not have to lie around incapacitated, helpless. More than once, too, when we talked about dying, she told me, "I am ready; God knows, I am ready any time." While we rejoiced with her in having been granted a death she had prayed for, we did feel sorry for Dad. Understandably, he was to miss her greatly.

On Saturday the fifteenth, in Saint Charles Borromeo Church, seated at the side of the casket, I led family and friends in the Rosary. Mom had had a lifelong devotion to the Rosary. Lying in the casket now, she had a Rosary around her hands, along with the little white cloth she had made for me over thirty years earlier, the cloth that was used to bind my hands together right after the bishop had anointed them at the Mass of my ordination to the priesthood. After the Rosary, accompanied by seven concelebrating fellow Jesuits, I offered the Mass of Christian Burial for my dear mother. For Dad's sake, I stayed on in Tacoma an extra day, returning to Fairbanks on the seventeenth.

My January 28, 1989, letter to Dorothy Jean began, "Minus fifty-three, dense ice fog, few planes flying, colder weather forecast, no end in sight. So much for the greenhouse effect! I should be heading for Tanana about now, but no flights."

Interior Alaska, at this time, was in the grip of what went down in history as the Great Cold of January 1989. In Fairbanks, we had temperatures in the minus-fifty range. In Tanana, it was really cold. Wrote Sister Maria Clarys, "Saturday the twenty-first, our pastor, Father Louis Renner, S.J., did not fly in. Sunday showed minus sixty-six degrees. On the twenty-seventh, Tanana broke its previous record. It got down to minus seventy-six." I was spared *those* extreme lows, but, as will be seen, I was to experience comparable ones two years later.

On May 29, Father Norm Pepin and I hiked the sixteen-mile Granite Tors Trail for the first time. We were to hike it, or parts of it, again numerous times. What makes that trail—off the Chena Hot Springs Road at mile 39 out of Fairbanks—so challenging is not so much its actual length as the fact that, in the course of hiking it, one climbs to an elevation of over thirty-three hundred feet above trailhead. Often the two of us hiked also the nearby, less challenging—but equally rewarding, as far as scenery goes—Angel Rocks Trail. Our favorite trail, however, especially in the late summer, when the blueberries were still plentiful and the low bush cranberries in their prime, was the White Mountains Trail northeast of Fairbanks. For shorter outings, we frequently hiked the Chena Lakes Trails just south of Fairbanks. We were blessed to have in one another a wholly compatible hiking partner.

"Left for Dillingham on Markair with Richard Dykema in middle afternoon. Slept on shipping container floor", reads my diary entry for June 13, 1989. This was the first of what was to be for me a series of twelve working vacations consisting of camping on the right bank of the Nushagak River near its mouth—below the Kanakanak Hospital seven miles southwest of Dillingham—and fishing commercially, as a member of the Dykema crew, in Bristol Bay, the world's leading sockeye salmon fishery. I was not a sharer in whatever profits were realized, as I was quite content with having all my expenses paid and, in return, to serve unstintingly as a full-fledged crew member. It was a perfectly satisfactory, mutually agreeable arrangement from the outset and remained such throughout more than a decade of fishing together as wholly compatible crew members, as friends, as "family".

My stays at the Dillingham fishing site lasted, generally, around three weeks, from about the middle of June through the first week of July. Eagerly, I anticipated the trips months ahead of time. True, they entailed much hard, physical work; long, irregular hours; being bathed alternately in one's sweat, then chilled to the bone; and also some danger. But all the logistics, the concerns about travel to and from, licenses, permits, regulations, equipment, and the like were in the hands of Richard and Gisela. I was carefree. What made those fishing ventures so attractive to me was that, in most all respects, they were in sharp contrast to my Alaskan Shepherd work. Like most everyone else, I found the Alaskan winters long. When spring did finally roll around again, much as I loved my Alaskan Shepherd work and little office, I felt an urgent need to get outdoors for longer stretches of time, to live close to nature, and to engage in some hard, physical work, even if under somewhat Spartan conditions. The words "working" and "vacations" each, in and of themselves, summarize well what those annual outings near Dillingham were all about for me.

The Bristol Bay area was a good place to get away to for a genuine outdoor experience. Nature there is raw and wild, abounding in a great variety of flora and fauna. One routinely sees rabbits, foxes, grizzly bears. My last year at Dillingham, I had little foxes playing on and under my tent platform. One year, we had a grizzly raid our food buckets. Another year, one came within a yard of my tent—while I was in it.

During the 1998 season, we watched as a sow paraded her two cubs along the beach just below the two porto-shelters. On land, the grizzlies were our major concern. In the water, it was the seals and beluga whales. Entangled in a net, they could make short work of it. Sea otters and beavers merely amused us, as did bald eagles, gulls, swallows, jays, and many other varieties of birds. A profusion of wildflowers and the lush green of a coastal spring added color to that whole expanse of wilderness.

Richard had fished commercially in Bristol Bay with his son-in-law, Mark Whitmire, the year before I joined the Dykema crew. Having retired from his position with the state of Alaska, Richard could use his time as he pleased. Convinced that he would enjoy commercial fishing and, hopefully, make a little money at it, he bought the permit and fishing gear of a fisherman who aspired to move up the ladder of commercial fishing. The basic fishing gear consisted of a twenty-two-foot aluminum skiff, a powerful outboard motor, nets, buoys, anchors, ropes, and plastic totes to hold the fish. Along with these items came also two porto-shelters, Quonset hut–like structures consisting of a skeleton of joined pipes mounted on a wooden platform and closed in all around with a waterproof covering. During the off-season, everything but the skiff was stored in a metal shipping container located on private rented property several miles from the banks of the Nushagak, where we set up camp for the season.

The first order of business for us upon our arrival at Dillingham was always to begin hauling to the campsite everything needed to get the porto-shelters up and basic items into them. In good weather, this was pleasant, if tiring, work. In rainy, windy weather, as was often the case, it was a matter of "grit your teeth and get the job done as quickly as possible." Normally, it took us about three long days to get the shelters up and all essential items into them. Generally, it was only Richard and I that spent the first several days at Dillingham setting up camp. We worked harmoniously together. Almost from the start, the left hand knew what the right hand was doing. A few times, Gisela was with us from the outset, but more often, she and other crew members came a few days after we did.

Richard and Gisela slept in one of the porto-shelters, the same one in which all the cooking and eating took place. The rest of the crew, except for me, slept in the other one. This was used also to store tools, fishing-related items of all kinds, life jackets, heavy overclothes, extra groceries, and much more. It, too, having an oil stove, served also as a drying room.

My nonnegotiable preference to sleep in a tent of my own was understood and honored. At first, my tent was a small two-man backpacker's tent. Except for a sponge pad, I slept on the ground. After several years—"as a concession to my advancing age and genteel upbringing", as I liked to say—I was provided a bigger, sturdier tent. This was pitched on a wooden platform. Thereafter, I was never again awakened by water seeping through the sponge and into my sleeping bag from below. One especially nice feature of a tent was that it was mosquito-proof. This was not the case with the porto-shelters. I slept well in those tents on the banks of the Nushagak, lulled to a care-free sleep, as I was—after a hard day's, or hard night's, work—by the wash of the waters, by the monotonous drone of clouds of mosquitoes, by the winds in the willows, by the gentle patter of rain on the rain fly over my tent.

Once the camp was all set up, days were spent hauling to it everything needed for the actual fishing, and readying all the gear and loading it into the skiff. Most years, new nets had to be rehung. Mending old or torn nets was a never-ending chore. An adequate supply of gasoline and oil for the outboard motor and the two pickup trucks—a newer Jeep and an old Dodge, the latter hitched to the trailer hauling the skiff—as well as heating oil for the two stoves had to be brought to the camp and safely stored there. A full tank of propane had to be hooked up to the kitchen stove and the fridge. The camp had no drinkable water. This had to be hauled from Dillingham. The collapsible outhouse had to be reassembled over a newly dug pit. There was no end to what needed to be done.

However, fishing for king and sockeye salmon was what Dillingham was all about. There were good seasons, and there were poor seasons. Some seasons, the run of salmon was so great that the canneries, when "the push" was on and they were swamped in fish, set a limit to what a given boat could deliver or simply refused to take any more fish. Other seasons, the run was so poor that permit owners could not even make expenses. There were seasons when the weather was ideal: cool and dry. One season, however, it was so hot and dry that tundra fires in the area kept us under a cloud of smoke throughout most of it. Several seasons were so rainy that the path to the outhouse was a constant little stream. Living so close to, and working so closely with, raw nature, one was forever conscious of the weather—and of the tides.

It is the moon that, by its waxing and waning, powers the ebb and the flow of the eternal tides. The Bristol Bay tides vary greatly. We saw tides as low as minus four feet and as high as plus twenty-eight. It is the tides that determine, to some extent, the movement of the fish. It was, ultimately, the tides that dictated virtually every move we made while at Dillingham. The tides determined the time of the "openings", the hours when nets are allowed to be in the water, as well as the "closings", when nets had to be out of the water. The tide book was our "bible", always at hand. The radio was generally tuned to the station giving the weather reports. The maritime weather tended to be unpredictable and could change rather unexpectedly. It can be calm one minute, then up comes the wind. It freshens. Up come the waves. Up comes the bow. Up comes the stern. And up comes—the kid's breakfast!

Ours was "set-net" fishing, as opposed to fishing from a moving boat dragging a net behind it. We had two assigned sites. These were on the right bank of the Nushagak, about a fifteen-minute run—depending on the winds and the rush of the incoming tide—downriver from our camp. Openings always began at midtide, when the tide was at seven to nine feet. Before the official minute of a given opening, we dragged one end of a twenty-five-fathom-long net out of the skiff and up the mud bank and there clipped it to a screw anchor firmly embedded in the mud bank. A buoy marked that end of the net. The main part of the net was still in the skiff. Clipped to the off-shore end of it were two ropes. One of these had an anchor tied to the end of it, the other a buoy identifying the owner. The net was so stacked that it could run out of the skiff moving at high speed without getting fouled up. No part of the net could be in the water before the exact minute marking an opening. At the first moment of an opening, the main part of the net was run out of the skiff as, with motor wide open, it zoomed out into the deep. Quickly, as soon as the off-shore end of the net was out, the attached anchor and buoy were thrown overboard. Generally, once the net was in the water, we had to hook onto the buoy rope and, under power, straighten the net out. A proper "set" on the first attempt was cause for self-congratulations. Sometimes, during a heavy run, the net started "poppin'" as soon as it hit the water. Nevertheless, we would leave it and roar off to put the second net in at the other site.

The nets we used were gillnets, so-called because the fish, on their way upriver to their spawning grounds, would swim into them headfirst and get caught by their gills. A net was ten feet from top to bottom. A corkline along the top kept it afloat. A leadline along the bottom kept it straightened out vertically.

Often, when the run was heavy, while we were tending one net, the other one, plugged with fish weighing around six pounds each, would "go dry", that is, settle into the mud as the tide went out. The fish, struggling to get free of the net, would get badly entangled in it and become totally covered with mud. Picking such fish out of a net gone dry and washing them free of mud was about the hardest of all the work any one of us ever did at Dillingham.

There were times when slogging through knee-deep mud to put in a screw anchor, or when dragging part of a net, along with rope and buoy, through a stretch of knee-deep mud—all the while dressed two-ply, as I was, in warm clothes under rubberized chest waders and life jacket—soon had me overheated, bathed in my sweat. It was then nice, at first, to sit back in the boat, to cool off, to relax, to snack while the nets were left to fish. However, the wet clothes, the darkness of night, the winds, and the rains soon cooled me off, so much so that I was chilled to the bone. During my forty years in Alaska, I was seldom as chilled as I was on some of those Dillingham nights. A number of times, it was only by getting out of the skiff and running up and down the mud bank that I was able to get warm again. Richard kept warm by jogging in place in the stern of the skiff. A certain amount of misery, to be accepted and endured, was simply part of Bristol Bay salmon fishing.

Those Dillingham days were, in part, also occasions for me to challenge myself, to see how well I could hold up under the pressure of hard work, of physical discomfort, of stressful, even dangerous, situations. They were occasions for me to practice patience, to resist complaining about the irregular hours, the raw cold, the mosquitoes, the flies, the foul weather, the intense heat of some summer days—or the slap of a slimy fishtail in my face.

But life on the banks of the Nushagak and on the waters of Bristol Bay was far from being merely an endless routine of hard work, discomfort, and misery. There were days when the waters of the bay were as calm as a millpond. And there were nights utterly serene, with silvery moonbeams dancing on the ripples of the river. There were also the congenial companionship of close friends, the leisurely lying back and reading in my tent, and the solo walks along the beach or over the tundra. There was time to pray the Rosary, to meditate, to reflect on how my work, as a commercial fisherman, was akin to that of Saint Peter and the other apostles who were also commercial fishermen. And there was time to play. Having always wanted to grow up to be a happy-go-lucky kid, I invented a game for myself. This I called "Stick-in-the-Mud". The trick of the game was to toss a stick—readily found on the beach along the river—up into the air in such a way that, coming down end-over-end, it would stick upright in the mud at the river's edge. A stick landing perfectly upright was worth a hundred points. The closer the top of the stick was to the mud, the fewer the points.

Richard and his son, Michael, were always the core members of a crew numbering, as a rule, around five. Richard, with rare exceptions, ran the motor. Michael handled the heavy, deep-water anchors and directed operations at the critical moments. Up to my last year at Dillingham, when the skiff was otherwise amply crewed, I was always a regular member of the crew. My experience as a deckhand on Foss tugs during my high school days now stood me in good stead. I was at home on the water and knew how to respect it without fearing it. I was familiar with ropes, knots, and anchors. The rest of the crew, varying slightly from season to season, consisted almost exclusively of immediate Dykema family members and in-laws.

My years of fishing at Dillingham, as a member of the Dykema crew, spanned from 1989 to 2001. I was not there for the 1994 season. That was the year of my golden jubilee as a Jesuit. I was in the Northwest for the celebrations, just when the fishing season was in full swing. I could write a book about my twelve seasons at Dillingham, but it is time to return to Fairbanks. After my first season at Dillingham, a relatively short one, I was back in Fairbanks by June 30.

On August 5, I flew to Tanana for the weekend. That evening, at a potluck dinner, I was a guest of Episcopal bishop George Harris in the Episcopal manse. Tanana has all along been mostly an Episcopal village, although the Catholic Church has had a mission there since 1904.

(The day I first arrived at Tanana, as I was walking along the river road, a fellow came up to me and asked, somewhat brusquely, "Who the hell are *you?*" When I told him who I was, his face lit up with a smile; and, with a warm handshake, he welcomed me to Tanana. He went on to tell me that he went to "the other Church" but that all in Tanana were like one big family.)

During the five years I had the care of the Catholic community in Tanana, I always found relationships between the two churches to be most amicable. Often members of the Episcopal Church came to our Mass when their church had no services. They were always welcome.

On Sunday, September 10, 1989, I enjoyed the most memorable of all my small-plane flights in Alaska. On that day, with Father Jim Sebesta at the controls of the Cessna 180, with Father Frank Fallert in the copilot's seat, with Father Joe Laudwein behind him, and with me to his left, we flew to Anchorage. It was already a golden autumn day in the high country. High country, in this case, was the Mount McKinley massif, through which we wove our way. The scenery was spectacular. We were on our way to attend a two-day diocesan ministries meeting at Holy Spirit Retreat House. That meeting ended at noon on the twelfth. We then went to the Alyeska Ski Resort, near Girdwood, to attend, along with the priests of the Archdiocese of Anchorage, three days of meetings on the subject of reconciliation. The scheduling allowed us ample free time. Mixing the useful with the pleasant, Fathers Dick Tero and Frank Mueller and I made an excursion to the Portage Glacier on the thirteenth and to the Crow Creek Mine the following day. On the fifteenth, I took the chair lift to its upper end, then hiked the rest of the way up to the Alyeska Glacier for some picture taking. That evening, in the Cessna 180, by the light of a full moon, we flew back to Fairbanks. The following evening found me in Tanana attending a potlatch feast for the dead.

By now, I had made numerous trips to and from Alaska but never overland. All were by air. An ideal, once-in-a-lifetime opportunity for me to travel from Tacoma to Fairbanks by road was offered me on September 20, when I was at the Dykemas' helping Richard with the annual rite of autumn, namely, digging up that year's crop of potatoes. He was soon to be in the Lower 48 to buy a Roadtrek van on a Dodge Ram chassis. He would do some touring in it before heading north to Alaska. Both he and Gisela thought it would be good if he had me as a companion for the drive north, to take place about the third week of October. I could not have agreed more with them. We settled on Sunday, October 22, as the day for our departure from Tacoma.

On the nineteenth, I arrived in Tacoma to spend a few days with Dad. Richard arrived in the evening of the twenty-second. However, because the van's defrosting system needed some work, we did not leave Tacoma until the twenty-fourth. We took the Cassiar Highway north through scenic British Columbia. We slept and ate all our meals in the van. Even in the cold and snows of northern British Columbia, we were perfectly comfortable in the van. All its systems functioned flawlessly. As we advanced north, there was little traffic along the highway. For long stretches, we were it. This gave us a wonderful sense of space, wilderness, and adventure. Near Whitehorse, we saw first a red fox, then a black wolf. Shortly after we crossed the border into Alaska, in the beam of the headlights, we saw an owl with a rabbit in its claws take off from the road just ahead of us. In spite of its length, the trip never became boring. I had reading material along but read none of it. As we approached Fairbanks at the end of our last day's drive of 476 miles, I said to Richard, "I could turn right around and head for Florida. This 'vanning' is addictive." I concluded my jottings of the trip with: "End of sixth day—and end of a wonderful 2,327-mile trip!"

Waiting on my desk for me upon my return to Fairbanks was a 235-page manuscript—already in the galley stage—entitled *Memoirs of a Yukon Priest* by Father Segundo Llorente, S.J. It had been sent to me by Father John B. Breslin, S.J., head of the Georgetown University Press, with the request that I proofread it and consider writing a foreword to it. Having at the moment no other "extracurricular" activity to engage me, I consented both to proofread the manuscript and to write the foreword. He urged me to do both as speedily as possible, for the book was already being advertised. On November 8, via Federal Express, I sent him both the manuscript and my foreword. The book, with my foreword, was published in 1990. It proved to be quite a success and was reprinted several times.

For Christmas 1989, I was again in Tanana. That year, a rather eventful year for me, ended on a Sunday, a minus-thirty-seven-degree day. I offered a morning Mass in Jesuit House. In the afternoon, I was transported to the sunny banks of the Egyptian Nile as I listened to the Metropolitan Opera's broadcast of *Aida*. My diary entries for the year ended with a fervent *Deo gratias!*

Chapter 23

The Earlier 1990s: 1990–1994

On February 23–25, 1990, I was in Ruby to attend the middle Yukon regional ministers meeting. Another drowning victim, again a young man, occasioned my trip to Tanana on May 7 to offer Mass and conduct graveside services. During May, I also frequently visited Father Frank Fallert, bedridden with leukemia in Fairbanks Memorial Hospital. On June 1, a Friday, I helped him move into a room in Jesuit House, where, it was hoped, a lengthy convalescence would restore him to passable good health. With shock, I learned the next morning that he had died during the night. That was my weekend to be in Tanana. On Monday, however, back in Fairbanks, I took part in the Rosary prayed for him; and, on Tuesday, I concelebrated at the memorial Mass offered for him in Sacred Heart Cathedral.

On Wednesday, June 6, I was again airborne, this time in a new twin-engine Piper Navajo *Chieftain* piloted by Father Jim Sebesta and copiloted by Bruce Hopkins. On board with us were Bishop Kaniecki and Father Fallert's two sisters— and Father Fallert's body. We were on our way to Tununak on Nelson Island, where he was to be buried. After making a refueling stop at Bethel, we continued our westward flight. When we came over the village of Toksook Bay, we flew low and circled the village. There, a big crowd was standing around the church and waving white flags, their way of saying a final good-bye to their much-loved pastor. On the road next to the church, in big, white block letters, was spelled out the one word: FAREWELL! On its third and last pass over the village, the plane tipped its wing in salute. In tear-choked silence, we on board flew the last few miles over to Tununak.

At Tununak, many people were gathered at the airstrip as we landed. On the back of a pickup truck, the casket was brought to the church. A procession of villagers on foot, singing hymns in Eskimo, Latin, and English, accompanied it. The sky was heavily overcast, the day foggy, windy, and cold.

The church was brightly decorated. A Rosary was said, then a Mass followed. At regular intervals, five more Masses were celebrated, all well attended. On Thursday afternoon, in a church crowded to overflowing, Bishop Kaniecki and six con-celebrating priests offered the Mass of Christian Burial. The body was then carried to the nearby cemetery and, with all appropriate ceremonies, laid to rest. With his burial in Tununak, his last request, "I want to be with my people", was honored. A potlatch followed. After it, we flew back to Fairbanks.

On June 17, as I was offering Sunday Mass in the church in Tanana during a thunderstorm, a bolt of lightning knocked out the power. Nature and grace in dramatic proximity! I had experienced power outages before, while offering Mass in villages, but this was the first one caused by lightning.

From June 19 to July 6, I was again at Dillingham for my second season of fishing. On September 12–17, I was at Saint Mary's attending a diocesan meeting about the importance of getting the laity involved in ministry. Both clergy and laity were all for more lay involvement in the catechetical programs and in the liturgies. Those were beautiful autumn days, with the tundra an endless carpet of brilliant colors. November 6–8 saw me in Galena attending a regional ministers' meeting.

To the joy, and great surprise, of the good people in Tanana, I appeared there unexpectedly on Sunday, December 23. I had been scheduled to arrive there the day before, but, because of unsuitable weather conditions, all commercial flights had been canceled. The same held true for that Sunday. However, one of the Tanana families, desperate to get home for Christmas, was able to charter a plane. At the last minute, I heard about this, inquired, and was given the last seat available. The church was filled for the 11:00 P.M. Christmas Eve Mass. After it, we socialized till 1:30 A.M. Christmas Day. The 11:00 A.M. Mass on Christmas Day drew only ten people. I returned to Fairbanks the following day.

When a prolonged high-pressure system turned interior Alaska into a massive deep freeze in January 1989, I found myself in Fairbanks, instead of in Tanana, as scheduled. When a cold spell to match that of 1989 struck the interior again two years later, I was in Tanana. "Stranded in Tanana; minus sixty-seven degrees!" reads my diary entry for January 15, 1991. I had been scheduled to return to Fairbanks two days earlier. During my forty winters in Alaska, I never saw a colder reading than that minus-sixty-seven-degree one in Tanana. To get some idea of what such a temperature feels like, I took a walk in it—a short walk. I found it to be instantly numbing. And yet it was not so much the cold as such that impressed me; rather, it was the utter stillness, the deathlike silence accompanying it that was so awe-inspiring.

Saturday, April 20, 1991, dawned heavily overcast. I was all set to be airborne, but the weather I saw out of my Fairbanks window left me with serious doubts about flying. Bishop Mike Kaniecki, however, looking at the big picture, saw enough green light for us to proceed as planned. By ten o'clock that morning, in the Cessna 207, we were airborne, with the Central Yup'ik Eskimo village of Newtok on the Bering Sea coast our ultimate destination. By 6:30 P.M., after stopping to refuel at Galena and Saint Mary's, we were at the tie-down area of the somewhat-soft gravel airstrip at Newtok, where Eskimo deacon Larry Charles and Jimmy Tom, arriving on their snow machines and pulling sleds, met us to bring us and our gear across a mushy pond to the priest's house.

That evening, we spent some time with Deacon Larry and his wife, Albertina, to discuss plans for the Mass and confirmation rite scheduled to take place the following day. It was Albertina who had prepared the sixteen young men and women to be confirmed. Fourteen children were due to receive their First Holy Communion at that same Mass.

Sunday dawned mostly sunny. Bishop Mike and I took a walk around the village to meet and greet people. At noon, there was a potluck dinner in the community hall, after which rehearsals were held in the church. Confessions followed. For quite some time, Bishop Mike and I were busy hearing first confessions and the confessions of people, in general.

Services began at 6:40 that same evening. They unfolded solemnly, leisurely. The church was packed and was warm and steamy even with the windows open. The small fry grew restless and squirmy. Some crawled up the aisles and had to be retrieved by older sisters or mothers. With the confirmation rite and the First Communions, everything came off as rehearsed. By 8:10, Bishop Mike had given the final blessing. The newly sacramented then posed with him for group photos. I was among the photographers. Later that evening, in the community hall, Eskimo drumming and dancing added a final, festive touch to the day's events. After snacking on a can of hash, pilot crackers, and coffee, Bishop Mike and I called it a day, a great day at and for Newtok.

The next morning, Monday the twenty-second, with Bishop Mike concelebrating, I offered the nine o'clock Mass. By

10:40, we were winging our way across the broad Yukon-Kuskokwim Delta—still mostly white but already splotched here and there with patches of brown tundra—toward the village of Hooper Bay sixty-four miles to the northwest. There we touched down at 11:05. Walter Naneng met us and, with his snow machine and sled, brought us to the church. Sisters Angela Fortier, C.S.J., and Julie Thorpe, S.N.D. de N., greeted us warmly and invited us to eat lunch with them and to discuss the events scheduled for that day and the next.

At 7:00 P.M. on Tuesday, in a church well filled—even though the seal-hunting season was under way—Bishop Mike offered Mass and confirmed six. Before the final blessing, he blessed an Eskimo drum specially made to be featured at the Tekakwitha Conference scheduled to begin later that week at Saint Mary's. In blessing that drum, he blessed Eskimo drumming and dancing, in general.

We arrived at Saint Mary's in the early afternoon of Wednesday the twenty-fourth. The conference began the following day. Close to two hundred people, mostly Native people from all over Alaska, were present for it. "One Voice in the Spirit" was its motto. Among its key themes were reconciliation, forgiveness, mutual support, family, return to cultural roots, and harmony between young and old and between generations past and present. There were daily Masses. But the conference was not all and only sacred and serious business throughout. There was time, too, for its attendants to relax, to bask in the warm April sun, to play a few games of cribbage, to socialize over a bowl of popcorn. A talent show, skits, clowning, and singing entertained the crowd on Saturday evening. A special Mass on Monday morning ended the conference. All who attended it agreed with Bishop Mike that it was "a huge success". My own role at the conference was little more than that of an observer, reporter, and photographer. Some of the photos I had taken at Newtok, Hooper Bay, and Saint Mary's were used to illustrate the accounts of those trips and doings that appeared in two separate issues of the *Alaskan Shepherd*.

As the year 1991 continued to unfold, so did my ministry as pastor of the Tanana parish. One Sunday, as I was walking to the Elders Home—wearing my Roman collar, as I always did when going there—a little Indian girl asked me, "Are you the God-Father?" Taken aback momentarily by such an unexpected and ambiguous a theological question, I could only stammer, "I—I guess so."

Normally, I left Tanana around the middle of the afternoon for the forty-five-minute flight back to Fairbanks. Once arrived at the east ramp of Fairbanks International Airport, where the bush air services had their operations, I always immediately set out to walk the three-mile stretch into town to Jesuit House, no matter what time of year it was or what the weather. Occasionally, I was offered a ride by someone who had been on the plane with me. I never hitchhiked, but sometimes I was offered a ride soon after I began walking. Always, as soon as I hopped into a given Good Samaritan's vehicle, I told him who I was, where I was coming from, where I was going, and that he could just drop me off at the Safeway store straight ahead, where I would take a right and walk a short mile to Jesuit House. Some insisted on driving me all the way home.

I met some interesting people on those Sunday afternoons. Several times it was ministers of other faiths. Sometimes it was a bush plane pilot just in from some village. One interesting meeting took place when a man pulled over and invited me to hop in. Seatbelt fastened, I told him I was a Catholic priest, just returning from Tanana, where I had offered Sunday Mass for the people. He all but stopped the van we were in, fixed his eyes on me, and asked, "How *can* you?" How can I, he wondered, be a member of that papist church, even a priest. He saw me as one on the sure road to hell. In all sincerity, he urged me, "Come out of it!" He assured me of his prayers for my salvation. I said little. He was all wound up. When we reached Safeway, I thanked him kindly and hopped out. He was a fundamentalist.

On May 19, 1991, as I was walking home from the east ramp, a man stopped, opened the passenger-side door, and invited me to jump in. I jumped in, thanked him, then told him the usual. He, in turn, introduced himself. He was an Irish Catholic from Chicago, a professor at the law school there. His hobby was flying. He had his own plane. When we got to the red light at Safeway, I made a move to get out. "No, no!" he protested. He would gladly drive me right to my doorstep. This he did. After some small talk, I thanked him for the ride, voiced a sincere "Well, God bless you!" and opened the door to get out. "Just a minute!" he said, as he grabbed my left forearm. He then reached into his pocket, pulled out his wallet, pulled out a bill, and handed it to me with, "Here. I don't have time to take you out to dinner, but I want you to have a dinner on me." It was a twenty-dollar bill.

Anyone who has read this far will have noticed that I spent a considerable number of days each year away from my office. This I was able to do because, with rare exceptions, I had a highly competent, dedicated, reliable Alaskan Shepherd staff on whom I could confidently rely. I myself, blessed with the gift of orderliness and the ability to plan ahead, always had everything under control. In my twenty years as editor of the *Alaskan Shepherd*, I never missed a deadline. I did much of my Alaskan Shepherd–related work in the quiet of the early morning hours. Some mornings, I was in my office by three o'clock. Often, after working several hours, I would go up to the chapel, sit on the floor before the tabernacle, rest my back against the wall, and pray till I nodded off. The nod-off I looked upon as a welcome "fringe benefit". Several times, Bishop Kaniecki, needing to pick up something in his office hours before he normally arrived there, found me—to our mutual surprise!—on the chapel floor dozing. To my explanation that I was "practicing falling asleep in the Lord", he observed, "I've noticed you're getting pretty good at it."

My 1991 diary records that, on November 19, I gave a slide lecture about King Island to a history class at the University of Alaska–Fairbanks; that, on December 7, I offered a Mass in the Elders Home in Tanana, at which we had an anointing of older Catholics; that, on December 8–11, I attended a regional ministers meeting in Galena; that, on December 16, I gave two lectures at Monroe Catholic High on the Catholic Church in Alaska and then helped out that evening with the penance liturgy and confessions in Sacred Heart Cathedral; and that, on December 23–26, I was in Tanana for my final Christmas there.

On Thursday, January 16, 1992, I found myself in Tanana, having received word two days earlier that Harper Antoski had died. A Rosary wake was held for him that evening. I offered the funeral Mass and officiated at the graveside ceremonies the following day.

Harper was somewhat special to me, ever since I had first met him during one of my early visits to Tanana, while I was walking along the banks of the Yukon River. We met and chatted often thereafter. After several years, he began to live in the Elders Home. There, after I had visited and brought Communion to the other residents, I would knock on his door. He knew who it was and would respond with a hearty "Come in!" We always began with small talk. When this began to wane, I would say, "Well, Harper, are you ready?" He knew what I meant and answered with his customary drawn-out

"Yes, Faawther." After a brief pre-Communion prayer, I would give him Communion, then fall silent to give him a little time to welcome the Lord into his heart and talk to Him. After a brief period of silence, and some more small talk initiated by him, I would say, "Well, Harper, about time for me to go. I have a plane to catch. See you in two weeks. So long, and God bless you." To this he would invariably respond, as I was getting up to leave, with a drawn-out "And Gaawd bless you too, Faawther." That never failed to touch my heart.

One Sunday, after I had given Harper Communion, I began to wonder if I might be in the presence of a mystic. For a much longer time than usual, there was nothing from him but silence. I glanced up. He was staring straight ahead out the window, out across the Yukon. Finally, he pointed and said, "You see that raven, Faawther? He hasn't moved a bit all this time." A mystic? A distracted child of nature? A harmonious blend of the two?

On May 23, I was in Tanana to offer a funeral Mass and hold graveside services for the last time there. This time, it was a young man. Harper was an elderly man. On Sunday, June 7, I offered my final ordinary Sunday Mass in Tanana. After it, the people put on a simple farewell party for me and gave me a mug to show their appreciation for my priestly ministry of almost five years among them.

The reader may recall what I wrote earlier, namely, that "by September 1972, the historian in me was beginning to stir", and that I was corresponding with Father Schoenberg about "a possible history of the Society of Jesus in Alaska", adding, "however, I know I'm not the man to do it." On August 30, 1979, Father Segundo Llorente had written to me, "Your German blood no doubt enables you to dig into facts and details and then to make them known to us. I am coming to the conclusion that you are the providential man to do what Father [Joseph] McElmeel wanted accomplished in good English: the history of the Church and of the Society in Alaska." On March 5, 1991, I wrote to Sister Antoinette Johnson, O.S.U., a veteran of many years on the Alaska mission, "I believe you know that I am asking—with mixed feelings—to be freed from my Tanana assignment so as to have time to write more. People await from me nothing less than a history of the Church in Alaska. A daunting prospect, indeed. I will know my superior's verdict in the weeks ahead." By January 13, 1992, I had that verdict. As of June 1992, I was to be relieved of my Tanana assignment. It was Father Ted Kestler, then general mission superior, who made the decision. *"Alaskana Catholica: An Encyclopedic Dictionary*—did organizational work on this." This entry, admittedly somewhat grandiose sounding, appears in my diary for August 19, 1992. That was the first time I used the phrase *Alaskana Catholica*. (It proved to be a durable one. My history of the Catholic Church in Alaska came off the press in November 2005 bearing the title *Alaskana Catholica: A History of the Catholic Church in Alaska; A Reference Work in the Format of an Encyclopedia*.) Freed from my Tanana assignment, I now had some extra time—after attending to Alaskan Shepherd–related work—to devote to the production of entries slated to appear in the projected history.

During the last two months of 1992, I wrote the article about the Eskimo Deacon Program mentioned in an earlier chapter. When I had finished writing the Michael Nayagak story, I sent a copy of it, with a cover letter, to Michael's daughter, Maria Boyscout, in Chevak. In response, Maria wrote to me on February 12, 1993:

Thank you very much for the letter you shared with us. But it is much more than a letter. Reading it, word for word, has given me a lot of encouragement to live my faith the best I could with my children. I've shared your letter with my fellow Eucharistic ministers, in hopes that it would give them encouragement never to give up regardless. I've also shared it with both of my sisters. One by telephone. My dad Michael Nayagak taught us to have strength through God and the Holy Spirit. Since I've gotten the letter, it's been like I've been not totally with the world around me. This faith I have of God grew a lot. I don't know how to express it in words, the joy it fills me with is so indescribable. Thank you again. In Christ we are a family—Maria Boyscout.

From the twenty-third to the twenty-eighth of December, having volunteered to fill in, I was at Kaltag for my one and only Christmas there. The morning I flew out of Fairbanks, it was minus twenty-nine. For the rest of December, temperatures hovered around minus thirty. In spite of the cold, that Christmas outing was a very consoling one for me. I was well received by the people and exceptionally well hosted and helped by Sister Ann Brantmeier. This turned out to be my last time at Kaltag.

Throughout the whole of the year 1993, I again worked on entries for my *Alaskana Catholica*. A fair number of these were solicited as autobiographical sketches written in the third person from people still alive. Information about various people and on different subjects, too, was solicited from living sources.

In March, from the twenty-seventh to the twenty-ninth, I was in Barrow. On the twenty-eighth, along with Father Frank Mueller, I concelebrated at the Mass at which Bishop Kaniecki blessed the new Saint Patrick's Church. I was principal celebrant at the Mass on the twenty-ninth. I was never to see Barrow again.

At the request of the sisters in Tanana, I returned to Tanana for the 1993 Holy Week and Easter services. On Holy Thursday, three children made their First Holy Communion. All the services were well attended. As a member of a tourist group, I was to visit Tanana again, and for the last time, on June 9.

During the latter part of April and the first part of May, I played host to, and helped, Sister Pauline Higgins, S.P., with her writing of *Providence in Alaska: Sisters of Providence; Education Ministry in Alaska, 1902–1978*. (This was published in Seattle in 1999 by the Sisters of Providence.)

May 9, 1993, was a red-letter day for me but even more so for my collaborator and very good friend Dorothy Jean Ray. On that day, in the Patty Gymnasium on the campus of the University of Alaska–Fairbanks, I had the joy and satisfaction of finally seeing the university, at its seventy-first commencement exercises, confer on her the richly merited honorary degree of Doctor of Letters. I had felt for years that the conferral of such a degree upon her, a onetime student at the university, was long overdue. The wheels of academe had turned, slowly; but they had turned.

Sometime in 1977, I had already brought up the subject with her about her being deserving of an honorary doctorate from the University of Alaska–Fairbanks. "I am flattered", she wrote to me on September 28, 1977, "that you think the University of Alaska should present me with an honorary 'Doctor' title." I proposed to make a case on her behalf with the university by drawing to its attention the fact that, among other things, she was "a distinguished scholar and writer, widely acknowledged and accepted as one who has achieved distinction in her profession." On November 10, she wrote to me, "Please don't be disappointed if you don't accomplish what you are setting out to do." On November 15, I addressed a letter to the president of the board of regents, Dr. Hugh B. Fate, remarking in the first paragraph that "the university conferring the degree will be as much honored as Ray, the recipient of the degree." No response. In a March 11, 1978, letter to her, I wrote, in passing, "As for that Ph.D., there will be another year." On March 30, 1978, to my surprise, I received a letter from the executive secretary to the board of regents apologizing for delaying so long in responding to my letter of November 15. That was all. Soon thereafter, Dorothy Jean asked me not to pursue the matter any further.

For over a decade, then, the Ray, Ph.D., matter seemed to be a dead issue. Somehow, however, it kept haunting me, so much so that, on July 20, 1992, I took it upon myself to write in a letter to the associate vice-chancellor at the office of University Relations and Institutional Advancement, Karen L. Cedzo:

> It is time for the University of Alaska–Fairbanks to correct an outstanding oversight.
>
> It is time for it to recognize, officially and formally, the distinguished scholarship of Dorothy Jean Ray and her major contributions to the fields of Alaskan anthropology, ethnography, history, and Native art. She is acknowledged as the undisputed authority on Eskimo and Aleut art. The corpus of her published Alaskana is singularly impressive.
>
> It is time for the University of Alaska–Fairbanks to seize the opportunity and to confer on her her first honorary doctorate. By so doing it will confer no less honor on itself than on the conferee.

On December 14, 1992, Dorothy Jean wrote to me, "I was absolutely flabbergasted to receive in the mail today news that the University of Alaska–Fairbanks was going to give me an honorary degree! How did that happen? Did you know about it?" No, I did not know about it until I received her letter; nor did I know how it happened. Whether or not my letters to Dr. Fate and Ms. Cedzo played a role in her receiving that honorary degree, I was never to learn—nor did it make any practical difference.

On May 18, 1993, Father General Peter-Hans Kolvenbach and American Assistant Father Francis E. Case—a onetime student of mine at Seattle Prep, as mentioned earlier—arrived at Jesuit House. There was a lengthy question-and-answer session with Father General that evening, and a concelebrated Mass, with him as principal celebrant, the following morning. After that, some group photos with him were taken. I then asked him to pose with me for a photo. This he graciously did. Toward noon, I was alone in the kitchen getting myself a bite to eat when—in walks Father General! What to do? What to say? What to offer him? I heaved a sigh of shy relief when moments later Father Case walked in.

I was in Dillingham on June 13–29. My early return was prompted by my having agreed to officiate, upon her request, at the wedding of Ginger Esmailka of Ruby to Jay DeLima of Manley Hot Springs. The wedding was to take place at Manley Hot Springs on July 3. I flew there around noon on the second for an afternoon rehearsal. This was followed by a dinner in the Manley Roadhouse. The nuptial Mass was celebrated at 5:45 in the afternoon of the third. It was an out-of-doors wedding, celebrated under a stand of tall spruce and birches. Two whole pigs roasted in a pit served as the main course at the wedding banquet. Leaving the dancing to others, I took a walk in the woods in the cool of the evening. At nine o'clock the morning of the fourth, I offered the Sunday Mass in Manley's Catholic church, a little log structure dedicated to Saint Joseph. That afternoon, along with a few others, I was flown back to Fairbanks.

In the forenoon of Monday, July 12, I received a long-distance phone call from Tacoma. It was my nephew Gary Ross, Julie's son, calling to tell me that Dad was in Saint Joseph's Hospital in Tacoma, and "sinking", and that I had better hurry down. By that afternoon, along with other family members, I was at Dad's bedside. He may or may not have recognized me. He had been anointed by then. He was ready and eager to die. In the evening, assured by the medical staff that Dad should make it through the night, I left the hospital, along with Al and Joanne. In a delicatessen, we bought some snack food, which we took to what on North Geiger Street had been Dad and Mom's home for several decades to eat and spend the night.

Early on Tuesday morning, the thirteenth, we were back at the hospital. At 11:30 A.M., I concelebrated at a Mass offered in the hospital chapel by Father Michael Feeney, O.S.B., one of the hospital chaplains. Dad's doctor attended that Mass. After it, I winked him aside and asked him to tell me how Dad was doing. "Father," he said, "your father is dying. He will not leave the hospital alive." Frankly, I was relieved to know that.

Except for a short lunch break, I spent the rest of that day in Dad's hospital room. Other family members came and went. At one point, one of them said spontaneously, "Let's all gather around Dad's bed and join hands, and you, Father Louie, will lead us in prayers." This was done.

As the day, then the evening, dragged on, there was no discernable change in Dad's condition. Around 11:00 that Tuesday evening, I told Joanne (my brother Al's wife and a registered nurse) that I was going to go to an empty room across the hall to nap a bit and that she was to call me if there was any change in Dad's condition. I went to that room and had one shoe off when she came running to tell me, "Hurry, Dad's dying!" With one shoe off, one shoe on, I ran across the hall to witness him breathe his last. It choked me up a bit—and made me smile a bit—when, shortly after Dad's death, Al, the sixty-year-old baby of the family, looked at me and, with a half-serious expression on his face, said, "Father Louie, we are orphans now."

At 10:30 A.M. on July 16, in Saint Charles Borromeo Church, I offered the Mass of Christian Burial for my dear father. There were no graveside ceremonies. By midafternoon the following day, I was back in Fairbanks.

"When I was in prison, you visited me", said the Lord. I had often given Him to eat when He was hungry; had given Him to drink when He was thirsty; had taken Him in when He was a stranger; and had clothed Him when he was naked. But I had never visited Him when He was in prison. I needed yet to do that. And the need for someone to do that, on a part-time basis, as a volunteer, was made known to me late in the year 1993. It was a priest that the Diocese of Fairbanks was looking for. I volunteered.

On October 18, in the afternoon, in the Presbyterian church in downtown Fairbanks, I attended a two-hour orientation session for those hoping to get a card certifying them to be qualified to do part-time prison outreach ministry. Without further ado, I had the card. In the afternoon of Saturday, October 23, I visited the jail—officially, the Fairbanks Correctional Center—for the first time, accompanied by Mary Therese "Tweet" Burik, Bishop Kaniecki's executive secretary, and Rosalie L'Ecuyer, a devout Catholic laywoman and former mission volunteer, both of whom had been to the FCC before. By the time I left it, I had signed in, had been cleared twice by security officers, and had gone through seven different doors, each of them twice, most of them clanging shut behind me, locked, after I had gone through them. As I went down the long corridors, I was escorted by an FCC staff member—and stared at, from behind iron bars, by inmates whose photos I had recently seen on the front page of the Fairbanks newspaper.

After passing through the seventh door, one with a big glass window in it, I found myself in the room that served as the prison chapel. There was no question of my offering Mass, even though the services to be held were announced as "Catholic services". The services were open to any inmate not in maximum security who cared to attend. They had, therefore, to be kind of nondenominational, rather freely structured. One never knew who, or how many, or of what faith, if any, might attend. A few times, the given service seemed to be, for some of the men and women attending it, no more than an occasion to flirt and flash cryptic signs back and forth. Numbers varied from a handful to as many as fifteen. Some of the services turned out to be genuinely grace-filled, moving experiences for all of us in attendance. One never knew from month to month what to expect.

I visited the FCC about once a month, always on a Saturday afternoon. Other priests visited it only upon request. Mostly, it was Tweet who accompanied me, having picked me up and driven me there in her car. Together we would sign in, then go to the chapel to arrange the folding chairs in a semicircle and put songbooks and missalettes on each chair. As people came in for the service, she listed their names. Generally, some song began the service. If we had guitarists in attendance, they would lead the singing. After making some opening remarks about the given day's liturgy, I would begin with the Sign of the Cross and follow this with a more-or-less typical penance liturgy and the readings for the following day. After commenting on the readings, I would invite comments from the assembled. Prayers of petition would then follow, then the Lord's Prayer, then a song, then the final blessing and dismissal. Generally, the room emptied rather quickly. Sometimes one or other would beckon me aside for a short private talk or for confession. After all were gone, Tweet and I would gather up the songbooks and missalettes, put them in a cupboard, fold away the chairs, and, through seven doors, exit the FCC. Tweet would then drive me home. During one of the drives home, I said to her, "You know, Tweet, I never really look forward to these visits; but every time I'm through with one, I'm glad I went." Turning to me, she said, "You know, that's exactly how I feel."

On December 25, 1993, I noted in my diary, "My first Christmas ever in Fairbanks! A peaceful, quiet one." I had spent the evening before in the FCC taking part in a rousing, revivalist-kind of nondenominational service. My principal reason for going to the FCC that evening had been to be available to any Catholics who might wish to go to confession. As it turned out, while many inmates stepped forward to be prayed over by the other ministers and to be forgiven by the Lord, none approached me for confession.

I was not a "natural" for prison ministry. By God's grace, however, I stayed with it for a little over two and a half years. On May 18, 1996, accompanied by Tweet, I visited the FCC for the last time.

During the early months of 1994, two miracles of modern technology began, unexpectedly, to be part of my life. I had heard of compact disc players and word processors but had never entertained the slightest thought of ever getting either. However, Christmas 1993 and my golden jubilee as a Jesuit changed all that. As a Christmas present, out of the blue, I received from my onetime Seattle Prep student and longtime friend John M. Hutchinson a compact disc player and some CDs. I soon discovered this to be a whole new world—new to me—of listening pleasure. In addition, on March 18, just one week before I celebrated my fiftieth anniversary as a Jesuit, a "mystery package" appeared on my desk. It was from Bonnie Graboski, a registered nurse, an Alaskan Shepherd benefactor become personal friend and correspondent. It was a Brother word processor. It turned out to be a most timely, providential gift, since my old IBM typewriter was, by then, beginning to give me trouble. Getting used to word processing on the Brother, in addition to making me a more efficient correspondent and writer, served, too, to prepare me to move on to become a full-fledged computer user a few years later.

As the feast of the Annunciation dawned on the twenty-fifth of March 1994, I found myself having difficulty believing that it was already fully fifty years since I had become a member of the Society of Jesus. It seemed to me I was too young to be a golden jubilarian Jesuit. When I first entered the Jesuits, it was only old men who celebrated golden jubilees. However, the figures added up, all right! That afternoon, in the Jesuit House chapel, I was the principal celebrant at a low-key Mass of thanksgiving. Fellow Fairbanks Jesuits concelebrated. A festive meal followed. Four days later, at 11:15 A.M., in the chancery chapel, with the whole chancery staff present, I celebrated a more-public Mass of thanksgiving. In my homily, I stressed how my vocation to the Society was all gift, grace, favor; likewise, my perseverance therein. I ended my homily with: "And the next fifty years? Most of them I will spend in eternity. I leave them all in the loving hands of the Lord. My past and my future, my living and my dying, my yesterdays and my tomorrows, my time and my eternity: I entrust them all into the merciful, caring, loving hands of the Lord."

All set to hike the Chilkoot Trail, June 23, 1980.

My living quarters at Healy while helping with the construction of the new church, August-September 1980.

A self-portrait of myself taking a tea-break on the shores of Norton Sound, near the mouth of Quartz Creek west of Nome, June 25, 1981.

In the cemetery at the site of the former Saint Mary's Mission, Akulu-
rak, praying at the grave of Jesuit missionary Father Jules Jetté,
August 4, 1981. Photo by Father Francis E. Mueller, S.J.

With Emmanuel Stanislaus, parents, godparents, and three newly baptized infants on the steps of Saint Ignatius Church in Alakanuk, December 30, 1981.

Working with Jesuit missionary Father Jim Sebesta at the cordwood saw in Kaltag, early June 1982. Photo by Father Mark A. Hoelsken, S.J.

In the social hall of Saint Charles Borromeo School, following the Mass offered in thanksgiving for twenty-five years of priesthood on August 6, 1982, cutting into the 25th anniversary cake. Photo by Kathleen Renner.

In Nulato, helping Jesuit missionary Father Charlie Bartles cut up the moose bagged by him down to meal-sized portions, October 1, 1982.

Splitting stove wood in Galena, October 7, 1982. Photo by Father Charles A. Bartles, S.J.

Ruby, a mostly Athabaskan Indian village on the left bank of the middle Yukon River, as seen from the cemetery bluff on March 10, 1984, the day the front-runners in the Iditarod Trail Sled Dog Race reached Ruby.

In the Ruby cemetery, leading the final services at the burial of Rubyite Harvey Albert, February 13, 1984. Photo by Sister Patricia A. Miller, O.P.

With Alfons Maria Cardinal Stickler, S.D.B., Prefect of the Vatican Library and Archives, in the Alaskan Shepherd office, September 25, 1985. Photo by Sister Margaret Pillette, S.N.J.M.

*With fellow Jesuit Father Frank Mueller on the banks of the
Copper River, June 12, 1986. Mount O'Neel and Childs Glacier in
the background. Photo by John P. Crowley.*

Relaxing in the Ruby cemetery with elder Altona Brown after the burial of Madeline Pitka Notti, June 16, 1986. Photo by Father Brad R. Reynolds, S.J.

West-facing Jesuit House in Fairbanks, in which I lived—upper, back, left corner room—from 1987-2002.

In the McMillan home, on July 24, 1988, offering a Mass of Thanksgiving on behalf of Dad and Mom for sixty-five years of married life together. Photo by Kathleen Renner.

The Dykemas' fish camp—on the right bank of the Nushagak River some seven miles downriver from Dillingham—as it appeared in July 1998. It consisted mainly of two porto-shelters, an outhouse, and a makeshift toolshed. My tent is barely visible above the pickup truck on the left. Photo by Kenneth Dykema.

With Richard Dykema, hauling sockeye salmon over the gunwale into the aluminum skiff, June 1989. Photo by Gisela Dykema.

Richard and Gisela Dykema visiting me in my Alaskan Shepherd office, January 5, 1990.

In the log residence attached to Saint John Berchmans Church in Galena, on November 7, 1990. Ministers to villages along the middle Yukon River pose, after a series of meetings, for a group photo. They are, left to right: Sister Monique Vaernewyck, O.S.U.; William E. Cardy, O.F.M.; Brother Kirby Boone, C.F.X.; Sister Ann Waters, S.N.J.M.; Sister Kateri Mitchell, S.S.A.; Father Louis L. Renner, S.J.; Father Joseph Hemmer, O.F.M.; Sister Maria Clarys, O.S.U.; and Brother Robert J. Ruzicka, O.F.M. Photo by Bishop Michael J. Kaniecki, S.J.

Whacking apart a piece of tundra—a sod island brought downstream to in front of our camp by the outgoing tide—to keep it from getting into some fisherman's net, July 1992. Photo by Gisela Dykema.

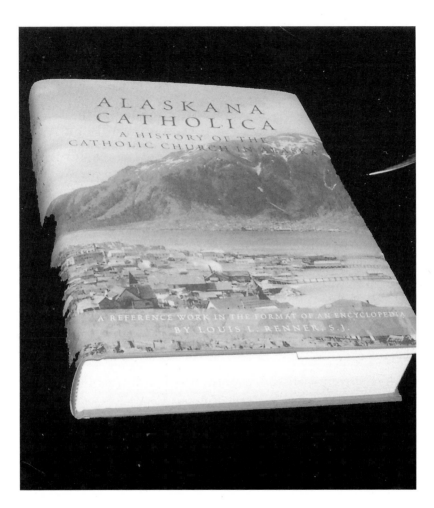

Photo by Father J. Alfred Carroll, S.J.

At the University of Alaska-Fairbanks, with Dorothy Jean Ray, May 9, 1993, the day she was awarded an honorary doctorate.
Photo by William S. Schneider.

In the foyer of Jesuit House, Fairbanks, with Father General Peter-Hans Kolvenbach, S.J., May 19, 1993.

At Manley Hot Springs, officiating at the nuptial Mass at which Jay deLima and Ginger Esmailka were united in Holy Matrimony, July 3, 1993. Deacon Walter H. Gelinas is assisting. Photo by Curt Madison.

In Saint Peter-in-Chains Church in Ruby, with Liza Kangas, who just made her First Holy Communion, Easter Sunday, April 3, 1994. Photo by Brother Kirby Boone, C.F.X.

The little cabin, uphill from the church, in which I often stayed while in Ruby, February 8, 1984.

On the Nenana airstrip, waiting out the weather with Brother Robert J. Ruzicka, O.F.M., April 4, 1994. Behind us is parked the Diocese of Fairbanks' plane, the Cessna 207, in which—with Bishop Michael J. Kaniecki, S.J., at the controls—I flew countless Alaskan bush air-miles. Photo by Bishop Michael J. Kaniecki, S.J.

On the riverboat Discovery III with the Partridges: Daniel, Alan, Cheryl, and Gayle, June 26, 1994. Photo by Brian J. Partridge.

On the Granite Tors Trail with Julie, Joanne, and Albert, May 24, 1995. Photo by Duncan S. McMillan.

In the Doyon Limited Building, Fairbanks, December 1, 2000, on the occasion of the book signing by and the reception held for Dr. Eliza Jones, co-author with Father Julius Jetté, S.J., of the Koyukon Athabaskan Dictionary. Photo by Stephen Paskvan.

At the Arctic Circle, en route on the Dempster Highway to Inuvik, Northwest Territories, Canada, August 13, 1996. Photo by Father Normand A. Pepin, S.J.

In the Alaskan Shepherd office, at the Christmas party hosted by the four Alaskan "Shepherdesses": Morva Hoover, Lucy Dalsky, Karen Schauer, and Pat Welborn, December 13, 1996. Photo courtesy of Morva Hoover.

At Dillingham, with Michael Dykema (back) and Steven (helping me hold the king salmon), and Daniel, sons of Ernie and Stephanie Dykema-Siemoneit, early July 1997. Photo by Gisela Dykema.

A grizzly leads her cubs along the bank of the Nushagak River immediately below our camp at Dillingham, July 1998. Photo by Gisela Dykema.

At Sunriver, Oregon, with William J. (Bill) and Bernice Renner and their children and grandchildren, gathered after the Mass offered in thanksgiving for fifty years of married life together, August 5, 1998. Photo by Fred Alexander/Sunriver Photography.

Enjoying a lunch-break and the view from the top of the Angel Rocks Trail with nephew Michael J. Renner's children Stephanie and Gregory, August 4, 2000. Photo by Michael J. Renner.

In the Carlson Center, Fairbanks, August 27, 2000, about to concelebrate at the Jubilee 2000 Mass.

My third, and rather palatial, tent at our fish camp downstream from Dillingham, June-July 2001.

From 1987 to 2002, I walked innumerable times a nameless path through the woods between Jesuit House and the chancery building. Early on the morning of April 25, 2002, I was surprised to see the RENNER WAY sign up at the Jesuit House end of the path. Some minutes later, I found it also at the other end. Patricia (Patty) Welborn-Walter—my successor as head of the Alaskan Shepherd program—was responsible for the sign, and this photo.

Father Louis L. Renner, S.J., September 17, 2005. Photo by Father Brad R. Reynolds, S.J./C00522-A352.

On the third of January already, I had received a phone call from Brother Kirby Boone, C.F.X., in Ruby asking me if I could be in Ruby to celebrate the 1994 Holy Week and Easter liturgies for the people. On Holy Thursday afternoon, Bishop Kaniecki dropped me off at Ruby on his way downriver to Holy Cross. As Brother Kirby was living in the priest's quarters in the back of the church, I happily spent my free time and nights in the little cabin up in the woods. A Monitor oil stove kept it warm. A microwave oven took care of all my simple cooking needs. A little cassette player provided wonderful music to put me in the spirit and mood for Holy Week and Easter: Rossini's *Stabat Mater*, Wagner's "Good Friday Spell" from *Parsifal*, and Slavonic sacred Easter music. In spite of the dog races taking place in Ruby at the time, services were well attended. The church was packed for the Easter Sunday Mass.

Bishop Kaniecki and Brother Robert J. Ruzicka, O.F.M., arrived in Ruby late Easter Sunday evening. The bishop, being tired, decided to spend the night there. At 9:00 on Monday morning, the three of us left Ruby for Fairbanks. That airport was reported to be shrouded in fog at the time. However, we had hopes the fog would have lifted by the time we got there. As we neared Nenana, the fog in Fairbanks had not lifted. We landed at Nenana and spent three hours at the airfield, waiting for favorable landing conditions in Fairbanks. It was a calm, sunny day, making for pleasant chatting, walking, and meditating as we paced up and down the airfield. At around 2:00 P.M., we landed in Fairbanks.

Annually, generally during the month of April, Bishop Kaniecki flew to the Yukon-Kuskokwim Delta Eskimo villages on a confirmation tour. He was scheduled to make his 1994 confirmation tour there during the latter half of the month. As editor and article writer for the *Alaskan Shepherd*,

I was always on the lookout for new material. Feeling I could use another field trip, I invited myself along. This trip was to be far more varied than the one I had been on with him three years previously.

In the Cessna 207, with Brother Kirby (in Fairbanks at the time) also on board, we left Fairbanks in the early afternoon of Thursday, April 14. After a two-hour flight, part of it through some rather "soupy" weather, we landed at McGrath. There we dropped Brother Kirby off and snacked on sticky buns as we visited with Father Bill Dibb, pastor of McGrath. Then, at 5:10 P.M., after gassing up, we took off for Saint Mary's. This leg of our travels took us almost exactly two hours. The weather was good throughout. However, we had barely landed and tied down the plane when snow flurries blew in, reducing visibility to next to nothing. A fierce wind out of the north and a temperature near zero degrees combined to create a chill factor of minus forty-five degrees. We were grateful to be met and driven the eight miles to the former Saint Mary's mission complex, where a hot meal awaited us. Knowing how unpredictable the weather in the Delta can be, Bishop Mike had wisely added a few extra days to his confirmation schedule to allow for days when flying would be impossible—and to gain time to attend to unforeseen business, to get a tearful earful here, a cheerful earful there, to give one of his shaggy shepherds an impromptu haircut, to relax, play a game of cribbage or two, and just to regroup. Saint Mary's was an ideal place for a break day. We spent Friday the fifteenth there.

On Saturday, assisted by a strong north wind on our tail, we flew the roughly one-hundred-mile stretch to Newtok in record time, where we were met by its pastor, Father Eugene P. (Gene) Delmore, S.J. We reconnected with Deacon Larry Charles and his wife, Albertina. The confirmation Mass began at 3:15 P.M. With the singing, and with the homily given in English and interpreted into Eskimo, and with nineteen confirmations, the whole service lasted around ninety minutes. A potluck of simple fare followed soon after it. In part, the potluck was held early, so that we could fly Father Gene and Jimmy Tom, at their request, to Chefornak. By 6:50, they were on the ground there; ten minutes later, we were airborne again and on our way to our next destination, the village of Hooper Bay, 113 miles to the northwest. This turned out to be a very pleasant flight. Part of it was along the coast. Much of the Bering Sea was still iced over, but there were also many leads and patches of open water for the evening sun to play on.

We touched down on the Hooper Bay airstrip at 7:50. After we had the plane secured, we began to walk toward the village. Soon, however, Walter Naneng—again our "tundra taxi", as he had been in 1991—came along on his snow machine, pulling a freight sled, to give us a ride to the village. Over rough ice and hard-packed snowdrifts, it was far from a smooth ride, but we were grateful for it. At the church, we were again warmly greeted by Sisters Angela Fortier and Julie Thorpe. With them, we shared an evening meal.

On Sunday morning the seventeenth, Bishop Mike was the principal celebrant at the eleven o'clock Mass. I concelebrated. The confirmation Mass began shortly after 5:00 P.M. Six were confirmed at it. Father Mark Hoelsken, pastor of Hooper Bay, having just returned on his snow machine from Chevak, one of his other stations, was my fellow concelebrant at that Mass. After it, refreshments were served in the parish hall. Eskimo dancing followed.

Monday, April 18, was one of our scheduled break days. We spent it and the night in Hooper Bay. In the early forenoon, noticing that the previous night's blizzard had so packed with snow the steps leading up to the sisters' second-floor quarters that they resembled a perfectly smooth slide, I decided to shovel them off. Shortly after I began, Sister Julie came out with two buckets and asked me to fill them with snow to be melted for wash water. Hooper Bay had no clean water supply.

On Tuesday, in the forenoon, Bishop Mike, Father Mark, and I flew the short hop to Chevak. There, Sister Rose Andre (Rosie) Beck—whom we met in an earlier chapter—invited us to her house for a turkey soup luncheon and to discuss plans for that evening's confirmation Mass.

That afternoon, in spite of the icy wind and a few snow flurries, I took a stroll through the village. It had changed considerably since I had last seen it in 1982, when I spent almost two weeks there helping move building materials for the new church from the riverside landing to the new church site.

The confirmation Mass began at 7:00 P.M. Young and old filled the church to see eleven of their community being confirmed. After the services, Sister Rosie served refreshments in her house to the many who had accepted her invitation. No Eskimo dancing followed. The dancing—rather, the whistling—was left to the wind howling around the church set high on the hill.

The Scammon Bay confirmations were scheduled for the evening of Wednesday, April 20. At 11:45 A.M., Bishop Mike, Sister Rosie, Father Mark, and I took off for Scammon Bay. Father Mark was in the copilot's seat to help Bishop Mike find the safest pass through the Askinuk Mountains just south of Scammon Bay. Shortly after noon, we were on the ground again. After lunch, I took off to explore the village and surroundings. I first visited the church, the oldest in the Fairbanks diocese at the time. I found the white, well-kept interior of the church to be bright and cheerful. I then climbed up the rocky outcropping behind and above the village to shoot some pictures of the village below. A friendly husky, looking somewhat bedraggled (he was just in the process of shedding his heavy winter coat) tagged along and kept me company.

The confirmation Mass that evening, although there were six to be confirmed, drew the smallest crowd of our whole tour in the Delta. But again, all age groups were represented. After the Mass, punch and cake were served in the church basement. As I was returning to the parish house, a group of kids, seeing me with my camera, gathered quickly to have their picture taken.

By the clock, it was already 9:25 P.M. before Bishop Mike, Father Mark, and I (leaving Sister Rosie in Scammon Bay) were ready to take off for Saint Mary's. As we were in far-western Alaska and on double daylight saving time, the actual time, sun time, was more like 6:30 P.M., and the sun was still high in the sky. That flight from Scammon Bay to Saint Mary's was, at least for me, the most beautiful one of our entire tour. The evening sun to the west, at times illuminating patches of light clouds, then playing on frozen surfaces below, created skyscapes and icescapes of rare, serene beauty. Just as we landed at Saint Mary's, at 10:10 P.M., the sun slipped below the northwestern horizon. After the Cessna 207 had been gassed up and secured against the cold and wind, we were ready to be driven down to the mission, where we arrived at 10:50. It was the end of a long, eventful, soul-satisfying day.

The next day, Thursday, April 21, 1994, dawned snowing and blowing at Saint Mary's. It continued to do so throughout the day and into the night. But let it snow! Let it blow! This was a scheduled break day. However, there was concern about whether or not the people expected for the potlatch honoring Brother Ignatius Jakes on the occasion of his golden jubilee as a Jesuit would be able to make it in. The potlatch was slated for the following day. At times, the airport was closed because of poor visibility and drifting snow. Even if planes could land, would passengers be able to get down to the mission?

There was a concelebrated Mass in the old mission chapel at 4:30 P.M. Shortly after it, Brother Jakes, beaming broadly, came up to my room to tell me that his two sisters and other family members, in spite of some weather delays, had arrived. He took me to meet them. It will be recalled that both he and I had entered the Jesuits in March 1944, so we were both now, in 1994, celebrating our golden jubilees.

Dinner that evening consisted of cornbread and stew, a real stick-to-the-ribs kind of dinner for a blustery day. After it, the fifteen of us Jesuits, gathered at Saint Mary's for the celebration of Brother Jakes' jubilee, assembled in the Brother Joe Prince House for ninety minutes of "faith sharing". This consisted of a Scripture reading, silent reflection, a period of silence before the Blessed Sacrament exposed, and prayers "that the Lord of the Harvest would bless our Church with Native priests, deacons, sisters, and brothers and that the Church in Alaska might truly become 'a Church of the people'." The faith sharing ended with us gathered around Brother Jakes, laying hands on him and praying in silence and out loud for him. Chess, cribbage, popcorn, and fraternal togetherness rounded out the evening.

The next morning, Friday, April 22, the big, long-awaited, long-planned-for day got off to a late start. It was also to have a late end. There was a concelebrated Mass at 11:00 A.M. in the old mission chapel. This was followed by lunch at noon and leisurely visiting and walks. Dinner was at 5:30 P.M. The Eskimo potlatch honoring Brother Jakes began at 7:30 P.M.

in the city hall, soon filled with people from near and far. The evening's ceremonies began with an opening prayer, followed by words of welcome and the introduction of honored guests. Father Ted Kestler, as general superior of Jesuits in Alaska, was the principal host of the whole affair. Eskimo drumming and dancing came next. After several hours of this, drums were put aside and the floor was cleared of dance mats. Following this, box after box of gifts to be distributed were brought in by the Jesuit priests present for the event. Then in strode Brother Jakes, wearing, in part, new, specially made Native clothes: an Eskimo parka, a fur hat, and beaded sealskin mukluks on his feet. Standing in the middle of the hall on a beaver pelt, he "presided" as gifts were distributed in his name to the crowd assembled to honor him. The distribution of gifts constitutes the heart of a potlatch. Part three of that evening's potlatch doings consisted of more drumming and dancing. It was near midnight before the last echo of the last drumbeat died out. My role, self-assigned, in the events of that memorable jubilee day was again mainly that of observer, reporter, and photographer.

The golden jubilee Mass was celebrated the following day, Saturday, April 23, also in the city hall. Bishop Kaniecki was principal celebrant, with fourteen priests concelebrating. Singing was in Eskimo, English, and Latin. After the Lord's Prayer, Brother Jakes, kneeling before the Sacred Host and chalice held by Father Ted, renewed his vows as a religious brother.

The whole potlatch celebration ended with a grand smorgasbord-type dinner in the city hall at 1:00 P.M. The early dinner hour was necessitated by the fact that Bishop Kaniecki was scheduled to hold confirmations that evening at 7:00 in Kotlik, another Eskimo village in the Delta.

With Father Henry G. Hargreaves, S.J., pastor of Kotlik, on board—and with that north wind still blowing stiff and fresh—we took off for Kotlik at 3:30 in the afternoon. During the first part of our flight, we had only broken clouds above us. Soon, however, a cloud cover began to form. We circled back to where we had better visibility to get on top of it. As we continued our flight north, the cloud cover below us became solid and so perfectly uniform that, as we flew along over it, there was no sense of forward motion whatever. Time seemed to stand still. I became a bit apprehensive. I noticed Father Henry, too, was watching Bishop Mike closely as the latter kept studying his maps and intently watching the instrument panel.

Then we began our descent. Slowly we lost altitude. The brilliant sun above us to the southwest first became obscured, then was gone. Uniform, luminous white all around us! It was like flying in a bottle of milk. Next thing Father Henry and I knew, we broke out through the bottom of the dense layer of clouds, and there, just a little ahead of us, lay the Kotlik airstrip. Pleasant surprise! To Bishop Mike, this was, of course, no surprise. He was relying on a GPS (global positioning system) to guide us to our destination. By 4:08 P.M., we were on the ground at Kotlik. While Bishop Mike attended to the Cessna 207, Father Henry and I, with our gear, headed for the village and the church. Four inches of new snow on, more or less, glare ice made the going slow.

Before long, Bishop Mike, too, was at the church. The evening confirmation ceremonies were discussed. Candidates came by for a rehearsal. After all had left, Father Henry served up a three-course—uh, a three-*can*—dinner for the three of us: ravioli, peas, and fruit. Instant coffee washed it all down.

The Kotlik confirmations were Bishop Mike's fifth on this tour. One might think that, by now, his celebration of the confirmation rites would have become somewhat routine, perfunctory. Not so. The initial freshness was still there. Every place was unique and had its own kind of excitement and community involvement. For each candidate, confirmation day was a special day, long awaited, long prepared for. Bishop Mike sensed this. To both him and to me, every confirmation day was a Sunday. The Kotlik confirmations had a simplicity and warmth all their own. Picture taking and refreshments ended them. That night, I slept my first, and last, night at Kotlik.

The last of the Delta confirmations were scheduled for the late afternoon of Sunday, April 24, at Alakanuk. The day dawned relatively mild, fairly sunny. It was to stay that way. What wind there was was still out of the north and helped get us to Alakanuk in just twenty-one minutes. By 9:35 A.M., we were there. After greeting the administrator of Saint Ignatius parish, Monica Shelden, in her home and discussing confirmation plans with her, Bishop Mike and I went to the church next door, more—to be honest—to "check it out" than to pay our respects to the Lord. The church had been moved to its new site just the year before. At noon, Monica put a simple lunch, boiled spaghetti and tomato sauce, on the table for Bishop Mike and me. She herself was too excited, too concerned about the doings scheduled for 4:00 that afternoon, to join us. In the middle of the afternoon, Bishop Mike and I took turns hearing confessions in the church. Just as the confirmation liturgies in the other five villages came off happily, so likewise at Alakanuk. This, too, was followed by picture taking and refreshments.

In spite of the much adverse flying weather we had encountered on our confirmation tour up to that point, we had been able to maintain our schedule. However, the weather on the coast was now forecast to deteriorate radically, and soon. With our work in the Delta done, Bishop Mike was not about to press his luck; he was, instead, eager to head inland right away. We said our good-byes to Monica, grabbed our bags, and headed out to the airstrip. We had originally planned to head inland by way of Unalakleet and the Kaltag Portage. However, a malfunctioning fax machine at Saint Mary's needed to be picked up and brought to Fairbanks. Before taking off for Saint Mary's, Bishop Mike phoned ahead to tell people there that we were coming and to meet us at the airfield. Before he could hang up, I suggested he ask them to bring us each a sandwich. It had, by then, been a rather long, and lean, day already—food-wise—and it would be a while yet before we would be at Aniak, where we planned to spend the night. As we landed at Saint Mary's, people were waiting for us with the fax machine and two bags containing considerably more than just a sandwich each. By 7:15, we were again airborne, on our way to Aniak, where we arrived just one hour later. That Saint Mary's–Aniak flight was, for me, the most pleasant of the whole confirmation tour. The pressure was off. We were ahead of the weather, droning along over scenery rich and varied, munching on bagged banquets. It was airborne contentment at its finest, enjoyed with grateful hearts!

At Aniak, Father William E. Cardy, O.F.M., was our gracious host. Over generous bowls of strawberry ice cream—served to make the eve of my sixty-eighth birthday a special occasion—we talked well into the night. On Monday morning, April 25, after a concelebrated Mass and breakfast, Bishop Mike and I were driven to the airfield. By 10:15, we were airborne, headed for Galena to take on some fuel there. Shortly after takeoff, we saw a big flock of swans. Another Alaskan spring was on the threshold.

We arrived at Galena shortly after noon, gassed up, then flew upriver to Ruby to pick up Brother Kirby. The Ruby–Fairbanks stretch was to be the last leg of our eventful, twelve-day tour. At 2:58 that Monday afternoon, the Cessna 207—making its fifteenth landing in less than two weeks—touched down in Fairbanks and taxied to its parking space in a hangar on the east ramp. Throughout our travels, the plane had performed flawlessly. Warm summerlike weather—midsixties—and the season's first mosquitoes greeted us as we got out. With me, in addition to my gear, I now had many rolls of film to be developed and enough material to fill six issues of the *Alaskan Shepherd*.

When on tours of greater length, Bishop Mike generally tried to keep up with his mail by dictating into a recorder letters to be typed up later in Fairbanks. A few days after our return there, I found on my desk a letter from him dated April 22, 1994. The letter began, "This letter is certainly overdue, and yet it still comes from the heart." From what follows next, it is evident that it was my fiftieth anniversary as a Jesuit that prompted the letter. The heart of the letter read: "Louie, your contribution to the diocese over the years is one worthy of note. Your quiet and steady ways, your striving for detail and perfection have certainly not gone unnoticed by me as bishop of this diocese. I formally want to thank you for all that you have done for the diocese over the years. Your writing has touched many souls, both locally and afar, but more than that, your warm and gentle personality truly reflects the spirit of Christ."

On June 6, 1995, in a similar vein, he wrote under "Comments from the Bishop" on my ministry performance review sheet: "Your articles are superb, and I think our reading audience justly recognizes that. You also have a fine sense of humor, and I encourage you to share even more of yourself with our staff and others. I know you are a bit shy, but we *do* enjoy your presence. Please spend even more time with us. Again, thanks for a superb job and all the support you have given me—and for staying in the saddle."

On June 8, I flew to Tacoma to spend time again with members of my immediate family. I visited Verne and Dorothy Jean Ray in Port Townsend on the fourteenth. Two days later, I was at Seattle University to concelebrate a Mass of thanksgiving and to enjoy a banquetlike dinner with fellow jubilarians. Two days after that, in Puyallup, I attended the wedding of my nephew David Carlin—whom I had baptized the week after my ordination to the priesthood—to Kassandra Williams. I returned to Fairbanks on the twentieth.

It may be remembered that, in Holy Cross Church in Tacoma on December 27, 1975, I had celebrated the nuptial Mass at which my niece Cheryl Ann Renner and Brian Partridge became husband and wife. On June 25, 1994, I welcomed them and their three children—Daniel (sixteen), Alan (fourteen), and Gayle (twelve)—in Fairbanks. For four days, it was a question of who could keep up with whom. On the riverboat *Discovery III*, we took a cruise out of the mouth of the Chena River and down the Tanana River a stretch and back, ate at the outdoor salmon bake at Alaskaland, hiked a good length of the White Mountains Trail, viewed a section of the Trans-Alaska Pipeline, and visited the musk ox farm at the University of Alaska–Fairbanks. In the Jesuit House basement, all had a room of their own to rest up in for the next day's activities. On the last day of their visit, the twenty-ninth, I offered Mass for them in the Jesuit House chapel at 10:00 A.M., after which they treated me to lunch at the Pumphouse. Good-bye hugs, and they were on their way south again.

Sometime in November, the people in Ruby asked to have me with them for Christmas 1994. I flew there on the twenty-third of December. On the back of a snow machine, I got a ride the two miles from the landing strip down to the village. At minus thirty-five, such a ride soon brings color to one's nose and cheeks. With Brother Kirby still living in the priest's quarters in the church, I again stayed in the little cabin in the woods. In the forenoon of Christmas Eve, I visited some of the older people in their cabins. Confessions were scheduled from 2:30 to 3:30 that afternoon. Business was not nearly as brisk as the weather. The 8:30 P.M. Christmas Eve Mass saw a full church, as did the Midnight Mass.

The Christmas Day Mass was moderately well attended. At it, we had the baptism of an infant and a First Holy Communion. The infant's father, recently from Germany, was pleasantly surprised to hear me speak to him in German. After the lunch following the Mass, I brought Holy Communion to some shut-ins in their cabins. For our Christmas Day dinner, Brother Kirby and I were invited guests in the home of Gary and Irene Kangas and family.

I returned to Fairbanks from Ruby on the twenty-sixth. As we were nearing Fairbanks, we had before us on the horizon the most striking mirage I had ever seen. You would have sworn you were seeing a high, flat-topped range of mountains ahead of you. As we lost altitude, the "mountains" began slowly to melt away. It takes just the right atmospheric conditions to cause such a natural phenomenon.

Chapter 24

The Latter Half of the 1990s: 1995–1998

"Real early at answering much Shepherd mail", "Answered a mountain of Shepherd mail", and similar notations recur almost on every page of my 1995 diary. Much of what I did throughout that year resembled, in large part, what I had done during the previous years. There were issues of the *Alaskan Shepherd* to be prepared, letters to be written and answered, budget and evaluation of staff members to be attended to, weekly staff Masses to be offered or concelebrated, meetings of all kinds to be attended, confessions to be heard, prison ministry turns to be taken, sick in the hospital to be visited, hikes to be taken and blueberries to be picked with Father Pepin, and professional sports on TV to be watched. At the Dykema place, there was wood to be split, the garden to be spaded up, potatoes to be dug—and many a "best meal in town" to be eaten. At Livengood, there was gold to be panned. And at Dillingham, there were king and sockeye salmon to be netted by the thousands. For all its being similar in many respects to previous years, the year 1995 had, nevertheless, its own special events and highlights. And everything else about it continued to remain for me new and fresh. I loved my formally assigned duties, as well as my freely chosen work and hobbies, as much as ever.

In January already, the people of Ruby made sure I would be with them again for the Holy Week and Easter services.

I flew there on April 13, Holy Thursday. Again, I stayed in the little cabin. During the days, there was much thawing. A bucket and cans caught the ceiling drippings from a leaky roof. No harm done. The services were all well attended, the people appreciative. By Monday the seventeenth, I was back in Fairbanks.

From May 22 to the morning of the twenty-fifth, I hosted Duncan and Julie and Al and Joanne on their one and only visit to Fairbanks. Among the attractions in Fairbanks, it was especially the little, old Immaculate Conception Church that impressed them. The cruise on the riverboat *Discovery III* proved to be a highlight, as did the hike along a good stretch of the Granite Tors Trail. Dinner at the Dykemas' had a family warmth about it that no "eating out" could have matched. Salmon on the grill was the specialty.

Our 1995 annual Alaskan Jesuit retreat differed considerably from previous ones. Instead of making this in Anchorage for eight days as usual, we met in Fairbanks from July 31 to August 3 for concelebrated liturgies, prayer and meditation sessions, and day-long meetings. On the third, we were all formally "missioned" by our general superior, Father Ted Kestler. I was "missioned" to continue on with my Alaskan Shepherd work and with my research and writing about the Jesuits and the Church in Alaska.

On September 14, 1995, life in Jesuit House changed significantly, both for me personally and for our community in general. On that day, Brother Jakes, having suffered a severely incapacitating stroke some weeks earlier, which deprived him of speech and the use of his right arm and leg and confined him to a bed or a wheelchair, became part of our community. His presence among us, while certainly a blessing, meant also a steady coming and going, even at mealtimes, of nurses, caregivers, therapists, relatives, and friends. To a degree, they, too, all became a part of our community. In all this, the Jesuit House community had a timely opportunity to practice what it had formally and officially espoused as its apostolic work as a community, namely, the extension of generous, gracious hospitality to any and all guests.

Brother Jakes and I, it will be remembered, had both entered the Jesuits in 1944. After novitiate days, we had been together at Mount Saint Michael's and at Monroe High. We had worked together on the new church at Chevak in 1982, and together we had celebrated our golden jubilees at St. Mary's in 1994. During his stay in Jesuit House, I was there for him. I frequently offered morning Mass for him, welcomed his visitors, and, with a monitor, took longer turns at keeping a sleeping ear alert to his possible needs during the nights. To shorten his days, I played many games of chess with him. Beating him at it was now no problem. He was no longer up to par—assuming my game was par. However, by handicapping myself and making ill-advised moves, I was able to keep making the game a pleasant enough diversion for him. He was almost always ready for a game or two. Conversation with him was wholly impossible, for he could not communicate verbally at all. Chess, and a few conventional signs, served us adequately as conversation. After he was taken to the Oregon Province infirmary on the campus of Gonzaga University on June 16, 1999, there was, for a time, a considerable void in my personal life. He died on August 23, 1999.

During the last quarter of 1995, I began directing Patricia Carey-Mohrmann, a former German student and advisee of mine at the University of Alaska–Fairbanks, in a "Nineteenth Annotation" retreat. We met roughly several times a month for about an hour. The retreat ended in May 1996. This was the closest I ever came in my life as a Jesuit to giving a retreat. I had made many a retreat on my own but had never directed one.

The end of 1995 found me again in Ruby. The Christmas Day Mass was especially festive, inasmuch as during it I baptized a young mother and her three children and gave her and her boy their First Holy Communion. The two girls, twins, were only sixteen months old. The day before, I had visited the mother and children in their home, more to put them at ease than to check out their preparedness for those sacraments. They had been well prepared by good Brother Kirby.

Stepping out into the predawn darkness on the morning of the twenty-sixth, I felt wet, fast-falling snowflakes on my face. Would I make it back to Fairbanks that day? I wondered to myself. As it turned out, the plane did make it out of Fairbanks but had to hold up in Tanana for a while because of snow showers in the Ruby area. It was not until 2:12 P.M. that we took off from Ruby, Fairbanks-bound. A mechanical malfunction made it impossible for the pilot to retract the landing gear. The added drag slowed our flight considerably. It took us almost two hours to get to Fairbanks. Buckled in and cramped into the copilot's seat, as I was, unable to squirm, I had a pretty sore bottom by the time we touched down in Fairbanks. That, however, was a small price to pay for what was, otherwise and in all respects, a fruitful, rewarding outing.

My Christmas homily in Ruby, subsequently repeated in Fairbanks, was on gifts. A chancery staff member found it worthy of publication. It is here attached as a kind of coda to the year 1995.

Around Christmastime, some people just seem to get carried away with gift giving. But how wonderful! How Godlike! How divine! Isn't that what Christmas is really all about? Did not God the Father Himself get carried away—loving the world so much that He gave His only Son to be the world's Savior? God is the greatest giver. Jesus is the greatest gift.

The gifts we receive are not just things but symbols, signs that somebody loves us. It is the love with which something is given that makes of it a gift. And it is not really a gift unless it is received with gratitude. Give with love! Receive with gratitude!

God is the principal giver of all gifts. We can give only what we have first received from Him. To Him all praise and all thanksgiving, especially for Jesus—of all God's gifts to us, the greatest.

The year 1996 was my three-score-and-ten year. On April twenty-fifth, I celebrated my seventieth birthday. As I wrote to Dorothy Jean, "I was treated royally." Earlier that April, I was again in Ruby for the Holy Week and Easter services. Except for the weather—"more like for Christmas: icy winds, new snow, twelve below on Easter Monday morning"— everything was rather predictable. By now, the people there were beginning to refer to me as "our Ruby Easter priest"— also as "our Ruby Christmas priest". At this time, Father Joseph Hemmer, O.F.M., had the care of both Kaltag and Ruby, about 135 miles apart as the raven flies. However, because commercial planes did not fly on Christmas and Easter, he was unable to cover both of those villages on those two solemn feast days.

I spent part of April 29 at the University of Alaska– Fairbanks discussing with Dr. James M. Kari and Dr. Eliza Jones what was four years later to be published by the Alaska Native Language Center as the *Koyukon Athabaskan Dictionary*. Dr. Kari is listed as its editor-in-chief, Jules Jetté and Eliza Jones as its coauthors. I am listed as the author of

"Jules Jetté: A Biography", a four-page article that appears in the introductory section of the dictionary. I was the logical one to write this mini biography of Father Jetté, having authored—as mentioned in an earlier chapter—the article "Julius Jetté: Distinguished Scholar in Alaska", published in the *Alaska Journal* in 1975. I am listed in the dictionary also as "editorial and bibliographic consultant". Before its publication in the year 2000, I was to devote a considerable amount of time, at irregular intervals, to this monumental work. It weighs exactly five pounds and seven ounces and has ninety-four pages of front matter plus 1,118 pages of text. November 2, 2000, was a red-letter day in my life. Before that day was out, I was to have, in hand, one of the only five copies of the dictionary in Fairbanks as of that date.

After another working vacation at Dillingham, I flew to Tacoma, on July 14, to visit family and, more in particular, to be present in Puyallup, Washington, on the twenty-first, when my sister Della and her husband, Don Carlin, celebrated their fortieth wedding anniversary. I returned to Alaska, to Anchorage, on the twenty-second to begin my retreat there the following day. After the retreat ended, on the thirtieth, I stayed on in Anchorage for three more days: to celebrate the feast of Saint Ignatius on the thirty-first with my fellow Alaskan Jesuits, and then, with them, to discuss and reflect on the documents produced by the Thirty-second General Congregation of the Society of Jesus.

Off and on, Father Norm Pepin and I had talked and dreamt about "the Dempster". On August 11, the time had finally come for us to do more than just talk and dream about it. At 2:00 P.M. that Sunday afternoon, we drove out of Fairbanks in anticipation of what was to be one of our greatest adventures. That day, we drove some 250 miles: southeast down the Alaskan Highway, through Delta Junction, and on to Tok, where we had a sandwich. A few miles beyond Tok, at Tetlin Junction, we headed north on the unpaved Taylor Highway. At the West Fork Campground, about halfway between the junction and Chicken, we spent the night: I, in my tent; he, on the back seat of the car. By 6:00 the next morning, we were on our way again, making Dawson in the Yukon Territory, Canada, by 10:00. After offering Mass there and eating, we visited the grave of Father William H. Judge, S.J., "the Saint of Dawson". It may be recalled that I had visited his grave before, with Father Frank Mueller, in 1980, after we had hiked the Chilkoot Trail.

We left Dawson around noon. A short drive brought us to the beginning of the Dempster Highway, a gravel lifeline north to the shores of the Arctic Ocean. The Dempster has to be one of the world's greatest wilderness drives. We found the scenery along it forever changing, eyecatching. There was plentiful wildlife and little traffic. Sometimes, for hour after hour, we were it. Our first night on the Dempster we spent at Eagle Plains, some 250 miles north of the Dawson junction. Here we were about halfway up the Dempster, halfway to Inuvik, its northern terminus and our destination. I again spent the night in my tent; Father Norm, in the car.

Around 8:30 on Tuesday morning the thirteenth, we left Eagle Plains. A half hour later, we were at the Arctic Circle, where we snacked a breakfast as we walked around the parking lot. By the Arctic Circle sign, we photographed one another. The Dempster is one of only two highways in the world that cross the Arctic Circle, the Dalton in Alaska being the other. About fifty miles above the Circle, we crossed over into the Northwest Territories. At 12:40 P.M., at Arctic Red River, we took the ferry across the Mackenzie River. At 3:00, we arrived in Inuvik. There we took in the sights, ate in a hotel, and, at 7:00 P.M., offered Mass in the Igloo Church. We spent the night in the Inuvik Campground.

On the morning of the fourteenth, we again offered Mass in the Igloo Church, had breakfast in a hotel, and did some more sight-seeing before we took a commercial flight on up to the Inuit village of Tuktoyaktuk on the very edge of the Arctic Ocean. We spent most of our time at "Tuk" taking a guided tour of the place. It was time and money well spent. Before that long, eventful day came to an end, we were back at Eagle Plains again for another night there.

By around noon on Thursday, August 15, the feast of the Assumption, we were back in Dawson, where, after concelebrating Mass, we had lunch before we were on the road once more for Alaska. The last night of our trip we again spent at the West Fork Campground. We had breakfast in Tok. By around 12:15 P.M., we were back in Fairbanks. The first thing we did upon arriving home was to concelebrate a Mass of thanksgiving for having been granted so satisfying and safe a trip. It bordered on the miraculous that, after a sixteen-hundred-mile drive, nearly a thousand miles of it over gravel roads, we had had not so much as even one flat tire, nor a single nick in the windshield. The Dempster Highway! We had now driven and seen the length and breadth of it—and had inhaled our fair share of it.

On August 29, Dorothy Jean inscribed for me a copy of her book *A Legacy of Arctic Art*. The inscription reads: "To Louis Renner, S.J., a wonderful friend and colleague, from Dorothy Jean Ray". On page 14 of that book, one finds:

> While I was working on the Eskimo art history, I was also involved in another project as editorial co-author with Louis L. Renner, S.J., for a biography of the pioneer missionary Bellarmine Lafortune.... I had jumped at the chance to work with

Fr. Renner, not only because he was writing history at its purest—almost exclusively from archival sources—but because the subject of Alaskan missions needed to be explored, and he was the foremost authority on Catholic history in Alaska.

My diary entry for September 23, 1996: "Spent an hour with Dr. Dorothy Jean Ray—11:30 to 12:30 in my office." She was in Fairbanks to deliver the Otto Geist Lecture at the University of Alaska–Fairbanks Museum of the North. This I attended. On October 1, I wrote to her: "Fondly I recall our time together last week. I felt so favored, being visited by you in my office for an all-too-short hour. It was kind of like a private audience, with the pope coming to you. Let me thank you again for giving me so much time out of your busy schedule."

During the latter months of 1996, I again had the satisfaction of helping students doing postgraduate work at the University of Alaska–Fairbanks with their writing projects. David Runfola produced a bibliography of writings by and about Jesuits relating to the Eskimos of western Alaska. With considerable help from me, Nicole McCullough began work on a thesis qualifying her, in part, several years later, for a master of arts degree. Her thesis bears the title "The 1951 Bristol Bay Salmon Strike". In it the names of Jesuit fathers Clifford A. Carroll, Jules M. Convert, and George S. Endal, as well as that of Bishop Francis D. Gleeson, S.J., are prominent. The thesis runs to well over a hundred pages. James H. Ducker, editor of *Alaska History*, eager to see it published, asked Nicole to do some revising. I was more than willing to help her. However, because of time constraints on her part, she did not pursue the matter any further.

I offered my 1996 Christmas Day Mass in the Jesuit House chapel for Brother Jakes and his faithful nurse, Deborah Emerizy.

In my annual self-evaluation report, dated February 18, 1997, I wrote to Bishop Kaniecki: "I am wholly happy with my work, and I am happy to be able to report that both Father Kestler and I, after our colloquy, see me continuing to do in the years ahead what I have been doing in recent past years."

That colloquy with Father Ted Kestler took place on February 4, 1997. In the course of it, my impaired hearing was discussed, and he directed me to see an audiologist. This I did. A need for twin hearing aids on my part was definitely indicated. By early March, Miracle Ear had me outfitted with a set. To make a long story short, I was never really able to get used to them. After using them off and on for a few years, I stopped using them altogether.

On April 3, from Fairbanks, I wrote a letter to Alaskan Shepherd benefactors. "I arrived back here from Ruby the other day", it begins.

> Everything went wonderfully well for me. The good Indian people of Ruby turned out in good numbers for the Holy Week and Easter liturgies, were appreciative of my ministrations, and served me two splendid dinners. It was cloudless the whole time, though on the cool side with a stiff breeze out of the north. Minus twelve on Easter Sunday morning. But then, it was an unusually early Easter. This was my fourth in a row there. How many more, God knows. Again I stayed in that cozy little cabin in the woods, took long walks, visited around, visited the cemetery, where lie six I helped bury.

In the morning of June 15, the fortieth anniversary of my ordination to the priesthood, after celebrating Mass, accompanied by Richard Dykema, I left for another season, my seventh, of fishing at Dillingham as a member of his crew. During that 1997 season, unlike previous ones, we had an unexpected, an unwelcome, visitor in camp, namely, a big grizzly bear. Four nights in a row he came, raiding the candy bucket we had sitting in a cooler-hole the first night. By setting out a lantern and keeping the burn-barrel going during the darkest hours of the night, we finally got rid of him.

On October 20, I drew up and signed, as did two witnesses, a brief document entitled "Donation of Bodily Organs". It reads:

> As of this date, 20 October 1997, I, Louis L. Renner, S.J.—in keeping with the spirit of the Jesuit principle of spirituality that we are to "give freely what we have freely received"— make conscious and formal donation of any and all of my bodily organs that may be of benefit to some other person or persons. I do this in a spirit of gratitude to God for having given me the use of them for over seventy years. May whoever receives one or other of these organs likewise receive it or them in a spirit of gratitude to God and use it or them, as I always tried, that is, solely to the greater glory of God and the good of neighbor.

This document I was to redate and re-sign during subsequent years.

That same October 20, I had occasion to write in my diary: "Early to chancery. Swept snow. A fortyish fellow came along. Was cold. I let him in to warm up. Gave him socks, gloves, hat, twenty dollars."

And early it was, that October Monday morning. It was around 4:40 A.M. Heavy, wet snow was falling on the four or so inches that already lay on the ground. I was out in front of the chancery building shoveling snow off the walk leading up to its front door. I always found it easier to clear walks of snow before the troops had trampled it down. There I was, busy with the shovel, when, all of a sudden, I was startled by a guy almost a head taller than I standing right next to me. Taken aback, I asked, a bit nervously, "Wha ... what can I do for you?" In a deep, hollow voice, he said slowly, "It's closed." "What's closed?" He pointed across the parking lot to Sacred Heart Cathedral. "Of course it's closed", I said. "It's not even five o'clock yet." In that same deep, hollow voice, he drawled out, "I'm cold." I could readily believe that he was cold. There he stood, a pair of soaked sneakers on his feet, no socks. No hat, just a layer of melting snow on his head. No gloves. A light jacket. I told him he could go and warm up at Safeway, less than a mile down Airport Way, or at Denny's restaurant, a shorter distance up Airport Way; they would be open. Again, in that same hollow voice, he simply repeated, "I'm cold."

The outer door of the chancery was unlocked by now. I had had to unlock it to get the shovel out. The alarm system was still set. There was a small radiator in that little entryway between the outer and inner doors. I told him he could step inside to warm up but to be sure not to go on in, because he would set off the whole alarm system. Without a word of thanks—but that was all right with me—he stepped inside. As I continued shoveling snow, I thought to myself, "You know, really, the best place for him to get warm would be down in the little room under the entryway, where the hot-water pipes from the cathedral come into the chancery. But that would mean taking off the alarm. Hey, he could conk me over the head and have the run of the place! It'd be hours before anyone else would be along." Then, however, after a little more shoveling, I thought to myself, "Oh, what the hell! Why not?"

I shut the alarm off, led him downstairs to that little room, and offered him a seat, the toolbox sitting on the floor. He sat down, not a word of thanks—but that was all right with me. I told him I would be back shortly.

As a kindly Providence would have it, some winter sports goods outfit had just recently sent to the Alaskan Shepherd office boxes and boxes of defective goods of various kinds, among them gloves, caps, and headbands. I provided my guest with one of each. Then I told him I would be back shortly.

I went to my office, more to give him a bit more time to warm up than to do anything in particular. Meanwhile, the image of those clammy feet in those wet sneakers was still with me. Then I remembered that pair of heavy woolen socks my niece Julie Ann had sent me some time before, a pair of socks I was saving for myself for just the right occasion. For a brief second, I thought to myself—to my shame!—"No, not those socks." But then I thought to myself, "Oh, what the hell! Why not?" I gave him the socks. He took them. Again, not a word of thanks—but that was all right with me.

Figuring he might be warmed up enough by now, I asked if he was ready to go. He nodded affirmative. I led him upstairs, saw him out the front door, and closed it behind him. Then, as he was slowly walking away, I thought to myself, "Hey, I'm sure that guy could use a few bucks for something to eat." I opened the door and yelled to him, "Hey, wait a minute!" I ran down to my office, grabbed a twenty-dollar bill, and brought it to him with, "Here, go up to Denny's and get yourself something to eat!" With his gloved hand, he took it and stuck it in his pocket, without, predictably, a word of thanks—but that was all right with me. Back in the chancery, I ran up to the second floor to look out of the chapel window to see where he was headed. As he gradually disappeared into the falling snow, he was headed toward Denny's.

For two years, this whole incident remained just a brief notation in my diary. However, when the snows of October were again falling heavy and wet, and it was my turn to offer the Thursday chancery staff Mass, on October 21, 1999, I thought about what had taken place at the chancery two years earlier almost to the day. At first, I hesitated even to think about it as a possible homily subject. But then, I thought to myself, "Oh, what the hell! Why not?" With a few words about the corporal works of mercy added, the homily, about as reproduced above, went over well. I was even asked, subsequently, to repeat it in the coffee room for those who had not been present at the Mass. At first, I did not consider it worthy of mention in this autobiography; but then, after weighing the pros and cons, I thought to myself, "Oh, ..."

On December 5, I was transported, in spirit, for several hours back to old Vienna. That evening, in the Hering Auditorium, the Vienna Boys' Choir performed. Father Dibb and I attended the performance in company and as guests of the Winston and Glenda Burbank family. During my years at the university, Glenda was both a member of one of my Latin classes and a fellow teacher in the foreign language department. Those associations marked the beginning of a lasting friendship. In 2005, the Burbanks made a generous contribution toward the publication of my *Alaskana Catholica*.

On November 24, I committed myself to be at Kaltag for my second Christmas there. However, on December 23, I had occasion to note in my diary, "Tried to fly to Kaltag via Galena with Bishop Mike. Got turned around by dense snow around Manley Hot Springs." On December 31, I wrote to a benefactor:

A week ago today I should have been at Kaltag. However, the forces of nature were contrary. Bishop Kaniecki, pilot of the Cessna 207, and I were forced to return to Fairbanks forty minutes into our flight by a dense snowstorm. Those were the worst flying conditions either of us, in our long years in

Alaska, had ever seen. When we lost sight of the Tanana, a major river, he decided to go up high enough to be safely above the highest elevations and to fly on instruments back to Fairbanks. After we had groped our way back to Fairbanks and were safely down, he said to me, "Well, we gave it a noble try!" Indeed we did! The next few days, the weather got only worse.

Holy Week and Easter 1998 saw me again at Ruby for what turned out to be another consoling, pastoral outing, even if fairly routine.

Sometime in June, Joseph Albino, a freelance writer-photographer and college English professor from Syracuse, New York, dropped into my office unannounced and asked if he could interview me. "Sure", I told him. It turned out to be a lengthy interview. The typed-up transcription of it ran to over thirty pages. He entitled it "Fairbanks: The Last Missionary Diocese in the USA". *Extension Magazine*, in its December 1999 issue, published a major portion of what they described as "this fascinating interview". Two photos of "Jesuit father Louis Renner, renowned chronicler of the life-and-death adventures of missionaries in northern Alaska", illustrated the *Extension* article.

In 1998, Bill and Bernice celebrated their golden wedding anniversary. On August 2, the three of us drove to Sunriver, near Bend, in central Oregon. The days there, in the high desert, were hot, but the nights were cool. Bill and Bernice's four children plus spouses and children were all there. There were twenty-one of us. We biked, canoed, played horseshoes, and ate leisurely meals on the deck in the cool of the evenings. It was most relaxing. On the fifth, in the Sunriver Community Church, with just the twenty-one of us present, I offered a Mass of thanksgiving. A multicourse dinner in the old lodge, with toasts and gift giving—and tearful, thankful words—followed. That whole week at Sunriver was all one prolonged, joyous, big family affair.

I returned to Fairbanks on August 10. By this time, that Brother word processor I had received four years earlier was getting to be more of a hindrance than a help to me as an editor, a writer of letters by the thousands, and a historian. When it functioned as it was meant to, I was perfectly satisfied with it. However, this was all too often not the case. Letters on the daisy wheels kept breaking off. From time to time, the word processor printed what the Sears repairman himself called "garbage". Finally, Sears simply replaced it. This replacement model, too, soon began to malfunction. At this point, I yielded to superior wisdom and let myself be persuaded by our finance officer and our in-house computer expert to switch over to a computer, something I should have done years before. However, I had been an "eke-er" all my life, always inclined to eke out, to get a little more use out of something, whether of clothes, tools, or whatever. By August 24, I had a rebuilt computer in my office. Soon thereafter, I was at home with it and wondered how I had ever gotten along without one.

In early November, exploratory surgery revealed that Father Don Balquin, pastor of Our Lady of Sorrows parish in Delta Junction and Holy Rosary parish in Tok, was suffering from inoperable cancer and would therefore not be available to hold Christmas services at those two places. Accordingly, even though I was aware that the people in Ruby would be disappointed not to have me, their "Ruby Christmas priest", with them that Christmas, to put Father Don's mind at ease, I volunteered to step in for him at Delta. Father Timothy (Tim) Sander, O.S.B., did likewise regarding Tok. On December 24, on his way to Tok, Father Tim dropped me off at Delta. There

I heard confessions, offered the 6:00 P.M. Children's Mass, the Midnight Mass, and the 10:00 A.M. Christmas Day Mass. In the early afternoon of that same day, Father Tim came by to pick me up, and together we drove back to Fairbanks, arriving there around 4:00. Just forty years earlier, I had spent my first Christmas in Alaska in Seward.

Chapter 25

Last Years in Alaska: 1999–2001

Off and on throughout the year 1999, I was again able to assist a number of students with their academic projects. Erica Dittmar, a high school student at Mount Edgecumbe in Sitka, interviewed me and received much material from me about the Pilgrim Hot Springs mission to help her with her writing project. With help from me, Robert Barnard—ordained to the permanent diaconate on October 16, 1999—successfully produced a term paper about Father Julius Jetté, S.J., for a course he was taking at the University of Alaska–Fairbanks. By December 1999, Katherine E. Price had finished her M.A. thesis on Father Bernard R. Hubbard, S.J. In her preface, she acknowledged my "valuable help, insights, research leads, and photographs" given her by me. She expressed thanks, too, that I had read various drafts of the thesis and had made welcome suggestions and corrections.

On April 1, while I was airborne between Fairbanks and Ruby in the Cessna 207, visibility was, at times, close to zero. In spite of that, Bishop Kaniecki, recognized as one of the best "seat-of-the-pants" pilots in northern Alaska, got me to Ruby for the 1999 Holy Week and Easter services. It snowed every day of the Holy Triduum. By the time Easter Sunday dawned, bright and sunny, eleven inches of new snow lay on the ground. Temperatures never got above zero. A white Easter! This was my sixth Easter in a row in Ruby.

After April comes May, the month the robins return to Fairbanks. By May 1999, chancery staff members attending the weekly Thursday staff Mass offered in the chancery chapel had come to expect, if it was my turn to offer the Mass, "Father Renner's robin homily". I quote it as I find it reprinted in *Focus*, a little publication by the Diocese of Fairbanks.

Worry, anxiety, fear, cares: basic, universal human emotions. We all experience them. Saints and sinners alike know these well. Even Jesus Himself had moments of fear and distress. Sacred Scripture, the liturgy, and spiritual writers recognize our proneness to fear, to worry, to anxious cares and offer us some words that can help us deal with and overcome these obstacles to peace of heart. Here are a few favorites of mine:

Psalms: "O Most High, when I begin to fear, in You will I trust."

First Peter: "Cast all your cares on the Lord, for He has a care for you."

Revelation: "He touched me with His right hand and said, 'There is nothing to fear!'"

Matthew: "I say to you, do not be anxious for your life, what you shall eat, or what you shall put on. Look at the birds of the air. They do not sow, or reap, or gather into barns. Yet your Heavenly Father feeds them. Are you not of much more value than they? Therefore, do not be anxious."

Said the robin to the sparrow: "I should really like to know why these anxious human beings rush about and worry so." Said the sparrow to the robin: "Friend, I think that it must be that they have no Heavenly Father such as cares for you and me."

"Please use caution and be alert. Large black bear seen 7/19/99. Aggressive moose has been encountered on Stations of the Cross trail." So read the sign posted on various doors of the retreat house in Anchorage, where my fellow Alaskan Jesuits and I had gathered for our annual 1999 retreat. While on that retreat, I met up with neither bear nor moose on the retreat grounds, but I did encounter, on my hikes in the nearby Chugach Mountains, on different days, a bull moose, two cows, a black bear, and a lynx. The blackie and lynx were first sightings for me. I met the bear as I was coming down a narrow trail. I had to backpedal up the trail and around several bends before he chose to go his separate way. Dillingham and fishing, Anchorage and retreat: nature and grace in abundance.

Writing letters to benefactors acknowledging grateful receipt of their donations was, in large part, what my Alaskan Shepherd work was all about. In the course of the two decades I devoted to the Alaskan Shepherd ministry, I wrote literally thousands of letters to benefactors. By the grace of God, I rarely found that part of my voluminous correspondence tedious. I saw it all as truly apostolic work, as an "apostolate of the pen". Through letters, written in my basement office, I was able to reach out and touch the lives of many, near and far. I thanked benefactors on my own behalf, as well as on behalf of the bishop, and, in a general way, of all the people in northern Alaska helped by their kind assistance. I assured benefactors, too, that their help was of critical importance to our missionary efforts and that it was well used in our service of the Lord and His people. I assured them that they, their dear ones, and all their concerns were daily remembered in my Masses and prayers, and in those of all who were serving in the missionary diocese of Fairbanks, as well as in those of all the people ultimately helped by their financial assistance. I almost always made my letters more than just brief thank-you notes. Small talk about the weather, the northern lights, and the flora and fauna interested them, as did news about my personal comings and goings and doings. I considered the personal touch to be the magic touch. That was one reason why I always put real stamps on outgoing letters. It was a relief when those self-adhering stamps, the "no-lick'em-stick'em" type, came into vogue. Many a correspondent, simply a name to begin with, became a personal friend after several exchanges of letters and remained such for years and years. Some sent me pictures of themselves and their dear ones, and even generous, "just for *you*, understand!" personal gifts.

One benefactor-correspondent was a religious education teacher who had the boys in his class write to me. They asked me all kinds of questions about Alaska, the missions, myself, and my interests and hobbies. Speaking a young boy's language, I wrote to them at length. It was the hope and prayer of both the religious education teacher and me that some of those boys might possibly start thinking of one day serving as priests in Alaska.

As an example of the kind of letters I wrote to benefactors in acknowledgment of a donation, I cite a whole one here, written on September 24, 1999, to a certain Bernard J. del Valle, an attorney-at-law in Pasadena, California.

Morning frosts have been with us for some time already. Great flocks of sandhill cranes, geese, and ducks—gathered earlier this month in the grainfields here to fatten up for their flight south to warmer winter climes—are gone. The birches and aspens, just recently fully robed in yellow and gold, are getting rather bare. The tundra floor, however, is still a riot of various hues and colors. The fur of the Arctic and snowshoe hares is fast turning white, camouflage against the snows of another winter now just around the next calendar corner. Autumn rains are dampening our days, but we welcome them. They keep water levels in the rivers high enough to make possible the late-season tug and barge traffic that brings heating fuel and other vital supplies to the villages scattered along the Yukon. Water for barging—and water for baptizing! Nature and grace are closely related, tightly interwoven, in this missionary diocese here in northern Alaska.

Know that, in a very real sense, you are part of it all. It is thanks to your prayers and generous financial help that we are able to carry out the basic ministries entrusted to our care in this cool corner of the Lord's vineyard. Along with good Bishop Kaniecki and all up here helped by your twofold support, I do very sincerely thank you for it, and now, in particular, for your recent so generous donation. God reward and bless you, bless all dear to you, look favorably upon you and all your concerns. We, for our part, will continue to remember you and all your intentions in our daily Masses and prayers. We appreciate being remembered in your good prayers.

A month later, addressing me as "Dear Father Renner", Mr. del Valle responded:

Sincere thanks for your most descriptive and satisfying letter of 9/24/99. It is a gem. I have sent copies to relatives and friends who are in complete agreement with my evaluation. It had a therapeutic effect on all its readers, and they will not be satisfied until I send them another that expresses your thought so beautifully and poignantly.

Therefore, to ensure an encore, I enclose a check for one hundred dollars for use in sprucing up the vineyard.

The people in Ruby wanted me with them again for Christmas 1999. In spite of considerable odds, I got there, thanks to a special Providence. Only at check-in time did I learn that the flight I was originally scheduled to go on was canceled. I tried another bush air carrier. Their only flight for the day had already left. The third carrier's flights were already both booked up. However, I was told, "We can put you on standby." So I had myself driven to the airport, where I waited, hoping anxiously that there would be a "no-show". There were several. I got on. It was Christmas Eve, cloudless, and around thirty below as we flew roughly three hundred miles, via Tanana, in the predawn darkness across a broad expanse of white wilderness on to Ruby. There Emmitt Peters—known as "the Yukon Fox" after he had won the 1975 Iditarod Trail Sled Dog Race—met the plane and drove me down to the church. Knowing that the flight I was expected to have arrived on had been canceled, the people were pleasantly surprised, and happy, to see me as I walked around the village to inform them of the times of the Masses. I received many a warm welcoming hug. Such a hug did my seventy-four-year-old heart good—just as the Christmas Day dinner, a turkey dinner with all the trimmings at the Ivan and Katie Kangas home, did my seventy-four-year-old stomach good. Again, the good people of Ruby saw to it that I neither froze to death nor starved to death. Now as a guest at this table, now as a guest at that table, I was again able both to see and to taste the goodness of the Lord.

The year 1999, as well as the second millennium, ended on the cold side. On December 31, Fairbanks had a reading of fifty-three degrees below zero.

As the third millennium dawned and began to unfold, little did I suspect that the year 2000 would bring with it events of major importance both for me personally and for the Diocese of Fairbanks in general. For the most part, insofar as my life and work were concerned, the earlier part of "the Great and Sacred Jubilee Year of Our Lord 2000" resembled previous years.

During my two years of teaching at Monroe High, 1958–1960, as part of my ministry, I had regularly offered morning Mass in one of the classrooms there. Forty years later, on April 14, 2000, I had the joy of concelebrating at the 9:00 A.M. dedication ceremonies and Mass offered in the long-awaited new Holy Family Chapel at the Catholic schools complex. Alaskan Shepherd benefactors, responding generously to a special appeal, helped significantly with meeting the costs of its construction.

Early in the year 2000, the Diocese of Fairbanks began planning to celebrate, in a major way, the jubilee year during the last weekend of August. The celebrations were slated to take place in Fairbanks, in the Carlson Center, with as many people as possible from all over the diocese present. A solemn pontifical Mass celebrated by Bishop Kaniecki and concelebrated by the priests of the diocese was scheduled to be the crowning event. Many, from near and far, were due to be confirmed at that Mass. Plans called for a major photo exhibit to greet the people as they came into the building. Responsibility for this was entrusted primarily to me. Accordingly, soon after Easter—again spent at Ruby—I began assembling photos, principally of the various churches in the diocese and of the men who had held ecclesiastical jurisdiction over the geographic region that had became the Diocese of Fairbanks in 1962. I wrote lengthy captions, actually, mini biographies, to accompany the photos of the different prelates. Madeleine D. Betz saw to the captions of the churches and the mini histories of the parishes. People were so impressed by this twofold exhibit that they urged it be given some permanency in the form of a book. In 2001, the Diocese of Fairbanks published the ninety-six-page volume, entitling it *A Brief*

Illustrated History of the Diocese of Fairbanks: Profiles of Prelates and Churches, Past and Present.

About the same time that I was working on the projected photo exhibit, I was culling through the files in the Diocese of Fairbanks Archives and those of the general superior of the Alaska mission in Jesuit House, for I had reason to believe that I would, any year now, be assigned full time to the writing of a history of the Catholic Church in Alaska. Photocopies of documents found in those two archives proved, subsequently, to be of inestimable value to me. Many of the entries in *Alaskana Catholica* were considerably enriched by material found in those two archives.

On May 1, 2000, I wrote to my father provincial, Robert B. (Bob) Grimm, as follows:

During our colloquy on October 26, 1999, you asked me to give thought to the matter of my writing for publication a kind of history of the Catholic Church in Alaska and to get back to you on this subject in May 2000. It is now May 2000. I am herewith getting back to you.

Over the years, but especially during this past half year, I have given the matter of my writing such a history much discerning thought and prayer. Over the years, too, I have amassed a considerable amount of manuscript and raw material toward such a history. And, over the years, a fair number of fellow Jesuits, scholars, historians, and people interested in things Catholic and Alaskan have urged me to produce a book on the general subject. They assured me that I was the one to do it and that, if I did not do it, it would never get done.

While I did gain time, after being freed of my Tanana assignment in 1992, to devote to writing of a more scholarly kind, I did not gain nearly enough to produce a history of the Catholic Church in Alaska. The Alaskan Shepherd work is virtually a full-time job. And I have, more or less, exhausted local archive resources. I need to do extensive research in the Jesuit Oregon Province Archives. Without going full time on this project, and in Spokane, I cannot produce the kind of history here in question.

How do I *feel* about all this? I love Alaska, have spent more years in Fairbanks than any other priest or Jesuit, am thoroughly "Alaskanized", am happy in my present work, and would be content to continue on in it. There would, naturally, be mixed emotions about leaving it and Alaska. But, with the help of God's grace, as in the past, so now, I am ready and willing to move on. When I weigh the good effected by my present work against the anticipated, long-range good hopefully to be effected by my successful production of *Alaskana Catholica* (my tentative title for the proposed history, since in format it will resemble an encyclopedia), then I see the scale tipped in favor of my being assigned, sooner rather than later, to the writing of the history.

Why now? The matter of my age is a major consideration in whatever decision seems at this time to be warranted. I celebrated my seventy-fourth birthday last week. While my health at present continues to be good, the shadows are, inexorably, lengthening. So I see some urgency in our arriving reasonably soon at a decision regarding my future work and place of work from the standpoint of time alone.

The contents of this letter are, at this time, wholly between you and me. Till I hear from you, I will say nothing to anyone about this whole matter. A relatively prompt answer from you would be welcome, since the bishop will need to be informed as soon as possible about whatever decision is arrived at. And I would want to initiate my successor to the position I would be vacating.

As I write this, my mind and heart are at peace. Strangely, somehow I now feel myself a younger man. May God's guiding Spirit and supporting grace be with us.

In a letter, Father Grimm asked me to discuss the contents of the letter just cited with Father Joe Laudwein, my local superior at the time. This I did. In a note to him, I made known that "I would like to be informed, sooner rather than later, formally and officially, in writing, preferably by the provincial—after the whole matter has been satisfactorily discussed by all parties involved—as to whether I am to continue on in my present assignment until such and such a date or to move on to the writing of the history in question." By mid-August, it was officially decided that I would continue on in the work I was then doing for the next two years.

On June 3, 2000, Father Frank McGuigan died in Fairbanks. Apart from the sadness I experienced at the loss of a Jesuit companion of many years, his death affected me only inasmuch as I took time out to attend wake and Rosary services, to concelebrate at the funeral Mass, to be present for the graveside services, and to write up a rather lengthy obituary. Later that year, I was to concelebrate at the funeral of the mother of a former Monroe student of mine, as well as at the funeral of a onetime fellow professor at the University of Alaska–Fairbanks. I concelebrated, too, at the Mass at which the daughter of one of the Alaskan Shepherd staff members was married.

It was now time to go commercial fishing again. From June 21 to July 9, as a member of the Dykema crew, I was working and relaxing once more in our fish camp on the banks of the Nushagak River downstream from Dillingham and fishing the waters of Bristol Bay. This was my eleventh season there. Even after a decade of commercial salmon fishing, an industry recognized to be one of the most dangerous of all of the Alaskan industries, I still had never suffered a mishap of any kind. That changed near the very end of the 2000 season. With fellow crew members, I was sitting in our skiff on the far side of Bristol Bay, near a tender, while we were waiting to offload a good day's haul, when, for no accountable reason, I felt a slight twitch in the little finger of my left hand. It was so slight that at first I did not even bother to take off my fisherman's glove to have a look at it. There was no pain. However, that little finger kept drawing attention to itself, so that I finally took off the glove to examine it. I found it to be stiff, to the point where I could not flex it. Some time later, in Fairbanks, I went to a doctor with it. After examining and x-raying it, he concluded that surgery might restore some flexibility. I opted to live with it as it was. That crippled little finger has served me, subsequently, as a constant reminder to be especially concerned for, to look out for, "the little guy", "the underdog".

On August 1, the day I returned to Fairbanks from Anchorage after making my annual retreat, my nephew Mike; his wife, Karen; and their three preteen children, Gregory, Stephanie, and Jason, arrived. In our Jesuit House suite of basement rooms they found lodging; in the kitchen, food; in our common room, pool and card tables for relaxation and games in the evenings after a full day of sight-seeing. Together, we took the riverboat *Discovery III* cruise and hiked part of the Granite Tors Trail and all of the Angel Rocks Trail before we drove on to Chena Hot Springs. While on our way, we spotted a cow moose feeding in a roadside pond. Mike got quite close to her for some fine photos. We visited the Trans-Alaska Pipeline and some of the in-town attractions Fairbanks has to offer. On Saturday morning, the fifth, I offered Mass for them before they went on their way again, heading south and east. Little did I suspect, as I blessed them on that August 5 and said a final good-bye, that things were about to change somewhat radically for the Diocese of Fairbanks.

Late in the afternoon of Sunday, August 6, 2000, just as I was about to take the final step of the flight of stairs leading up to the second floor deck at the back of Jesuit House, a highly excited Father Richard L. (Dick) McCaffrey, S.J.—sitting in the shade on the deck and having himself a smoke—blurted out, "Have you *heard?*" "Have I heard *what?*" I asked. "He's dead!" "*Who's* dead?" "He himself, *Mike!*" That was the first I heard of the wholly unexpected, sudden death, of a massive heart attack, of Bishop Kaniecki, at Emmonak, an Eskimo village near the mouth of the Yukon, where he was about to celebrate a confirmation Mass at 11:00 A.M. It was the feast of Our Lord's Transfiguration.

My first order of business, after the death of Bishop Kaniecki, was to get a letter out to all the Alaskan Shepherd benefactors informing them of his death, asking them for their prayers for him and the Diocese of Fairbanks, and telling them what now lay ahead for the diocese, insofar as we knew. The media turned to me for information about him, photos of him, and my thoughts concerning the interim and future status of the Diocese of Fairbanks. They wanted to know who might possibly be his successor and details of the process leading to the appointment of a new bishop. The apostolic delegate in Washington, D.C., solicited my input regarding a possible successor. Letters of condolence and letters loaded with questions poured in from near and far, from prelates in high places and people in the Alaskan bush. All called for answers. Editors of various publications asked me for an obituary. Having, by this time, produced a lengthy caption—in reality, a mini biography—to go with the photo scheduled to be part of the upcoming Jubilee 2000 exhibit, I had, virtually, already in hand a well fleshed-out obituary, as well as a most timely article for an issue of the *Alaskan Shepherd*. I needed to do little more than merely change present tenses to past tenses.

Along with trying to keep up with the additional desk work occasioned by the death of Bishop Kaniecki, I attended the morning prayer services held for him in the chancery chapel on the seventh and eighth. On the ninth, I was in Sacred Heart Cathedral when his body was brought in. That evening, I attended the Rosary prayed for him. The following morning, in the chancery chapel, I participated in a concelebrated Mass offered for him. On the eleventh, I again participated in a concelebrated Mass, and in the Office of the Dead. The solemn Mass of Christian Burial and the graveside ceremonies took place on the twelfth. A reception followed. The sudden death of Bishop Kaniecki—a big man at over six feet—with whom I had for some fifteen years worked so closely, and with whom I had flown thousands of Alaskan bush miles, left a big hole in my personal life.

Meanwhile, life went on. In addition to work occasioned by the death of Bishop Kaniecki and the usual Alaskan Shepherd work, there was still much that needed to be done in preparation for the Jubilee 2000 doings that had been planned and were still slated to take place before the end of that eventful August. Gradually, however, everything got done in due time. In the afternoon of Saturday the twenty-sixth, I was in the Carlson Center for a rehearsal of the events scheduled to take place there the next day. While a certain cloud of sadness, owing to the unexpected death of Bishop Kaniecki, hung over the festivities of "the Great and Sacred Jubilee Year of Our Lord 2000" that took place that Sunday, they were, nevertheless, for the most part, of a joyous nature. This was due, in no small part, to the tone set by Francis T. Hurley, archbishop of Anchorage, who stepped in for the deceased Bishop Kaniecki and, at 10:00 A.M., offered the solemn Jubilee 2000 Mass. Many priests concelebrated. Many people were confirmed. Many signs of love and peace were exchanged.

Sometime during the year 1992, all the members of the Oregon Province were asked by their father provincial the two-pronged question "Where do you see yourself in the year 2000, and what do you see yourself doing?" My answers:

> In the year 2000, assuming I live at least another eight years, I will be seventy-four. Given the good health I have been blessed with, I hope to be still fully active. After going through a personal prayerful discernment process and talking my status over with superiors, I see myself, during the next decade, continuing to live in Jesuit House here in Fairbanks, continuing on as editor of the *Alaskan Shepherd* and as fundraiser for this missionary diocese of Fairbanks and as a formally assigned writer. These two formal assignments would translate into a solid, full-time load. I would make some time, however, for ad hoc "helping out", for doing occasional, more directly pastoral work.

I went on to add: "When my days of active ministry are over, I hope to continue praying constantly and fervently for the Church and the Society and to love and support my Jesuit brothers by a patient, cheerful acceptance of whatever trials, sufferings, and crosses the Lord lays on me." As shall be seen in a subsequent chapter, a kindly Providence saw fit to let what I wrote in 1992 be a remarkably accurate "prophecy".

In an earlier chapter, I mentioned that November 2, 2000, was truly a red-letter day in my life as a writer, for, on that day, I was handed one of the only five copies of the Jetté-Jones *Koyukon Athabaskan Dictionary* in Fairbanks. A month later, on December 1, from 4:00 to 7:00 P.M., in the Doyon Building in Fairbanks, I had the joy of seeing Dr. Eliza Jones honored at a signing and reception party. As was to be expected, many Koyukon Athabaskan Indian people were there to honor, in Dr. Jones, one of their own. Much signing was done, not only by Dr. Jones, but by others who had contributed to the project. Many photos of those of us who had worked on the dictionary were taken.

On November 7, Father Hemmer informed me that the people of Ruby wanted me with them for yet another Christmas. I arrived there in the early afternoon of the twenty-fourth. That evening, Christmas Eve, I offered Masses at 7:00 and 11:00. Some people attended both. There was no Mass on Christmas Day. I slept in, took a long afternoon walk, enjoyed a family dinner in the home of Ivan and Katie Kangas, and, pondering in my heart the mysteries and joys of Christmas, went to bed early, letting another Christmas be history. I returned to Fairbanks on the twenty-sixth. With a lengthy evening visit to the Blessed Sacrament in the Jesuit House chapel, I ended "the Great and Sacred Jubilee Year of Our Lord 2000".

Throughout the year 2001, in addition to tending to my routine Alaskan Shepherd work, I kept working away at producing entries for my proposed *Alaskana Catholica*, gathering information, and soliciting autobiographical sketches for it.

On January 30, Father James F. Garneau contacted me about the possibility of my writing the entry, "Alaska, Catholic Church in" for *The New Catholic Encyclopedia* (a second edition of *The Catholic Encyclopedia*), then already in the process of being compiled. In short order, I had the article completed to his satisfaction. It was published as I had written it.

Before the year 2001 became history, I was involved with the publication of *Frost among the Eskimos: The Memoirs of Helen Frost, Missionary in Alaska 1926–61*. Early in the year, the Reverend Ross F. Hidy, a Lutheran historian, turned to me for my thoughts regarding some sensitive matters in the manuscript as it had come from the pen of Helen Frost. By that time, Reverend Hidy and I had already met in Fairbanks and become good friends and regular correspondents. In my January 24, 2001, letter to him, I commented:

> I share your most legitimate concerns about being "sensitive to the feelings of the Natives". Some of the comments made by missionaries about the Native people, their beliefs, mores, lifestyle, etc., are painful to read in light of today's under-standing. But what they wrote, they wrote! The historian has to come to grips with it. Readers of the historian's findings have to feel confident that they are getting an accurate pic-ture of reality—as it was, as it was seen. Readers should know—through glosses, comments, notes—that the present-day historian or editor or publisher does not approve of some of what was said, of some of the expressions used, by writ-ers, diarists, letter writers, etc., of yesteryear. Prudence and good judgment may, however, in some cases dictate that some quote or expression be better omitted in order to avoid leav-ing a bad taste in the mouth of readers and rendering them less favorably disposed toward the subject of the biography or autobiography. It's a challenge to maintain a delicate bal-ance: to do justice to the original text and its author, to respect the sensitivities of the people or person written about, to give readers credit for being understanding of differences between then and now, and to maintain one's integrity as an historian.

On the back cover of the published book, we read: "Cath-olic Historian, Fr. Louis L. Renner, S.J., Univ. of Alaska, Fair-banks, wrote: 'As one who has made the Seward Peninsula—its geography and history—the primary focus of his historical research, I can honestly say that without the publication of the Helen Frost book a significant piece of the mosaic that makes up the cultural, spiritual, and Christian history of the Seward Peninsula would be lacking. We owe a special debt to Rev. Ross Hidy for publishing *Frost among the Eskimos.*' "

During the year 2001, at the request of Bradley Collins, the editor of *Extension Magazine*, I produced also the article about burials in Alaska entitled "All They Want Is a Simple Pine Box—and Prayers". This was published in the November 2001 issue of *Extension*.

Father Dick Case, flying the Cessna 207, dropped me off at Ruby on April 12, Holy Thursday, for the 2001 Holy Week and Easter services. We had planned to travel the day before, but weather conditions were too marginal for safe travel. At Ruby, everything went routinely well. As on other Easter Sundays, the church was full to overflowing.

On Monday, I returned to Fairbanks commercially in a four-passenger bush plane. Our departure from Ruby was delayed by a heavy snowfall in the area. The first part of our ninety-minute flight saw us "treetopping" and "flying the river". To make sure that the infant girl we had on board would not suffer from the cold, the pilot kept the heat on high, turning the little Piper Chieftain into a flying sauna. Once arrived at the east ramp in Fairbanks, I started immediately to walk into town. I had no sooner taken my first steps when along came John Huntington—known to me since my days as pastor of the Tanana parish, of which he was a member—who insisted on driving me to the very doorstep of Jesuit House.

I had my annual colloquy with Father Provincial Bob Grimm on May 29. After it, I made the simple notation in my diary, "G. U., here I come!" I was now about to begin my last year in Alaska before heading to Gonzaga University.

My twelfth, and last, "working–fishing vacation" at Dillingham began on June 17 and ended on July 7. This season differed from previous ones mainly in that I did not go out in the skiff to join in the actual fishing. The skiff was adequately crewed without me. I helped set up camp; I also helped with chores around the camp and, especially, with the subsistence fishing: the netting, cleaning, and putting up of king and sockeye salmon for personal, noncommercial, use. Did I miss going out in the skiff? Not really. It was nice not having to get up at all hours of the night, in all kinds of weather, because an "opening" demanded as much. I was able to do more walking along the beach, even to do some genuine loafing. During some nights, my sleep was somewhat disturbed by two little foxes running around on my tent platform. However, it was easy to forgive the rascals.

My final retreat in Alaska I again made in Anchorage, with fellow Alaskan Jesuits, on July 23–30.

Robert L. Whelan, S.J., the retired bishop of Fairbanks, living in Spokane at the time, died there on September 15. The following day, I readied an obituary. He was to be buried in Fairbanks. I was among those who met the body at Sacred Heart Cathedral on the twenty-eighth, took part in the wake service that evening, concelebrated at the Mass of Christian Burial the following day, and assisted at the graveside ceremonies.

While the golden leaves of autumn were still on the birches, Father Joe Hemmer asked me if I would again be willing and able to be in Ruby for yet another Christmas. Being aware that that would almost certainly be my last Christmas in Alaska, and being willing, and anticipating that I would be able, I said, "Sure!"

When I arrived in Ruby that Christmas Eve, it was thirty-one below down by the river. It was a little warmer higher up in the village. After discussing Mass times with Harold and Florence Esmailka, I decided that there would be two Christmas Eve Masses, one at eight o'clock for the little ones, and another at eleven. No Christmas Day Mass. Experience had taught that the two Christmas Eve Masses—along with several services in "the other church"—seemed always to suffice the people. For the first Mass that evening, the church was moderately filled; for the second, it was packed—despite the fact that the mercury at 10:30 P.M. stood at minus thirty-six. Some people attended both Masses. For my homily, I spoke about some of the key words found on Christmas cards: joy, peace, light, hope, and love.

On Christmas Day morning, in a church empty save for the spirit of Christmas, I offered Mass for family, friends, and the benefactors of the Alaska missions. When, at 11:00 A.M., I walked to the bottom of the village to bring Holy Communion to an elderly shut-in woman, the town of Ruby, except for some early rising and howling dogs, was still nothing more than just one big dormitory. For my last Christmas Day dinner in Ruby, I was invited by the Ivan and Katie Kangas family, with whom I had eaten my first Ruby Christmas dinner eighteen years earlier. What were then preschoolers were now university students home for Christmas. A somewhat turbulent flight had me back in Fairbanks on the twenty-sixth. Before I left Ruby, the people asked me to be with them again for the Holy Week and Easter 2002 services.

Chapter 26

Post-Alaskan Years: 2002–2006

As the New Year of Our Lord 2002 dawned, so also dawned a year that was to bring with it some major changes in my life.

On January 16, 2002, I wrote to Dorothy Jean Ray:

> My godmother is going on ninety-seven! Longevity seems to be the lot of more and more people. Facing the writing of a history of the Catholic Church in Alaska, I can use a good chunk of longevity. More and more, the move to Spokane is on my mind. I'm rather looking forward to it, though leaving Alaska after calling it home since 1958 will be done with mixed emotions. However, I shall press on, confident that the same kindly Providence that has guided my life so satisfyingly—even if, at times, rather mysteriously—up to now will continue to guide it in the days, weeks, months, and years (?) ahead. I've always been a positive thinker. Among the many nice, and major, touches of Divine Providence, I number my contacting you, meeting you, collaborating with you, knowing you, dear Dorothy Jean, as a most cherished friend.

Throughout the early months of 2002, when not preoccupied with Alaskan Shepherd–related work—and not busy easing my successor, Patricia (Patty) Walter, into her new position—I spent much time reading documents on microfilm dealing with the Catholic Church in Alaska, producing

452

entries for my projected *Alaskana Catholica*, soliciting many autobiographical sketches, and gathering relevant information of all kinds from a great number of people.

In mid-August 2000, as mentioned above, it was officially decided that I would continue on with my Alaskan Shepherd work for two more years. A letter dated February 26, 2002, from Father Provincial Grimm to me read:

Let me begin by expressing the gratitude of the Society for your many years of faithful and dedicated service to the Church of Alaska. Your scholarship, fundraising, and pastoral care have been wonderful gifts to the people of the Fairbanks diocese. Your Alaskan Shepherd ministry has been most important for sustaining the diocese financially and has enabled many others who have not been to Alaska to appreciate the wonderful work of the Church on the northern frontier.

Now, however, it is time for you to take up a new mission. On behalf of the Society, I mission you to a ministry of scholarship. I mission you to continue your work of writing a history of the Catholic Church in Alaska and ask you to go to the Gonzaga University Jesuit Community as a scholar in residence to carry out this ministry.

I pray that you find joy and consolation in taking up this mission. I am confident that the fruit of your labor will be an important gift to the Church in Alaska and for the Society. May the Lord bless you and give you the strength and wisdom you require to bring this mission to completion. I pray that this time of transition may be peaceful and full of gratitude for all the Lord has accomplished through your labors in Alaska.

On March 3, grateful to Divine Providence that it was Father Grimm who had taken the initiative in this whole matter of my undertaking the writing of the history in question, I responded to his letter:

Many very sincere thanks to you for writing me so very kind and gracious a letter and for missioning me to "a ministry of scholarship", to the writing of a history of the Catholic Church in Alaska. I pray God to grant me the grace to carry out this mission to a satisfactory conclusion. I will happily make the move to Gonzaga University as a scholar in residence as I devote myself full time to this mission. Again, I thank you most sincerely for your very kind, heartening words concerning my years of ministry in Alaska and for the new mission, which, with God's grace, I undertake to the greater glory of God.

On Holy Thursday, March 28, after a commercial flight, I noted: "Barely made it to Ruby because of blowing snow." Again, Holy Week and Easter Sunday services were well attended. This was my final trip to Ruby; and, as a Holy Week–Easter one, it was one of the shortest. On Easter Sunday evening, after a festive dinner with the Harold and Florence Esmailka family, I flew with Harold, Florence, and their son, John, back to Fairbanks on a special flight. After securing the plane, our pilot drove me to Jesuit House.

During the first ten days of April—after having anguished for quite some time as to what to take or not to take with me to Spokane, and after having finally decided that, if at all in doubt about a given item, to take it—I packed and shipped forty-four boxes of books, photographs, various papers, and manuscripts. It turned out to be a wise decision. Shortly before heading south, I shipped also a dust-collecting microfilm reader plus forty-two rolls of microfilm. The reader and microfilm proved, subsequently, to be of inestimable value to me, as having them in my room for viewing whenever I wished, or had need to, greatly speeded up my research. On those forty-two rolls, I had the major portion of the Jesuit Oregon Province Archives material relevant to my research literally at my elbow. I shipped also three trunks and some big boxes containing an assortment of various items, including two pictures behind glass. One of these was the watercolor view of King Island Village by artist Nancy Taylor Stonington, mentioned already in an earlier chapter. The other was the copper etching by Albrecht Dürer, dated 1514, of Saint Jerome at his desk in his den, *Hieronymus im Gehäus*, one of my favorite works of art. Thanks to the careful handling and shipping by Consolidated Freight Lines, everything I shipped arrived at Jesuit House on the campus of Gonzaga University in as good a condition as I had shipped it. Cause for gratitude!

"Longtime Fairbanks Educator, Spiritual Leader Says Goodbye" read the front-page headline in the June 2002 issue of the *Senior Voice*, a publication produced monthly in Anchorage. The article was based on the interview Peggy Frank Freeland had had with me on April 12.

"Father Renner Bids Adieu" read the front-page headline of the April 29, 2002, issue of the *Fairbanks Daily News-Miner*. Three days previously, I had been interviewed by *News-Miner* staff writer Mary Beth Smetzer. The interview served as the basis for her feature article. A big front-page photo of me by *News-Miner* photographer Eric Engman accompanied the article. Mary Beth began her article with, "A string of titles, accumulated over a long career, trail after the Rev. Louis L. Renner's name." This she followed up with, "Author, academic, teacher, linguist and doctor of philosophy are a few. But most important to the scholar are the initials S.J., which signify the Society of Jesus." She then quotes me to the effect: "I have had but one desire in my life, to fulfill God's will for me. My whole life has consisted in offering myself totally—bodily, mentally and spiritually—to the will of God. I have no plan for myself. I have only tried to do what God wanted of me." With the insight of a professional reporter, she summarized, referring to me, "All his interests coalesced here. He credits Divine Providence for bringing together his love of languages, philosophy, Alaska and writing."

With the month of May at hand, the time for final good-byes and farewell luncheons, dinners, and parties was also at hand. On May 23, from 12:00 to 4:00 P.M., the Alaskan Shepherd ladies hosted a grand farewell party for me in the big common room in Jesuit House. The warmth of the party was matched by the warmth of the day, sunny and eighty-two above. Over a hundred people attended. Among them were former students and former fellow teachers of mine, from both Monroe High and from the University of Alaska–Fairbanks. Before the afternoon was over, there was much camera clicking, many a mutual hug, and more than one tear-dampened cheek. I had to keep reminding people that I was going only to Spokane and not to Birch Hill—a Fairbanks cemetery with a burial plot for priests.

On May 27, I paid final farewell visits to members of the Dykema family. The following day, to my considerable surprise, I received a letter from no less a personage than the vice-president of the United States, the Honorable Richard B. Cheney.

The May–June 2002 issue of the *Alaskan Shepherd*—produced by Patty Walter, my successor as editor thereof—bears the title "Priest in Alaska, 1958–2002: Louis L. Renner, S.J." The issue is about me but ends with a somewhat lengthy farewell letter by me addressed to the many who had helped make the Alaskan Shepherd fundraising program a success. After praying blessings upon one and all, and expressing my sincere gratitude to all, and assuring them of remembrances in my Masses and prayers, I ended the letter with: "And now I bid you all farewell!—till merrily we meet, yonder, where breaks a new and glorious morn, where the dreams we do not even dare to dream really do come true."

The Friday, June 7, entries in my diary begin with, "Early at answering Shepherd mail." This was the last of literally thousands of such or similar entries made by me in the course of the two decades I headed the Alaskan Shepherd fundraising program. But as I answered Shepherd mail that morning, I did so in a spirit of rare excitement. Before that day began, none of us had, as yet, any idea as to who might be the next bishop of the Diocese of Fairbanks, or as to when he might be appointed. There was, however, one exception, Father Richard Case, the diocesan administrator. On the night of the sixth, after he was sure all had left the chancery, he went there to put on the bulletin board a photo of Monsignor Donald J. Kettler, whose appointment as bishop-elect of the Diocese of Fairbanks was to be made public the next day. When I went into the Jesuit House kitchen at around 7:15 A.M. to get myself something to eat, who should walk in but this six-foot-four giant of a man! At the time, I did not know that he had spent the latter part of the night in one of our guest rooms. Having seen the photo on the chancery bulletin board, I knew immediately who he was. I began to introduce myself, but that was hardly necessary. He told me he had been receiving and reading the *Alaskan Shepherd* for some years. We had a pleasant, relaxed chat together. Before the day was out, he had met the chancery staff and held a press conference.

Early in the morning of the eighth, I took a final, leisurely, nostalgic walk up to the University of Alaska–Fairbanks campus. On Sunday the ninth, at 10:15 P.M., Father Joe Laudwein drove me to the Fairbanks International Airport. At 1:05 A.M. on the tenth, I flew out of Fairbanks, bound, via Seattle, for Spokane. There was something rather unique about the whole of that two-thousand-mile flight. I experienced it more as a passage across a threshold of time than as a flight across a stretch of space. Throughout much of it, I found myself not so much anticipating what lay ahead of me as reflecting, gratefully, in my heart, on how God, in His Divine Providence, had called me, guided me, and used me over my long years in Alaska to achieve certain ends in keeping with His will—ends often not foreseen by me, nor always clearly understood by me.

By around 8:30 the morning of my arrival in Spokane on that memorable June 10, 2002, I was sitting in the dining room of Jesuit House on the campus of Gonzaga University eating breakfast. Father James M. (Jim) McDonough had kindly met me at the Spokane airport and brought me to my final destination. That afternoon, he took me on a shopping tour. I needed some additional office-type furniture for my north-facing room on the third floor of Jesuit House. It was not long before I was ideally set up, except for a computer, to begin in earnest the writing of *Alaskana Catholica*. A new, quality computer was provided for me a few weeks later. Meanwhile, I was roughing out entries for my proposed encyclopedia by longhand. It was psychologically, if for no other reason, good for me that I got down to work without delay. I was now out of Alaska, but Alaska was not out of me.

Well before I left Alaska, there was talk in the family circle about a family picnic. It was by now four years since I had last been in the Northwest. It was left up to me as to when the picnic should take place. Wanting to be well settled in at Gonzaga and in full stride with my writing before taking a break, I suggested August 10. That date was agreeable to all concerned. As a kindly Providence would have it, Len and Marty were in Spokane the third weekend of July. With them, on the twenty-second, I drove to Tacoma. From the twenty-third to the thirtieth, I made my retreat at Bellarmine. On Saint Ignatius Day, the thirty-first, I took the Amtrak to Vancouver, Washington, to spend several days with Bill and Bernice. At nephew Gary Ross' home, on August 10, the clan gathered for the scheduled picnic. The following day, I took a Greyhound bus back to Spokane.

Settled again in Spokane, I soon fell into a fairly predictable daily rhythm, or routine, consisting of morning Mass, work, a prebreakfast walk of about an hour—the while getting some exercise, praying the Rosary, and making a distracted meditation—breakfast, more work, lunch, a nod-off, more work, another walk, work, dinner, light work, early to bed. Breviary prayers and visits to the Blessed Sacrament punctuated this daily routine at more-or-less regular intervals. With that routine, I soon had the writing project in full stride.

Dorothy Jean Ray, who had, for years, been urging me, prodding me to write a history of the Catholic Church in Alaska, wrote to me on August 23, 2002, "This is just a note to let you know that I received the letter and preface and am happy, happy, happy that you have indeed plunged into your project with full force." She gave my rough-draft, dry-run preface quite a working over, something it badly needed, and I welcomed it. Mainly, she scolded me for being too apologetic about my qualifications to write the history in question. In my September 6 letter to her, after thanking her "most especially for the very valuable suggestions given me for improving greatly my preface", I assured her that I much preferred "a cruel editor", as she had described herself, to a cruel book reviewer.

In that same letter, I also gave her a progress report: "Fairly steadily I'm moving ahead with the production of entries and with the production of the bibliography and list of entries. I do find my situation here quite ideal for this project. I have a great deal of material, including forty-two rolls of microfilm plus reader, right here in my room. I have, actually, to spend relatively little time in the archives. This house, the campus, the surroundings are very much to my liking, great for walking."

Gaining access to archival materials for *Alaskana Catholica* was no problem for me. On September 30, 2002, David A. Kingma, curator of the Jesuit Oregon Province Archives, wrote to Father Provincial John D. Whitney, "I received in good order your letter of September 16, granting full archival reference access to Father Lou Renner. I look forward with pleasure to assisting Father Lou in any way I can. Patrons like him, organized, scholarly, and respectful of the preservation and arrangement of records, are a treat to work with."

A surprise—and a distraction from the writing project— awaited me when I received a letter dated September 23, 2002, from Ira Perman, president of the Alaska Humanities Forum. The letter began:

> It is with pleasure that we announce that you have been selected to receive the 2002 Governor's Award for Friend of the Humanities, awarded to that individual who has advanced the humanities through his lifelong efforts. To celebrate your achievement, Governor Tony Knowles will present this award in a public ceremony honoring a select handful of individuals and organizations that have made lifelong contributions to both the humanities and the arts. This event, the 2002 Governor's Arts and Humanities Awards, will be held Friday, October 25, 2002, at the Fourth Avenue Theater in Anchorage. We understand that Father Richard Case, S.J., will be accepting the award for you.

They understood correctly. When Alaskan Shepherd staff members first considered recommending me for the award (unbeknownst to me!), they already suspected, and correctly so, that I would be reluctant to return to Alaska to receive it, and they let me know that Father Case would be willing to step in for me if I wished. That was my wish, and he did receive the award on my behalf. This is a big, heavy, bronze medal on a blue ribbon, accompanied by an official certificate. My name, and what the medal is all about, appear on the front and back of the medal.

My article "Last Christmas [2001] on the Yukon" appeared in the December 2002 issue of *Extension Magazine*. My diary entry for December 25, 2002, reads, "Took memories of Christmases past on a long early morning walk." I ended my Christmas 2002 letter to family and friends with, "The writing's bumping along fairly well, but the road ahead still stretches beyond the horizon—so, spare a prayer!"

Annual calendars have to be prepared well ahead of time. The 2003 calendar was the last one I was to create as editor of the *Alaskan Shepherd*. "Annual calendars", I began my introduction to it, "serve to keep us aware of the inexorable passage of time. They remind us that our days are numbered, that we do not have here a lasting city, that we are only wayfarers on this earth, and that, as individuals and as a people of God, we are but pilgrims on the road to everlasting life, to where time is no more."

Unlike the year 2002, a year of major changes and highlights in my life, the years 2003 and 2004 were mainly years of more "bumping along" the road that was eventually to lead to the publication of *Alaskana Catholica*. Throughout that two-year period, especially during the earlier part, I devoted most of my time to producing and polishing entries for it. During the latter part, I began also to send out queries to prospective publishers. During intervals, while I awaited responses, I kept "touching up" my manuscript.

Alaskana Catholica, as an encyclopedia, is unique in that all the entries were written by only one person, me. Throughout its composition, I was its sole writer—but I was not its sole editor. I was extremely fortunate and blessed to have, all the while, the willing and able editorial services of Sister Margaret Cantwell, S.S.A. Years earlier, I had helped her with her book *North to Share*. As archivist of the Archives of the Sisters of Saint Ann in Victoria, British Columbia, she was now in a position to help me. Before she was through with her editorial collaboration, she had seen all the entries and had made her suggestions for improving them. She had also drawn my attention to the fact that certain called-for entries were lacking. These I supplied. As I produced entries, I e-mailed them to her. In short order, I had her comments. E-mail proved to be a great saver of money and time. Indebtedness to Sister Margaret, a historian and writer of things Alaskan, while it may not be overly evident to the reader of *Alaskana Catholica*, is considerable and gratefully acknowledged in the introduction to the book.

Long before *Alaskana Catholica* began to take on a life of its own, Father Armand Nigro, fellow Jesuit and classmate, had already encouraged me, pleaded with me, to preserve in writing for future generations the lives of early-day Jesuit Alaskan missionaries. As I produced entries for *Alaskana Catholica*, I mailed them to him in batches for his comments. He favored me with many welcome comments and kept heartening me with his positive, encouraging words.

However, working away at the encyclopedia did not absorb me totally throughout the years 2003 and 2004. During spells when I considered the encyclopedia press-ready and was waiting for word from a prospective publisher, I spent longer periods of time in the archives organizing my personal archive file and my King Island and Little Diomede Island photo collections, or helping David Kingma identify and organize the vast Father Bernard R. Hubbard, S.J., photo collection. In my room, too, I spent many hours identifying and organizing photos I had taken or collected.

And there were times when I was away from Spokane. On June 15, 2003, at 11:10 A.M., David Kingma and I, in his Windstar sport-utility vehicle, left Spokane for western Washington. We spent that night in Anacortes. The following morning, we took the ferry across to Sidney, British Columbia, and drove into Victoria. There we visited with Sister Margaret Cantwell, filled the Windstar with books and other archival materials the Sisters of Saint Ann were donating to the Jesuit Oregon Province Archives, ate dinner, and stayed the night at Mount Saint Angela, the main Victoria residence of the Sisters of Saint Ann. On the seventeenth, we took the ferry to Port Angeles and drove on to Port Townsend. There we visited briefly with Verne Ray, in a care home, and with Dorothy Jean in the Ray home. For the evening meal, she treated us to dinner at the Manresa Castle Hotel. David and I spent the night there. Early the next morning, we took the Bainbridge Island ferry to Seattle. By around 4:15 that afternoon, we were back in Spokane.

On July 18, I flew to Vancouver, Washington, where I spent the evening and night with Bill and Bernice. The following day, the three of us drove down to Sunriver, Oregon, where the whole Bill Renner family had gathered again for a week of visiting and vacationing. Before returning to Spokane on the twenty-ninth, I stayed several more days with Bill and Bernice in Vancouver.

Verne Ray, almost a hundred years old at the time, died on October 3. He had willed his archival materials to the Jesuit Oregon Province Archives. On November 18, via Tacoma and Bremerton, David Kingma and I drove to Port Townsend. We again spent the night in the Manresa Castle Hotel. The whole of the next day we were at the Ray home, visiting with Dorothy Jean and loading box after box of Verne Ray archival materials into the Windstar. Early in the morning of the twentieth, after another night in the Manresa Castle Hotel, we left Port Townsend. Having decided to return to Spokane by the northern route, by way of Stevens Pass, we took the Whidbey Island ferry to Mukilteo. After driving awhile, we stopped in Monroe for breakfast. We made a brief stop also in Leavenworth. By around 4:30 we were back in Spokane.

Unlike the year 2003, the year 2004 proved to be a stay-at-home one for me. Except for a few drives up to Mount Saint Michael's cemetery to attend the burials of fellow Jesuits, I was never on wheels.

A memorable spiritual celebration was my sixtieth anniversary as a Jesuit. It will be remembered that I joined the Society of Jesus on March 25, 1944. Accordingly, on March 25, 2004, I celebrated my diamond jubilee as a Jesuit. The anniversary day itself passed rather quietly. However, on June 9, in the Jesuit House chapel, with fellow Jesuit jubilarians and some priests from the Diocese of Spokane, and with William S. Skylstad, the bishop of Spokane, presiding, I concelebrated at a Mass of thanksgiving.

On July 14, 2004, Father Provincial John D. Whitney wrote to me:

> With great joy and thankfulness, I forward to you the enclosed letter from Father General on the occasion of your sixtieth year in the Society of Jesus. Speaking for myself, I want to thank you for your great contribution to the Society and to the province, especially in the area of scholarship and service to the Alaskan missions, where you have served so generously. With quiet grace and constancy, you have brought

to these areas the gift of your priesthood, the strength of your intellect, and the gentleness of your person, through whom Christ has blessed this work.

With joy, then, Louis, I join Father General and your brothers throughout the province and the Society in congratulating you at this milestone. I hope this year of jubilee is one of consolation, deepening in you the fires of faith, hope, and love for your vocation and for all of God's people.

My September 9, 2004, diary entry reads: "Mass. At genuflection after the consecration of the chalice, momentary blackout. Gashed right cheekbone on edge of altar. Finished Mass as usual. Felt at peace."

I had never before experienced a blackout, nor did I experience such a one subsequently. It was a deep, spiritual peace that came over me when I was again fully conscious. I can honestly say that I felt ready to die, there and then. Not wanting to be deprived of my dying as a conscious, free, personal act—as a knowing and willing and loving acceptance, for the final time, of the will of God for me—it had, for many years, by then, been a key part of my evening prayer to tell the Heavenly Father that I accepted from His merciful, loving hands (with the help of His grace, of course) whatever kind of death, with all its pains, anxieties, and uncertainties, He, in His wisdom and love, should decree for me. I had often prayed, too, "O Lord, grant me the grace that nothing in my life may so become me as the manner of my leaving it." By that September day, I had long since ended each day praying also, "Abba, Father, with Jesus dying on the Cross, into your hands I entrust my spirit."

I had scarcely made myself at home in Jesuit House on the Gonzaga University campus on June 10, 2002, when I began to lament the fact that Gonzaga University Press was no longer a going concern. Prospects of finding a suitable publisher for my history in the Spokane area seemed poor indeed. Working with a publisher at a distance was not an attractive option, especially when I dwelt on the thought that the history would be a book of around eight hundred pages with nearly four hundred photographs.

By early January 2005, I had contacted a number of prospective publishers in hopes that they might see fit to publish my history. All had kind words concerning the generous sampling of the manuscript I had submitted to them. None, however, saw fit to take on the publication of the history. Was I disappointed? Naturally. I could not know, at the time, that the rejections were, in reality, true blessings in disguise.

Enter a kindly Providence! On January 6, 2005, in the vault of the Jesuit Oregon Province Archives, David Kingma and I were digging through a box of books in search of a particular book when, all of a sudden, a great big tome all but jumped out at me. It was Monsignor Francis J. Weber's *Encyclopedia of California's Catholic Heritage*. I had never so much as heard of the book or of its author. Immediately, I checked to see who had published it. It was the Arthur H. Clark Company, located almost literally right next door, in Millwood, Washington, a suburb of Spokane. I had never heard of this publishing firm, though it had been in existence for over a century. That very same day, I contacted Robert A. (Bob) Clark, grandson of Arthur H. Clark, the founder of the company, and mailed him a generous sampling of my manuscript. We met on January 19. After a very satisfying, confidence-inspiring talk with Bob, I was firmly convinced, then and there, that a kindly Providence had so ordained that the Arthur H. Clark Company was meant to be the publisher of *Alaskana Catholica*.

Meanwhile, on January 13, I had had my annual colloquy with Father Provincial Whitney, in the course of which he assured me that the Oregon Province was prepared to finance the publication of *Alaskana Catholica* to the extent necessary. Without delay, in consultation with Father Whitney and William L. Lockyear, chief financial officer of the Oregon Province, Bob and I began to work out the details leading to a contract wholly agreeable to all parties concerned. This was signed by the third week of March.

By the end of that memorable January 13 colloquy, Father Whitney had also asked me to contact Tina M. O'Brien, director of the Oregon Province development office, about raising funds to help finance the publication of *Alaskana Catholica*. Working along with Darlene J. Allred, database manager in the Oregon Province's Portland development office, Tina and I elaborated a way of proceeding. I would draw up an appeal letter to be sent out of Portland to the province's donor list. I myself would mail it out to members of my family, to friends, and to other prospective contributors, among them former students and fellow academic colleagues of mine. Donations were to be sent to the Portland office and duly tracked by Darlene. I would personally acknowledge all donations. The appeal letter was mailed out in early February. People responded generously. By mid-May, it had produced somewhat more than 100 percent of the dollar amount contracted for with the Clark Company.

The appeal letter, addressed to "Dear Friends of Things Catholic and Alaskan", read as follows:

After some twenty years of research and writing, I finally have my history of the Catholic Church in Alaska, *Alaskana Catholica*, ready for publication. It is now only a matter of time—and money. We are talking here of a big volume, expensive to publish. The Oregon Province will, of course, help in a major way to finance the publication of *Alaskana Catholica*, but it needs help and has asked me personally to turn to you for whatever help you might be able to give us. I personally will gratefully acknowledge receipt of all donations.

The names of those helping with the publication costs of *Alaskana Catholica* will be listed in the book, though not the dollar amount contributed. They will be listed in the book under the heading: *The publication of* Alaskana Catholica *was made possible by the many kind and generous friends whose names are listed here below. May Saint Thérèse of Lisieux, "the Little Flower", to whom this history is dedicated, obtain special blessings and favors for them!* If you do not wish your name listed, kindly let me know. Let me know, too, how you wish to be listed. Know that contributions may be made also in the name or in the memory of someone.

Know that I will be sincerely grateful to you for whatever help you give us in this matter. And, if you are unable to give any, I understand and am still grateful to you for having felt free to turn to you for help. God bless us everyone!

With the contract signed and the dollar amount contracted for toward the publication of *Alaskana Catholica* in hand, it was now only a matter of seeing the manuscript transformed, step by step, into a hardbound published book.

During that same January 13 colloquy mentioned above, Father Provincial, on his own initiative, asked me to write my autobiography. Accordingly, the following day already, I began to cull my archive file for such materials—letters, diaries, notebooks, official documents, photographs—as I thought might help me recount my life in a more-or-less chronological order. What I considered pertinent materials I photocopied and lined up chronologically in three-ring loose-leaf binders. Meanwhile, I was still working on the photos intended to illustrate *Alaskana Catholica* and was rechecking the text, as well as routinely proofreading articles to appear in upcoming issues of the *Alaskan Shepherd*. On March 29, I delivered the *Alaskana Catholica* photos to the Clark Company. By April 4, I felt the text was ready to be put on a compact disc; and, by the sixth, the whole text, on one compact disc, was in the hands of the Clark Company. On April 20, I began with the actual writing of my autobiography. Two days later, I noted in my diary, "Good progress on my autobio."

May 4 proved to be a day of major importance in the process of *Alaskana Catholica*'s moving along toward publication. On that day, Bob Clark met me in the Jesuit Oregon Province Archives to deliver into my hands the initial set of proofs, the galleys. With him, he had a young lady, Ariane C. Smith, a member of the Clark Company staff. We were introduced to one another and, with that introduction, began a most satisfying writer-publisher working relationship. Almost single-handedly, Ariane, with a high degree of professionalism and personal concern, saw my manuscript—"our book", as she referred to it almost from the outset—through to its successful publication. In a letter of May 19, she commented: "This book is going to be done in record time, and I have to say it is due in large part to your perfectly organized materials; it has made a big project into a relatively easy one."

I spent the better part of May checking the galleys. By May 26, I had them back in Ariane's hands and was relaxed enough to continue on with the writing of my autobiography.

On June 3, the feast of the Most Sacred Heart of Jesus, in the Jesuit House chapel, I concelebrated at a special Mass honoring the jubilarians of the Oregon Province. After Mass, I joined some of my classmates at a dinner. The following day, in Saint Aloysius Church, I concelebrated at the Mass at which Sean M. Raftis was ordained a priest. I shared in the banquet that followed it. After the solemnities at the altar, and the convivialities at the table, I was back at my desk working on my autobiography.

On July 18–28, I proofread the second stage of the *Alaskana Catholica* proofs, the formatted pages. On August 2, Ariane showed me the proposed dust jacket design. Finding it a true work of art, I insisted she add to it, "Dust jacket design by Ariane C. Smith". This she did. On August 9, she brought me the index page proofs. Proofreading these kept me preoccupied for the next two weeks. On September 14, I began checking the "final author's copy". This was soon done. Thereafter, everything was in the hands of the publisher. I was back to work on my autobiography.

On August 25, Father Frank Mueller kindly volunteered to drive me to the Fred Meyer store, where I needed to do some shopping. We had a pleasant visit during the drive to and from the store and while I shopped. This may seem like a matter of minor importance to note. However, that was the last time the two of us were to be in one another's company. Father Frank and I had first met in 1944 at the novitiate at Sheridan, Oregon. We had lived together in Fairbanks for many years. For most of those years, he was my superior. Together we had hiked the Pinnell and Chilkoot trails, floated the Copper River and dipnetted salmon out of it, worked on the Healy church, concelebrated Mass at the dedication of the new church in Barrow, tented at Akulurak, and driven almost every mile of Alaska's highways and byways. Early in the morning of September 28, I was shocked to read the notice on the Jesuit House bulletin board announcing Father Frank's wholly unexpected death. He had died peacefully in his bed that morning. On October 4, I concelebrated at the Mass of Christian Burial offered for him. His death left a significant feeling of emptiness in my life.

Although as a member of the Regis Community, he had lived in Bea House, across the street from Jesuit House, my residence, we had seen one another fairly often.

Around mid-October, Pat Ferguson, a Gonzaga University senior, contacted me about helping him with a major term paper he was proposing to do on the subject of the evangelization of the Seward Peninsula–area Eskimos by Jesuit missionaries Fathers Bellarmine Lafortune and Thomas P. Cunningham. My biographies of the two men had steered Pat to me. I told him I was more than willing to be of whatever help I might be in the matter. This was an area I had specialized in and that continued to interest me. We met for the first time on October 29. I was glad to be able to help him see his project through to a satisfactory conclusion.

November 17 proved to *the* red-letter day of red-letter days for me. On that day, around 4:30 in the afternoon, Ariane delivered into my hands a copy of *Alaskana Catholica: A History of the Catholic Church in Alaska; A Reference Work in the Format of an Encyclopedia*. I was more impressed by its physical appearance than I had anticipated. With its dust jacket, it was a real eye-catcher. Put on display for fellow Jesuit community members to see, it evoked many favorable comments.

I now had the answer to the oft-asked question "How's the book comin' along?" Soon after its appearance, I found myself being asked the not-unexpected question "Whatya workin' on now?" The answer was simple: "My autobiography!"

November 22 found me, for the first—and only—time, in Millwood, in the venerable establishment of the Arthur H. Clark Company. This I discovered to be a one-floor, split-level, sprawling space containing individual desks and computer and work stations. At the same time, I experienced it as an art gallery, a library, and a cozy den permeated with an aura of history, a modern publisher's place of business. My business—rather, my pleasure—there that day was to autograph several dozen copies of *Alaskana Catholica*. Most of these were to be mailed out to people far and wide; some were for the Clark Company staff. The autographing, done with considerable care, took me almost two hours. I was not about to put pen and ink to an eighty-dollar book casually.

Just as a thing, the book, hardbound in blue linen cloth, is a beautiful object. The dust jacket, as mentioned above, is a true work of art. Three photographs grace it, as well as a number of comments concerning its contents. In the words of Father Francis Paul Prucha, S.J., professor of history emeritus, Marquette University: "This fascinating volume offers an intimate picture of the activities of the Catholic Church's Alaska Mission, from its beginning in the nineteenth century to the present. . . . Father Renner, with a historian's concern for the facts and a writer's eye for a good story, has produced a valuable work."

Dr. Robert C. Carriker, the book review editor of *Columbia: The Magazine of Northwest History*, made the dust jacket with:

> Alaska has long deserved a comprehensive history of its religious foundation. *Alaskana Catholica* justifies the wait. Louis Renner, S.J., has expertly crafted a volume that is a combination historical narrative, biographical dictionary, and encyclopedia of notable Alaska events. . . . The preparation of such a volume required attention to detail and, happily, Father Renner took on the task, making use of his forty years of experience in the Land of the Midnight Sun as an author and documentary scholar. This effort will not soon be exceeded.

Donald J. Kettler, bishop of Fairbanks, commented: "Through years of dedicated research, writing, and documentation, Father

Renner has created a succinct yet comprehensive guide detailing in total clarity and conciseness the history of the Catholic Church in Alaska.... Father Louis L. Renner, S.J., has accomplished in *Alaskana Catholica* a momentous feat—a magnum opus."

Two words end most of my diary entries for any given year: "DEO GRATIAS!" And, addressing those same two words to a kindly Providence, I write to this autobiography: FINIS!

INDEX